The Undesirable Many

The Undesirable Many

Black Women and Their Struggles
against Displacement and Housing
Insecurity in the Nation's Capital

. . . .

ROSEMARY NDUBUIZU

The University of North Carolina Press Chapel Hill

Set in Charis by Westchester Publishing Services
Manufactured in the United States of America

Library of Congress Cataloging-in-Publication Data
Names: Ndubuizu, Rosemary author
Title: The undesirable many : Black women and their struggles
   against displacement and housing insecurity in the nation's capital /
   Rosemary Ndubuizu.
Other titles: Justice, power, and politics
Description: Chapel Hill : The University of North Carolina Press, 2025. |
   Series: Justice, power, and politics | Includes bibliographical
   references and index.
Identifiers: LCCN 2025015423 | ISBN 9781469689678 cloth |
   ISBN 9781469689685 paperback | ISBN 9781469689692 epub |
   ISBN 9781469689708 pdf
Subjects: LCSH: Discrimination in housing—Washington (DC) |
   Poor African Americans—Housing—Washington (DC) | African
   American women—Washington (DC)—Social conditions | African
   American women—Political activity—Washington (DC) | Rental
   housing—Political aspects—Washington (DC) | Sex discrimination
   against women—Washington (DC) | BISAC: SOCIAL SCIENCE /
   Ethnic Studies / American / African American & Black Studies |
   SOCIAL SCIENCE / Sociology / Urban
Classification: LCC HD7288.76.U62 W186 | DDC 363.5/109753—dc23/
   eng/20250618
LC record available at https://lccn.loc.gov/2025015423

Cover art: Housing activists in Washington, DC. Reprinted with the
permission of the DC Public Library, Star Collection © Washington Post.

For product safety concerns under the European Union's General Product
Safety Regulation (EU GPSR), please contact gpsr@mare-nostrum.co.uk
or write to the University of North Carolina Press and Mare Nostrum
Group B.V., Mauritskade 21D, 1091 GC Amsterdam, The Netherlands.

Dedicated to Phyllissa Bilal and all the ONE DC mamas
who chose justice, not silence

Contents

Illustrations

Acknowledgments

It is a well-known African proverb that it takes a village to raise a child. A similar sentiment can be applied to my book—it took a village of caring supporters to bring my book to fruition. Over the nearly five years it took to produce this book, I have enjoyed the beautiful company and support of many people, within and outside academia.

I am eternally indebted to the movement-building community of Organizing Neighborhood Equity DC (ONE DC). Without them, my research and lifelong commitment to affordable housing and transformative learning might never have materialized. Since 2006, I have met and organized alongside hundreds—possibly thousands—of ONE DC members and leaders. The vast majority of these wonderful people warmed my spirit and encouraged my success as a scholar-organizer. While this list is not meant to be exhaustive, I pray it represents the scope of ONE DC members who supported my academic work and allowed me to organize alongside them. I thank Patricia Penny, Jessica Gordon Nembhard, Gwendolyn Smart, Ka Flewellen, Akosua Dosu, Luci Murphy, Michelle Hamilton, Jourgette Reid-Sillah, Kalfani Turé, Kimberly Butts, Nadia Johnson, Khadijah Huggins-El, Nakeitha Cates, Nicole Newman, Brook Hill, Katheleen Maloy, Heather Burns, Nzingha Hooker, Mona Triplett, Linette Robinson, Timeca Latrice Roundtree, Paulette Matthews, Serita El-Amin, Phyllissa Bilal, Keisha Harden, Janice Underwood, Dewayne Brown, Haley Clasen, Medea Benjamin, Claire Cushman, Charles Turner, Kami Steffenauer, Sarah Rooney, Virginia Lee, Tim Kumfer, Ollie Micheal Lesile and Rasheed Van Putten. I also acknowledge and note my respect for ONE DC's current and former staff. I am grateful for the care and labor they gave to ONE DC during their organizing tenure. A special shout-out goes to Dominic Timothy Moulden, Kelly Iradukunda, Gloria Robinson, Claire Cook, Patrick Gregoire, Grace Guber, Nawal Rajeh, Reece Chenault, Nkechi Feaster, Nia Nyamweya, Jessica Rucker, Imani Fox, Shakeara Mingo, Jamee "Poncho" Garland, Serena Jones, Melody Zhang, Jojo Morinvil, Gio Hardy-Gerena, Isabella Dominque, Harriet "Bunny" Jackson, Taniya Rogers, and Joel Kesterson.

I appreciate the funding support I received from Georgetown University, the Ford Foundation, the National Women's Studies Association, and Rutgers University. I also thank the librarians and administrative staff at Georgetown University, Rutgers University-New Brunswick, Catholic University, the Ronald Reagan Library, the National Archives and Records Administration, the DC Office of Public Records, George Washington University, the Moorland-Spingarn Research Center at Howard University, the Wisconsin Historical Society, and the People's Archive at the DC Public Library.

Many scholars and editors helped me improve my book and scholarship. I appreciate Heather Ann Thompson and Rhonda Y. Williams, editors for the Justice, Power, and Politics series at The University of North Carolina Press, for their support and acceptance of my book. I am grateful to the editorial board at the press for their support too. My book's peer reviewers were impressive; their comments were generous, comprehensive, and thoughtful. Their feedback improved my book, and I hope they find the final product as strong and compelling as I do. My book also benefited from fantastic editorial assistance. I thank Dawn Durante for her great stewardship of my project throughout the review and production process. I appreciate the production staff at The University of North Carolina Press for their assistance as well. I also recognize Dylan White and Brandon Proia for supporting my project during their time at UNC Press. Lastly, I treasured Alix Genter's support. As my copyeditor, Genter provided meticulous feedback and first-rate editing.

I extend a warm hug and big thanks to my colleagues in the Black Studies department at Georgetown University. I feel lucky and honored to count myself among this esteemed group. I especially thank Robert Patterson and Soyica Diggs Colbert for their consistent availability and generous mentorship since my arrival. I also thank LaMonda Horton-Stallings, Zandria Robinson, Dayo Gore, Anita Gonzalez, Melanie Y. White, Brienne A. Adams, and Kelsey Moore. Your gentle and sincere support has meant the world to me as I walked the long trek toward this book's completion. Other Georgetown scholars (both current and former) have supported my scholarship: I thank K-Sue Park, Samantha Pinto, Marcus Board Jr., Marcia Chatelain, Corey Fields, Maurice Jackson, Olúfẹ́mi O. Táíwò, Amani Morrison, Mecca Jamilah Sullivan, Kwame Edwin Otu, Jamil Scott, Carla Shedd, Ebony Gisom, Eva Rosen, You-Me Park, and Nadia Brown. I also appreciate my research assistant Major Elliott and our department's excellent office staff: business manager Elaf Alchurbaji and office assistants Sebastien Pierre-Louis, Keturah Crawford, Elise Merchant, and Autumn Davis.

Additionally, I want to express my deepest thanks to my students. Our lively and thought-provoking discussions helped shape my work in innumerable ways. I hope all of you continue to experience success, joy, and principled civic engagement in your various walks of life.

I also appreciate the feedback I received on my book at conferences and workshops held with the Black Thought Collective, the Black Studies: Imagination Abound Symposium, the Society for American City and Regional Planning History, the National Women's Studies Association, the American Studies Association, the Organization of American Historians, the National Conference of Black Political Scientists, the International Labor Organization Conference, Connecticut College, Princeton University and the University of Maryland-College Park.

Outside Georgetown University, I appreciate the wonderful scholars and organic intellectuals who read chapters, provided professional advice, and lent a supportive ear. I especially thank Nancy Racquel Mirabal, Johanna K. Bockman, Sarah Shoenfeld, Amaka Okechuckwu, Mary Sies, La Marr Jurelle Bruce, Gwendolyn Beetham, Neha Kagal, Monica White, Tanya Golash-Boza, Amara Enyia, Ashanté M. Reese, Sade Ajala, Paris Hatcher, Savannah Shange, Jamala Rogers, NTanya Lee, Lisa Owens, Charlene Carruthers, Julian Hill, Sally Bonet, Robert Choflet, Derek Musgrove, Tracey Deutsch, Eduardo Contreras, Marques Vestal, Sarah Tobias, Nicole Fleetwood, Ethel Brooks, Zaire Dinzey-Flores, Mary Trigg, and Abenia Busia.

I extend special thanks to a select number of Black women scholars who were invaluable to me as they modeled academic excellence and compassionate camaraderie. I deeply value my relationship with Donna Murch. Since my last two years in graduate school, Donna Murch has been an amazing source of friendship and mentorship. She embodies the fact that brilliance can exist alongside big-heartedness and political integrity. I also value Nikol Alexander-Floyd's support. Graduate school was unfamiliar terrain for me and I am thankful for her model of productive discipline and intellectual rigor. I admire Barbara Ransby, Premilla Nadasen, Rose Brewer, and Keeanga-Yahmatta Taylor for modeling the principle that high-quality scholarship and academic communities can and should be in service of liberatory aims. I appreciate Lisa Young, Taida Wolfe, Ashleigh Wade, and Akira Rodriguez for their friendship and support. Writing can be a lonely vocation, but their company made this intellectual journey worthwhile.

In addition to scholars, I thank my movement comrades and dear friends. I consider these people to be my chosen kin—those who listened and comforted me as I wept, lamented, fretted, or cheered with delight. They were my invisible armor, helping me navigate the difficult balance of knowledge production, community organizing, and wellness. Dara Cooper, a dear friend and movement comrade, has always created a safe space for me to be my messy and authentic self. She is also an amazing model of visionary leadership and Black feminist praxis. M. Adams is a dear friend and movement thought partner. They have always been a brilliant movement strategist and a consistent source of intellectual honesty and political determination. Since college, Jennifer Rae Taylor has been a soul-nourishing friend, encouraging me to claim my intellectual and authorial voice. Donna Davis is a dear friend who since the COVID-19 global pandemic has been an excellent source of fun, tennis, and positivity. I want to give another special shout-out to Dominic Timothy Moulden. Since we first met in 2006 at ONE DC, he has been an enduring model of ethical leadership and principled accountability. I pray life continues to grant him the blessings and recognition he deserves.

My family of origin remains a trusted and steadfast support system. My parents, Wilfred and Mary Ndubuizu, are my biggest supporters, always cheering for me as I reach new academic milestones. My siblings, Emelda Ndubuizu, Irene Ndubuizu, and Christopher Ndubuizu, are wonderful embodiments of kindness, courage, and talent. I thank my sister Emelda's beautiful family, who has been a welcome source of joy: Edozie Okolo (Emelda's husband and my brother-in-law) and Chidera and Arinze Okolo (my delightful niece and nephew). My extended family has also been exceptional. The Dike and Anyikwa families always support my passions and remain a beautiful source of loving fellowship. I cherish the lifelong support the Ndubuizu clan has given me too. I pray we all continue to sustain our family's legacy of achievement and service. I give a special thanks to my four-legged family member, Ah-yo (aka Big Mama), who has always been a faithful companion and walking partner.

Lastly, to all the well-wishers who encouraged me when I shared random updates about my writing and research, thank you! Your goodwill never went unnoticed. May we all continue to march closer to liberation, love, and authentic belonging. Onward!

The Undesirable Many

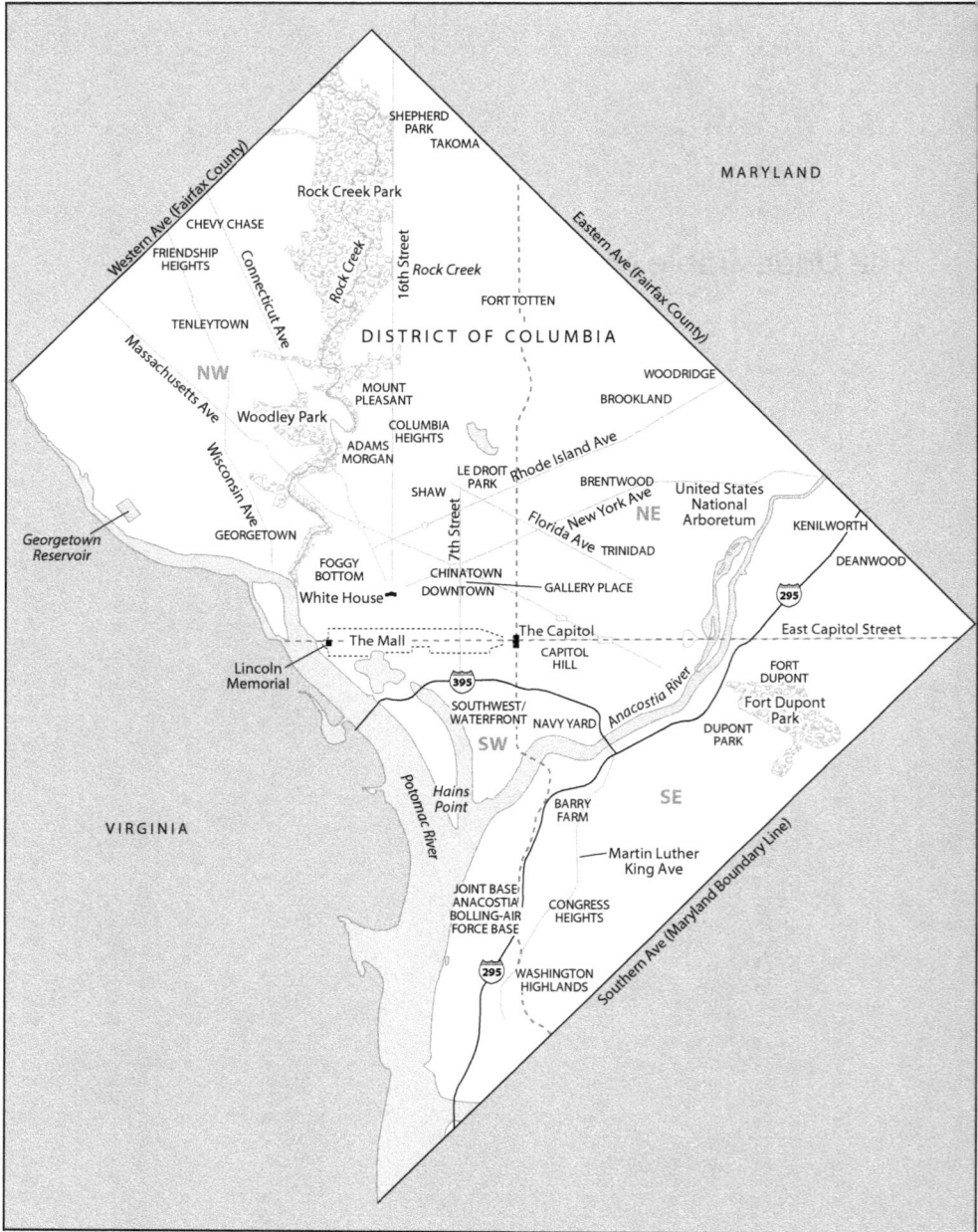

Map of select DC neighborhoods

Introduction

Who Belongs in the City?

· ·

It was sometime in 2008 or 2009; I am hazy about the exact year. I was a full-time community organizer at the height of a campaign. Things were hectic and fast-paced. I was working with Organizing Neighborhood Equity DC (ONE DC), a group headquartered in Shaw, a historically Black and working-class neighborhood in the District of Columbia. ONE DC advocates for economic and racial equity in DC. A membership organization, ONE DC recruited working-class residents to design and execute local direct-action campaigns on affordable housing and living wage work.[1] As an affordable housing organizer, I recruited and worked with ONE DC's housing campaign members, primarily Black women. Together, we petitioned elected officials to allocate local resources to enable DC's working-class families to gain or retain affordable housing units.

Back then, our affordable housing agenda focused on compelling the city to fulfill a community benefits agreement brokered in 2006. At that time, ONE DC had led a successful campaign to urge public officials to put aside a higher number of deeply affordable units on a parcel of public land in Shaw that was set to be sold to a private developer. ONE DC came to an agreement with the District of Columbia's advisory neighborhood commissioner (a neighborhood-level public official meant to represent community interests) and the city's National Capital Revitalization Corporation (NCRC). The NCRC was a quasi-public agency established in the late 1990s to amass and sell public lands for economic development. A core feature of the compromise was that the NCRC would set aside another piece of public land, known then as Parcel 42, to be fully developed at the deepest affordability levels. This meant that the site's future units would be affordable for households earning less than 30 percent and less than 50 percent of the DC metropolitan's area median income (AMI), with monthly rents for one-bedroom units estimated to start in the $500 range.

This compromise was a historic victory for two significant reasons. One, Shaw was on fire: gentrification had thoroughly seized the entire neighborhood. By the early 2000s, Shaw had earned the dubious title of the most gentrified neighborhood in the country.[2] Two, the city had not seen rents that low since the project-based, rent-assisted properties of the late 1980s. But, of course, with politics, nothing is guaranteed. And we at ONE DC were in for a rude and rapid awakening when it became clear that the community benefits agreement was falling apart.

Shortly after the deal was signed, DC's Ward 4 council member, Democrat Adrian Fenty, won the city's mayoral seat in 2006, replacing two-time incumbent Anthony Williams. Fenty ran a campaign championing affordable housing as a vital way to address the city's rising rents that disproportionally affected working-class Black Washingtonians. However, while in office, Fenty struggled to listen to these residents, who grew more frustrated with the city's persistent embrace of gentrification. Even though Fenty was ultimately not responsible for ushering in this gentrification wave, he maintained his predecessor's goal of recruiting one hundred thousand new residents, leaving existing residents feeling devalued and vulnerable.[3] Fashioning himself as a bullish urban reformer, Fenty quickly moved to dissolve and reabsorb the NCRC back into the mayor's administration. At ONE DC, we understood Fenty's agency integration presented a political opportunity. We met with Fenty's administration to secure their support for protecting the community benefits agreement brokered for Parcel 42.

Much to our surprise, we learned that the city was getting cold feet. My fellow tenant activists and I listened as the administrators questioned the desirability—or, in the language of housing officials and developers, the feasibility—of a deeply affordable rental community at Parcel 42. In the context of the city's tight budget, they reasoned that Shaw already had a number of rent-assisted developments that had been built in the 1970s after residents organized and demanded that urban renewal benefit rather than displace Black Washingtonians.[4] Their argument floored us. What did these earlier victories have to do with our current objective? In response, we explained that alongside DC's gentrification wave, the city was experiencing a rise in affordable covenant opt-outs as private landlords sought to take advantage of neighborhoods' rising rents. Given this context, we could not assume that any past victories would remain secure in the future.

Nonetheless, the officials doubled down on their objections to making Parcel 42 a deeply affordable rental property. They countered that building properties with deeply affordable rents in Shaw would bring together welfare-dependent families with poor behavior and would perpetuate concentrated poverty. By the end of the discussion, their message was clear: low-rent housing invites the undesirable and unruly poor to live there. City officials seemed ready to block the Parcel 42 project. I, in particular, left the meeting heated for reasons that went well beyond a failed negotiation.

When we returned to the office, we knew we could not let the administration's choice to ignore the deal stand. But we were not sure about our response yet. As we brainstormed our political options, I had an epiphany. Later that day, and admittedly, with the righteous indignation typical of organizers in their early twenties, I furiously wrote an email to ONE DC's Parcel 42 campaign leadership and staff. I shared my realization: that the city used cultural messages about DC's poor to obscure its political and economic agenda. In this case, officials at the meeting used racialized stereotypes about welfare-assisted families to justify their support for the unspoken promise of gentrification: lower crime rates and (white) middle-class revanchism. These were ideological messages about who belonged in the city, who did not, and why. I understood then that we were not simply in a battle for resources but were also in a battle of ideas. In hindsight, it was a deceptively simple insight, but at the time, it was eye-opening.

As I continued organizing over the next decade and beyond, I heard these cultural messages baked into public officials' arguments for defending gentrification as a goal of urban development. Variations of the same cultural message appeared when different mayors and housing officials advocated the demolition of public housing, supported landlord opt-outs of rent-assisted affordability covenants, or approved luxury housing construction over deeply affordable multi-family rentals. In one such incident, a housing official in Vincent Gray's mayoral administration cautioned against extending affordability covenants. He reasoned that support for long-term affordability would indirectly encourage low-wage households to remain dependent on welfare and entrench intergenerational poverty. For us, these arguments were misplaced and offensive. Because we organized with working-class DC renters, we believed that discrimination, low wages, and government cuts to welfare were more responsible for urban poverty. We also knew that these cultural arguments were gendered and racialized. Black women were the primary demographic living in the city's public and rent-assisted housing. We maintained that the city's choice to ignore these structural factors would lead to more displacement and poverty. And yet, we understood that these cultural messages about the city's "undesirables" would help absolve DC officials from addressing the city's increasing loss of deeply affordable housing.

The Undesirable Many: Black Women and Their Struggle against Housing Insecurity and Displacement in the Nation's Capital historicizes why affordable housing projects that directly benefit working-class Black families perennially confront the challenges we faced in our Parcel 42 campaign. I argue that the housing insecurity of low-wage Black women and their families is not the result of colorblind financial considerations of the state or real estate. On the contrary, it is due to cultural stereotypes about these families that work to legitimize and exacerbate affordable housing scarcity.[5] In this book, I investigate three related issues that show how gender, race, and class intricately work together to sustain the marginalization of low-wage Black women and their families in rental housing markets. The first issue is how gendered narratives about the Black family have historically legitimized how the real estate industry and public officials treat the residential spaces of Black families differently. The second issue is how these intertwined narratives about low-wage Black families ultimately justified a political defense for conditional access to affordable housing. The third issue is the way these intertwined narratives evolved to explain and condone the local entrenchment of housing inequality for low-wage Black women and their families.

By centering low-wage Black women and their families, I offer a fresh take on why the housing affordability crisis persists in the United States. In the post–civil rights era, soaring home prices have dramatically outpaced household earnings.[6] As critical urbanists have pointed out, these rising housing costs followed historic spikes in inflation. Deregulation and financial instruments like mortgage-backed securities made it easier for corporations, households with generational wealth, foreign capital, and other moneyed interest groups to expand and concentrate their real estate holdings.[7] By the 1990s, the tech-driven stock market boom had exacerbated housing unaffordability in many urban centers. Since the Great Recession and the COVID-19 global pandemic, this structural tendency toward housing unaffordability has only deepened as federal monetary policy changes and limited construction have decreased the housing supply and increased housing prices.

However, affordability crisis explanations that focus on market forces (and only hint at political decisions) often fail to adequately explain why low-wage Black women and their families continue to be subjected to the highest rates of displacement and housing insecurity. Urban sociologists aim to fill this knowledge gap with descriptive snapshots of how prejudice shapes landlord-tenant relations. These scholars limn racialized social interactions leave the poorest vulnerable to eviction, a practice that structurally hurts their chances of being reabsorbed into the private or public housing market.[8] Yet this area of study disproportionally attends to users—namely, small-scale landlords and tenants—and fails to capture how these discreet market transactions evolved historically. They miss opportunities to examine institutional, political, and economic factors that developed over time to shape housing market conditions and differential consumer outcomes. Moreover, these scholars rarely interrogate how welfare state politics evolve and shape affordable housing.

Affordability crisis explanations that recognize the interconnected relationship between cultural narratives, policy, and real estate get closer to a comprehensive analysis of housing inequities in the United States.[9] Critical urban scholars have historicized the fundamental role of race in etching racial segregation in the country's residential real estate markets over the last several decades. In a field dominated by local studies, critical urban historians have identified how racist practices hardened in the first half of the twentieth century with the help of federally backed institutional tools such as restrictive covenants, zoning discrimination, and redlining.[10] Relatedly, these scholars have documented how racism has systematically undermined the distribution, production, and maintenance of public housing.[11] Notably, only a few scholars have traced the constitutive role gender played in the history of public housing in the pre–civil rights era. Rhonda Williams's *The Politics of Public Housing: Black Women's Struggles against Urban Inequality* is one of the most prominent studies to address Black women's marginalization in the history of public housing and to feature Black women's powerful activism against mistreatment. In recent years, more critical urban historians have sought to close the gap between studies of public and private housing, arguing that both forms of real estate are intertwined and interdependent.[12] Toward that end, newer research has presented how the marginalization of Black people underwrote the institutional governance of private and public housing and eventually motivated government officials to pursue urban growth policies that supported displacement and gentrification in the second half of the twentieth century.[13]

Despite the immense value of this body of research, there are opportunities for additional insights. This research typically focuses on the pre–civil rights era and rarely interrogates how housing disparities evolved in the post–civil rights era. Moreover, since this field usually separates studies of public and private forms of housing, it is rarely understood how different privately managed, affordable housing measures that emerged in the post–civil rights era sometimes get conscripted into and replicate historical segregation or displacement patterns. Additionally, this scholarship often focuses only on race, seldom giving systematic attention to the role that gender—particularly narratives about gender expectations, family, and sexuality—has played in historical practices of racial segregation and contemporary realities like gentrification.

The Undesirable Many centers Black women and their families to demonstrate the complex ways cultural forces evolve and impact market behavior and state practices. As such, this book examines the housing experiences of low-wage Black women and their families from the pre–civil rights to the post–civil rights era to illustrate how gender, class, and race work together to shape the political economy of urban rental markets. As a social group, low-wage Black women and their families occupy intersecting identities that can illuminate different aspects of the real estate market and rental housing politics. Overlapping narratives about race, gender, ownership status, and family composition, for example, affect real estate market fundamentals such as property availability, property values, and (preferred) land use. Focusing on Black women and their families also elucidates how welfare politics shape real estate and affordable housing politics. Lastly, the experiences of these families in private and public housing markets uncover the linkages between finance, real estate, and discrimination. Indeed, by centering the housing experiences of low-wage Black women and their families, *The Undesirable Many* helps give a fuller account of the political economy of rental housing in the United States.

Black Feminist Materialism

I employ Black feminist materialism as a methodological framework in order to understand the complex dynamics between cultural narratives, market behavior, and state actions.[14] Black feminist materialism is an intersectional mode of analysis that traces the constitutive role that culture and meaning making play in a political economy. By applying this interpretative methodology to political and economic issues, Black feminist materialism can help expose how meaning making and culture underwrite political and economic behavior.

Black feminist materialism gives a name to a long-standing intellectual and political tradition within Black feminism.[15] Broadly, Black feminist theory contends that intersecting race, class, and gender dynamics shape social structures and understands how these social vectors intersect to reproduce structural inequities such as labor exploitation as well as political and civic marginalization. This intersectional oppression affects Black people in tiered and gendered ways, and only an intersectional analysis can enable scholars to trace the dimensions of Black people's subjugation. Black feminist theory also acknowledges the powerful force of culture—and its ideological narratives about marginalized populations—in anchoring this intersectional oppression. Given the historical silence on Black women's experiences with intersectional oppression, Black feminists often use Black feminist theory to underscore how oppressive systems impact Black women.

Within this intellectual tradition, Black feminists develop grounded assessments to address contemporary inequities. More specifically, Black feminists often use their political work to challenge "effective system[s] of social control," elevate public consciousness, and sharpen their theoretical thinking.[16] Take, for example, Claudia Jones, a Communist Party member and labor activist who organized in the 1930s until her death in 1964. Offering grounded assessments of trends in labor organizing, Jones argued that the labor movement must attend to its blind spots within its activism. Organized labor's failure to recognize Black women's community work as alternative sites for working-class organizing allowed movement leaders to discount Black women's value and role in organizing and community leadership.[17] Radical Black feminists in the 1970s built upon this political tradition. The Combahee River Collective—a queer, Black, feminist, and socialist organization based in Boston, Massachusetts—contended that multidimensional recognition of oppression required multiple sites of struggle. "We might, for example," the collective's statement averred, "become involved in workplace organizing at a factory that employs Third World women or picket a hospital that is cutting back on already inadequate health care to a Third World community, or set up a rape crisis center in a Black neighborhood. Organizing around welfare and daycare concerns might also be a focus. The work to be done and the countless issues that this work represents merely reflect the pervasiveness of our oppression."[18] Thus, Black feminists have long used community work to finetune their theoretical assessments of how intersectional oppression harms Black women.

There has been a notable departure from this intellectual tradition in recent years. As Black feminism became more institutionalized within academia, the dominant analytical trend moved toward applying Black feminist theory to questions related to culture and representation.[19] Toward this end, Black feminists impressively used Black feminist theory to understand Black women's cultural marginalization in many facets of social life, including law, media, and politics.[20] This analysis has enabled many Black feminists to advance incisive critiques about unfair power differentials and the state's complicity in Black women's historical marginalization.

Notwithstanding these worthwhile contributions, contemporary inequities resulting from economic factors need more attention within the Black feminist intellectual community. Prominent Black feminist figures like Angela Davis, Keeanga-Yamahtta Taylor, and Barbara Ransby remind us that a thorough Black feminist analysis necessitates a deep understanding of economics and political economy.[21] To study economics, one must analyze "the production and distribution of the goods and services we need and want."[22] Moreover, since economic activity is a social practice, it is also important to observe how political decisions shape economic activity. A political economy analysis examines the interactions and political tensions between fundamental institutional actors in producing and distributing goods and services. Take, for example, the political economy study of housing. One must analyze the production of housing, noting how government officials, housing agencies, builders, finance, and real estate agents work together to produce and sell residential units. This analysis must be paired with a close study of consumption that traces who purchases housing and why. This institutional analysis of consumption must also consider how different actors, including housing officials, developers, property managers, media, judges, academics, (tenant) activists, nonprofits, or homeowners, shape housing consumption patterns.

Despite the limited number of Black feminist materialist studies, there are representative examples of how this work can be conducted. Black feminist materialists identify the intersectional dynamics of oppression within a society's political economy and have long argued that race operates as a central anchor in capitalist economic activity—a framework that most critical race scholars refer to as racial capitalism.[23] In the United States, Black feminist materialists document how race (and racial messages) enable institutional actors such as corporate leaders or politicians to reproduce racial *and* gender stratification in labor, capital, and consumption patterns. Black feminist geographer Ruth Gilmore is one example. She combines Marxist theory with Black feminist insights to illustrate how the state of California addressed its post–1970s economic downturn by expanding its stock of rural-based prisons and by increasing the criminalization of low-wage Black urban men at an alarming rate.[24] Sarah Haley, a Black feminist theorist, blends deconstructionist methodological tools with Marxist and Black feminist theories to uncover the gendered tactics of the racialized terror the carceral state perpetrated in the early twentieth century to demonstrate the vulnerability of low-wage Black women to state imprisonment and forced labor.[25] Black feminist historian Keeanga-Yamahtta Taylor historicizes the central role that negative narratives about Black people played in the real estate industry's predatory inclusion schemes for urban Black households in the post–civil rights era.[26] Black feminist sociologist Rose Brewer uses similar tools to prove that negative cultural images of Black women opened political pathways for states to disinvest in public housing and dispossess low-wage Black residents at the start of the twenty-first century.[27] These scholars and many more have demonstrated that political-economic analyses must address the cultural and social discourses that legitimize inequitable market and political behaviors.[28]

I build on this methodological practice of Black feminist materialism in three ways. First, I center a racialized analysis of social reproduction. Every capitalist society must replenish its labor supply by determining how to address the care and socialization needs of (future) laborers alongside care for others, including the elderly, disabled, and infirm. Materialist feminists call this process social reproduction and have long argued for the necessity of analyzing social reproduction within studies of capitalism.[29] They add that in order to properly study social reproduction, it is necessary to examine local norms of care provision, delineating how social reproduction needs are met through the market, the family, the community, and/or the state.[30] Much of the care work for laborers is considered a familial responsibility in the United States: parental figures or legal guardians are expected to earn enough wages or income to purchase the social reproduction goods and services a family needs such as housing, health care, childcare, food, and clothing in the marketplace. Within most families, care work is often bifurcated into gender roles, with nurturing care work responsibilities gendered as female and validated by narratives, laws, and social institutions such as religion. Materialist feminists argue that gender inequities arise in part because this gendered division of care work has facilitated the societal devaluation of women's personal and professional care work and a cultural expectation that women will turn to men to subsidize their domestic stability.[31] Black feminist materialism takes the necessary step of addressing how race complicates the social reproduction of Black families.[32] Black feminist materialists understand that race, as a sociological category, is not based on biological fact but allows societies to classify certain people as racial groups—groups that carry complicated relational, historical, and cultural meanings. It also helps justify uneven resource distribution and functions as a "fundamental organizing principle of social stratification."[33] Consequently, I give special attention to understanding how political actors use race (racial narratives) about Black families to justify disparate treatment in the housing market and welfare politics.

My second contribution to Black feminist materialism is recognizing that gender plays a decisive sorting role in working-class Black families' inequitable access to the goods and services meant to address care and socialization needs. To be clear, gender is also a social category with a complex meaning-making system. It helps societies decide which humans should do certain types of labor and why. This labor category and its various rationales are wide and encompass reproductive (mainly unpaid work to sustain life), productive (labor that happens in the formal economy), emotional, behavioral, and social labor.[34] As such, gender affects political economies in particular ways. Gender not only shapes who gets access to jobs and welfare resources in market-based economies, but it also impacts these economies' negative consequences like poverty and economic inequality. Materialist feminists argue that because capitalism produces cyclical downturns and extended periods of sluggish wage growth, laborers and their families are prone to social reproduction crises—a reality that emerges when the costs of social reproduction outstrip wages earned. Marxist feminist Nancy Fraser adds that contemporary social reproduction crises have only worsened, especially as corporations and other businesses explore new ways to intensify the commodification of social reproduction.[35] For example, Black feminist materialism recognizes that as housing costs continue to soar, gender plays a key role in the political and economic arguments that are given to defend these costs.

In the United States, gender provides a powerful framework for political actors to understand and address social reproduction crises. For example, over the last fifty years, the US economy has shifted to a knowledge-based service economy, in which laborers often need more postsecondary education to secure high-wage work (unlike the high-wage manufacturing work that dominated in the postwar era). In this different labor market, many more men experience higher rates of downward mobility, whereas many women and other marginalized laborers endure more precarious work.[36] Working-class men's limited economic mobility has encouraged many political actors, ranging from politicians to social media influencers, to use gender as a way to defend male entitlement to state and business support. For example, during the COVID-19 global pandemic, more men received entertainment content that spoke to their grievance of labor competition with women.[37] As they expressed their entitlement to certain forms of wage labor and higher incomes, they articulated resentments against institutions and political decisions that they believed elevated other gendered groups like queer, trans, and gender expansive people over them.[38] For many of these men, they understand their social reproduction crisis through the historical script that nuclear heterosexual households with wage-earning men should form the basic economic unit in free-market societies. By adopting this script, many political officials believe the social reproduction crisis these men face can be best addressed through social and economic policies that shore up traditional heteropatriarchal families.[39] Notably, this cultural script about the interconnection between heterosexual family norms and policy has a longer history. It has been used to justify not providing social reproduction support (e.g., affordable housing assistance) to low-wage and nontraditional Black families.[40] My Black feminist materialist analysis traces how mainstream cultural narratives about gender help naturalize uneven outcomes and obfuscate structural causes of social reproduction crises by blaming Black people's supposed lack of allegiance to heteronormative gender scripts.[41]

Third, my approach to Black feminist materialism documents how cultural scripts about race and gender evolve to justify business actors' profit-making strategies. In the commodification of necessities for social reproduction—like housing—low-wage Black women are often devalued as consumers. Their poverty and substandard housing are typically read as evidence of poor character. Businesses or other capital interests may use these narratives to condone differential and sometimes discriminatory business practices. I use Black feminist materialism to trace how these negative narratives about Black women and their families shape market behavior and inform political justification for their distinct consumer treatment.

Rental Housing Politics Meets Cultural Narratives

The Undesirable Many tells the story of how low-wage Black women and their families remained vulnerable to a social reproduction crisis of housing unaffordability in the rental housing market of Washington, DC, from the early twentieth century to the start of the twenty-first century. Washington, DC, provides an excellent case study site for three reasons. Significantly, the nation's capital was the country's first majority-Black city. In the decades leading up to that transition, the real estate industry and local politicians expressed their beliefs about the impact of Black people on the city's rental housing market. As the Black population continued to rise, other institutional actors—such as the federal government—weighed in, providing an opportunity to examine how various institutions used race, gender, and other ascriptive differences to shape the city's rental housing market. Further, the location of and unique mode of governance in DC illuminate national and local perspectives about low-wage Black women and their families by studying the interplay between the federal government and local politics.

DC not only reveals the enduring connection between state and cultural scripts about race, gender, and place, it also offers an opportunity to examine the success and weakness of tenant protest. Since the height of the civil rights movements in the mid-1960s, DC has housed a strong tenant activist community that is anchored by Black women. In the past, this broad tenant alliance has successfully lobbied for some of the country's most robust tenant protections, like stronger housing code enforcement and rent control. These protections were partially meant to challenge the uneven effects of commodified housing on working-class Black families. However, organized real estate interests rolled back many of these protections in the post–civil rights era. The DC context, where a full spectrum of interests is represented in city politics, demonstrates how shifts in rental housing market practices impacted different groups.

The city also provides a unique opportunity to analyze Black politicians' responses to battles between organized tenants and the real estate industry. Black people earned historic access to governance positions in the post–civil rights era, especially in DC. As institutional actors, Black politicians navigated rental housing politics with varied allegiances and outcomes. These politicians not only shaped DC's rental housing market but also had a consequential impact on the perpetuation of inequities within it.

This study is a multiyear and mixed-method project. It uses archival and interview material from six national and local archives that hold housing policy documents of business leaders and politicians, organizational correspondence, and minutes from tenant meetings with public officials. Congressional hearings, newspapers, and other local publications are also critical primary and secondary sources. In addition, I collected ethnographic observations over eighteen months and conducted more than fifty interviews with Black women tenant activists and nonprofit housing providers, developers, and property managers. This data reveals how elected officials, business leaders, property managers, public housing administrators, and landlords used stereotypes about Black women's parenting, homemaking, and household maintenance to justify consumer mistreatment in the city's rental housing market.

This research reveals the power of culture in shaping market and state behavior. More specifically, this study demonstrates that Black people have been historically subjected to what I identify as a *gendered trope of Black tenant irresponsibility*. It traces how this stereotype operated as a shadow discourse in the city's affordable housing politics and uncovers the foundational belief that Black households fail to adequately care for private property. In the first half of the twentieth century, real estate representatives used the stereotype of Black tenant irresponsibility to depress Black households' property values, charge higher rents, and keep Black families marginalized in the country's oldest and worst housing stock. The combination of this structural housing shortage and price discrimination exacerbated a social reproduction crisis for many working-class Black families who struggled in overcrowded and comparatively costly housing. The city's affordable housing market emerged within this racialized context. Most prominent in urban locales, affordable housing markets offer housing prices that are deemed affordable for those who earn at or below a locale's median income. In the District of Columbia, housing officials and progressive activists in the early twentieth century sought to counter real estate interests' refusal to build for the city's working-class by institutionalizing what I call *disciplinary housing governance*—an approach to tenant management that argues that low-wage Black families' access to new or improved housing should be conditional on state regulation and/or private surveillance of their domestic lives.

The trope of Black tenant irresponsibility evolved alongside shifting real estate practices that ensured racial segregation and profitability. In the postwar era, this stereotype became more focused on low-wage Black women and their families. With the help of sociological studies, the state launched different experiments in disciplinary housing governance, with affordable housing—particularly public and rent-assisted housing—the preferred testing ground. These measures most often implicated (single) Black mothers and included mandatory casework, housekeeping checkups, and invasive personal interviews about the composition and household dynamics of families. Ultimately, the city's reliance on disciplinary housing governance helped vindicate racist real estate practices that differentiated consumers by their ability to pay and scrutinized and assessed the domestic practices of Black households.

However, this study understands that culture is a battleground, with protest serving as an essential tool to challenge inequities found in civic life. In the 1960s, Black working-class tenant activism emerged as a powerful counter to the gendered trope of Black tenant irresponsibility and disciplinary housing governance. At the height of the civil rights movement, Black women became the vanguard and primary base of tenant activism in DC.

Their activism, which included rent strikes, direct-action protests, and legislative campaigns, compelled the city to redirect its attention to regulations about real estate and landlords. However, despite Black women's powerful influence, national and local housing officials continued to perpetuate the narrative that low-wage Black women were irresponsible tenants who needed disciplinary regulation of their domestic lives. Moreover, adapting to the political context of increased tenant activism, real estate representatives often used negative cultural messages about Black women's domestic practices to defend reactionary experiments with disciplinary housing governance. For example, in response to Black women's demand for universal housing code enforcement in the 1960s, real estate championed mandatory housekeeping courses.

The gendered trope of Black tenant irresponsibility enabled real estate interests to defend their profit-making strategies in the District of Columbia. In the wake of substantial tenant victories in the 1960s and early 1970s, the real estate industry employed the stereotype to lead counterattacks against tenant protections, particularly rent control. In the 1970s, a multicultural, working-class tenant base with an active leadership that consisted of Black women successfully pushed city officials to adopt rent control as a universal and colorblind tenant protection. However, by the 1980s, real estate leaders and housing officials viewed rent control as a drag on the local real estate economy. Consequently, organized real estate interests worked with conservative think tanks and the mainstream press to link rent control politics to cultural narratives about the Black urban poor, especially welfare-assisted Black women and their families. This negative depiction eventually compelled some Black politicians to side with moneyed interests in rejecting rent control. Gender ideologies animated and legitimized their stances. Black male politicians often embraced masculinist interpretations of racial uplift, suggesting that welfare-assisted Black women and their families destroyed rent-controlled properties. In the wake of this alliance between real estate and some Black politicians, housing officials increasingly backed speculative real estate practices that left low-wage Black women and their families more vulnerable to housing insecurity and displacement.

Certain political actors' enduring defense of the gendered trope of Black tenant irresponsibility required different racial and gender performances in the post–civil rights era. As numerous institutional actors circulated blame narratives that targeted welfare-assisted Black women, social reproduction crises among the poorest Black urban families, especially those who lived in public housing, worsened in the 1980s. However, the gendered trope of Black tenant irresponsibility disguised the complexity of these crises, working in tandem with the discursive dichotomy of "honorable" versus "undesirable" Black poor that the institutional actors governing affordable housing perpetuated. Utilizing both narratives, conservative elites promoted a stance that became pivotal in increasing political tolerance for welfare retrenchment and housing insecurity. Moreover, they utilized Black people themselves, curating voices from urban communities to argue that welfare-assisted Black women and their children exemplified the category of "undesirable" public housing residents. Conservatives reprimanded this group for their purported inability to adopt heteronormative gender practices in their households and condoned their exposure to carceral measures, disinvestment, and, in some cases, displacement. Conversely, conservative federal officials tapped "respectable" Black women tenant activists like DC's Kimi Gray to back their call to privatize public housing through tenant management and public housing ownership. The few who would qualify for this limited access were assumed to be representatives of the so-called honorable poor.

As the nation entered into the twenty-first century, conservatives were not the only ones who deployed the gendered trope of Black tenant irresponsibility and disciplinary housing governance. By the 1990s, the gendered trope of Black tenant irresponsibility was firmly fused with a damaging gendered depiction of the Black underclass. This negative stereotype encouraged Democratic politicians to link public housing reform to urban growth initiatives and state-sanctioned displacement. This included supporting the demolition of public housing and calling for new affordable housing units to be occupied only by the "honorable" poor. However, this social category did not prioritize welfare-assisted families. Instead, it valued senior citizens and the original beneficiaries of affordable housing: smaller families and income-restricted but upwardly mobile young professionals. In this context, updated experiments in disciplinary housing governance emphasized credit and background checks, resulting in structural marginalization of families with carceral and eviction histories. This political moment produced a net decrease in public and project-based assisted housing. At the start of the twenty-first century, the gendered trope of Black tenant irresponsibility persistently followed low-wage Black women and their families as they privately navigated a real estate market awash with capital that helped shift existing rental housing into higher-yield use. Inevitably, serial displacement and housing insecurity became a permanent reality for low-wage Black women and their families.

To some, *The Undesirable Many* may feel like a story far removed from their reality. They may counter that these damaging cultural narratives impact only a segment of the country's poorest and reveal little about the rest of the (un)housed population. On the contrary, these stories help sharpen our analysis of how housing inequities remain ubiquitous in many urban areas. Joining critical urban studies published by Keeanga-Yamahtta Taylor and N. D. B. Connolly, this study illustrates how the inequities and profitability schemes of the housing market require the mobilization of evolving cultural tropes that devalue the housing consumption of different populations. My work demonstrates how gender has increased its systematic salience since the postwar era to become a critical way to justify the differential treatment of marginalized groups. By deploying the gendered trope of tenant irresponsibility and correctives like disciplinary housing governance, vested political and market interests can successfully naturalize inequitable market outcomes such as disinvestment and dispossession, arguing that both reflected tenants' cultural undesirability. *The Undesirable Many* contends that the gendered trope of Black tenant irresponsibility endured and evolved in part because of the bias of the US welfare state toward the middle class, thereby encouraging various stakeholders, including segments of the Black middle class, to support multiple iterations of disciplinary housing governance. This perspective adds nuance to existing welfare state studies. With a focus on the intersection of housing and welfare state politics, this book offers a compelling synthesis of different institutional factors that shape affordable housing in urban locales like the nation's capital while also underscoring the constitutive and adaptive force that gender and race play in such politics.[42] Importantly, this book also provides the crucial insight that if working-class tenant activists hope to regain some of the political strength many enjoyed during the tenant activist heyday of the 1970s, more attention has to be paid to the underwriting and sometimes corrosive influence culture has on market practices and political formations.

The Undesirable Many tells this complex story chronologically. Each chapter addresses a distinct political era in DC's rental housing history. Chapter 1 focuses on the first half of the twentieth century, tracing how negative racial stereotypes impacted real estate market practices and housing options for Black working-class families. It also examines how local housing officials and affordable housing developers embraced disciplinary housing governance as an institutional response to negative stereotypes about working-class Black families. The next chapter uncovers the significant impact Black women's tenant activism had on local and federal debates about tenant protections in the 1960s and early 1970s. This activism served as an indirect challenge to disciplinary housing governance's underwriting stereotypes about Black working-class domestic lives. The third chapter documents the harmful effect of stereotypes about resource-poor families on local debates about rent control in the 1970s and 1980s. The fourth chapter considers the recalibrated alliance of conservative elites with select Black women tenant activists during the height of federal welfare retrenchment in the 1980s. Conservatives used these connections with Black women tenant activists to validate their reforms to public housing. The fifth chapter recognizes the alliance of federal and local governments in urban growth politics and the tacit support for the displacement of the "undesirable" Black poor in the 1900s and early 2000s. It links these stereotypes to contemporary reforms in disciplinary housing governance that further entrenched the housing insecurity and forced displacement of low-income Black women and their families.

Finally, because the cultural implications of housing potentially affect everyone, this book offers an opportunity for self-reflection. The stories and names in the ensuing chapters may move you to place yourself in the context of history. Consider how you or your family would have coped with the challenges that working-class Black families confronted in rental housing politics. Perhaps you or your family knew one or few troublesome Black tenants and decided to champion conditional measures to ward off any future distress. Consider if those measures were merely self-protective or perpetuated a more extended history of exclusion that reinforced unhelpful hierarchies and housing unaffordability. Your reflective orientation to the material may open up new possibilities for alliance and generate a shared understanding of the cultural underpinnings of structural inequities.[43] And since some of us bear the brunt of this cultural and structural marginalization more than others, it is only fitting that this book concludes by sharing Black feminist insights for pathways toward a more equitable housing economy.

1 Finding "Problem Families"

The Origins of Disciplinary Housing Governance

· ·

With a radiant smile and deep dimples to match, Patricia Penny could shift the mood in a room with her youthful spirit alone. A native Washingtonian now in her sixties, Penny grew up in Shaw, a historically Black neighborhood near the city's center in Northwest DC. We met when I joined ONE DC as a full-time community organizer in July 2007. Penny, one of ONE DC's most influential leaders, devised campaign strategies while also conducting outreach with me in Shaw. Door knocking with her was a treat because she always regaled me with funny childhood stories intermixed with Black residential history. Neighborhood cookouts, school crushes, and sibling rivalries were just a few of her positive childhood memories. These tales from her youth complemented the robust history of elite African Americans who lived in Shaw, where luminaries like Carter G. Woodson and Duke Ellington studied and celebrated Black life. Yet as we talked, Penny's joy slowly dissolved when she recounted her mother's struggles to find low-rent but quality housing for herself and her seven children.

Recalling the early 1960s, when her mother had just separated from her husband, Penny described how her family's housing struggles began: "Back then, you couldn't move into an apartment with seven kids. So, pretty much, you had to lie about it. Back then, she couldn't fill out an application for herself. . . . So back then, my mother had to ask her friend's husband, Jerome, because even Doris [Penny mother's friend] could not fill out an application for her best friend to help my mother get a place."[1] Since men were expected to be household representatives in housing market transactions, Penny's mother would occasionally invite Uncle Jerome to the house to keep up appearances. Penny remembered that her mother told her children that only two of them could play outside at a time in order to avoid lease infractions for overcrowding. Her mother's efforts to allay suspicion were short-lived, however, as someone reported them for defying the building's occupancy standards. The owner soon told Penny's mother to vacate the premises.

If the press or local housing officials had heard of Penny's mother's decision to lie to secure affordable shelter, they would have promptly labeled hers a "problem family." They would have counted her among those irresponsible tenants who destroyed property and brought so-called blight to neighborhoods. They also would have suggested that families like Penny's made it harder for the city to enforce its housing code—a minimum set of standards for building maintenance that outlined landlord-tenant responsibilities.[2] Housing codes became a mainstay in the United States after the federal government incentivized their passage in local areas using urban renewal funding in the 1950s. These codes were part of a broader spectrum of twentieth-century urban planning measures, such as building codes and zoning regulations, that were meant to improve the housing stock and stabilize property values. However, housing codes would become a powerful tool that Black mothers used to demand better living conditions through universal enforcement in the mid-1960s. But until then, local officials and landlords used housing code enforcement as a political way to fine-tune anti-Black arguments that have long justified residential segregation and housing insecurity.

For the first half of the twentieth century, most real estate interests and politicians considered Black people a threat to property values. They justified higher rents and implemented state-sanctioned exclusionary measures to curtail this supposed risk. In the postwar era, housing officials and real estate tweaked this trope, focusing on subgroups like single mothers and suggesting that insufficient maternal care produced persistently disinvested communities. As a result, gendered stereotypes about Black tenant irresponsibility operated as a shadow discourse that shaped the affordable housing market and housing policies such as code enforcement. Within this loaded ideological context, low-wage families in urban centers, particularly Black families, had to prove that they deserved better housing, a process that subjected them to disciplinary housing governance. Many state and social welfare actors hoped that offering access to improved housing after families agreed to attend housekeeping classes or consented to some other form of behavioral oversight would act as an effective hedge against property decline.

This chapter charts the institutionalization of disciplinary housing governance in the nation's capital from the Progressive Era to the post–World War II period. While welfare and housing officials experimented with different approaches to disciplinary housing governance, the gendered trope of Black tenant irresponsibility legitimized each iteration. This stereotype allowed various institutional actors to defend legal and social measures that protected a racial hierarchy in real estate in order to justify rising property values. Many of these actors saw disciplinary housing governance in low-rent housing and housing code enforcement as a necessary complement to the era's racial regulation. Attention to the thematic history of disciplinary housing governance reveals the intersectional role of race, gender, and class in the housing market and affordable housing politics. This ideological context both produced and concealed obstacles such as those Penny's mother had to navigate privately as she worked to shelter her family.

Progressives and the Origins of Disciplinary Housing Governance

Abraham Lincoln's signing of the District of Columbia Compensated Emancipation Act in April 1862 outlawed enslavement in the nation's capital and prompted Black people to flock to the "city of freedom" in the war-torn South.[3] Less than ten years later, Washington, DC, housed the highest percentage of Black residents in the country. From the Civil War until the end of the nineteenth century, most Black migrants came from Maryland, Virginia, and the Carolinas. Many settled in Georgetown, one of the city's oldest neighborhoods, located in DC's upper northwest quadrant. Like other neighborhoods in the United States, Georgetown developed over time. Adjacent to the C&O Canal, which channeled water from the Potomac River between DC and Maryland, Georgetown was initially inhabited by the Indigenous Nacotchtank people called Tohoga. But after English settlers began to colonize the neighborhood in the seventeenth century, Georgetown grew from a trading post into an industrial hub where raw materials and enslaved Africans were bought and sold.[4] But after DC's emancipation law, the neighborhood blossomed as Black migrants created and stewarded powerful institutions such as churches, civic clubs, schools, and local businesses.[5]

Yet while Black Georgetown residents served as an indisputable model of Black excellence (once they were granted democratic inclusion), Black migrants as a collective were not treated as desirable newcomers. In a housing market that was strained by the speculative real estate boom resulting from the Civil War and ensuing public works projects, Black migrants encountered a real estate market that unevenly enforced a color line. Anti-Black discrimination was pervasive, even for wealthy families. As Black journalist John Wesley Cromwell wrote in 1881, "There seems to be a multi-understanding among the capitalists and real estate dealers who have been conspicuous in contributing to this development of our city, that the colored man, no matter how respectable, how intelligent, or how thrifty is not to enjoy in common with other citizens the right to live in as good a style as his means will allow him." He added, "If a house becomes vacant, if it has modern improvements, if it be in a decent neighborhood, the word is invariably given that no colored tenant shall occupy it."[6]

Discrimination ultimately shaped Black families' settlement patterns in "freedom city." Because few landlords were willing to build explicitly for Black migrants, they often had to move into communities with a high concentration of Black people and/or immigrants. In response to the city's post–Civil War housing crisis, Congress agreed to expand the construction of alley homes. Many of the original tenants were European immigrants, but as those residents found new homes, Black families became the dominant population.[7] By the end of the nineteenth century, close to 20,000 Black families lived in alley homes, constituting over 95 percent of DC's alley residents. As not quite a quarter of DC's resident population, Black people were overrepresented in alley housing.[8] Placed within alleys and with limited access to main streets, these hastily constructed homes often had dirt floors and typically lacked indoor bathrooms, plumbing, and windows. Rooms were as small as ten feet long by ten feet wide (imagine a slightly oversized pool table), and entire families were sometimes forced to live in one room.

Black migrants' typically deplorable housing conditions inspired some of the city's first organized housing activism. By the end of the nineteenth century, educated and well-resourced activists known as Progressives began challenging the uncoordinated ways that cities and real estate interests housed (im)migrants. Progressives were part of a political reform movement that advocated a mixed economy guided by government regulation. They championed a policy platform that ensured social protections for consumers and vulnerable populations and advocated for public goods such as parks, public education, and public health infrastructure. To coordinate their advocacy, Progressive activists created groups such as the National Housing Association to champion state reforms to curb the death and disease that threatened residents of overcrowded and poorly built homes packed into city centers. However, since building codes fell under local and not federal responsibility, DC constituted a unique circumstance. Since DC lacked statehood and local governance, Progressives had to lobby Congress and the city's three federally appointed District of Columbia commissioners to address their housing concerns. They pushed for building reform that moved beyond the city's focus on aesthetics, materials, height, and building placement to include housing code measures that protected the health and safety of occupants.[9]

Progressives linked their housing reform goals to the city's urban planning project to compel Congress and local officials to act. At the end of the nineteenth century, the federal government wanted the nation's capital to become a city befitting a rising imperial power. To realize this vision, federal officials supported the City Beautiful movement. City Beautiful represented a national movement led by urban planners and architects who sought to improve cities with beautification projects like building monuments and expanding green space. Progressive activists pushed congressional and local leaders to include working-class families' poor housing conditions in City Beautiful goals. In 1892, their successful lobbying resulted in a local building regulation that mandated that new alley homes be built with a modicum of building code standards—sewage, water mains, electricity, and public street connections.[10] The Board of Public Health, the city's leading enforcement body for this law, struggled to keep pace with condemning unsanitary alley homes, while local officials tried to accelerate the elimination of alley neighborhoods and buildings by turning them into streets, parks, playgrounds, or garages. The law's ultimate effect, however, was to freeze alley home construction, which enabled landlords to continue renting existing unsafe units primarily to Black families.[11]

Unlike Progressives, many landlords and developers believed the city's poor housing conditions for Black families were an unavoidable fact of urban life. Furthermore, they believed Black families' inadequate housing reflected cultural and racial character traits, not class divisions. The gendered trope of Black irresponsibility anchored this discussion. These business actors were not the only ones who accepted this trope. Many local officials viewed alley dwellers as members of the "idle class" and blamed them for much of the city's crime, even though they constituted a small minority of the population.[12] Nevertheless, developers and landlords who housed Black alley dwellers utilized this stereotype to justify higher prices with economic logic: you charge higher prices to offset risk. For these real estate representatives, Black families were risky investments who were broadly assumed to be irresponsible and more likely to destroy property or skip payments. Such depictions emboldened real estate interests and white Washingtonians to resist the efforts of Black families to seek better shelter in majority-white neighborhoods.

The gendered trope of Black tenant irresponsibility was so pervasive that it impacted Progressives too. While many Progressives challenged some racist tropes, they often accepted the Jim Crow stereotype that Black people were culturally underdeveloped due to their African origins. For Progressives, morality was the primary determinant of character and tenant desirability. One of the country's most famous muckrakers, Jacob Riis, typified this approach in *How the Other Half Lives*, in which he praised Black people's supposedly cheerful disposition toward American life: "Poverty, abuse, and injustice alike the Negro accepts with imperturbable cheerfulness. His philosophy is of the kind that has no room for repining. . . . His home surroundings, except when he is utterly depraved, reflect his blithesome temper. The poorest Negro housekeeper's room in New York is bright with gaily-colored prints of his beloved 'Abe Linkum,' General Grant, President Garfield, Mrs. Cleveland, and other national celebrities. . . . In the art of putting the best foot foremost, of disguising his poverty by making a little go a long way, our Negro has no equal."[13] Rhetoric like this attempted to distinguish the moral and thus deserving recipient of better housing from the dissolute or undeserving tenant. Progressives contended that the latter thrived in poor housing environments and believed that irresponsible and unscrupulous tenants chose to live there to avoid public reproach and detection by police.

Far from rejecting the trope outright, some Progressives embraced it to justify their advocacy for housing reform. Unlike New York and other cities with a higher percentage of immigrants living in the worst housing, in DC, it was predominantly Black people living under such conditions, mainly in the city's feared alley homes. There, Progressive activists made pronouncements similar to Riis's, creating moral hierarchies of Black deservingness. Reproductive labor, such as domestic work, parenting, and coupling practices, quickly became the signifier of a family's morality or deviance. Charles Weller, a social worker turned journalist, studied DC alley homes for seven years in the early 1900s. His published results used women as a symbolic index for a family's ideal reproductive labor practices. For example, Weller characterized dishonorable families as those with women who lived in "houses of ill repute" (brothels or homes were sex work was conducted) and "un-moral" homes (which often did not practice male-centered leadership). According to Weller, if neighbors identified a home by a woman's name and ignored "her male companion," that was also evidence of Black women's undesirable reproductive labor practices.[14] Seen as household leaders, these Black women also sometimes troublingly, according to Weller, subsidized "a common class of [Black] men whom the alley folks call 'lovers,'" who financially contributed little to the household.[15]

This implicit bias among Progressives inspired different interventions for certain racial groups. Negative descriptions of the reproductive lives of poor Black families contrasted with explanations that defended white ones, such as families who lived in the all-white Caucasian Alley (located in the city's Northwest Dupont Circle neighborhood). Social workers often saw these white families through empathetic frames as victims of circumstance (e.g., an alcoholic husband who lost his job and a virtuous wife with a teachable spirit). For them, Progressive social workers preferred private welfare interventions such as a "drink cure" for the husband and a new home for the family away from the alley, where tenants would not be able to taunt the husband for becoming "a goody goody, an' likewise a fool."[16] Conversely, they viewed Black families as inherently pathological due to their African origins and the "social irresponsibility of country life" from which many came. As a result, social workers like Weller enumerated Black mothers' alleged parenting failures and advised stronger measures such as the removal of children.[17]

Gendered understandings of tenant morality soon became a hallmark of Progressive inroads into creating an affordable housing market. One of their interventions was establishing limited dividend companies that enabled mission-oriented business groups to develop low-rent housing. The Washington Sanitary Improvement Company, which subscribed to a business philanthropy model fashioned after similar endeavors in European and other American cities, is one of the most well-known examples in DC. Founded in 1897 by prominent white Progressives, the company grew from an alliance between social scientists and the city's leading white businesspeople. Seeking to disprove the developer maxim that housing working-class families was unprofitable, the company secured congressional approval to issue and sell stock to investors willing to build deeply affordable housing in exchange for a dividend payout capped at 5 percent. This business model contrasted mightily with that of alley property owners, who often netted 10 to 20 percent profit margins.[18] The Washington Sanitary Improvement Company used the accrued capital to purchase lots on which to build homes with housing code standards that Progressives had long championed, including indoor plumbing, bathrooms, front and back doors, and kitchens with modern appliances. Only a few miles from the White House, the company built its first eight rental properties on Bates Street NW near North Capitol Street NW.

Given that Black families were the city's primary alley dwellers, it stands to reason that they would have been first in line to occupy most of the company's new homes. The opposite occurred. By 1904, 110 white families and only thirty Black families had secured these new houses.[19] Most of these new tenants represented rising middle-class workers, including engineers, policemen, teachers, doctors, and tailors.[20] The company's leadership defended this demographic decision, stating, "It was considered best to begin this movement by providing improved dwellings for the better class of wage-earners, in the belief that the next grade would rent houses vacated by them, and so on until the bottom of the ladder was reached."[21]

This company's filtering strategy rested on subjecting working-class tenants to an external evaluation of their moral deservingness and fitness for new low-cost housing. This ethos of conditional access helped legitimize one of the conceptual anchors of disciplinary housing governance—the endless defining, sorting, and distinguishing between "deserving" working-class tenants and "undesirable" ones. The Jim Crow–circulated stereotype of Black tenant irresponsibility meant that even Progressive groups like the Washington Sanitary Improvement Company took great care to identify "respectable colored tenants" deserving of code-compliant new housing (i.e., those who were heterosexual, married, did not drink, were law-abiding, and had suitable work).[22] The company's tenant selection model validated Progressives' earlier moral evaluations of the city's poorest, keeping those marked as "un-moral" and nonnormative out of the desirable tenant pool.

The Washington Sanitary Improvement Company eventually extended its business model to low-wage tenants. In 1906, the company adopted a new funding model practiced by New York business philanthropist Henry Phipps. It expanded its tenant criteria to include "people of humble means," such as male day laborers and laundresses and their families.[23] The company selected Foggy Bottom, then an industrial and working-poor neighborhood in the city's southwest quadrant near the Potomac River and Rock Creek, for some of this new housing. Seeking to provide a model for sheltering the city's poorest, it built in some of DC's oldest housing stock in Black-only alley communities such as Snow Court and Hughes Alley. Residents of these renovated properties were expected to accept the "guidance" of agents, who collected rents and lived on site. Although archival evidence of what such "guidance" entailed is scant, these agents, who often had social work backgrounds and were often employed through the Associated Charities of Washington, DC, assisted in judging the potential character fitness of tenants and most likely provided services to adjust their household practices.[24]

The Washington Sanitary Improvement Company's model inspired others to follow suit. Charlotte Everett Archibald Hopkins was one of the city's most prominent proponents of tying disciplinary housing governance to low-rent housing. A wealthy white philanthropist, Hopkins successfully petitioned Congress and First Ladies Ellen Wilson and Eleanor Roosevelt to support alley demolition in Washington, DC. To replace these demolished dwellings, Hopkins envisioned code-compliant and family-centered communities for deserving "laboring" families that included a library, a playground, a wading pool, laundry facilities, a medical clinic, and a social hall.[25] Fearing that Black residents would not "successfully" transition from alley homes to apartment or single-family living without strong character management, Progressive women like Hopkins offered these amenities alongside what critical theorist Saidiya Hartman has called the "scrutiny of the stranger's gaze."[26] In this instance, disciplinary housing governance was not simply a matter of correcting the behavior of undeserving tenants but was also a method for acculturating deserving tenants to middle-class homemaking standards. To facilitate this cultural adjustment, Hopkins wanted existing settlement houses and social workers to oversee the character development of former alley dwellers and shape Black women's reproductive labor by insisting, for instance, that they attend cooking classes.[27] With a social worker supervising how Black people used their homes, Hopkins and other Progressive women hoped to meticulously cultivate what feminist theorist Melinda Cooper describes as the "social conservatism ethos of African American domesticity."[28]

For Progressives like Hopkins, disciplinary housing governance was a necessary hedge against property decline and a way to achieve middle-class cultural integration. Progressives regarded such practices as a liberal way to acculturate DC residents and saw them as a necessary counter to the mainstream cultural belief that poor Black people preferred substandard housing conditions. It was a political choice that would have numerous consequences on affordable housing politics in the future. Chief among these political outcomes was that public officials and real estate interests would justify the argument that the state or private actors needed to judge and assess which working-class Black families deserved new housing while leaving the racialized housing market unchallenged.

The city's Progressive movement for affordable housing and disciplinary housing governance stalled once the United States entered World War I in 1914. The federal government conscripted raw materials, triggering a national housing shortage. Hopkins's vision never materialized, and the Washington Sanitary Improvement Company struggled to raise capital and amass land amid a speculative housing crisis. As 100,000 residents migrated to DC, including 75,000 as wartime workers, the intense demand for housing strained the city's real estate market. The limited housing supply pushed many to reject government employment offers, while some government workers chose to canvas "the residential sections of the city, ringing doorbells until some private family, taking pity on their plight, should agree to house them under the family roof."[29] Congress rushed to hold hearings on the matter. In those sessions, Congress members learned that speculators were seizing older homes and large apartment buildings so they could sublet rooms and charge higher rents. With low overhead, nonexistent vacancies, and limited prospects for new low-rent development, speculators knew they had captive consumers and hiked rents and issued evictions accordingly.[30] Their next step was to accelerate homebuying, driving up resale prices beyond the financial reach of most Washingtonians.

The gendered trope of Black tenant irresponsibility once again colored the political response to the city's affordability crisis. Because building new homes was not feasible, Congress focused on regulating the racial use of existing homes. In congressional hearings, white Washingtonians shared horrid stories of landlords threatening to evict them and replace them with Black tenants. In their defense, landlords claimed that Black people were irresponsible and duplicitous renters. "Colored people would move into a property and throw it to nothing," one landlord testified. "We have no law here to prevent colored people from moving next door to you in any section of the city and when they do we either move out and the property can not be rented to anybody else but colored people, or else it goes down to nothing."[31] These harmful scripts about Black recklessness allowed Congressman Ben Johnson (D-KY), who served as the House of Representatives chair to DC's oversight committee, to attach an amendment to Senator Willard Saulsbury Jr.'s (D-DE) resolution to freeze rents and halt evictions during the war. His amendment sought to prevent "colorable sales of real estate for one year after the war."[32] Congress ultimately agreed with Johnson and passed the Saulsbury resolution, which froze rents, issued a moratorium on evictions, and prohibited real estate sales to Black people on May 31, 1918.[33]

The measure illustrated Congress's peculiar and reactionary role in DC's affordable housing politics. Sensitive to public pressure, Congress conflated its need for personnel stability with local (white) demand for racial segregation. White southern male rule dominated District oversight committees, so it is not surprising that Congress gave in to this political pressure even as northern congressmen insisted that the nation's capital should represent American modernity and liberal ideals. Despite the inconsistent local involvement of Congress, the resolution was a historic measure that made DC the first city in the country to implement a rent freeze and a moratorium on evictions. That action later paved the way for DC to become the first city to implement rent control.[34] Nonetheless, the federal Saulsbury resolution exposed an institutional alliance between members of Congress, landlords, and many white Washingtonians regarding race, thus ensuring that Black residents would continue to be the city's undesirable many.

The Saulsbury resolution also perpetuated a political silence about Black Washingtonians' experiences in and strategies against the city's racialized housing market. Black people's exclusion from the debate enabled Congress to follow the national trend of using state power to intervene in the housing market to ensure that white households had access to affordable housing while restricting Black residential mobility. Localities throughout the country were experimenting with similar goals using zoning regulations. In 1910, Baltimore implemented the first racial zoning ordinance in the United States. Other cities, including DC, built upon Baltimore's invention, establishing planning commissions to implement exclusionary zoning measures.[35]

Although the Saulsbury resolution provided economic relief through its rent freeze, it proved to be a weak measure for stopping Black migration and halting real estate speculation.[36] Black people continued to find single-family homes to buy or rent in white neighborhoods in the nation's capital. In the early 1920s, employed Black families typically located a white seller to purchase a home, usually in the middle of the block, while earning the problematic moniker of "invader."[37] Occasional violence emerged, as in other places in the country, but more often panicked whites fled the area. Consequently, as one Black sociologist explained, "It is only a matter of a few months before one may see scores of colored children roller skating on the sidewalks or playing contently on the lawns, symbolizing the fact that the area which once belonged exclusively to white people has become a Negro neighborhood."[38] White residents in other neighborhoods tried with varying degrees of success to use racially restrictive covenants to ban future sales to Black owners. However, the combination of the profit motive and white panic kept the racial turnover of white neighborhoods going strong, especially in areas with comparatively lower land values that were located close to commercial districts such as Georgia Avenue, U Street, and Florida Avenue.[39]

Black residents generally gained access to existing middle-grade housing stock. Developers who built Grade A and Grade B homes that included top finishes and the best amenities often exercised restrictive covenants, a tactic that some wealthy Black people also used. Most Black families employed in working-class professions could purchase Grade C homes, which typically were several decades old and had just been vacated by white families of similar means. Black renters occasionally gained access to Grade C homes too, but compared to homeowners, they experienced greater difficulty finding higher-grade homes. Instead, Black renters were overrepresented in Grades D and E homes, where landlords effectively abandoned maintenance.[40] Regardless of their ownership status, DC's increased Black presence contributed to higher housing prices citywide during the 1920s.

While forgoing serious consideration of how race shaped the city's real estate practices, white real estate representatives and homeowners demanded state enforcement of racial segregation to protect their property values. As the Great Migration led more Black residents to DC in the 1920s and 1930s, white real estate interests and homeowners lobbied Congress and District commissioners to enforce stricter racial restrictions on property use. They argued that Black settlements near or in white neighborhoods drove down the value of the property of white homeowners. Again, their defenses were tied to the racist trope of Black irresponsibility. In congressional hearings about the city's housing stock and property values, landlords and property tax assessors described how this racist principle became an economic fact. Landlords repeated the long-held racist belief that Black families triggered lower rental values because it was assumed they would destroy property, skip rent payments, and hike litigation costs.[41] The city's real estate tax assessor, William P. Richards, offered a more nuanced perspective on why Black families threatened property values. He said that property value assessment required the dual assessment of the owner's desired rent and the public's perception of the property's economic value. Richards explained, "If a man purchases a piece of property he purchases it with the idea that it is going to derive a certain income from it; that fixes the price in his mind, but if we determine both the revenue that is derived from property and the prices that are paid, we become acquainted with what the public is willing to accept in the way of an income from properties, so that all these things together influence the judgment of the assessors in their final conclusions as to what property is worth."[42]

This seemingly colorblind explanation of property values suggested that Black residences would not trigger declining value, especially if they paid more than previous white residents. At least one congressman, Henry George Jr (D-NY), pointed this out in a congressional hearing about DC's tax assessment practices. However, Richards argued that property value assessments were also influenced by demographic continuity, land improvements, local amenities (e.g., schools, grocery stores), and other comforts such as public safety.[43] He added that when low-wage Black families moved into existing low-wage white neighborhoods, property values rarely decreased. Only when Black families moved into "fine residences" once held by people the assessors believed to be more desirable residents did tax assessors reduce property values. Richards described this phenomenon in LeDriot Park, located next to Howard University in DC's northwest quadrant and, by the early 1910s, home to the city's Black elite such as civil rights activist Mary Church Terrell and Black feminist Anna Julia Cooper. He said,

> That neighborhood [LeDriot Park] in that section in 15 years' time has changed entirely from a white residential section to a colored tenant section. Now here is the peculiar condition of values. With all the houses worth in the neighborhood of from $3000 to $3500, the rental values are probably the same that they were before; but on T Street and some of the cross streets . . . there were some very fine residences. Persons formerly owned their own houses and had yards around them and were content to stay there as long as it remained a white neighborhood. This change has caused those people to move away and sell their houses at a sacrifice, and the rental value from those large houses will not compare with the rental value of the small houses. The large houses are too good for the neighborhood.[44]

Sharing a sentiment expressed by his peers nationally, Richards believed the downgrade in property values reflected real estate economics: the highest and "best" use of large houses was for wealthy white (family) homeowners. Richards argued that after these families departed and large homes were sold or subdivided and rented to supposedly less desirable Black people, a value reassessment was warranted.

The city's racialized property value practices left Black renters and owners vulnerable to ongoing public attacks because white homeowners and landlords often blamed them for economic and social consequences like overcrowding and disinvestment (both of which often meant "blight" in urban planning discourse). White landlords and homeowners' fear and anger at a possible property value downgrade compelled many to unite in the institutional presumption that Black families, no matter what their income status was, were expected to be in the city's oldest stock and smaller units because it was assumed that was what they could afford—and what they deserved. It was this racialized and classist hierarchy of property use that

$5.50 Int. Rev. Stamps affixed.

DISTRICT OF COLUMBIA, TO WIT:

I, George H. Campbell a Notary Public in and for the District of Columbia, D O HEREBY CERTIFY That Henry Boesch add Anna M. Boesch, his wife, parties to a certain Deed bearing date on the twenty-third day of March A.D. 1922, and hereto annexed, personally appeared before me in said District, the said Henry Boesch and Anna M. Boesch, being personally well known to me as the persons who executed the said Deed, and acknowledged the same to be their act and deed.

GIVEN under my hand and seal this twenty-third day of March A.D. 1922.

George H. Campbell

(NOTARIAL SEAL)

Notary Public

Notary Public for the Dist. of Columbia

(NOTARIAL SEAL)

My Commission expires Apr. 20, 1924

-----0----------

Minnie Wittlin   )
    to   )Deed
)
Blanche K. Towson)

No. 215. Recorded April 5, 1922,
at 2:59 P.M.

THIS DEED, made this Third day of April, in the year one thousand nine hundred and twenty-two, by and between Minnie Wittlin, of the District of Columbia, party of the first part, and Blanche K. Towson, of the same place, party of the second part:

WITNESSETH, That in consideration of Ten ($10.00) dollars, the party of the first part does hereby grant unto the party of the second part, in fee simple, all that piece or parcel of land, together with the improvements, rights, privileges and appurtenances to the same belonging, situate in the District of Columbia, described as follows, to wit: Lot 8, in Square 2701, of Mary G. Machen's subdivision of part of the tract of land known as "Indolence, as per plat recorded in Book 55, at page 179, in the Surveyor's Office of the District of Columbia. Subject to the conditions and covenants that when a builing is erected on said lot it shall not be located within 15 feet from the North line of Webster Street, except as to bay windows and porches; and that all buildings erected or to be erected on said lot shall be built and used for residence purposes exclusively, except that a stable, carriage house, or private garage, sheds, or other buildings to be used only in connection with such residence, may be erected on the rear of said lot, and not abutting on Webster Street, or situated in proximity to the building line thereof. During the period of 20 years from June 17, 1916, the said lot of ground shall not nor shall any part thereof, nor any building nor part of a building thereon, be used for trade, business, manufacturing, or commercial purposes; and no hospital, asylum, apartment house or flats of any description, hotel public house, livery stable or public garage shall ever, during said period or term of 20 years be erected or maintained on said Lot of ground. The said lot of ground shall not, nor shall any part thereof, nor any building, or part of any building to be erected thereon ever at any time whatsoever, be sold, leased, transferred or conveyed unto or in trust for, or for the purpose of occupation or use of any negro or colored person, and in case of a sale, and conveyance of said lot by the purchaser, he shall require the grantee to covenant to this effect therein

An example of a racially restrictive covenant in Washington, DC. District of Columbia Recorder of Deeds.

Subject , however, to a certain incumbrance of record of Forty five hundred ($4500.00) Dollars.

A N D the said party of the first part covenants that she will warrant specially the property hereby conveyed, and that she will execute such further assurances of said land as may be requisite.

W I T N E S S her hand and seal the day and year hereinbefore written.

In presence of   Minnie Wittlin (Seal)

J.C. Kennedy Campbell

$17.00 Int. Rev. Stamps affixed

DISTRICT OF COLUMBIA, TO WIT:

I, J.C. Kennedy Campbell a Notary Public ,in and for the District aforesaid, H E R EBY C E R T I F Y That Minnie Wittlin who is personally well known to me as the grantor in, and the person who executed the aforegoing and annexed Deed, dated April 3rd A.D. 1922, personally appeared before me in the said District,and acknowledged the said deed to be her act and deed.

G I V E N under my hand and seal this 3rd day of April 1922.

(NOTARIAL SEAL)   J.C. Kennedy Campbell

                                     Notary Public.

----0--------

Blanche K. Towson   )
)
      to   ) Trust
)
Union Trust Co. D.C.   )

No. 216. Recorded April 5, 1922, at 2:59P.M.

T H I S   I N D E N T U R E Made this 4th day of April A.D. 1922 by and between Blanche K. Towson, widow, of the District of Columbia, party hereto of the first part and The Union Trust Company of The District of Columbia, a body corporate in the said District, party of the second part, W I T N E S S E T H:

W H E R E A S, the said party hereto of the first part is justly indebted unto The Washington Loan And Trust Company, in the full sum of Eighty-five Hundred Dollars ($8500) for money loaned for which amount she has made and delivered her eight certain promissory notes bearing even date herewith, numbered 1 to 8 inclusive, Notes Nos. 1 and 2, being for the sum of Two Thousand Dollars ($2,000) each. Notes Nos. 3, 4 and 5,being for the sum of One Thousand Dollars($1,000) each, and Notes Nos. 6, 7 and 8,being for the sum of Five Hundred Dollars($500) each; all of said notes being payable to the order of the said The Washington Loan and Trust Company, three years after date with interest at the rate of six and one-half per centum per annum, from date and until paid,payable semi-annually, each instalment of interest to bear interest after maturity, if not then paid, at the rate of six and one- half per centum per annum. Principal and interest payable at the Office of The Washington Loan and Trust Company, Washington, D.C.

A N D W H E R E A S, the party of the first part desires to secure the prompt payment of said debt, and the interest thereon, when and as the same shall become due and payable, as well as any renewals or extensions thereof, with any increase in the rate of interest on said debt, and of all costs and expenses incurred in respect thereto, and of all costs and expenses,including reasonable counsel fees ...incurred or paid by thesaid party of thesecond part or substituted trustee, or by any person hereby secured on account of any litigation at law.or in equity which may arise in respect to this trust, or the property hereinafter mentioned while this trust continues, and of all money which may be advanced as herein provided for, with interest at the rate of six and one-half per centum per annum on all such costs and sums so advanced from the date of such advance.

(continued)

This photo documents the controversial shift in residential occupancy from white to Black residents. Renowned photographer Carl Mydans seems to have captured the prevailing white public sentiment regarding this issue with the photo's charged caption: "A once proud section of Washington, D.C. These houses are now overcrowded with a Negro population and are in great need of improved sanitary conditions." Library of Congress, Prints & Photographs Division, Farm Security Administration/Office of War Information Black-and-White Negatives.

emboldened even poor white families, whose homes were not likely to experience reduced values, to join wealthier white homeowners and landlords to lobby elected officials (and urban planning and zoning officials) to keep Black residents and their social reproduction needs in select neighborhoods in DC's northwest, southwest, and southeast quadrants.[45]

Notably, the city's firm embrace of residential segregation in the wake of World War I exposed the limits of affordable housing advocates' private solutions to DC's affordability crisis. The racial discrimination in private housing undermined private filtering of higher-grade units to nonwhite tenants and kept Black families stuck in older homes. Additionally, limited dividend companies like the Washington Sanitary Improvement Company could not compete in a market that remained disproportionally oriented to single-family homeownership. The companies' advocates admitted that if forced to purchase higher-priced land, they would need to recoup the higher development costs, making rents out of reach for the neediest families.[46] The national housing shortage and these companies' limited capacity ultimately pushed housing advocates to argue for code-compliant public housing as the most pragmatic solution.[47]

Public Housing and Disciplinary Housing Governance

In the fall of 1929, the country plunged into the Great Depression after the New York Stock Exchange lost half its value in ten weeks. By 1932, one out of every four American adults was jobless and two million were homeless. In DC, Black manual and domestic workers suffered the most extended periods of unemployment. Unemployed workers across the country increased their labor militancy and demanded state assistance with work and affordable housing.[48] With national unrest as a political backdrop, President Herbert Hoover commissioned a series of White House papers to study the national state of homebuilding and ownership. Wide-ranging in scope, these eleven papers informed Hoover's reluctant decision to back federal intervention in the housing market.

One of these papers focused exclusively on Black people's housing conditions. It offered a critical account of the policy recommendations of select Black elites for addressing the chronic lack of affordable housing for Black households throughout the country. The report's committee consisted of the who's who of influential Black leaders in real estate and social welfare, including committee chair Nannie Helen Burroughs, a Black feminist leader who founded a prominent industrial school for Black girls and women in DC, and esteemed Black sociologist Charles S. Johnson, who had trained at the University of Chicago and later became the first Black president of Fisk University. Johnson authored the report of the committee's findings.

The Report of the Committee on Negro Housing (1932) confirmed that what happened in DC happened in most cities with rising Black populations.[49] Significantly, it provided an outright rejection of much of the real estate industry's insistence that Black families were irresponsible. Instead, the report provided an alternate perspective to the debate on the alleged unfitness of Black households for quality new homes and called for a real estate market that recognized the class and moral differences of Black people and built accordingly. The committee also chastised housing reformers' disproportionate focus on social protections for people experiencing poverty while sidelining the need for additional homes for deserving middle-class Black families who also struggled. Public education was necessary, the report argued, to rid real estate interests of this racist stereotype. This education was essential for Black families too. For those in the middle class, the report recommended and celebrated Black participation in local chapters of the Better Homes Movement, a national campaign that emerged after World War I and promoted segregated homeownership and homemaking classes. The movement celebrated homemakers, usually women and mothers, whose fiercest advocates wanted them to become experts at "perfection in essential routine" while continuing to stay up to date about new housekeeping products and practices.[50] The report suggested that resource-poor Black families, mainly recent migrants, participate in privately sponsored, neighborhood-based civic groups to acclimate them to middle-class domestic standards. It proposed that Black community workers like Emily Cook, who worked in Blagden's Alley located on Ninth and M Streets in DC's Mount Vernon neighborhood, organize youth and women's clubs on gardening and homemaking as an appropriate intervention.[51] Stopping short of suggesting mandatory participation, the report concluded that these programs would act as a shield against the decline of new homes under Black stewardship.

The stance of Black liberal elites on public education reflected a partial critique of disciplinary housing governance. Although the report accepted the premise of the conditional behavior of and character oversight of tenants, that was secondary to its call for labor protections to ensure that Black workers had wages high enough to purchase newer units and prohibitions against racially exclusionary measures and extralegal violence.[52] However, while the committee conceded that "anti-social tendencies" like criminality existed among Black people, it argued that it was a cultural and often temporary maladjustment, not a mark of racial inferiority. While evaluator bias often determined who constituted "the maladjusted," poor (im)migrants, single mothers, substance users, and individuals involved in illicit work usually typified the category.

The committee's stance on public education to counter "anti-social tendencies" in urban Black communities reflected a growing embrace of sociological studies on Black urban poverty. By the 1930s, academic sociologists dominated the urban poverty studies initially led by business leaders and social workers.[53] The University of Chicago's sociology department shaped the field with its disorganization theory. Chicago-trained sociologists like Johnson saw cities as akin to organisms that developed ecologically. According to proponents of this theory, industrial capitalism introduced a disequilibrium in cities and individuals, forcing urban migration and pushing the poorest migrants to the city's core. At the same time, more educated and successful residents established norm-shaping institutions such as churches, civic organizations, nuclear families, and patriarchal households in newly developed urban zones. The theory argued that the maladjusted would model responsible behavior with time and participation in these norm-setting institutions. Johnson saw self-help race work, a product of educated Black elites' uplift movement of the late nineteenth century, as critical in guiding the maladjusted toward normative cultural standards. Quoting an affordable housing developer in the committee's report, Johnson expressed the belief that "where respectability ends, slum conditions begin."[54]

Although the insights of the report of the Committee on Negro Housing would prove more significant in the post–World War II era, its immediate impact was support for placing Black residents with more resources in public housing before including resource-poor families. In 1933, President Franklin D. Roosevelt and Congress inaugurated government-run public housing when it passed the National Industrial Recovery Act (NIRA). The act included a mandate that the Public Works Administration lead "construction, reconstruction, alteration, or repair under public regulation or control of low rent housing and slum clearance projects."[55] Like other New Deal policies, the law aimed to stimulate the economy by subsidizing the private sector and encouraging cooperation between labor and capital.

Under the NIRA, localities were required to establish housing authorities in order to receive federal funds. After extensive local lobbying led by DC's progressive housing organizations, district commissioners and Congress created the Alley Dwelling Authority (ADA) in October 1934. The agency was granted limited authority to reclaim condemned buildings in or near alleys, redevelop this land into housing or other uses, and lease any remaining holdings to private interests. John Ihlder, a white Progressive who worked closely with the National Housing Association and scores of local housing groups, was tapped to lead the ADA as well as its successor, the National Capital Housing Authority (NCHA). (The agency's name changed after the Housing Act of 1937 permitted the city to acquire land outside of alleys and identify financing to build public housing.)

In the nation's capital, select Black people benefited immediately from public housing. Racial progressives like Ihlder facilitated this measure by insisting that poorly housed families should get access to public housing first. Local developers worked with Black architects and built Langston Terrace Dwellings to signify Black progress in DC, making it one of the country's earliest all-Black public housing communities.[56] Located on cleared land in the city's Northeast neighborhood, just south of the United States National Arboretum, Langston Terrace Dwellings was named after Black luminaries George Washington Carver and John Mercer Langston. It was designed by acclaimed Black architects Hilyard Robinson and Paul Revere Williams and was built 1935–1938. The result was a 274-unit, garden-style apartment complex with a central courtyard featuring sculptor Daniel Gillette Olney's signature terra-cotta frieze, *The Progress of the Negro Race*. Although local developers constructed the community, they eventually transferred management to DC's public housing authority. The city wanted to prioritize families with young children as residents of Langston Terrace Dwellings. However, it wanted to ensure that tenants were members of the "submerged middle-class"—families who "retained their middle-class culture and outlook" but had fallen into poverty during the Great Depression.[57]

Tenant eligibility measures became the primary instrument for administering disciplinary housing governance in public housing.[58] To that end, Langston Terrace Dwellings implemented a strict admissions policy focused on identifying "members of the honorable poor." After submitting applications confirming that candidates met the requirements for income and housing need, NCHA staff, both Black and white, conducted employment checks and house visits with eligible applicants. These visits also allowed agency workers to assess whether applicants were desirable neighbors, good housekeepers, and diligent parents and to ensure that prospective resident families were currently living in overcrowded and poor housing conditions.[59] This character-contingent measure, according to officials, elicited pride among Black tenants who understood the rigorous selection process to distinguish them from the more than 12,000 Black applicants seeking one of only 2,000 public units built for Black families before 1940.

Black people's deservingness of new public housing in DC often required social confirmation from white authority figures. While optional, letters of recommendation from members of Congress and other influential white people provided "evidence as to the desirability of the applicant."[60] Citing good housekeeping practices as the most valuable trait, recommenders sought to demonstrate that these particular Black people were not irresponsible tenants. As an example, in November 1938, white socialite Agnes Proctor wrote to Ihlder with a desperate plea on behalf of Mrs. Irene Peterson, an elderly Black woman who lived with her family in Southwest DC. Peterson's home lacked an indoor bathroom, plumbing, and electricity and the family suffered under a landlord who demanded higher rents but made no improvements. Proctor begged Ihlder to accept Peterson and her family into public housing, arguing that Peterson consistently kept her dilapidated home clean.[61]

Proctor's recommendation letter offered more than simply a white paternalistic assessment of Black domestic life. It raised troubling questions about applicants that were not considered desirable or honorable. Were tenants undesirable if large families could not dedicate daily or weekly time to cleaning their decrepit homes to white middle-class standards? Were the housekeeping standards of the low-wage mothers who were denied access to public housing in the 1930s and 1940s seen as unacceptable too? Was keeping these allegedly undeserving families in poor housing conditions a form of social purgatory that was similar to a jail sentence until families chose to repent and change their behavior? These unspoken and gendered questions of deservingness loomed large and were not addressed.

Nevertheless, conversations about tenant worthiness and race continued to shape the NCHA's internal politics. Building materials were conscripted and housing was inadequate during World War II, and the agency mobilized the politics of deservingness within a racial frame. Some segregated buildings assigned to Black families drew protests from white real estate interests, who continued to argue that Black housing would prevent future sales to white buyers. As the NCHA navigated segregationist politics, it struggled with decisions about which buildings should go to which racial group while also straining to meet the federal mandate to house wartime workers. The quality of public housing construction invariably suffered as funding limits worsened wartime shortages of building materials.[62]

Debates about who deserved access to public housing also informed arguments against public housing as critics grew louder and more organized toward the end of the war. In the early 1940s, real estate interests treated DC's public housing policy as a testing ground for arguments against state participation in the housing market. They insisted that the government overreached with its production of low-rent housing and undermined free-market competition between for-profit developers. Conversely, public housing officials rebuked private real estate companies for refusing to build low-rent housing for residents unable to pay market rents and argued that the NCHA had closed this gap in the real estate market. They asserted that the NCHA's behavioral model of governance—including a strict admissions policy that favored the honorable poor and a firm property management approach that required compliance with a strict lease—distinguished the agency as a necessary participant in the real estate market.

Public housing officials like Ihlder saw public housing as a corrective social institution that taught residents tenant responsibility. This included socially appropriate parenting, housekeeping practices that met middle-class standards, and nuclear family household dynamics. Property management was, therefore, essential. "The key to good housing is good management," Ihlder insisted. "No owner of a factory would dream of turning it over entirely to his employees, but many house owners seem to think that their only function is to collect rents."[63] Ihlder argued that property management actually benefited the working poor because it improved both tenant behavior and the longevity of buildings. This was a bold and progressive proclamation at the time. In the first half of the twentieth century, property management was considered a luxury service, a high-end amenity for wealthier families who lived in new apartments with air conditioning, landscaping, and modern kitchens and appliances. But during the post–World War II era, property management slowly expanded in American cities as owners increasingly agreed with Ihlder that the practice was necessary to maintain property grounds, oversee repairs, and comply with local regulations, thus ensuring that buildings appreciated in value. However, the owners of the older homes and apartments that low-wage Black families were confined to had little incentive to invest in upkeep, let alone hire property managers. Instead, they relied on real estate agents to lease units and collect rents. Public housing property managers, in contrast, focused not only on grounds and building maintenance but also on regulating homemaking standards and correcting tenants' "social problems." For example, Ihlder contended that issuing fines to poor housekeepers would engender the "creation of the right environment for the building up of [a] satisfactory home life."[64]

As public housing critics pressed on with their battle against public housing, they refined their policy critique to argue that the state should use disciplinary housing governance and focus on the city's poorest and leave the rest of the population in the private market.[65] Ihlder strenuously disagreed. He countered that the NCHA's 25 percent cap on welfare-assisted families kept it from becoming a "poorhouse." He claimed that removing that cap would hurt the agency's ability to help the poorest families improve their economic situations.[66] Critics countered that Ihlder and the NCHA should focus on its original mission: clearing inhabited alleys, selling reclaimed sites to private redevelopers, and building new housing only when it was "appropriate" and reflected "neighborhood needs."[67] Ultimately, Congress agreed and approved the District of Columbia Redevelopment Act of 1945, which required the NCHA to prioritize families displaced by slum clearance. The law signaled a national push toward urban renewal. This government-led endeavor aimed to turn disinvested neighborhoods—labeled "slums" or "blight"—into higher-yielding land.

Urban Renewal and the (Gendered) Trope of Black Tenant Irresponsibility

Despite the growing discontent among political conservatives and business leaders who decried the country's emergent welfare state, the federal government expanded its role in the economy and urban centers in the 1940s.[68] In addition to public housing and public works initiatives, the Roosevelt administration and Congress used New Deal policies to install the modern welfare state in response to the Great Depression. With these policies, the federal government articulated a new political standard of New Deal liberalism, suggesting that the state must invest in citizens' economic and social well-being. These New Deal programs assisted capital and labor through subsidies to stimulate housing ownership and construction, protections for organized labor, unemployment aid, and banking regulation. Yet, due to long-standing bias, the federal government denied these benefits of the modern welfare state to large swaths of Black and immigrant communities by restricting access and demonizing their welfare needs.[69] Nevertheless, the jobs produced through this government expansion were indispensable to many Black Washingtonians, especially after President Roosevelt issued Executive Order 8802 in 1941, which banned discriminatory employment practices within federal agencies, unions, and companies engaged in defense-related work.[70]

Increased government services meant more economic opportunities that inspired more than 100,000 Black migrants to resettle in the nation's capital during the 1940s. But the reasons many chose to stay there extend beyond the realm of wage work. Walter Fauntroy, a DC native and the city's first nonvoting congressional delegate, was among the new Black migrants. Fauntroy experienced a childhood that celebrated Black fellowship. He has fond memories of attending sporting events at Griffith Stadium, an arena that once stood on Fifth Street between W and Florida Avenue NW, now the site of Howard University Hospital. As an adolescent in the 1940s, he enjoyed watching the Capital Classic, where Black universities fought for bragging rights to football titles.[71] While Black youth relished recreation, their parents enjoyed cultural institutions rooted in Black leisure such as the Howard Theatre, also located in Shaw, where they could party to DC's jazz maestro Duke Ellington and Virginian jazz vocalist Ella Fitzgerald. While many Black migrants came to DC because it was where they could find a "GGJ," a good government job, they often stayed because the city had respected places of Black belonging. From educational powerhouses such as Howard University and historic places of worship such as Mount Zion United Methodist Church, the city's oldest and first Black congregation, Black families carved out affirming spaces where they could learn, share, and support one another.

Sadly, these Black-led cultural and educational spaces did not engender the development of sufficient housing to accommodate the historic rise in Black migrants. In the private housing market, Black families continued to deal with discriminatory treatment. In 1935 to 1940, almost no private housing was built for low-income households. The private rental units that were available to Black working-class families were appreciably inferior in that period.[72] In the 1940s, landlords routinely exploited the social reproduction crisis Black families were forced to navigate privately. Marking up prices for smaller subdivisions of residential space, landlords raised rents to the highest in the country. With a vacancy rate of "only eight-tenths of one percent" in Black neighborhoods, one landlord proudly shared, "During the war years, you could rent anything. A tenant could move out one day and you'd have the place rented the next day. It was amazing how much you could save without repairs or decorating."[73] Many landlords eagerly took advantage of the high number of Black migrants who relocated to the city. Even though they constituted close to 40 percent of DC's Black population, these migrant families fared the worst when it came to securing well-maintained rental options. They were often expected to live in the lowest-grade dwellings, housing that lacked running water, electricity, windows, and even walls.

The Redevelopment Act of 1945 kickstarted a federal response to disinvested hovels in DC. The law established the Redevelopment Land Agency (RLA) and endowed it with the power to "acquire and assemble real property, including the use of eminent domain" and to resell or lease acquired property for redevelopment purposes. The National Capital Park and Planning Commission devised a comprehensive plan that mapped out desired land uses, density projections, and slum clearance areas. Zones marked as slums were subject to the RLA's eminent domain and redevelopment authority. Although many individuals displaced by urban renewal were enti-

A rental home in predominantly Black Alexander Court, located in the Dupont Circle neighborhood, just a few blocks away from the White House. In 1941, a mother and her two children rented rooms in this home. It lacked indoor plumbing; water was available only in an outhouse located in the backyard. Photo by Marion Post Wolcott. Library of Congress, Prints & Photographs Division, Farm Security Administration/Office of War Information Black-and-White Negatives.

tled to the agency's relocation referrals, the RLA directed those who could not afford rent in the private housing market to the NCHA, which the law had also converted into a redevelopment agency. Yet private enterprise's first right of refusal hampered the NCHA's ability to assemble and develop public housing. Legal challenges and Congress's failure to appropriate funds also undermined the powers of the NCHA and the RLA during the first several years of the law's implementation. However, when Congress passed the Housing Act of 1949, it made urban renewal a federal goal, providing federal aid to localities for slum clearance and urban redevelopment while empowering local authorities to build 810,000 public housing units. The NCHA was authorized to build 4,000 of those units.[74]

The Housing Act of 1949 reignited the debate in DC about the housing code for existing units. Local advocates working with the Urban League and the Washington Housing Association (of which Ihlder was a founder and leader) believed that a housing code was necessary to improve housing conditions.[75] However, other local officials resisted implementing a code until the Redevelopment Act of 1954 made it possible to secure funding for slum clearance and urban redevelopment. For planning officials, a comprehensive and citywide housing code had two interrelated goals: it could help stop the further deterioration of so-called blighted neighborhoods and stabilize property values by ensuring a higher floor for housing conditions. According to these officials, blight resulted from overcrowding and reflected a neighborhood's "depreciating and declining character and value."[76] But they also noted that a housing code provided public benefits and social good; for example, by extending the life of buildings and indirectly providing better conditions for low-income households in the city's older housing stock. With the prospect of federal aid underwriting their development projects, key business leaders joined planning and welfare officials in backing a proposal to pass a housing code in DC.

Landlords grew increasingly frustrated as political support for a housing code for existing units grew. They expressed their concern using the familiar gendered trope of Black tenant irresponsibility. An anonymous op-ed titled "Tenants Make Slums" in the *Washington Evening Star* reflected this perspective, written by a landlord who blamed Black parental neglect for "blighted" neighborhoods. The landlord wrote: "I know of a section of five and six room row houses, formerly all occupied by owners. Now, if you ride through you can pick out the rented housing by their appearance. Dogs and cats are fed on lawns defaced with bottles, cigarettes, candy and ice cream wrappers and papers. There are broken screens and flower boxes, dirty children digging and defacing front yards. Evening attire for men and boys is little or no shirt, girls in sun suits or seaside slacks and permanent-waved women in shorts."[77] Unlike these irresponsible parents who eschewed social decorum, apartments for "first-class residents," the author claimed, "allow no pets, permit clothes hung out in fixed hours only and control the number of residents per house and the demeanor of the same." While he admitted there were some "poor colored alley dwellers [who] have homes sweet and clean," he suggested that most of these parents were irresponsible and in need of external correction. For this landlord, following the social rules of middle-class respectability reflected and protected property value. This alleged lack of discernable order and value rested on a critique of Black mothering: the landlord mocked "permanent-waved women in shorts" and suggested that lax Black mothering was to blame for children's filth and the decline in property upkeep. This landlord advised disciplinary housing governance for undesirable parents who sought improved housing. He recommended that public housing executive Ihlder "acquire some of the alley houses as a barrack for relief accepters, erect a public washhouse and employ inspectors, then give the supervision to our society charitable workers."[78]

Gendered stereotypes of Black irresponsibility prevented any complex discussion about Black family life in disinvested neighborhoods. For example, in alley communities, single Black mothers were essential in supporting extended and chosen kin.[79] In older and long-demonized neighborhoods such as Foggy Bottom, where urban renewal officials debated redevelopment, Black mothers and grandmothers were vital to facilitating belonging. Waldo (Petey) Greene Jr., a community activist turned national radio personality, grew up in Foggy Bottom in the 1930s and 1940s. Greene's memoir *Laugh If You Like, Ain't a Damn Thing Funny* notes with sly humor that he and his Black working-class neighbors were adept at trickery:

> Where I lived in [Foggy Bottom] (the West End) it was a residential section, which is now made up of condominiums and things. It was between L and M on 23rd Street and it was a street where everybody knew everybody. On each corner, we had a store owned by Jews, and they were into the community as far as groceries and knowing everybody and things. Everybody was buddies. All the neighbors were friendly. . . . It was a real camaraderie in that neighborhood. A white person could come round there asking for somebody: "No we don't know." Then they would see the person and say: "See that white guy over there, he was looking for you." Sometimes it was the police. Sometimes it was a guy doing him a favor, you know. And the white guy would say: "Well, man, I thought you said you didn't know this man." They'd answer: "It wasn't him I didn't know. It was you I didn't know."[80]

In addition to this sort of protective camaraderie, Greene reflected with pride that Black maternal care—be it through mothers or grandmothers— was at the core of Black working-class neighborhood life.[81] With his father in and out of prison and his mother struggling to balance youthful pleasures with adult responsibilities, Greene's grandparents raised him.[82] In their low-rent household that had a coal-fired stove and an outdoor toilet, he learned how to create spaces of comfort, even without modern appliances:

> Like we didn't have no air conditioner. When it was real hot, they'd get a 15-cent block of ice, set in the middle of the floor. Take a big blanket and put it behind the ice. Then take a fan and turn the fan to blow on the ice. The cold air would hit that blanket, the blanket would catch the air and the air would come back cool. Just like central air. It would be 95 outdoors, feel like it's 20 in the house. . . . Another thing we used to do, we used to take two bricks and heat 'em and go upstairs and put 'em in the foot of the bed when it was cold. Cause we didn't have no radiator or heater upstairs at the time. Then when you go get in the bed, the bed would be warm, like an electric blanket.[83]

In a home filled with such ingenuity, Greene learned much about social norms, including the nuances of racial relations, family dynamics, and gender expectations. His grandmother Maggie Floyd, affectionately known in the neighborhood as A'nt Pig, adored her children and grandchildren. Greene recounted with delight that even though she had no formal education, she raised and sustained their multigenerational household on the meager and precarious wages she pooled from her laundry service and her husband's construction wages.[84] In a household rooted in the value of sharing, Greene's grandmother taught him to cook and how to use his natural humor to build affirming Black communal spaces.

Yet Greene also recognized that the unacknowledged, omnipresent reality of racialized uneven development that produced his overcrowded home indirectly contributed to family tensions. Greene's youngest sibling, Jackie, often turned to the family to take her in when her relationships with men frayed or her precarious work left her vulnerable to nonpayment and eviction. When Jackie moved in, arguments would inevitably erupt between her and A'nt Pig as well as petty squabbles between Jackie's five siblings. Knowing that these arguments scarred everyone in the household in unspoken but countless ways, A'nt Pig cautioned Greene against reproducing such pain. "Boy, don't never hurt nobody's feelings," she warned. "It's the worst thing in the world to have your feelings hurt, because your feelings control your heart and your heart hook up to your mind, and make you just do simple things when your feelings hurt. If you don't want your feelings hurt, then don't hurt nobody's feelings."[85]

However, Black maternal philosophies, complex family dynamics, and resilient domestic labor were invisible to landlords and urban renewal officials,

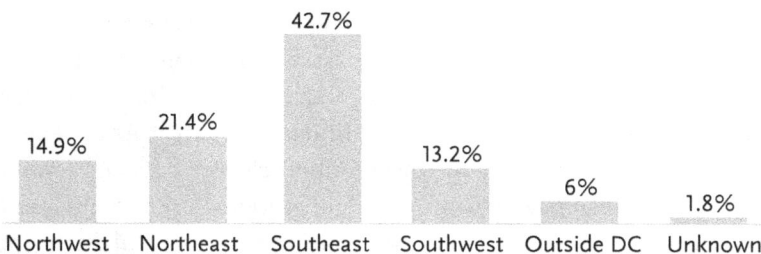

		42.7%			
	21.4%				
14.9%			13.2%		
				6%	1.8%
Northwest	Northeast	Southeast	Southwest	Outside DC	Unknown

In its annual report for 1960, the DC Redevelopment Land Agency presented this chart from the Southwest Urban Renewal Project showing where displaced Southwest residents had been relocated. Courtesy of the District of Columbia Redevelopment Land Agency.

who were focused on debating housing code standards and initial sites of displacement. The Redevelopment Land Agency selected most of DC's southwest quadrant for its first slum clearance project. The disinvested neighborhoods in the site, which was located in the oldest section of the city and was dotted with brick rowhouses, were a stone's throw from the Capitol, a fact that eased the city's decision to demolish the entire area.[86] Starting in 1950, the RLA divided the Southwest Urban Renewal Project into three smaller development projects. Spreading over 550 acres and affecting over 5,600 units, these projects involved close to 25,000 individuals, the overwhelming majority of whom were Black renters.[87] The RLA moved these families out to make way for over 2,000 luxury apartments and townhouses as well as spaces for high-end retail and other commercial uses. In its annual report, the urban renewal agency praised its makeover of Southwest. The new residents were 90 percent white and represented a new "cosmopolitan community with residents from the diplomatic corps who formerly lived in distant lands as well as those in the government service and private employment."[88]

In the 1950s, the city engaged in two other major urban renewal programs that also primarily impacted and displaced poor Black families. Unlike the Southwest Urban Renewal Project, which focused on slum clearance, the RLA prioritized enforcement of housing codes in its other urban renewal projects. The Northwest Urban Renewal Area was one such project, which spanned over 900 acres with boundaries that roughly corresponded with the city's second police precinct (then known as the city's "wickedest" area).[89] The Adams-Morgan Program, the other urban renewal project, emphasized the conservation and rehabilitation of existing units that were considered to be at risk of future decline.

Local officials set out to finalize a housing code while urban renewal projects were underway. For years, city officials and housing advocacy groups had unsuccessfully lobbied for a housing code. The Housing Act of 1954 provided the final push that enabled DC to pass a comprehensive housing code since federal urban renewal funds came with the conditionality that localities provide a strategy for curtailing additional "blight."[90] As a member of DC's board of commissioners, Engineer Commissioner Louis W. Prentiss coordinated the housing code draft and deliberations. Prentiss invited fire, police, and health agencies to work alongside business and real estate groups to contribute to the stipulations of the housing code. Like localities in major northeastern and midwestern cities, the draft housing code for the District of Columbia included provisions for indoor plumbing, heat, screens, occupancy limits, and habitability standards for basements.[91] On November 30, 1954, a public hearing was held to solicit feedback on the draft. Most of the participants that testified supported the code, including local advocacy group the Washington Housing Association.[92] Carey Winston, president of the Washington Real Estate Board, also backed the code. He testified that the code provisions were "a far-reaching step towards slum prevention," adding that many property owners would be "put to considerable expense" as they worked to comply with its new requirements.[93]

Owners of low-rent properties were most likely to bear the expense of new code stipulations. Unsurprisingly, those owners protested the code. "We have cheap people living in cheap houses," insisted Raymond Ruppert, the owner of 600 homes in areas selected for urban renewal.[94] Ruppert founded the Small Property Owner Association, a group created to oppose the housing code, and denounced the code as a form of socialism. He warned city officials that property holders would abandon the low-rent housing market if the state did not grant cash-strapped owners leniency and exemptions.[95]

The accepted housing code set "rock bottom" standards that marked any noncompliant housing as "deleterious to the health, safety, welfare and morals of the community and its inhabitants."[96] The regulations laid out different responsibilities for tenants and owners. Owners were responsible for structural safety, maintenance, light, ventilation, rat-proofing, electricity, heating, plumbing, bathroom facilities, and window screens. Tenants were responsible for housekeeping, occupancy levels, cleaning alleys and backyards, and appliance upkeep. If an owner or a tenant failed to comply with their assigned responsibilities, someone—a citizen, a tenant, or an owner—could contact housing inspectors and issue a complaint.[97] The Department of Licenses and Inspections, an agency that was revamped to administer the updated code, would be responsible for housing inspections. In addition to addressing citizen complaints, the Department of Licenses and Inspections had the power to conduct enforcement sweeps, particularly in areas where planning officials wanted "blight" remediation. Owners generally had up to ninety days to rectify any infractions of the housing code. Failure to comply precipitated fines or worse. The housing code gave owners of properties that inspectors had condemned sixty days to repair them or tear them down. Notably, the length of these compliance periods was a response to low-rent property landlords' pleas for leniency. In addition, after compliance notices expired, the Department of Licenses and Inspections could grant owners extensions "as long as necessary," especially if they demonstrated a "serious effort to comply." Owners could also petition a seven-member Board of Appeals if they believed the rehabilitation would result in "exceptional or undue hardship by reason of excessive structural or mechanical difficulty or impracticability."[98]

For almost a decade after enacting the housing code, the city had a mixed record with eradicating blight. Administrative slowdowns hindered the immediate impact of the code in the first several years. In a city with approximately 250,000 homes, inspectors focused on the more than 35,000 units labeled as blighted or obsolete. Enforcement sweeps started in neighborhoods such as Capitol Hill, Marshall Heights, and Adams-Morgan, where inspectors urged citizens, tenants, and landlords to improve living conditions by removing litter and repairing structural damage.[99] Yet undertrained and limited staff made that level of success inconsistent.[100]

These early years of code enforcement exposed three subpopulations to greater housing insecurity: elderly homeowners, large families, and single mothers. With limited funds, each group struggled to readjust to living in a city that was improving its housing stock and increasing its costs. Elderly Black homeowners in Marshall Heights, a majority-Black neighborhood, typified this dilemma. Marshall Heights is located on the edge of the city in the southeast quadrant. Shortly before the Great Depression, Black families settled there in greater numbers because there were fewer restrictive covenants on the land. Many Black residents built makeshift homes using their own savings because local banks had stopped investing in the neighborhood. Limited city infrastructure plus capital abandonment kept Marshall Heights underdeveloped well into the 1950s. Planning officials hoped to demolish the neighborhood along with Southwest, but Marshall Heights residents successfully lobbied Congress to block the measure. The neighborhood was instead subjected to code enforcement, and elderly Black homeowners had to decide whether to take on enforcement costs or face prosecution (although housing inspectors routinely insisted that they preferred issuing additional compliance time rather than starting court proceedings).[101] Even though they had access to federal funds that could offset rehabilitation costs and potential lawsuits, many elderly Black homeowners balked at the prospect of accruing debt to repair homes they had built with limited or no state assistance.[102]

Even confronted with the possibility of debt, impoverished elderly Black homeowners had access to more state resources than large families, especially those led by single mothers.[103] In addition to urban renewal funds, the Housing Act of 1954 made building public housing for the elderly a federal priority. Even though the NCHA had great difficulty finding sites for public housing in general, public housing for the elderly was rarely subjected to the same public scrutiny and backlash as multifamily public housing. Large families (defined as households with more than four children) struggled to find affordable accommodations, even in public housing communities. Rooming homes and apartments were typical destinations for these families because they cost the least. However, enforcement sweeps and citizen complaints often exposed the living arrangements in such households, leading some inspectors to openly consider whether it was cruel to enforce occupancy standards for overcrowding when tenants attested that they had no affordable alternatives. Some housing code inspectors defied the rule. One said, "If a man and wife have seven children or any number of children they should be permitted to live in an apartment regardless of size if they can . . . without jeopardizing [the] health of the community."[104] Business leaders and planning officials disagreed and steadfastly enforced the occupancy restrictions of the code, arguing that "overcrowding was a major cause of slums."[105] In these circumstances, the best hope families had was that a housing inspector would refer them to private charities or city welfare services to help them relocate.

Leaders who insisted that overcrowding caused slums ignored the fact that the private housing market used discriminatory practices that ensured overcrowding. The city's flood of urban renewal funds did not fully address the decades-long undersupply of new units for Black families. The trope of Black tenant irresponsibility underwrote capital and state bias against building en masse for segregated Black neighborhoods. The federal government perpetuated this stereotype by linking working-class Black neighborhoods to declining property values. As a result, the Federal Housing Administration (FHA) condoned redlining by offering mortgage insurance coverage to approved lenders who built housing in putatively desirable and mainly white neighborhoods.[106] Postwar manuals for property appraisers enshrined this philosophy. One popular manual ranked Black- and Mexican-inhabited neighborhoods as lowest in land and property values and thus closely tied to depreciating or disinvested areas.[107] In order to ensure that property values would increase, planning officials locally and nationally allowed developers to continue racial segregation.

Federal protection of white households' property values enabled urban and suburban developers to perpetuate racial discrimination. In the postwar era, suburban communities dominated the frontier of new construction while vigorously upholding the color line. New construction in cities followed the same development logic.[108] As was customary, the federal government condoned this practice. The FHA's urban renewal loan program enforced racial quotas for new construction built to rehouse those who had been displaced by development projects. In the 1950s, officials increasingly turned to neighborhoods in Southeast DC, which had comparatively more white flight and undeveloped land, to build public housing. Many private developers involved in these urban renewal projects preferred racially segregated communities. In Congress Heights, an essentially all-white working-class neighborhood in Southeast, white developers attempted to prevent a racial transition by using FHA loans for the construction of a white-only dwelling in 1959. Even though most displaced residents were Black and white residents were more likely to leave the city, the developer defended the move. Citing federal regulations, he argued that he was allowed to rent to any race as long as urban renewal projects in other locations built a minimum number of units for Black residents.[109] Alongside such debates about racial occupancy in new construction, urban renewal developers increasingly chose not to build family-size apartments at rents that displaced people could afford. They made the same excuse that private developers of previous years had: additional federal and local regulations and higher land acquisition and construction costs meant higher rents, and those who could not afford the higher rent baselines should turn to the city for assistance or support elsewhere.

Inadequate construction and uneven housing code enforcement left single mothers and large families vulnerable to predatory landlords. In the late 1950s, it was well known that some landlords preferred renting to families with children because their parents were most likely captive consumers who were forced to purchase services from a limited number of suppliers who controlled the prices and quality of service.[110] In the summer of 1959, the *Washington Post* released an investigative series on housing inspectors' checkered success with enforcing the city's housing code. The series revealed that landlords in disinvested neighborhoods willingly rented to single mothers if they accepted certain conditions. In one example, a landlord asked a homeless single mother of four to "write the names of her husband and two of her children on the registration card," pay two weeks' rent in advance, and rent the room sight unseen.[111] Single mothers like Patricia Penny's sometimes put on more elaborate fronts, bringing a man to act as a proxy leaseholder if they wanted better negotiating leverage. Nevertheless, the practice of renting properties sight unseen enabled many landlords to skirt housing code regulations. This tactic seemingly proliferated after the Department of Licenses and Inspections advocated for an enforcement modification that encouraged apartment owners and property managers to submit affidavits of code compliance to speed up compliance verifications.

Violations of codes related to a building's structure such as defective plumbing that led to carbon monoxide exposure went unchecked. These harmful violations put single mothers and their children at particular risk since they were often shuttled into basement and attic apartments.[112] When complaints or enforcement sweeps finally reached these neighborhoods, households were regularly evicted and were not always promised relocation services. Predictably, homelessness among families led by single mothers increased. However, the predatory low-rent housing market also had submarkets that catered to tenants who were willing to pay for inferior housing. Some landlords rented to large families who paid in advance for noncompliant subdivided single-family homes with individually rented rooms.[113] Others rented to single mothers on welfare assistance because they believed these tenants were a "good rent risk." After all, a third of their welfare checks would go directly toward their rent.[114] The treatment of welfare-assisted single Black mothers in this discriminatory housing market underscores the nuanced aspects of what historian Keeanga-Yamahtta Taylor terms predatory inclusion.[115] The housing needs of welfare-assisted single Black mothers and their families were often treated with contempt.

Unfortunately, the discourse urban planning officials used to express their growing frustration with these families overshadowed any discussion of structural mistreatment. Toward the end of the 1950s, displacement due to housing code violations and public works initiatives outpaced displacement from the Southwest Urban Renewal Project.[116] Many of these displaced families sought public housing. Overwhelmed with this rising need, public housing officials could not secure enough construction sites to meet urban renewal development goals. Business leaders made matters worse by blocking the NCHA's attempts to buy existing private dwellings and convert them to public housing.[117] The RLA provided minimal assistance and openly reprimanded public housing officials for not absorbing more displaced families into existing units. NCHA executive director James Ring, who took the helm after Ihlder retired in 1952, resisted the RLA's pressure by insisting that the agency remain self-sustaining on rental income. Prioritizing only rehousing families displaced by urban renewal, Ring warned, would be "indefensible" and would leave the agency susceptible to violating its own governance standards. Ring revised the NCHA's tenant selection process to accept 5 percent more families from the District of Columbia's lowest income levels as a compromise. Ring insisted that the rest of the applicants must pay the NCHA's economic rent to keep the agency solvent.

"Problem Families" and New Experiments in Disciplinary Housing Governance

Shortly after the city's housing code passed and displacement efforts began, the NCHA began to rehouse a greater number of displaced families. The NCHA's uptick in low-income Black tenants prompted Ring to launch a campaign to encourage tenant responsibility. In December 1955, Ring called on private citizens and public housing property managers to assist in this initiative. Borrowing an emerging postwar sociological term, Ring suggested that many displaced residents were "problem families" that were prone to irresponsible behavior that they would bring to their new dwellings in both private and public housing. "The concern in this regard," Ring explained, "results from the assumption—which experience indicates is largely a certainty—that many such persons will, upon relocation, transfer to new housing the abuse of household equipment, negligence in maintenance and rent-paying and antisocial attitudes characteristic of slum living."[118] Endorsing the social services the 1932 report of the Committee on Negro Housing had lauded, Ring appealed to private groups to provide mothers' clubs, youth programs, and parenting and homemaking classes to help displaced families limit their slum habits in their new residences.[119] Insisting that the NCHA "cannot give to [these] programs the degree of assistance and encouragement which they require," Ring saw this supplementary education as vital.

In sounding the alarm about families he feared would subvert the urban renewal goal of upgrading and sustaining the existing housing stock, Ring echoed a refrain that was spreading across the country. Public housing officials from Boston to Hawaii criticized the federal mandate to evict higher-earning families in order to ensure that there would be enough vacancies for populations displaced by urban renewal. They were also frustrated because they now had to house more "problem families" instead of the "honorable poor" they were accustomed to serving.[120] In the 1950s, numerous reports commissioned by public housing authorities decried the rising number of these tenants, sometimes described as "multi-problem families," "hard to reach multi-problem families," or "hard-core" families. These reports wrestled with the repercussions of housing a higher number of "families with low standards of living, physical and mental health problems and anti-social behavior."[121]

In addition, the problem of categorization troubled welfare leaders and private welfare organizations. Like Progressive Era sociologists who defined maladjusted tenants by evaluating their desire for upward mobility (or lack thereof), welfare agencies in the urban renewal era identified problem families through similar metrics and/or on the degree to which family members had received public assistance or had been jailed or imprisoned. Difficulties emerged about which moral evaluations should serve as objective truth and which cases were worthy of institutional intervention. Some agencies and officials defined "problem families" as those who had marital, housekeeping, parental, and mental health issues.[122] These were broad categories. The concept of marital dysfunction, for example, included "broken families, widowed, divorced and separated (without regard to the legal status of the marriage)" and "conspicuous situations: those involving open fights, calling of police, desertion." Others attempted to classify problem families primarily through their interactions with the state. As one New York social service organization noted, "Perhaps the most naïve approach is to define 'problems' in terms of 'being on an agency caseload' and thus to count a family as multi-problem if it is on the caseload of two or more agencies."[123] That organization argued that such a description left room for confusion, as there were plenty of families that required public assistance when a parent was chronically ill or one child out of several demonstrated behavioral challenges in school. The group subsequently refined its definition of "multi-problem families" to include only those that exhibited a "multiplicity of problems; chronicity of need; resistance to treatment; handicapping attitudes." Each subcategory required assessing a family's capacity or desire for a "normal, self-sufficient, socially approved pattern of living" in order to identify "multi-problem families." Refusing services and/or ignoring caseworkers' advice constituted markers of "resistance to treatment," while "handicapping attitudes" included "hostility toward the school," a "lack of middle-class drive," "fear and suspicion of social workers and social agencies, hostility toward and fear of the police and law-enforcing authorities, the feeling that everybody (truant officer, children's court, bill collectors, teachers, social workers) is trying to 'pick on people like us,' lack of respect for one's own or others' property, evaluation of uncouth language and sexual aggressiveness as desirable male traits, [and] lack of appreciation for values of good health and preventive hygiene."[124]

Proponents of classifying households as problem families maintained that the categories they used did not indicate racial bias. However, the most prominent advocates—academics and social welfare officials—infused gendered narratives with implicit racial meanings. Take, for instance, the inclusion of "sexual aggressiveness as desirable male traits" as an example of a "handicapping attitude." While this category was not explicitly about race, proponents' analytical focus on urban Black families meant that such critiques of gendered performances as undesirable and culturally underdeveloped were inherently racial. These assessments discounted that postwar American culture praised youthful male (sexual) aggression as a rite of passage when the young men were white.

Postwar behavioral scientists popularized these coded meanings by shifting the analytical conversation about poverty away from the Progressives' earlier focus on moral character, wages, race, and political economy. Within the context of a historic economic boom, postwar sociologists increasingly no longer saw poverty and the associated cultural underdevelopment of poor people as a racial ailment but as a condition that afflicted only a small minority. This perspective compelled behavioral scientists to place greater weight on culture and social psychology, a field that was attentive to how external factors shape people's thoughts, feelings, and actions. Historian Alice O'Conner attributes this postwar intellectual turn to behavioral scientists who viewed the roots of poverty through a "psychological understanding of the family, and specifically of gender relations within low-income, and particularly within Black families." This gendered conceptualization of poverty "heightened attention to poor women's reproductive behavior while ignoring their economic role."[125]

Drawing on this variant of behavioral science, housing and welfare officials advanced similar arguments, suggesting that poverty was merely a by-product of poor personal or cultural choices. RLA executive John R. Searles approved of this emerging sociological consensus, identifying the "social problems" of families displaced by urban renewal as a chief concern. James G. Banks, chief of the agency's Relocation Division and one of the city's top Black urban renewal officials, agreed with Searles: "Other social problems are more important than the financial problems. Solve the other problems and, by and large, the financial problems solve themselves."[126]

To that end, welfare and public housing officials argued that public housing management required a shift toward behavioral regulation. Instead of focusing on building maintenance and lease compliance through property management, they called for a service-oriented approach that emphasized the character transformation of tenants. Localities throughout the country tested different strategies to accomplish this new management goal. In DC, welfare officials also vetted ideas. In the summer of 1958, the District Commissioners youth subcommittee recommended that the city apply a Dutch reacculturation model to public housing. The proposal advised placing problem families—defined as those with children who had repeated encounters with police and who relied on welfare as primary assistance for an extended period—in select public housing communities to be reeducated. The NCHA and welfare authorities would not coerce the families they chose but would invite them to join these therapeutic communities. As with the Dutch program, officials would provide "detailed instruction in such routine matters as budgeting, cooking, housekeeping, hygiene and choice and care of clothing in addition to needed medical and psychiatric aid."[127] The proposal's architects hoped to make participation in these communities mandatory in order to receive welfare but said nothing about how to reintegrate families who completed the program.[128] While city officials, home builders, and realtors did not express support for this specific plan, some backed its intent. They shared elsewhere their belief that no new public housing would be necessary if "real problem families" were assigned to such communities and were under "intensive supervision."[129]

This therapeutic isolationist plan seems to have gone nowhere. Instead, public housing officials listened to recommendations from the Urban League, a long-standing civil rights organization committed to racial and economic justice, which advocated for coordinated social service delivery to displaced Southwest families. In 1954, the NCHA agreed to work with the RLA to conduct a massive behavioral study of these residents in order to identify best practices for interagency service delivery. Notably, it was generally not the case that civil rights groups could influence a city's urban renewal policies. However, it was not unusual for a Black civic organization to have such influence in the nation's capital, where Black political influence—particularly

Black middle-class advocacy groups—helped shape DC's implementation of federal welfare policies. Positions in the city's public housing and urban renewal sectors eventually became an informal pipeline for later appointments to city and national roles for Black leaders.[130]

James G. Banks was one of those leaders. Selected to oversee the Southwest behavioral study, Banks's rise to the position reflected a lasting ambition to serve the public and assist the city's poorest residents. Born in 1921 in Washington, Banks was raised in the Barry Farm public housing community during its "honorable poor" era. At Howard University, Banks studied under E. Franklin Frazier, a Black sociologist trained at the University of Chicago who believed in the theory of disorganization and the assimilative power of norm-setting institutions like marriage. Predictably, Frazier's work marked Black female-headed households as maladjusted and therefore prone to social pathology.[131] Banks earned a graduate degree in sociology from the University of Pittsburgh and then joined the NCHA, where his job involved interviewing and screening public housing applicants. He was later promoted to the position of relocation chief for the RLA's Southwest Urban Renewal Project, which included managing its behavioral study. In addition to overseeing the forced relocation of 5,000 families, Banks led a public-private partnership between welfare agencies and community groups that had been brought together to execute the nearly $300,000 study (close to $3 million today when adjusted for inflation). Banks hoped the study would uncover "the kinds and manner of social and health service which must be provided to reduce the likelihood that slum habits among displaced families will continue in new and better neighborhoods."[132]

The study followed the qualitative research methods of behavioral science. Caseworkers conducted a door-to-door survey that identified over 1,000 participant families and the potential services they would need. Friendship House, Southwest House, and Southeast House—local settlement houses with social work histories dating back to the Progressive Era—agreed to provide these services to encourage the assimilation of displaced tenants into three public housing communities, Arthur Capper, Greenleaf, and Kenilworth, all of which had been established through urban renewal efforts. The organizations worked together to identify approximately 200 of the surveyed families to participate in experimental and control groups for the study. The control group would receive only healthcare and educational services from the summer of 1958 to the spring of 1959, while the experimental group would receive mandatory casework for at least six months after the families moved into their new homes.

The study identified four types of "problems"—economic, health, behavior, and family relationships—and like other midcentury casework studies, these categories shaped caseworkers' perceptions and emphases. Focusing on family dynamics, the study concluded that low-wage Black households were usually "multi-problem" families that fit into more than one category. Although the study also included white problem families, they were more likely to be nominated for release from mandatory casework, even the white single-parent households.[133] Consequently, Black women and girls constituted the majority of participants in mandatory casework and community programming, as photographs from the cooking, babysitting, and home repair classes substantiate. Centered on domestic labor, the classes viewed markers of desirable character transformation through the lens of white middle-class norms. The mostly Black participants learned "good grooming habits" and appropriate dress for different occasions, as defined by books written by white authors who emphasized middle-class consumption and domestic practices. For example, the presenter for a "Personal and Family Health" workshop taught participants about constructive parental discipline, good manners and language, suitable approaches to leisure, and how to properly care for the sick in the home. Notably, at least one session focused specifically on the "unwed mother."

Given the postwar sociological rebuke of Black single mothers, it is not surprising that a majority of them were recommended for casework. Miss J, described as a Black thirty-two-year-old "mother of 5 illegitimate children, ages 11 to 5 months, by two different men," offers a representative example.[134] Although Miss J was not married, she did have a partner, Mr. D, "47 years old and father of the three youngest children." According to the report, Mr. D was "Miss J's paramour for 15 years, alternately abusive and beneficent, cruel, kind and, notwithstanding the mood, drunk." He had left Miss J several times but the two had reconciled whenever he returned. Facing the imminent demolition of their home due to urban renewal, the caseworker submitted that Miss J and her family were undesirable candidates for relocation because their income and union were unstable. In addition to criticizing Miss J as an "out-of-wedlock mother with an ever-increasing number of children, depending on support from an inadequate, irresponsible man who was 15 years her senior," the caseworker described her as "hostile, uncooperative, and dependent." As such, social service agencies considered Miss J—and cases like hers—to be "hopeless."

Even so, caseworkers employed strategies to overcome tenant resistance and attempt to fashion desirable candidates. Miss J's caseworker encouraged her to modify her behavior in the hope that she and her family could qualify for relocation and services. Since public housing would not accept common-law marriages or cohabitation, convincing Miss J and Mr. D to get legally married was key. The report notes that the caseworker first had to work to gain Miss J's trust, which she accomplished by purchasing consumer goods such as toys and clothes for her children. Eventually, Miss J agreed to attend some of the workshops while the "RLA applied pressure to Mr. D." This pressure from an unnamed person ultimately compelled Mr. D to accept the recommendation that he marry Miss J and secure a job that earned enough for the family to move into public housing.

To the study's authors, Miss J and Mr. D's marriage exhibited the success of the mandated casework approach. Yet it simultaneously signaled its limitations. Through omission, the study suggested that so-called problem families, especially those led by single Black mothers, lacked any desirable albeit nontraditional lifestyle practices and overlooked existing systems of mutual aid and cultural vibrancy among Black people.[135] Vickey Nelson, who was raised by her mother in DC public housing, spoke to this sentiment. Her mom anchored the community as an "other mother" who cared for neighborhood children. She explained that single Black mothers frequently pooled resources, hosted celebratory events, and looked out for each other. Rather than searching for value in different ways of living and supporting women like Miss J in their autonomy, the study presumed that heteronormative marriage and nuclear families were ideal markers of character rehabilitation. This criterion of heteropatriarchal marriage belied the thorny reality of the quality of the union—a substantial issue considering Mr. D's history of abusive behavior.

Ironically, the study actually exposed the limits of demanding that resource-poor Black families replicate middle-class domestic and gender norms. As the program's leading participants, Black women were taught to master labor that was traditionally considered male housework, such as reglazing a window sash, replacing light switches, splicing wires, and restoring cracked plaster. Moreover, the workload of Black women in public housing upkeep was simply higher than that of the middle-class white women they were advised to mimic. Such contradictions made the normative, heterosexual, middle-class domestic life featured in white-centered home economics books almost impossible for participants to achieve.

Finally, the study normalized the unspoken assumption that the racially tiered housing and labor market were insignificant factors in the experiences of Miss J and others with urban renewal displacement. Instead of acknowledging harmful structural discrimination, the study helped institutionalize the postwar belief that poor housing conditions were connected to nonnormative household and gender dynamics. By conflating participants' "chronic sense of defeatism, negative self-images, and inadequate motivation" with poor housing conditions in urban renewal areas, public housing and urban renewal officials could reframe tenant irresponsibility as an ostensibly apolitical understanding of poverty.[136] Accordingly, the NCHA coordinated its new ideal for disciplinary housing governance with casework services that demanded acceptance of heterosexual standards of reproductive labor. To aid in this acceptance, caseworkers, private social agencies, and property managers needed to act as the critical frontline disciplinarians of public housing residents, reducing Black mothers to clinical subjects who needed to (re)learn submission to state and private regulation.

While the NCHA's behavioral governance model enabled liberal housing officials to reframe Black tenant irresponsibility as objective truth, other housing officials interpreted the same evidence as proof that punishment, not casework, would be a more effective approach to character rehabilitation. In the late 1950s, DC housing inspectors who regularly enforced leniency with owners began to emphasize punishment for tenants, such as increased eviction for overcrowding. In 1959, over 500 households were displaced by eviction. Less than half were relocated to public housing and the status of the rest is unknown.[137] In addition, the Department of Licenses and Inspections implemented a tenant-focused compliance program to combat (Black) tenant irresponsibility. J. J. Ilgenfritz, director of the city's Division of Housing Inspection, defended the need for the plan, citing landlords' insistence that Black tenant irresponsibility manifested in ineptitude with housekeeping, yard and alley maintenance, and appliance and plumbing upkeep. Ilgenfritz appointed seven housing inspectors to curb the irresponsible behavior and "slum-breeding habits" of problem families.[138] Taking this mission to heart, housing inspector Thomas I. Jones said that his job was "to help break the slum habits of people who for generations have hardly known what it feels like to wear a clean shirt. . . . I also work with kids before bad habits are too far developed."[139] This program eventually contributed to an increased emphasis on a punishment-oriented enforcement model in which inspectors issued costly citations to families who shirked code-related responsibilities.[140]

By the end of the 1950s, the evolved trope of Black tenant irresponsibility enabled more political actors to demand harsher penalties for public housing residents. In 1959, just before the RLA was supposed to release its final report of the coordinated service delivery study, political disputes hampered federal funding, leaving the NCHA unable to absorb all eligible families into public housing. The agency's waitlist ballooned to the thousands.[141] With a pressing need for public housing and a prominent narrative of destructive problem families, John A. Remon, the long-term chairman of RLA's board, suggested punishment as a core tactic in property management. Remon accused the NCHA of covering up rising problems such as youth scribbling on the walls and children running unsupervised throughout public housing communities. Walter Washington, a Black DC native serving as NCHA director of management, cautioned that declining federal funds prevented the agency from hiring enough maintenance workers to keep up with the need. In response, Remon retorted, "I am going to try to stop these places from being reduced to plain slums. We have provided good places for these people, and they ought to appreciate it." He added, "I think that when people destroy government property, they should be criminally prosecuted. I do not think it is enough to evict them."[142] Although Remon sought a return to the NCHA's original character-vetting model, he wanted it to include a punitive twist that emphasized eviction and criminal prosecution for rule-breaking tenants. Remon's call was typical of a growing chorus of critics who openly attributed declining conditions in public housing to irresponsible Black tenant behavior.

· · · · · ·

By the end of the 1950s, there was a clear consensus in affordable housing politics: (Black) tenant irresponsibility was to blame for the persistence of disinvested and declining housing conditions. Sociological discourse repackaged the language so it was no longer explicitly about race but about undesirable cultural and personal choices. As a result, single motherhood, welfare assistance, and households affected by the carceral system became the representative face of the undesirable many after World War II. An evolving gendered trope of Black irresponsibility drove a popular and institutional demand for disciplinary housing governance that linked access to improved housing with character assessment and surveillance. As officials focused on the putative psychological problems and cultural dynamics of low-wage Black households, they successfully diverted analytical attention away from the structural forces that reproduced racial and gendered hierarchies in the urban housing market.

But what if policymakers had considered the structural factors and the institutional actors who sustained the discriminatory housing market? Would disciplinary housing governance have had the same resonance and enduring allure? Could experiments in disciplinary housing governance have been reoriented to address these structural factors? Interventionist measures suggested in the Committee on Negro Housing's report, such as guaranteed living-wage work, abolition of workplace and capital discrimination, and elimination of segregated housing, offered worthwhile alternatives. Or would the endurance of the gendered trope of Black tenant irresponsibility have ensured that even these measures failed?

The Black feminist materialist analysis applied here uncovers the deliberate but evolving way that reproductive discourse came to anchor property and tenant desirability. This analysis also shows how policymakers' narrow focus on the allegedly psychological problems and cultural dynamics of low-wage Black households successfully diverted attention away from the structural forces that caused the social reproduction crisis of housing insecurity for low-wage Black families.

Despite this lack of critical inquiry among postwar officials, Black civil rights activists began to stress the need for structural solutions to poor housing conditions in urban centers. The 1960s introduced an explosion of Black tenant leaders who willingly confronted the urban renewal and public housing officials who resisted or ignored them. These leaders, particularly Black mothers, unapologetically claimed their political voices and demanded that the city apply structural reform to housing code enforcement and public housing policy—or else.

2 Silent No Longer

Black Mothers, Tenant Revolt, and Evolving Opposition

• •

The year 1963, a turning point in the civil rights movement, also triggered a national groundswell of urban Black tenant activism. With civil rights activism heightening Black people's racial consciousness, many Black people throughout the country simmered with anger and frustration when they saw Governor George Wallace (D-AL), an avowed segregationist, declare, "Segregation now, segregation tomorrow, segregation forever," in his inaugural gubernatorial speech on January 14, 1963.[1] Their collective frustration and righteous indignation only deepened when they learned that civil rights leader and preacher Martin Luther King Jr. and dozens more had been violently arrested in Birmingham, Alabama, on April 12, 1963, for "parading without a permit." Arrested for the thirteenth time, King sat in jail and penned his now-famous "Letter from Birmingham Jail." Written in his signature style that blended theological wisdom with moral clarity, King reminded civil rights organizers to embrace their moral obligation to engage in nonviolent direct action and "bring to the surface the hidden tension that is already alive . . . where it can be seen and dealt with."[2] Civil rights activism eventually inspired Black tenants nationwide to challenge their mistreatment.

Just as Martin Luther King Jr. was writing his powerful call to action, a glimmer of tenant resistance emerged in DC. On April 14, 1963, a *Washington Post* article featured Black mothers' growing frustration with housing inspectors' lax enforcement of tenant complaints about landlords' code violations. From October 1962 to January 1963, Black tenants living in a subdivided single-family house at 1358 Columbia Road NW called housing inspectors seventeen times to report structural damage, including holes in walls, missing stairs, and open electrical sockets. In one example, a mother said that she had asked the landlord to replace the front doorknob to "keep out drunken strangers."[3] The landlord scoffed at her request, claiming, "It wouldn't last more than two days. . . . The first one that forgot his key would smash it in, then the housing inspector would come by tell me to put a new one." Despite its repetition of the landlord's reference to the trope of Black tenant irresponsibility to defend his noncompliance with the housing code, the article conveyed a subtle change in the tone of Black tenants. Their public rebuke of their landlord represented a decisive break from years past when tenants traded landlord criticisms privately and avoided any markers of identification in the media.

Over the next five years, Black mothers became the city's largest organized tenant base. Youth-led civil rights groups like the Student Nonviolent Coordinating Committee (SNCC) encouraged Black mothers to embrace rent strikes, litigation, and protest as necessary tactics for increasing public awareness of their declining housing conditions. By the mid-1906s, Black women tenant activists in private and public housing were leveraging the city's housing code to demand state protection of tenant rights using civil rights organizing tactics and, later, War on Poverty funds.

Unafraid of controversy, Black women reshaped affordable housing politics to emphasize the structural disadvantage their families experienced in the rental housing market. Putting their leadership and courage on full display, their actions indirectly contested the stereotype of irresponsibility that helped legitimize their mistreatment. In public hearings, lawsuits, and campaign speeches, the testimonies of Black mothers exposed how real estate representatives and urban officials were exploiting the composition of Black families and their status as recipients of public assistance to enhance profitability and inform methods of disciplinary housing governance. Their experiences exhibited what can only be considered a Black family tax, a penalty that compounded their poverty and contributed to wealth accumulation for real estate interests.

However, Black women's powerful advocacy was not always seen as politically strategic. Officials often treated their testimonies as individual grievances that did not constitute a structural critique. Within this limited framing, members of Congress and local leaders continued to push for disciplinary housing governance. This political position, with members of both political parties agreed, asserted that conditional measures were critical for both curbing rampant Black tenant irresponsibility and incentivizing landlords to comply with the housing code.

After the four-day rebellion in the nation's capital in response to King's assassination in April 1968, federal leaders began to promote more punitive modes of disciplinary housing governance. Richard Nixon, a California conservative who won his presidential campaign on a platform of law and order, quickly appointed conservative-minded local judges who believed that irresponsibility—whether evidenced by family composition, protesting, or poor housekeeping—was responsible for property decline. Socially conservative and middle-class Black men played a key role in legitimizing this punitive turn in disciplinary housing governance. Mobilizing masculinist interpretations of racial uplift, these Black leaders helped justify a broader conservative turn toward the punitive in affordable housing policy—a turn that was most evident in the early 1970s when DC's House Oversight Committee sought to ban welfare-assisted public housing tenants from participating in rent strikes.

This chapter traces this interconnected history of Black women's tenant activism and backlash politics to illustrate the discursive ways that disciplinary housing governance endured through the 1960s and 1970s. Black women's activism and leadership skills did not weaken the power of the gendered trope of Black tenant irresponsibility, which continued to pervade the political spaces Black women entered to demand housing policy reform and legal redress. Members of Congress, judges, and housing officials validated this stereotype by linking gendered and racialized interpretations of "problem families" to building decline and social unrest and by circulating negative portrayals of low-wage Black mothers in their efforts to get disciplinary housing governance measures passed. This conservative backlash affected Black women's tenant activism in DC. Public housing tenant activists struggled to regain political strength, but they eventually regrouped and found other structural and organizational means to continue their activism well into the next decade. This historical moment underscores the powerful social currency that misogynoir discourse (a discourse against Black women) carried as well as the effectiveness of the state's gendered attack on Black tenant protest in the early years of welfare retrenchment in post–civil rights DC.[4]

SNCC: Planting the Seeds of Black Tenant Revolt

Although 1963 provided the launchpad for Black tenant organizing, persistent racial marginalization meant that dissent was inevitable even though housing was increasing in the city. In 1957, the nation's capital became the country's first majority-Black city. This historic first did not change housing discrimination in the region. In 1960, Black people constituted 25 percent of the population of the DC metropolitan area, 80 percent of which lived in the District of Columbia. Within the city, a notable 45 percent of white Washingtonians lived in neighborhoods (mostly west of Rock Creek Park) that were 90 percent white.[5] Black residential mobility remained severely restricted as new homes continued to be built with racial exclusions that were illegal but nonetheless expected and applied. As a result, less than 3 percent of DC's new homes were sold and less than 10 percent of new apartments were rented to Black people.[6] This hypersegregation meant that Black people continued to bear the brunt of living in the region's worst housing conditions. Disinvestment—or "blight" in urban planning discourse—spread in working-class Black neighborhoods in the nation's capital. By the early 1960s, urban renewal officials and business elites were publicly lamenting that increasing signs of disinvestment—inconsistent public services, lower property values, cluttered alleys, declining property conditions, and abandoned buildings—threatened the city's prospects for economic growth.[7] To curb these markers of disinvestment, the city refined its building code in 1961, expanded code enforcement sweeps, and stepped up enforcement against recalcitrant landlords who failed to upgrade their properties to meet the new standards.[8]

On May 16, 1963, a public scandal revealed the inadequacy of such measures. Two *Washington Post* investigative journalists revealed that the city had crafted a gentlemen's agreement with landlord John D. Neumann to pause housing code enforcement. Neumann owned more than 300 properties in DC, that housed 11,000 tenants, most of whom were Black. He allegedly met with city officials in November 1961 to plead for leniency, insisting that full code compliance would bankrupt him. Officials agreed to a tiered repair schedule, maintaining the city's practice of leniency for landlords who claimed financial hardship or showed good-faith efforts toward compliance. Thirty-six of Neumann's properties needed immediate Grade A repairs—homes with conditions rated hazardous such as missing windowpanes or defective flooring. The remaining properties were ranked Grades B to D with code violations related to the 1961 Building Code, certification of occupation problems, and other housing code stipulations.[9]

The city's culture of owner leniency enabled landlords like Neumann to increase the number of disinvested properties that abandoned maintenance but generated large profits. The *Washington Post* article noted that housing inspectors failed to enforce the agreement with Neumann for seventeen months. Although tenants complained that their requests for maintenance went unanswered, housing inspectors shuffled internal memos with responses such as "property may be on untouchable list," and "supervisor stated that John D. Neumann's property will receive special consideration until further notice."[10] The city's hesitance about enforcing the law allowed Neumann to receive more than $10,000 a year in rents on one of his properties with the worst violations while paying less than $675 in real estate taxes.

Black women used the article to expose the degrading experience of landlord property neglect. Notably, with only one exception, all of the tenants featured in the article were women. Neumann had purchased many of his properties in Northwest neighborhoods entering postwar decline, and Black mothers and their families rented subdivided single-family homes that had seen grander days. For example, Rosa Broadus, a thirty-nine-year-old Black mother of three lived at 703 Sixth Street NW in the city's Northwest Penn Quarter neighborhood. Located next to downtown DC, the area was populated with historic sites like Ford's Theatre, where President Abraham Lincoln was assassinated, and was within walking distance of the soon-to-be-built National Portrait Gallery. However, when Broadus moved into her home, she witnessed the walls crumbling around her. She recounted the terror she felt in early 1963, when her family was awakened by the sink hitting the floor and flooding her bathroom. When she notified Neumann's maintenance crew, workers reattached the sink with a "makeshift arrangement of wooden blocks."[11] They left little evidence that they dealt with the water that had sprayed up into the ceiling and seeped into the floor, surely causing mold. Shirley Taylor, a twenty-eight-year-old mother of five, also endured the pain of living in declining conditions. Taylor's family resided at 1772 Corcoran Street NW in Dupont Circle—an upper Northwest community named after decorated admiral Samuel Francis Du Pont, whose family had amassed its original fortune in gunpowder sales. Once home to business and political elites, Dupont Circle contained mansions and large townhomes. But with postwar white flight, Taylor's family lived in a dwelling that Neumann chose to barely maintain. Rats scurried around her house even though the housing code stated that it was the responsibility of landlords to rat-proof their properties.

With a bureaucratic scandal now in public view, the city ordered swift code enforcement. Housing officials began to vet and process housing code complaints for court prosecution quickly. Less than a month after the article was published, housing inspectors recommended that 1,200 cases be reviewed for possible prosecution, prompting one official to comment, "We are so loaded nobody has a chance to catch a breath."[12] The *Post* published more articles that exposed the depths of the ineffectiveness of the city's housing bureaucracy. Housing bureaucrats publicly admitted that they had repeatedly failed to follow up on Neumann's properties.[13] The *Post* then uncovered a leniency deal between housing code officials and another landlord.[14] Under increasing public scrutiny, the city's housing officials pressed Neumann and other landlords to correct the violations as promptly as possible.[15]

For many landlords, increasing public support for stricter housing code enforcement was a new threat to their business model, and they again mobilized timeworn cultural scripts of Black tenant irresponsibility as their defense. In response to the *Post* exposé, Neumann insisted that he was a good landlord and dismissed his noncompliance as "a problem of coordination and the honest errors thereof." In addition, Neumann blamed his tenants if there were notable code violations in his properties. He claimed that his monthly plumbing bill was upward of $3,500 a month because families were "throwing ham-bones, dolls, hair combs down the toilet. We've had to replace commodes because they couldn't get the bones out."[16] Tenants' laziness and incompetence were responsible for broken windows and missing balusters, Neumann said, adding that "rats are caused by lazy people." Other landlords rallied behind Neumann. A week after the explosive article came out, Frank Calcara—founder and president of the DC Property Owners' Association and a fierce opponent of the housing code—expressed sympathy for the property owners who had to house "the great influx of a minority level of citizens overcrowding dwellings with facilities already taxed to the maximum."[17] Housing inspectors, he said, understood that property owners had to deal with "the constant struggle to keep up with willful damage done by many tenants and vandals with repairs often destroyed soon after they are made." Through subtle racial references to the "minority level of citizens" and "ham-bones," Calcara and Neumann used signifiers related to geography, food, and domestic labor to promote the stereotype of Black tenant irresponsibility to defend their (in)actions. They argued that inadequate upkeep was an unavoidable reality with "moderate and low-priced urban housing."[18]

In contrast to earlier decades, when local legislative and advocacy measures hoped to secure better housing conditions for working-class residents, in the 1960s, the protest-driven civil rights movement provided an organizational infrastructure and political language that Black people used to challenge the structural marginalization they endured in multiple facets of life, including housing. By the summer of 1963, Black tenants in the nation's capital and throughout the country were publicly rejecting Calcara and Neumann's stance on disinvested urban housing. As early as 1960, Jesse Gray, a Baton Rouge native who had relocated to New York City in the 1940s, was threatening rent strikes against landlords who abandoned maintenance in majority-Black Harlem.[19] This threat became real in August 1963 when Gray called for a march on City Hall to deliver a message to New York City's mayor: "We are not going to pay any more rent on these blocks until the violations in our homes are corrected."[20] The civil rights group Congress of Racial Equality (CORE) supported Gray's call. The organization's New York program director Gordon Carey asserted, "We've got to go into the Negro slums and try to make the lot of people who live there better."[21]

The 1963 March on Washington surely primed Black Washingtonians to demand improved housing conditions locally. At that event, numerous civil rights organizations, including the Southern Christian Leadership Conference (SCLC), the National Association for the Advancement of Colored People (NAACP), CORE, and SNCC, partnered with labor unions such as the United Auto Workers and social justice groups such as the American Jewish Congress to host a historic protest for jobs and freedom in the nation's capital. On August 28, 1963, 200,000–300,000 protesters poured into the city to recognize the 100th anniversary of the Emancipation Proclamation and denounce the persistence of racial and economic inequality.[22] Standing on the steps of the Lincoln Memorial, civil rights activists presented a vision of racial and economic justice. SNCC chair John Lewis called for organizers to "get in and stay in the streets of every city, every village and hamlet of this nation until true freedom comes, until the revolution of 1776 is complete."[23] Concluding the march, Martin Luther King Jr. gave his moving "I Have a Dream" speech that condemned racism. King warned, "We cannot be satisfied as long as the Negro's basic mobility is from a smaller ghetto to a larger one."[24]

This rousing message of freedom and protest most likely motivated SNCC's local affiliate chapter to offer organizing support to DC residents. A cohort of Black students at Howard University had established a SNCC affiliate chapter, the Nonviolent Action Group (NAG), in 1960, inspired by the young Black college activists who had led the Greensboro sit-ins.[25] Although NAG never gained official recognition from Howard University, it made its mark as a powerful student group through political action and study.[26] Every second Sunday of the month, NAG members met at Newman House at 2717 First Street NW, located near the university and next to the McMillan Reservoir. The group held its first sit-in at the People's Drug Store in Arlington, Virginia, on June 9, 1960. Stokely Carmichael (later renamed Kwame Ture), NAG member and eventual SNCC chair, described NAG participants as "[a] diverse a group of youth as one could expect to encounter, even though most of us were Africans from America."[27] Indeed, NAG's membership was broad and unique. Members' involvement extended beyond Howard to other universities; some participants had no formal ties to a college, and members hailed from the nation's capital, other parts of the United States, and the Caribbean. Such a broad membership base aligned with NAG's commitment to different sites of political action. Carmichael explained that "[NAG] was struggling on at least two very different fronts: one to organize the campus, the other to end racism in the nation. Each required different strategies and different kinds of organizing. The approach to organizing on campus, to influence student attitudes and political awareness, was different from the work off campus, where the focus was both local—discrimination within the District and outright segregation in Maryland and Virginia—and national, getting the attention of the Congress and the incoming Kennedy administration." He added, "Because we were in the nation's capital with the proximity of the African and Caribbean diplomatic corps and with their student presences at Howard, international questions were also a part of our discussions."[28]

Seeing that many Black families had lost faith in the city's housing enforcement process, NAG decided to use direct action to expose social injustices in DC's housing. In the fall of 1963, one of its local campaigns focused on housing code enforcement. The group offered organizing support to Katherine Schuler, the mother of NAG member and DC native Lorenzo Schuler. Forty-one-year-old Katherine and five of her children were getting evicted from their apartment at 1414 Girard Street NW in Columbia Heights. Schuler's Northwest neighborhood had undergone a postwar racial transition. Like the mothers in the *Washington Post* exposé on lax housing code enforcement had done, Schuler and her neighbors appealed to housing inspectors to act as intermediaries to improve their living conditions. In May 1963, inspectors ordered Schuler's landlord to repair over thirty violations in the building, and by the end of the year, fifteen more inspections had been conducted. Schuler's apartment was in the worst condition; "huge chunks of plaster [were] missing from her walls" due to a defective roof. Seeking repairs and maintenance, Schuler refused to pay rent or to move out. Shortly thereafter, her landlords, Mr. and Mrs. Frank A. Vicek, secured an eviction order.

NAG saw Schuler's impending eviction as an opportunity to expose the institutional failure of housing inspection and articulate a new consumer protectionist standard for Black working-class tenants. Schuler wanted to remain in her home because the options elsewhere were limited for households of her size. She also believed that most of the rent she had paid

Katherine Schuler's son, Ricky, was photographed near a hole in the wall that Schuler had asked the landlord to repair. Her maintenance request was met with a retaliatory eviction. This prompted the Nonviolent Action Group, SNCC's DC affiliate chapter, to organize the city's first publicized rent strike. Wisconsin Historical Society, WHI-Gray71–508 00093.

should have gone to maintenance. NAG supported her vision and believed that tenant solidarity was one of the first steps toward realizing this social right. CORE's DC chapter, which was led by civil rights activist Julius Hobson, agreed to support NAG's lead, likely providing infrastructure and support during protests. CORE had initially led Freedom Rides to compel the desegregation of interstate transit. By 1963, it had expanded its advocacy work to include supporting rent strikes throughout the country.[29] In December 1963, NAG members began knocking on doors at the homes of Schuler and her neighbors.

One can only imagine the content of the conversations between the activists and the building's tenants, which engendered a shared investment in the risky tactic of rent strikes. How many times did the activists talk with tenants? Did NAG members break bread with them while discussing the campaign around kitchen tables? Or did they take families to nearby carryouts and Black-owned restaurants like Big Ben's Chili Bowl and the Florida Avenue Grill? Did NAG help with childcare while parents planned the strike? Were NAG activists attentive to tenants' fears of landlord

Katherine Schuler was one of the first tenants to use the housing code to defend her rent strike claims in Washington, DC. Reprinted with permission of the DC Public Library, Star Collection © Washington Post.

retribution? Whatever trust-building approach it used, NAG's organizing bore positive fruit. By the week of January 17, 1964, seven households in Schuler's building, over forty people, mainly members of large families, agreed to be the first rent strikers in Washington, DC. The same week, NAG blocked the Viceks' attempt to evict Schuler and her family. In their rental building, they handed a petition signed by tenants to Francis X. Barry, the landlords' real estate agent, demanding repairs to the entire building and a stop to the eviction of Schuler.[30] Given near-total tenant support, NAG hoped Barry and the Viceks would recognize that working-class Black tenants deserved quality maintenance and habitable conditions at affordable rents.

On January 25, 1964, NAG made the first rent strike in DC public. The District of Columbia became the second location in the nation to have a rent strike, after Harlem and Brooklyn.[31] NAG, Schuler, and her neighbors agreed to use Schuler's eviction as a test case to link rent payments to livable conditions—the strategy that had succeeded in New York City the previous year. Six of the seven rent-striking households withheld their January rents and placed them in an escrow account SNCC had established. "We're cooperating because everyone else is," explained Mrs. Bernard McCoy, a mechanic's wife who was the mother of six.[32] With tenant solidarity intact, NAG turned to the courts in the hope of convincing one judge to recognize rent strikes as a legitimate tool for compelling landlords to respect the consumer demand of low-wage Black families for code-compliant housing.

Schuler's tenant rights claim was subjected to judicial interpretation. On January 28, 1964, Schuler testified in Landlord-Tenant Court, arguing that rent should be tied to livability. Schuler said on the witness stand, "When it rains, or snow melts on the roof, only two rooms in the five-room apartment are livable," adding that the water sometimes became ankle deep.[33] Housing code worker Coleman Homes and NAG member Eugenia Bell substantiated Schuler's testimony. All argued that since the landlords had not upheld the landlord's mandated responsibilities for maintenance in the housing code, Schuler should not have to pay rent until repairs were made.

However, the housing code law stipulated responsibilities for both landlords and tenants, and the Viceks decided to tie their claim that they were not liable for repairs to proving that Schuler had failed to uphold her tenant responsibilities because she was a lax mother. For example, the landlord's building manager testified that he once saw some of Schuler's "11 children" playing on the roof and that she had invited a man to whom she was not married to live in her apartment.[34] Whether this attempt to impugn Schuler's moral character and her parenting affected the judge's decision is unclear. What is clear is that her landlords' argument rested on the "problem family" stereotype that dominated the press and public opinion after World War II. Judge DeWitt S. Hyde ultimately sided with the Viceks, upholding the landlords' right to private property and to evict, especially since Schuler lacked a lease and thus proper legal grounds for appealing the eviction.[35]

This disappointing outcome deviated sharply from the recent successes in New York City, where a December 1963 ruling supported similar tenant rights claims and local officials passed legislation that approved rent strikes when conditions were hazardous to the health of inhabitants. After Schuler's legal defense failed, NAG tried to convince another DC judge of the validity of these arguments using her neighbors' petition and rent strike. That judge also rejected their claim, arguing that as consumers, tenants had the right to move but not to contest habitability. He maintained that tenants must trust the housing inspection process and press inspectors to enforce codes that made landlords responsible for making repairs. The same judge predicted anarchy if tenants could deny rent for inferior housing services, insisting that there would not be "enough judges to handle the cases."[36]

NAG, Schuler, and her neighbors witnessed state repression in the aftermath of their defeat in court. On April 10, 1964, twenty-five NAG members helped the newly displaced families pack their belongings as six US marshals and fifty District of Columbia police officers stood watch to make sure the evictions went as planned.[37] This dramatic show of police force hinted at the city's fear that this wave of Black tenant activism would become widespread. Their fear was soon realized. NAG's legal loss did not spell the end to tenant activism. Within months, the city experienced an explosive growth in organizing infrastructure. Numerous civil rights and housing advocacy groups like the DC chapter of CORE, the Ad Hoc Committee on the Housing Crisis, a group called Associated Community Teams, and another group called the Coalition of Conscience began coordinating rent strikes and popularizing tenant rights discourse.

Some tenant rights advocacy groups focused on conducting grassroots research. In April 1965, All Souls Unitarian Church, a progressive church located in Columbia Heights, released *The Girard Street Project,* a damning report that suggested that the Department of Licenses and Inspections not only condoned but also rewarded landlords who willfully chose not to comply with the city's housing code. Based on a three-year study of housing conditions in Columbia Heights, the report revealed that landlords regularly transferred ownership of properties deemed noncompliant in order to avoid prosecution. Once ownership changed, housing inspectors invalidated previous code violations and renters were forced to repeat the process of requesting code enforcement. Despite such flagrant noncompliance, housing inspectors continued to preach and practice a policy of "friendly collaboration and gentle persuasion" with landlords.[38] The report showed that tenants were more likely to be punished and evicted when they did not uphold their housing code responsibilities. In July 1965, the United Planning Organization (UPO), a private social welfare agency that received President Lyndon Johnson administration's War on Poverty funds, conducted a massive survey that found similar results. The survey, for which UPO staff and 1,000 volunteers interviewed 13,000 residents, confirmed that these code deficiencies were citywide.[39]

Public Housing and Housing Code Tenant Activism

Federal funding was a vital way that the UPO and other social welfare groups throughout the country began to address Black working-class families' long-standing battle over poor housing conditions. A year before to the release of UPO's housing survey, President Lyndon Johnson passed a slew of legislation that expanded the federal government's budget and its reach into public life. In addition to signing the Civil Rights Act of 1964 and Voting Rights Act of 1965, Johnson implemented his domestic policy agenda called the Great Society in May 1964. These federally sponsored programs increased federal involvement in education, employment, healthcare, transportation, and cities to address poverty and safeguard civil rights.[40] Known as "War on Poverty" initiatives, these federal measures allowed the White House to redistribute funds to local groups like the UPO, hoping these groups would seed community organizations to address these various concerns.

War on Poverty funds ultimately financed an organizing infrastructure that enabled the emergence of public housing tenant activism. In 1962, James G. Banks stepped down from his leadership position in urban renewal and became the UPO's first executive director. As the city's distributor of local War on Poverty grants, the UPO financed local social welfare groups that were willing to hire local workers to conduct community action programs aimed at poverty reduction and community engagement. Southeast House, a settlement house established in the 1920s, received an infusion of civil rights leadership just as Black tenant activism was sweeping the city. Ralph Fertig was a community organizer with a social work background who gained civil rights organizing experience when he participated in Freedom Rides and helped organize the 1963 March on Washington. Fertig became Southeast House's executive director in the early 1960s. He and his team used a $133,000 grant from the UPO to hire thirteen antipoverty workers, mostly formerly unemployed public housing residents, eleven of whom were African American.[41] The team's earliest work included supporting public housing residents by creating tenant councils.

Fertig tapped Pharnal Longus, a native Black Washingtonian who was also trained in social work and civil rights activism, to head Southeast House's Barry Farm organizing campaign. Barry Farm, a 443-unit multifamily public housing community built in the city's Southeast Anacostia neighborhood near its namesake river, was one of the city's earliest public housing communities built for Black families. Developed on land the Freedmen's Bureau had earmarked for post–Civil War homesteading, Barry Farm public housing struggled to maintain its original allure as urban renewal funds and private capital were routed away from Southeast neighborhoods like Anacostia, leaving its residents to cope with isolated poverty, fewer city services, and limited quality and affordable retail options. Longus hoped to change Barry Farm's bleak economic and social outlook with an infusion of transplanted civil rights activists who would galvanize the tenants to create "strong, large, militant organizations (independent of Southeast House)."[42] According to historian Anne Valk, Longus hired nine men and only one woman because he believed that men motivated campaigns oriented toward "collective action" rather than individual grievances, which he assumed women organizers were more likely to support.[43] But at Barry Farm, Longus quickly learned that Black women had no problem designing campaigns or building organizations oriented toward collective action.

Public housing tenant activism extended beyond building-specific concerns and demanded that tenants be included in policymaking. In mid-February 1966, Southeast House community organizers met with Barry Farm tenants living on the 1100 block of Stevens Street SE to discuss their thoughts about improving their public housing community. The list was long. They wanted street lamps to illuminate the sidewalks that went dark every night. They wanted pest extermination and better maintenance. They wanted a well-stocked supermarket, a laundromat, and bus transportation for the community's 2,600 residents.[44] In response, Longus told them to either organize or stop complaining. The tenants chose the former and got organized.[45]

Mothers from Barry Farm formed the Band of Angels and teenagers from Barry Farm and neighboring Congress Heights started a youth group called Rebels with a Cause. These two groups decided that their first collective demand would be the inclusion of tenants in Barry Farm's renovation plan. Barry Farm was slated for a renovation project projected to cost over $300,000. Even though the community was less than twenty-five years old, it already showed the need for extensive repairs due to poor construction.

Although Walter Washington, the NCHA's first Black executive director, believed in community involvement, he chose to engage the long-standing Central Tenants Council for discussions about the city's renovation plans, much to the surprise of Barry Farms tenants. On February 26, 1966, Rebels with a Cause and the Band of Angels held a press conference to denounce Washington's decision not to include Barry Farm tenants. "Since we live here, we are best qualified to advise Mr. Washington on how the funds should be spent in the best interests of our community," argued Lillian Wright, a mother of four who chaired the Band of Angels.[46] Wright warned that if Washington did not meet with the tenants soon, they would sit in the NCHA's main office until he did.

The next day, February 27, 1966, Barry Farm tenants took their protest directly to Walter Washington. Fifty parents and their children held the first reported public housing tenant protest outside Barry Farm's recreation center, where Washington was scheduled to meet with the Central Tenants Council. Accosted at the doorway by protesting youth with their parents, Washington advised the tenants to join the meeting instead of protesting outside. Lillian Wright rejected his offer, recounting a disrespectful exchange

Etta Horn (*third from left in the protest line*) was one of the city's most prominent leaders in public housing activism and welfare rights. Horn later led a local welfare rights organization and a daycare center until her passing in 2001. Reprinted with permission of the DC Public Library, Star Collection © Washington Post.

she had with Washington's secretary, who had informed her that Washington's time was "valuable" and refused her request to meet.[47] After Washington failed to dissuade the protestors from assembling at the NCHA's office, tenants succeeded in getting Washington to agree to discuss their concerns about the renovation proposal for Barry Farm and the lack of desirable recreation, counseling, and employment opportunities for youth in their public housing community. Notably, twenty-nine-year-old Marion Barry, then a SNCC organizer who had relocated to DC the year before, was in attendance, watching the protest unfold, passing out pamphlets, and defending a boycott against racist business owners.[48]

On February 28, 1966, the Band of Angels met with Washington at his NCHA office to present their demand that Barry Farm's renovation plan emphasize preventive maintenance. Roof repairs, bathroom upgrades, new plumbing, and consistent maintenance were the tenants' chief requests. They learned that NCHA officials were not receptive to their recommendations. Washington and other agency leaders told the Band of Angels that their recommendations were too costly and that some of their maintenance

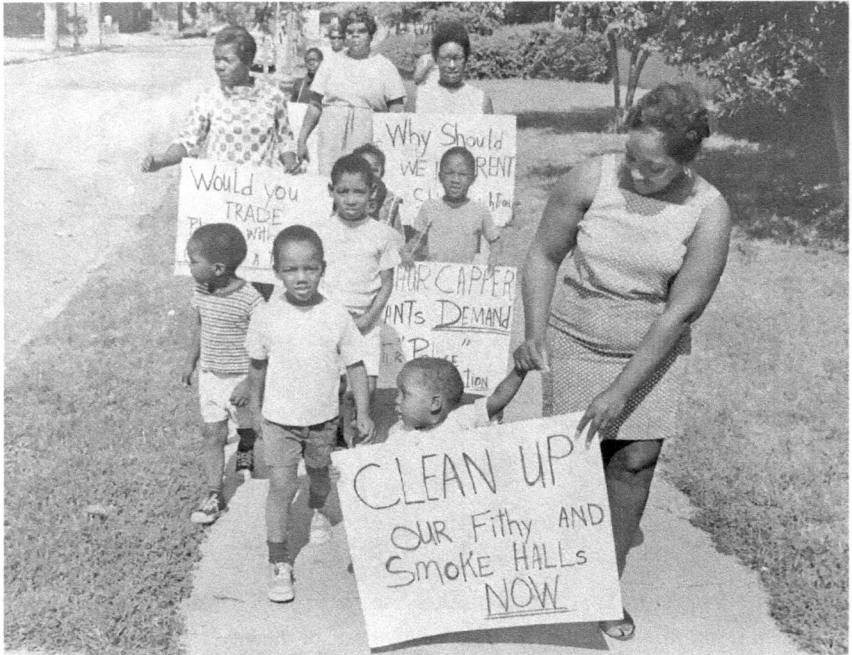

A public housing protest led by Black mothers and their children who lived in Arthur Capper/Carrollsburg public housing in Southeast DC. Reprinted with permission of the DC Public Library, Star Collection © Washington Post.

and renovation requests were the responsibilities of tenants, not the NCHA. An example is Band of Angels leader Rachel Lawrence's suggestion that scheduled replacements of doorknobs and screen doors be folded into the renovation process in order to stop the practice of charging tenants individually for maintenance due to natural wear and tear or weather-related damage. She explained that "if a screen door is broken by a storm, we are charged for it."[49] In response, an NCHA official told Lawrence, "The door is your responsibility," a comment that suggested that her request was misplaced and perhaps reflected her lack of knowledge about the tenant obligations outlined in her lease. Unmoved, Lawrence replied, "A storm is the work of God. Do I have to pay for that?" The meeting ultimately failed to bring the results the Band of Angels desired.

Tenants involved in community action groups eventually decided to join forces and create the city's first public housing tenant union. The project began at Friendship House, another local settlement house that dated back to the Progressive Era. Friendship House shared the commitment of

Southeast House to encourage public housing tenants to serve as antipoverty workers and tenant rights leaders. Friendship House hired Black mothers living in public housing like Lillian Johnson to improve the conditions in the Arthur Capper/Carrollsburg public housing community (hereafter Capper). Designed by famed Black architect Hilyard Robinson and built in 1958, Capper was a 707-unit high-rise multifamily community located in the city's Southeast Capitol Hill neighborhood. After Capper tenants described their frustrations with toxic fumes and poor plumbing in a survey conducted by Friendship House, Johnson and her colleagues held a mass meeting in March 1966. Over a hundred tenants from across the city attended the meeting, where they created the Citywide Tenants Union of National Capital Housing (CTU). Within a few months, the CTU's membership expanded to include over a hundred representatives elected from twenty-one public housing communities.[50] In a series of tenant meetings, union leadership compiled a list of seventeen demands. Similar to Black renters in private housing, CTU leadership wanted rat-proofing: "Rats and mice are ruining these homes, destroying food and clothes and biting children. We want extermination." They wanted preventative maintenance: "Small children eat plaster that falls from holes in the wall around bath tubs. We want tile on the walls around the bath tubs." And they wanted rents that included maintenance: "We pay for maintenance men in paying rent. We feel that we should not be paying for labor again when fixtures are replaced and repaired."[51]

However, tenant leadership quickly learned that their demands needed to be vetted and approved by the NCHA. To complicate matters, the CTU still had to fight for institutional recognition. On May 3, 1966, the NCHA announced the formation of its Interproject Tenants Advisory Council and invited elected representatives from all forty public housing communities into meetings with agency leadership. The next day, the CTU made a surprise visit to Washington's office to notify him of their demands and push back against the NCHA's alternative tenant advocacy group. CTU leaders told Washington that most of the agency's elected officials would not be effective. Tenants viewed them as "company people" who received "special privileges" from property managers.[52] Unconvinced by their argument, Washington invited both groups to a meeting on May 16, 1966, where he presented the agency's response to tenant concerns. According to local reports, "a hostile clash started almost as soon as the director opened the meeting at NCHA offices."[53] CTU representatives lambasted the NCHA, while tenants from the NCHA-approved group scolded the CTU as discourteous. Despite this tension between tenant leaders, Washington conceded to some of their demands, promising rat extermination in all properties and no additional charges for repairs due to normal wear and tear. The meeting seemed to reassure some tenants, but much of the union's leadership stated that they would not back down until all of their demands were met.

Black Mothers' Dissent and Congressional Testimonies

The brewing citywide tenant revolt eventually compelled the federal government to intervene in local affairs again. The US Department of Housing and Urban Development (HUD), a cabinet-level agency established by President Johnson in September 1965, was tasked with integrating and developing federal housing programs. In January 1966, HUD issued a harsh directive to city housing officials: DC needed to "develop (and put in effect) procedures to reduce the amount of compliance time for those cases that involve willful and persistent housing code violators."[54] HUD cited *The Girard Street Project*'s report and UPO's survey as evidence of the city's continued struggles to ensure that codes were enforced. The agency warned that DC's failure to carry out a housing code enforcement program that elevated all of the city's 157,000 dwelling units to a code-compliant standard would result in reduced federal funding.

A Democrat-controlled Congress supported HUD's position, hoping to address tenants' demands for legally protected rent strikes and better housing code enforcement with legislation. The same month HUD passed its directive, the Washington Planning and Housing Association (WPHA) established a committee headed by local lawyer Edward S. Cogen. The WPHA drafted a bill that would, among other measures, prevent landlords from using Landlord-Tenant Court like "a collection agency" for tenants who fell behind on their rent by a couple of days.[55] In addition to stopping the retaliatory evictions that plagued rent-striking tenants like Schuler and her neighbors, the bill authorized rent strikes when tenants paid their rents in escrow with the city and prohibited punitive rent hikes when tenants complained about housing code violations.

However, when Congress entered the local debate, familiar cultural scripts about Black tenants informed the discussion. In the spring of 1966, Joseph Tydings (D-MD), chair of the Senate District Committee, agreed to hold hearings on a bill that the WPHA had initially drafted. In the leadup to the hearings, Tydings met with other stakeholders, including real estate representatives, for the purpose of revising the WPHA bill. On June 14, 1966,

Tydings held a press conference in front of homes in the Truxton Circle neighborhood (also referred to as East Shaw) to announce his intention to back key aspects of the WPHA bill, including legal protection for rent strikers. But he added a key provision: the creation of a landlord and tenant school, similar to "the Police Department's Traffic and Pedestrian Schools, which would be conducted at night primarily to teach tenants to take better care of their living quarters."[56] This ostensibly colorblind proposal reflected the desire of real estate interests for state action to reduce property damage caused by tenants, and left an opening for landlords and other real estate representatives to validate the long-circulated gendered trope of Black tenant irresponsibility.

Now organized and organizationally supported, Black people, particularly Black mothers, would not allow the congressional hearing to devolve into another session about Black tenants' alleged cultural deficiencies. Civil rights organizations, housing advocacy groups, and tenant activists with ties to UPO community action groups participated in congressional hearings held on July 19 and 21, 1966. There, these groups engaged in a political battle over the meaning of the housing experiences of Black working-class families. Notably, eleven Black women testified as tenants of private and public housing.

The Black women tenant activists who testified understood how cultural narratives underwrote practices in the housing market. The real estate industry, they argued, operated with the shared assumption that the worst housing should go to the least desirable tenants, a category that was directly tied to family composition. For example, Rosa Robinson, a mother of eight, said, "About 2 years ago I lived in a two-bedroom apartment. I have eight children, the oldest one is 12, the youngest one is 18 months, so it was overcrowded. I had received 30 days' notice that I had to move, so I went to the real estate agency to find a place to move to. When I told them that I have more than two or three children they would tell me, 'Well, we can't rent you a house because there are too many children.'" As her eviction date neared, Robinson grew nervous. But she soon found a place on Selma Street and asked her husband to negotiate the lease and rent. The rent would be $139 per month, but if they wanted the broken windows and screen doors replaced that would increase to $149. They agreed to the rent hike but once the family moved in, they endured a rodent infestation. "You can be sitting down and the rats underneath the floor are squealing like they are fighting, under the floor you can hear them all night," Robinson testified.[57] Forced to navigate a racially restrictive housing market with time-sensitive eviction notices, families like Robinson's were at the mercy of landlords who knew that the city's dwindling low-rent inventory incentivized higher rents. If tenants wanted lower rents, they needed to put up with less maintenance.

Black mothers also understood that these negative cultural scripts about Black families enabled racialized profitability schemes. Mrs. Annie West, a mother of four, said that real estate agents treated her children like they were "some kind disease." Her agent only offered her a recently vacated single-family home with a broken porch and a missing kitchen floor. Like Robinson, West was desperate for a home and she accepted the dwelling, hoping she could convince the agent to make repairs later. West suspected that agents felt that working-class Black families deserved poor housing: "It seems to me that most real estate brokers just usually hand these white elephants off to people, especially people with children, and it just does not seem to matter to them in what condition they hand it to you." West clearly believed that real estate interests colluded to direct large Black families to noncompliant, disinvested housing because they were considered undesirable tenants. Indeed, one agent said, "The Negro costs infinitely more to rent to. There's no getting around it. He beats up the property more; he moves more people into it; he has no concern about it. The cost of repair goes up appreciably."[58]

Refuting the persistent argument of real estate interests that Black tenancy should be managed with the monetization of risk, Black mothers suggested that majority-Black tenancy enabled landlords to protect profit margins by transferring all maintenance to tenants. Debbie Washington was the cofounder of the nonprofit tenant-led advocacy group CRUST, which consisted of local residents seeking to ensure that urban renewal in the overwhelmingly Black Shaw neighborhood was equitable and prevented Black mass displacement. Washington noted, "A number of landlords now force their tenants to make major repairs of their homes. We feel that this is a responsibility of the landlord, and a burden which the tenant should not be forced to carry, since the rents that tenants pay is already out of proportion to values received by the tenants."[59] Harris Weinstein, chair of the WPHA, substantiated Washington's claim. He reported that after the housing code passed, many landlords inserted provisions into their leases that stipulated that renters were responsible for maintenance. As an example, Weinstein provided one lease that specified that the tenant was responsible for "all necessary repairs" and "replacements to the heating plant, pipes, radiators, or plumbing fixtures caused by freezing, or by the negligence, lack of proper care or improper use."[60] Weinstein added that many landlords also included provisions in leases that prohibited renters from petitioning the Department of Licenses and Inspections. In light of these loopholes, Debbie Washington's demand to negotiate tenant responsibilities was powerful. She directly challenged an industry practice that allowed landlords to neglect the upkeep of disinvested homes and encouraged them to retain properties until the land value appreciated to where they could sell and pocket the profit.[61]

Black women argued that the city needed to defend an industry-wide standard of maintenance to stop this racialized hierarchy of tenant mistreatment. Marion Byrd, the chair of the 1600 Block Tenant Association on Twelfth Street NW, shared her experience: "I used to live in 1633, but due to the fact that we had a blowout [electrical fire] on Easter Sunday, I am not living there anymore." She continued, "We had been complaining about a short circuit through the switches, and the bathroom, for five years so when we got this wreck up there, he didn't say anything about it, but he wanted to pass the table [transfer repair responsibility to tenants]. . . . I didn't feel it necessary for me to put out money to do something that the owner had known about for 5 years."[62] After Byrd was evicted due to the electrical fire, she and her family moved into housing that was marginally better because her landlord offered maintenance, albeit only on weekends. When Byrd complained about her new landlord's sluggish approach to repairs, her housing inspector preached patience since many landlords would not provide maintenance at all.

Public housing residents sought the same standard of housing maintenance that renters of private housing demanded. CTU president Precious Smith wanted Tydings and his colleagues to broaden the scope of the WPHA bill to include public housing residents. CTU leadership argued that the city's public housing agency did not have to comply with the housing code, which left public housing residents, particularly Black mothers, exposed to discriminatory treatment. Mrs. Louise Davis, a Barry Farm tenant, testified to support this point: "My son was sitting outside on the morning of June 6, when a big rat came out of the vent that leads into the basement or storeroom that is in the exclusive control of the NCHA. This rat bit my son and went back into the same vent."[63] Davis continued, "I then had to take him to the hospital. Two or three days [later] the housing inspectors came out and gave me a notice to fill the rathole around my house. I did not think that was my responsibility." For Davis and many public housing residents, the city's notice to Davis was evidence of a troubling double standard: the NCHA's operational and maintenance deficiencies fell outside the boundaries of state accountability, but accusations of tenant negligence did not.

Without a citywide maintenance standard, public housing residents worried that they would continue to suffer from discriminatory treatment and "sloppy management."[64] Public housing residents resented that they were expected to develop personal solutions to managerial neglect while also being left unclear about the details of tenant responsibilities. In one example, public housing tenants said that they were held responsible for interior painting, which included clearing and repainting multiple rooms within a limited timeframe. They argued that this was an unreasonable expectation for the elderly residents and single working mothers who constituted the majority of tenants in public housing in the 1960s. The result was that families who could not adhere to property managers' unreasonable expectations were often mistreated and humiliated.[65]

Black women also suggested that stronger state regulation of landlord behavior would protect tenants from landlord intimation and retribution. Dorretha M. Dade, chair of the 4929 Foote Street Residents Club in Northeast DC's Lincoln Heights neighborhood, testified that fifteen families in their sixteen-unit rental community joined their tenant association after it became clear that their landlord, Maurice Rosenbloom, was more interested in rebuke and paternalism than in management that responded to tenants' needs. Dade said, "We attempted to confer with him as a group about our problems. We wrote to him expressing our desire to live in a decent place; we also listed what we felt needed to be repaired. Our only reply was notices to many of the members of the club, that our rent had been increased."[66] She added, "Since our decision to continue our fight for better living conditions, we have been verbally intimated by threats from the owner. . . . He has notified some of us that we must move within 30 days; he has used profane language in talking with many of the families, and has sent notices to some, to appear in court for nonpayment of rent, when in fact, the rent has been paid." Rosenbloom accused Dade and her neighbors of waging an "international Communist conspiracy" and instituted a new punitive managerial approach.[67] After tenants collectively requested additional maintenance services, Rosenbloom enforced collective punishment for any act of property damage. He also issued a stern directive related to character oversight: "There will be periodic monthly inspections of each apartment to ascertain general condition and cleanliness. . . . Those tenants who do not maintain their apartments and have roaches will be given orders to clean up premises within a specified time. If not followed through, the orders to move will be given."[68]

The testimonies of these Black women were a powerful response to landlords' insistence that poor housing conditions reflected poor housekeeping.

Miss CAROLYN A. BAKER,
Washington, D.C.

DEAR MISS BAKER: Since it cannot be determined who is responsible for the disassembling of the heavy-duty steel anchor fence belonging to the property, which was maliciously perpetrated last month, then the tenants will be held equally responsible for this vandalism. Equally important, all tenants will also be charged for the extensive vandalism perpetrated in apartment 303 this past week.

Your rental account with our office has been charged $7.50 as your share to help defray the replacement cost of this fence and $18 for damages to the vacated apartment.

Rent due	Date due	Court cost	Repairs due	Amount received	Balance due on rent
$89.50............................	June 2, 1966	....	....	1 $89.50	....
$95.00............................	July 2, 1966	$3.25	{ 2 $7.50 3 18.00 }	4 $9.50	$34.25

1 June 6, 1966.
2 For fence.
3 For apartment damage.
4 July 5, 1966.

There is an outstanding amount of $34.25 due as of July 2 rent. You are requested to pay the amount outstanding on your rent.

We, therefore, are hoping that you will reconsider the situation and will desire to make an amicable settlement of your account. However, if we do not hear from you within the next five days, you leave us no alternative but to have our legal representative contact the Personnel Department at the Federal Bureau of Investigation and inform them of your collaboration with this criminal activity.

Yours truly,

MAURICE H. ROSENBLOOM,
Rental Manager.

This letter from a landlord to tenants in Southeast DC attempted to charge all tenants for an act of vandalism that had happened on the property. This landlord later attempted to charge tenants additional fees for numerous arbitrary infractions, including poor housekeeping. "Housing in the District of Columbia," 1966, pp. 405–406. Published with permission from the US Government Printing Office.

In a postwar housing economy that valorized women's purchasing power, Black mothers' articulation of the multiple ways the market and state devalued their housing consumption was particularly poignant. Their testimonies underscored the intricate link between landlords' assumptions about the housing services their tenants deserved and the race of tenants, the size of their families, and the domestic labor performed within those families. While antiblackness anchored these discriminatory housing market practices, Black women understood that single Black mothers and large families bore the negative effects of what could only be considered a Black family tax. Excessive costs, time lost, stress, and dysphoria were inherent components of this regressive tax, and housing inspectors' inconsistent code enforcement only compounded this negative reality. The testimonies these women gave offer a nuanced understanding of the Black tax for renters, a concept that scholars often discuss in the context of Black homeowners.[69]

Congress and the Specter of Disciplinary Housing Governance

Heteropatriarchal cultural scripts about male leadership and male policy expertise may explain why Tydings and his colleagues seemed to miss the structural analysis of the Black women who testified. After each testimony, the committee focused more on determining whether tenants' testimonies were accurate than on identifying themes in what they said.[70] Perhaps, like some male civil rights organizers who saw low-wage Black women as unstrategic but effective articulators of grievances, members of Congress may have believed that the appropriate political contribution of these women was to provide lists of mistreatment in isolated disputes between tenants and slumlords. Members of Congress did not ask the tenants how they felt about Tydings's most controversial proposal: a landlord-tenant night school. It was a notable omission that suggested that Black women tenant activists were hypervisible as political subjects but minimally influential in this legislative debate.

Because members of Congress felt that male leaders were the desirable representatives for expressing Black tenant dissent, it fell on men to address the gendered and racial bias that Tydings's proposed school might perpetuate. Only two men—one Black and another white—spoke directly against the school. Channing Phillips, a thirty-eight-year-old Black minister and civil rights activist involved in several affordable housing groups, including the nonprofit Housing Development Corporation, objected to the proposal.[71] Phillips wanted Congress to increase the supply of new low-rent housing and worried that the proposed landlord-tenant night school would harm low-income Black families because of prejudicial judgment and human error. Phillips also warned that this legislative measure might negatively harm Black families, citing a hypothetical example in which children might have caused a mess on the day of a court-appointed evaluation of an accused tenant's home that the evaluator could improperly blame a parent for. Bruce Terris's objection was more forceful. A thirty-two-year-old white public interest lawyer who assisted Better Homes, another nonprofit housing development corporation, Terris believed that landlords with numerous properties were most likely to mistreat tenants and unlikely to correct their actions in a night school. Terris rejected the idea of the school for tenants because housing inspectors already used code enforcement disproportionately against tenants, so a school would not serve as an effective corrective. He also pointed out, "I don't think many of these people are very ignorant, many of these people will keep my house clean, keep houses clean in the suburbs and get paid to do it."[72] But when presented with the racial and gendered undernotes of the night school, Tydings remained unmoved: "It is obvious to me that there are areas which need improvement with respect to tenants, cleanliness, and sanitary items. Tenant responsibility is a problem."[73]

With the trope of (Black) tenant irresponsibility kept at the fore of the congressional debate, real estate representatives continued to argue for state regulation of Black consumer behavior. The city's board of realtors advised Tydings to make his proposal part of the housing code: "While it is true that poor housekeeping and living habits are the cause of many code violations, it is not realistic to think that either the threat of fines or even jail, can be effective in changing habits which developed over a lifetime and were the legacy of several hundred years of deprivation. Shotgun tenant education programs cannot be effective under these circumstances. . . . Rather than experimental tenant programs, why not make such programs an integral part of the code enforcement process?"[74] Real estate representatives sought another mode of disciplinary housing governance by making the school compulsory to correct Black people's alleged collective underdevelopment in domestic practices.

Tydings's response to real estate representatives suggested that he embraced a postwar behaviorist mode of governance that focused on a subset of tenants, most likely "problem families" identified by landlords, courts, and housing inspectors. His investment in behavioral regulation also enabled welfare and housing officials to use the congressional debate to legitimize their disciplinary housing governance initiatives. For example, housing officials highlighted the large-family demonstration program the NCHA had launched in 1961 as evidence of the city's ability to ensure that low-wage families adhered to their tenant responsibilities. The program was connected to DC's first scattered-site housing program, in which the NCHA leased private dwellings and rented them to qualified tenants. In the agency's official report on the large-family demonstration program, housing officials returned to moral character assessments as preconditions for tenant qualification. Accepted applicants exhibited a "stable, cohesive unit in which both parents were present and whose behavior could not reasonably be subjected to extensive criticism." Heterosexual gender norms were implicit within this appraisal of tenant stability and desirability: "In almost all cases, the family's total income was derived from the husband's employment. . . .

Few of the mothers were employed, and most of these held part-time domestic or other service jobs."[75] Referencing this program at the hearing, housing officials suggested that low-wage tenants required behavioral supervision.

Welfare officials promoted stronger character oversight for families who fell outside the category of the honorable poor. At the time of the hearing, nearly 10,000 families received welfare assistance in the nation's capital, over 90 percent of whom were Black. The Department of Public Welfare was under fire for its failure to properly vet private housing and ensure that its rent-assisted homes compiled with the city's housing code (notably, the NCHA was exempt from this requirement). The Department of Public Welfare proposed that caseworkers evaluate and develop tenants' housekeeping practices more frequently in exchange for higher welfare allowances and more consistent checks of housing quality. Because the gendered trope of Black tenant irresponsibility was accepted as a self-evident truth in welfare-assisted homes, the agency's recommendation of stronger character oversight was a predictable outcome.[76] Its promotion of this practice ran counter to an emerging urban policy trend in cities like Chicago and New York of empowering welfare-assisted tenants to contest poor housing conditions with rent strikes when code enforcement failed. However, welfare officials and real estate representatives were able to convince members of Congress that Black tenants were irresponsible instead of seeing recipients of public assistance as people with agency.

The congressional hearing on the WPHA bill did not yield a new law, but it did usher in a post–civil rights political posture that attempted to balance tenant rights with landlord protections. In the nation's capital, this institutional response accepted the trope of Black tenant irresponsibility. Some tenant rights organizers challenged this latent discourse, but much of this battle was led by local welfare rights activists such as Etta Horn and Lillian Wright. These activists created or participated in welfare rights organizations that critiqued measures that tied welfare with disciplinary schemes like "no-man-in-the-house" rules or housekeeping checkups.[77] For the next several years, they disrupted congressional hearings, protested to welfare officials, and rejected the repeated political insinuation that their poverty and poor housing conditions were the result of poor parenting and tenant irresponsibility.

Congressional inaction in defining and protecting tenant rights in the nation's capital meant that tenant activists eventually pivoted to legal recourse. This strategy relied on court rulings and a strong organizing

Many of the objectives treated here involve problems of neglect concerning the basic elements of sound housekeeping habits. Together with shelter, cleanliness is a fundamental must because it contributes a substantial share of preventing the deteriorating conditions of many properties and neighborhoods. No housing program can be sound unless the premises occupied for residential purposes are kept in a clean and sanitary condition. In licensed premises, i.e. apartment, tenement or rooming house, sanitation for common space is the landlord's responsibility. In non-licensed premises, i.e. single family and two family houses the tenant has responsibility in the following: areaways, walkways and yards should be clean and free of ashes, filth, litter, refuse, garbage, human and animal waste or any other insanitary matter. In those parts of a dwelling occupied and under the exclusive control of a public assistance family, it shall be their responsibility to maintain good housekeeping standards to include:

1. Floors, floor coverings and other walking surface should be kept clean and free of dirt, dust, filth, garbage, human or animal waste, litter, refuse or any other insanitary matter.
2. Walls, ceilings, windows and doorways should be kept clean and free of cobwebs, dirt, dust, soot or any other insanitary matter.
3. Furniture should be kept clean and free of dirt and dust.
4. Bedding and linens should be kept in a clean and sanitary condition.
5. Stove and refrigerator should be kept in a clean condition and free of dirt and greasy film, or any other insanitary matter. In those parts of a dwelling occupied and under
6. Food should be properly covered so as to protect it from flies, dust or other types of contamination. Storage for food should be kept clean and free of any insanitary matter.
7. Dishes and cooking utensils should be properly washed within a reasonable time following each meal.
8. Garbage and trash should be stored in lawful and separate containers kept properly covered at all times.
9. Bathroom facilities (toilet, wash basin, tub or shower) should be kept in a clean, sanitary condition and free of dirt, filth, human waste or any other insanitary matter.

The District of Columbia's Department of Public Welfare administered a housing improvement program in the early 1960s that placed public housing families into code-compliant but privately owned housing. Department of Public Welfare representatives defended their housing program by stressing how welfare workers closely monitored public housing tenants' housekeeping practices. This excerpt reflected the different metrics welfare workers used to assess public housing tenants' housekeeping. "Housing in the District of Columbia," 1966, p. 460. Reprinted with the permission of the US Government Printing Office.

infrastructure that was willing to engage in long-term advocacy and legal battles. For private housing, this strategy eventually yielded positive results. The antipoverty group Neighborhood Legal Services Project (NLSP) hired a number of lawyers to assist residents with legal concerns. One of these hires, Florence Roisman, a Harvard Law graduate in her twenties, quickly distinguished herself in the small but growing field of movement lawyering in the nation's capital. She once said, "I believe the law can respond—it must respond—to groups to which it was totally unresponsive to in the past. If it fails to respond, fails to change—then I think we will have a revolution."[78] Roisman and other NLSP antipoverty lawyers had a number of victories related to housing code enforcement.[79] Chief among these was a

December 1967 court ruling that interpreted leases as contracts. The court ruled that if landlords failed to provide code-compliant maintenance, the tenant's obligation to pay also lapsed.[80] An appeals court upheld this ruling in May 1969, as did the Supreme Court, ending the decades-long legal principle that backed landlords who argued that maintenance was a tenant responsibility. As the appeals court judge maintained, tenants should not be "jacks-of-all-trades" when it came to property maintenance.[81]

Disciplinary Housing Governance and Backlash Against Public Housing Activism

Public housing residents hoped to use the same strategies—community organizing and legal recourse—to improve their living conditions through universal housing code enforcement and better maintenance. However, public housing residents relied on federal funding to maintain their homes. Some conservative congress members soon learned that withholding federal monies could become a punitive tool used to punish certain forms of activism. By 1965, the civil rights movement morphed into numerous social movements that responded to many political issues. For instance, shortly after the federal government entered into another Cold War proxy war in Vietnam, young college students launched a national antiwar movement, challenging the country's foreign policy priorities and military conscription policy. At the same time, young women across the country expanded the feminist movement, demanding the abolition of policies and social practices that devalued women and girls. Meanwhile, Black civil rights groups evolved or transitioned into Black Power or pan-African solidarity movements, ushering in a new wave of cultural institutions and political militancy. What united these disparate movements was what historian James Patterson describes as a commitment to "rights-consciousness"—a belief that the government should and can assist historically mistreated groups through state protections and resources.[82]

These groups' political demands and controversial protests aroused the ire of conservatives, who quickly mobilized white Americans who worried that this era of protests was moving the country in the wrong direction to vote for them. This fear was expressed at the ballot box. In the fall of 1966, conservative actor turned politician Ronald Reagan was elected as California's governor, ousting the two-time Democratic incumbent Pat Brown. In office, Reagan led attacks against Black Power groups like the Black Panther Party, campus protesters, and welfare recipients.[83] A staunch segregationist,

Lester Maddox, who defended states' rights, including the "right" to reject civil rights, won the Georgia governorship. The Republican takeover wave continued in Congress, with over forty Democratic members of Congress losing their seats in the House and Senate.[84] With a conservative resurgence, President Lyndon Johnson understood the political tide toward his grand vision of a redistributive federal government, as evidenced in his Great Society initiatives, was turning, and his political compromises became more conservative.[85]

Less than six months after DC public housing tenants testified for federal support of their request to make the NCHA comply with the city's existing housing code, Congress and President Johnson took steps to undercut the organizing infrastructure that public housing residents relied on. Congress slashed $166 million from its 1967 budget for community action programs in order to pay for the Vietnam War.[86] In DC, these cuts were implemented immediately: $4.5 million was cut from the community action program. The UPO was forced to terminate half of its community action staff. While community organizers mounted a vigorous campaign to stop these cuts, the endeavor failed, and community groups struggled to maintain coordinated citywide advocacy.[87] Another blow to the organizing infrastructure came in late 1968 on the heels of the social unrest that swept the nation after Martin Luther King Jr. was assassinated. Large swaths of the city were engulfed in flames, prompting one federal official to decry that DC "looks like Vietnam."[88] The backlash against these uprisings and other social movements arguably propelled millions of Americans to elect Republican candidate Richard Nixon to the presidency. Nixon aimed to fulfill his law-and-order campaign promises by appointing conservative-minded officials to oversee War on Poverty initiatives, further gutting the federal financing for community organizing.[89]

While conservatives led campaigns to roll back the welfare rights efforts financed through War on Poverty initiatives, the country's weakening economy provided another opportunity to embolden conservatives' calls for welfare austerity. The country's economic slowdown in 1968 exposed the structural weakness of public housing—a growing gap between operating expenses and tenant income.[90] By the 1960s, the tenants in public housing had shifted overwhelmingly from largely employed two-parent households to low-wage tenants with less stable income sources. Public housing now consisted primarily of the elderly, individuals with disabilities, welfare-assisted mothers, and large families, all of whom struggled to pay the rents that the original architects argued were necessary to sustain the financial health of public housing. Yet federal law required that most operating costs, including maintenance, come from rents.[91] By the mid-1960s, public housing authorities had begun to run operating deficits. During most of that decade, federal welfare expenditures provided a temporary reprieve. That reality changed when the Nixon administration tried to rein in federal spending on public housing. In the fall of 1969, the NCHA was again in the red. The agency needed an immediate infusion of federal cash, or it would not be able to make payroll. HUD agreed to a one-time subsidy on the condition that the NCHA raise rents to solve its recurring budget shortfalls.

HUD's demand that the NCHA address its long-standing fiscal issue with rent hikes drove public housing residents to launch their own community organizing and legal campaign. For at least three years, public housing tenants had organized and pressured NCHA leadership to respond to their demands regarding maintenance and code compliance, but their protests had yielded little change. So when the NCHA notified tenants on October 3, 1969, that it was implementing an across-the-board rent hike of $11.00 ($95.21 in 2025 dollars) starting on November 1, tenants were shocked that the agency failed to mention any provision for code compliance.[92] Tenants quickly turned their shock into clarity and got organized. While the CTU, Friendship House, and Southeast House were smaller after budget cuts, they provided assistance. Herman Kitchens, a Black Friendship House organizer with Carolina roots, played a leading role in organizing tenants.[93] On October 13, 1969, more than one hundred NCHA tenants met at Ballou High School in DC's Anacostia neighborhood and voted to launch a rent strike and legally challenge the rent hike due to poor code compliance and poor management. Shortly thereafter, the NLSP filed a court injunction to stop the rent increase because the NCHA had not issued the statutory thirty-day notice.

After the tenants obtained the injunction, they learned that the federal government would continue to play an out-sized role in their housing campaign. The tenants visited NCHA executive director Edward Arnov to present their demands and were probably surprised to learn that Arnov was sympathetic to their concern that increased rents would eat into their limited income. He likely brought up the successful rent strike in St. Louis that had inspired Black moderate Republican Edward Brooke (R-MA) to back what became known as the Brooke Amendment of the Housing and Urban Development Act of 1969. While the law authorized the HUD Secretary to give land and finances to localities for various development uses, including housing and parks, the amendment capped public housing tenants' rent contribution at 25 percent of a tenant's income and tasked HUD with covering a more significant percentage of the operating costs of public housing. However, the Brooke Amendment did not become law until late December 1969. Until then, Arnov could not rescind the rent hike because it was fiscally and legally necessary. This news most likely offered tenants some relief, but they still believed the rent hikes were unjust. Reverend Chester C. Thompson, a spokesperson for the campaign against the rent hike, said, "My moral convictions tell me that they [the NCHA] are wrong. They are in violation of so many laws, first the golden rule, and then the housing code. Why should the private housing industry be made to comply with the regulations and the National Capital Housing Authority go free?" With fierce moral conviction, public housing residents began a rent strike in November 1969. Campaign representatives estimated that 1,000–2,000 public housing residents withheld rents.

As the rent strike entered the 1970s, internal politics within the Nixon administration indirectly undermined the public housing residents' goal of code compliance. With the passage of the Brooke Amendment, tenants may have believed that budgetary relief was imminent, but bureaucratic politics got in the way of policy execution. Sensationalistic news coverage about rising crime rates and shifting demographics in public housing made some Nixon officials hesitant to allocate more federal dollars to public housing. The administration increasingly saw public housing as a "money-eating monster out of control."[94] Not all conservatives shared this view. Like moderate Republican Edward Brooke, HUD secretary George Romney wanted to maintain funds to keep public housing afloat. Conversely, Nixon's Office of Management and Budget (OMB) wanted to introduce fiscal austerity.[95] The latter group of conservative leaders won, and HUD failed to enforce the Brooke Amendment. The department repeatedly asked Congress for fewer operating funds than were required for public housing and made localities responsible for meeting the deficit. In turn, localities with rising operating costs chose to defer maintenance, making the change DC tenants had demanded in their rent strike impossible. Complicating matters further, tenants could not count on HUD administrators as allies since the agency was undergoing a leadership crisis. Romney was increasingly isolated within Nixon's cabinet and had to deal with embarrassing ethical scandals involving HUD officials. One of the first involved HUD's deputy secretary Lawrence M. Cox, who was accused of financial wrongdoing and questionable leisure choices (he frequented an all-white country club that enforced a gentlemen's agreement to exclude Black and Jewish people).[96]

The extent to which tenants knew of these internal conflicts within the Nixon administration is not clear. However, what is clear is that HUD insisted on interfering with DC's public housing leadership politics as the rent strike took hold. After a year of stalled negotiations between the NCHA and the Rent Strike Coordinating Committee (the body established to represent the different groups supporting the rent strike), Walter Washington, now DC's mayor-commissioner (and appointed to the post by President Johnson), fired Arnov and issued a freeze on any new public housing commitments. Hoping to generate goodwill among the organized tenant leadership, Washington and NCHA officials invited them to interview candidates for the NCHA's executive director position. Elsewhere, HUD officials weighed in on the hiring process and backed one candidate: James G. Banks. After resigning from the post of the UPO's executive director in May 1967 to join HUD as director of community development, Banks returned to city government several months before the public housing rent strike. He served as Washington's special assistant for coordinating DC's housing activities from April 1969 to July 1970.[97] Washington had been integrally involved in the rent strike negotiations, and HUD officials most likely saw him as an ideal choice given his experience in federal and local government. DC's public housing tenants saw it differently. They found Banks's leadership style to be "condescending" and contested his candidacy.[98]

Despite tenant resistance, Mayor-Commissioner Washington appointed Banks to serve as the NCHA's executive director in the summer of 1970. Shortly thereafter, Banks signaled that his vision for public housing management was another reason he had gained HUD's favor. He launched a public relations campaign in the summer of 1971 to share why he believed that new behavioral regulations were necessary for public housing residents. In an interview with William Raspberry, a Black columnist for the *Washington Post*, Banks explained that he wanted public housing management to focus on shaping Black women tenants' domestic lives. Irresponsible parents—whom he suggested were often single and sometimes teenage mothers—were creating intolerable conditions in public housing. To rectify this, he supported minimum age requirements and new domestic arrangements in public housing. Specifically, Banks recommended reconfiguring public housing from private individual apartments to communal living. Single Black mothers and their children would eat together, wash their clothes together, and learn about proper homemaking from their elderly neighbors. These management interventions, Banks argued, would give "people the motivation and the means for providing their own internal discipline.

Unfortunately, too many Black people are being kept from advancing because of a lack of this sort of discipline."[99]

However, while this measure was speculative and perhaps even progressive for Banks, he soon clarified that he understood discipline and its physical embodiment as a gendered task that was best performed by men. In October 1971, Banks presented his NCHA public housing reform plan to the wealthy and largely white Washingtonians of the Potomac chapter of the National Association of Housing and Redevelopment Officials. Declaring the agency's needs-based admission approach of the urban renewal era a failure, he called for a new administrative direction that ensured the stability of Black heteronuclear families. For Banks, the NCHA's problem and solution hinged on Black men. Noting that public housing "clustered hundreds of families with few male adults," he blamed the absence of Black fathers for the rise in crimes against property, such as broken windows and stolen appliances, as well as the declining property value of public housing. Banks recommended several policy initiatives that would "virtually revolutionize" the NCHA, including prioritizing the hiring of young Black men to do repairs, maintenance, and security and encouraging private management companies to oversee low-rent housing.[100]

Banks's proposal directly translated sociologist Daniel Patrick Moynihan's stance on welfare. A racial liberal who argued for corrective welfare policy as a remedy for past racial injustices, Moynihan gained fame in 1965 with his report *The Negro Family: The Case for National Action*. Moynihan's report cited sociological data that noted the postwar rise of divorce and pregnancies out of wedlock among low-wage Black families. This trend, Moynihan claimed, resulted in more urban Black families drifting toward a "matriarchal structure" in which men and women reversed gender roles and manifested a "tangle of pathology."[101] Moynihan agreed with family disorganization theories that had been popular at the beginning of the twentieth century, contending that single-mother households perpetuated maladaptation, such as children, especially boys, seeking "immediate gratification of their desires" outside the home. He advocated increased enrollment in the military to give young Black men a "needed change: a world away from women, a world run by strong men of unquestioned authority, where discipline, if harsh, is nonetheless orderly and predictable, and where rewards, if limited, are granted on basis of performance."[102]

Unlike the women who led welfare rights activism and demanded child-rearing support, Moynihan and Banks saw Black men as the truly aggrieved party in welfare policies and sought to remedy the problem by making them welfare's privileged beneficiaries. For urban officials with sociological training like Banks, family reform measures felt familiar, harking back to a time when public housing served as a corrective institution that taught tenants to embrace heteronormative middle-class domestic ideals. But unlike Moynihan, Banks was a Black man who had once lived in public housing; no one could accuse him of being racist. Banks most certainly understood that as a Black man he had the social capital to articulate family reform policies that would help public housing residents regain the social prestige of the "honorable poor"—a prominent distinction before urban renewal. For him, that meant following the tenets of racial uplift, including compulsory heterosexuality. At the start of 1972, Banks began promoting another behavioral regulation measure: "father substitutes."[103] Instead of privileging women, Banks wanted to rewrite eligibility standards to ensure that more men would gain admittance to NCHA housing. His hope was that these men, particularly veterans and graduate students, would provide the physical discipline that multifamily public housing allegedly lacked. HUD agreed with his proposal and awarded a three-year grant to kickstart its implementation.

While Banks's eligibility reform was small in scale, it contributed to a conservative political dialogue that directed attention away from the demands of public housing tenants and reinscribed the NCHA's institutional belief that single Black mothers and their children were the prototypical problem families. To be sure, there were certainly many women—and men— who agreed that a more supportive male presence would benefit public housing. It was (and continues to be) a well-known practice among single mothers to enroll their sons in sports and educational or mentoring programs to provide opportunities to interact with adult men who would ideally model healthy adult behaviors. However, Banks's proposal ignored the men who actually lived in public housing, even the ones who modeled the paternalism he encouraged. Although Black women dominated the leadership of public housing resident councils, a number of Black men lived in these communities and supported public housing activism.[104] Men like George E. Jackson, Robert Oden Sr., Herman Taylor, Woodrow Ingram, William Colter, John Jackson, Victor Corley, B. T. Jefferson, Larry Key, and Leon Sharp sat on tenant councils that challenged public housing officials.[105] But Banks, like Moynihan, erased their presence and support by suggesting that the problem with public housing—and welfare in general—was the lack of men.

Officials' focus on Black women's alleged deficiencies as parents provided another cultural explanation for the faults of public housing. Bureaucratic attention to household composition notably sidestepped important structural forces, including gendered labor inequities and the government's increased reliance on the carceral state to contain urban Black poverty, both of which generated changes in household composition and personal relationships among public housing tenants.[106] Moreover, shifting postwar expectations about mating practices was a notable cultural trend many Black women welfare rights activists embraced. As feminist historians have noted, many low-wage Black women began to exercise greater autonomy over their life partnerships by leaving violent or unfulfilling relationships as they continued to demand better welfare services, more wage labor, and affordable childcare options.[107] But in the absence of a comprehensive and mindful discussion about structural and ideological factors that shape family life, Banks advanced the socially conservative argument that a one-size-fits-all heteronormative model was public housing's best management solution, one that erased the value of nontraditional yet equally valuable queer or intergenerational households where care work and parenting can also thrive.

No longer silent and afraid, Black women welfare rights activists expressed their frustration with this conservative turn in welfare politics. Black women welfare rights activists resented the fact that housing officials often pointed to their marital status as indisputable evidence of their parental and domestic irresponsibility. They understood that officials had deep-seated cultural biases against their households and parental autonomy. Their feelings were best captured by welfare activist Annie McLean, who asserted, "Investigators don't know what it is like for us because they're middle class. They don't know what the people really feel when they come in and treat us like they do." Black women welfare rights activists like Etta Horn demanded that the city focus less on their personal choices and ameliorate poverty through better schools, guaranteed incomes, well-resourced recreational outlets, and living-wage work.[108]

Conservatives Respond: The Public Housing Rent Strike and the Courts

Despite welfare rights activists' persistent efforts to gain state support and respect, a conservative resurgence undermined their efforts. More specifically, a conservative-leaning court and the House Oversight Committee ensured the ultimate demise of the campaign public housing tenants conducted to demand code-compliant housing. During the Nixon administration, local judges deliberated about how to counter the lawsuits that NAG, CORE, and Black tenant activists had initiated. Judge Harold Greene of the District of Columbia Court of General Sessions (who, interestingly, was the first judge to rule against retaliatory evictions) recommended reorganizing the courts and reconsidering legal disputes regarding the housing code. He argued for a redesigned Landlord-Tenant Court and for more conservative legal rulings. Greene's vision for reform slowly came to pass. In 1971, judges in Landlord-Tenant Court, now a subdivision of DC's Superior Court, began to issue more conservative rulings on housing code violations. Community lawyers noted the shift in legal opinion after two DC judges ruled that tenants could no longer use rent strikes to compel landlords to address housing code violations unless the violations were considered life-threatening. These rulings ensured that landlords were entitled to partial rent payments even when they failed to correct code violations.[109] It was within this shifting judicial context that a DC court ruled on the legality of the DC rent strike.

The judges President Nixon appointed reintroduced the gendered trope of Black tenant irresponsibility into the debate surrounding the rent strike against the NCHA. In February 1971, the agency began to process eviction cases against the thousands of NCHA tenants who participated in the rent strike. The cases went to different judges, but the NLSP believed that jury trials would be the best strategy to allow DC citizens to shape the legal outcome. The first round of 250 NCHA eviction suits came before Judge Bryon W. Sorrell. A white native Washingtonian, Sorrell had been a lawyer in private practice for twenty years before President Nixon appointed him to serve on the District of Columbia Superior Court in 1969. His service on the bench was controversial, including his review of the NCHA eviction suits. Although closed meetings during court proceedings were considered professionally improper, it was customary for Judge Sorrell to hold such meetings in his chambers to determine a settlement or plea deal. During the NCHA eviction cases, Sorrell called NLSP lawyers, the NCHA's lawyer, and James Banks into a closed meeting. According to an affidavit submitted by NLSP lawyer Sharon P. Banks, Sorrell admonished NLSP lawyers for pressing what he saw as a case that failed to place the responsibility on the appropriate party: the tenants. Sorrell contended:

> The law says that they must be given housing, but you social work lawyers are saying that the government must give them adequate housing. I don't think the law and the taxpayers are required to give them adequate housing. The trouble with those people is that they

want something for nothing. . . . I remember when I was growing up that my family had rats in the house, but we killed our own rats. We got rid of the trash that caused the rats. We didn't expect the government to kill rats for us and we paid our rent every month. . . . My mother always said that you can be poor, but you don't have to be dirty. What those people need to do is go to work. I am of the opinion that if they have a roof over their heads, then they should pay at least 50 percent. . . . If the Good Lord gives you health and strength and a bar of soap, then the battle is half won.[110]

Judge Sorrell's comments are another example of normalizing backlash against NCHA rent strikers through negative discourse about low-wage Black families' domestic lives. Black women, according to Sorrell, needed to embrace the belief in civic dignity gained through silent struggle and perseverance. It did not matter that most of the public housing residents Sorrell demonized were employed. He also implicitly defended disgust, contempt, and frustration as rational emotional responses to the political demands of public housing tenants by implying that low-wage Black mothers were ungrateful and undeserving welfare recipients.

The state's investment in a behaviorist mode of governance may explain why James Banks did not protest Sorrell's racial and gender bias. In fact, Banks doubled down on demanding rent payments regardless of housing conditions. Although he agreed in principle that the housing code should apply to the NCHA, Banks told rent strikers that for the foreseeable future the agency could not invest in the maintenance needed to ensure compliance. He insisted that tenants pay at least 70 percent of their rent, with or without repairs. Fearing that they would be duped into paying for repairs that would never come, public housing tenants refused to comply with Banks's demands. Instead, they hoped that local courts would force the NCHA to comply with city law.

Unfortunately, the courts did not do that. Tenants witnessed mixed results with the cases under Judge Sorrell. The jury trial strategy garnered significant wins in approximately sixty out of two hundred fifty NCHA eviction suits. In the first forty-five cases, the jury agreed to apply the DC housing code to the NCHA, voided fifteen leases, and significantly reduced or canceled rent payments for all but one of the cases.[111] However, in the next fourteen cases, most tenants had to pay half or 90 percent of the funds they had withheld during the rent strike.[112] While these disparate results left rent strikers unsure if their strategy would achieve their goals of rent forgiveness and improved maintenance, they remained committed. In August 1971, 2,000 rent strikers who had withheld over $1 million (more than 10 percent of the NCHA's operating budget) refused to pay until they received a guarantee of improved maintenance for all tenants.

More Congressional Backlash and Protest Fatigue

In 1971, conservative members of Congress once again ventured into local affairs when the House Oversight Committee began to circulate legislative proposals to ward off what they saw as wasteful state spending, rising crime rates, and unscrupulous welfare rights activism in the District of Columbia. Landlords who owned low-rent housing helped shape this discussion and began petitioning congressmen as early as March 1970. These private property owners—many of whom were battling lawsuits about their failure to comply with the housing code—asked the committee to pass legislation to "protect them against the growing powers of tenants."[113] Without some legislative relief, these landlords threatened a strike of their own—large-scale property abandonment. The following year, the House Oversight Committee decided to act. Every year, DC was expected to submit a revenue bill, detailing the city's funding sources for its operations and services. The measure enabled Congress's Fiscal Affairs Committee to attach a rider to the District of Columbia's revenue bill that would deter welfare-assisted mothers from participating in rent strikes.

In September 1971, the Fiscal Affairs Committee did just that. The rider to DC's revenue bill mandated that welfare agency officials investigate and verify all tenant allegations of housing code violations and that welfare-assisted strikers put their rent into a particular escrow account while waiting for their claims to be adjudicated.[114] If the officials determined that the violations were not severe or if welfare-assisted tenants did not comply with the escrow rule, the city would step in to remunerate their landlords for any withheld rents, taking the money from tenants' welfare payments. The rider was a bipartisan compromise between liberal and conservative committee members. The former believed that rent strikes were acceptable when justified, but the latter opposed them completely. The rider established a welfare garnishment system to ensure that welfare recipients paid their rents. This bold congressional move unsettled local leadership, including Banks and Mayor-Commissioner Washington, but there was little they could do. The rider required that they implement the mandate in order to receive the city's annual federal payment from Congress in lieu of a tax for occupying city land.

The welfare garnishment rider and local attacks on the rent strike's organizing infrastructure crippled the campaign. Up until the rider's passage, welfare recipients accounted for about one-third of the $1.7 million in rents withheld from the NCHA.[115] But without the power to protest their housing conditions, welfare recipients were forced to once again place their trust in social workers and landlords rather than political action. Further, the remaining public housing rent strikers watched a direct attack on their organizing staff. According to campaign leaders, City Council chair Sterling Tucker singled out key organizer Herman Kitchens and convinced the board of Friendship House to fire him.[116] Phyllis Martin, another Black rent strike coordinator, reported that Kitchens's termination sent protestors into a panic, resulting in a split in leadership. Some campaign leaders argued that tenants should set up escrow accounts to set aside rent payments. The other camp insisted that their experience of poor housing nullified their need to pay rent and encouraged tenants to spend their rent money on other necessities.

The internal weakening of the leadership and tenant base of the public housing rent strike left protesters vulnerable to state-driven solutions. In late 1971, as the rent strike was losing ground, the NCHA established a thirty-three-person tenant advisory board that included leaders from the rent strike, including Martin. However, their inclusion did not yield the changes the rent strikers desired. According to Martin, when Banks began to enforce the evictions of nearly eight hundred tenants who had not settled their back rent payments, the tenant council stopped holding the NCHA accountable for poor housing conditions. Martin said that members of the tenant advisory board "were not dealing with . . . the maintenance problems of National Capital Housing. They were dealing with people that were on the rent strike." She recounted what she remembered as the thought process of the tenant advisory board:

If they [tenants with back rent] don't have their money, throw
them in the street. So, I felt that you want to put hundreds of people
out in the street that have families and not deal with what was the
problem . . . what we can do to help, then I have problems with that.
So I cut loose and came back on the local level. The only one that
came up with the best solution to deal with the problem is Jim Speight

[director of Southeast House] 'cause he started a Rent-a-thon which collected something in the order of $28,000. And those that had the large families, even though some of them was riding on the coat tail of the rent strikers, we paid that [back] rent and stopped them from putting people in the streets.[117]

This disappointing end to the tenants' years-long rent strike demonstrates the enduring power of the assumption that low-wage Black families should have conditional access to improved housing. During the strike, Congress, judges, and the NCHA's leadership all insisted that Black women—not structural disinvestment—were to blame for the decline in the quality of public housing, at least in part. In response to strikers' demands for improved maintenance and better management, these institutional actors had the power to design solutions as they saw fit. Behavioral supervision and the ideological bias on which it rested—the belief in Black domestic dysfunction—provided a ready-made answer.

· · · · · ·

The anticlimactic end to DC's historic public housing rent strike corresponded with shifting conservative tactics to challenge the country's civil rights movement and other social movements. Urban scholars tend to distinguish between public and private housing residents in their analyses of tenant activism, but this approach masks how the institutional mechanisms of backlash against these protests were incremental and followed the institutional histories of agencies, which were partially shaped by gendered discourses about the Black poor. The Black feminist materialist analysis I use in this study illuminates the complex ways that negative stereotypes about Black domestic life shaped housing and welfare politics and enabled officials to repeatedly advance disciplinary housing governance as a desired policy measure over structural reform.

The bipartisan consensus on disciplinary housing governance enabled a number of institutional actors to blame Black families for their poor housing conditions. In the private rental market, Black women were seen as poor housekeepers. In public housing, Black women were framed as entitled gender disloyalists who rejected marriage yet expected state protection from poor housing conditions.

As the District of Columbia entered a post–civil rights era, the bipartisan articulation of these gendered blame narratives survived and intensified in part because it was legitimized by some Black people, particularly

Black men who gained access to more positions of authority. HUD rubber-stamped the conservative turn in urban housing politics during Nixon's second term by appointing socially conservative Black leaders. As this chapter shows, one's gender did not necessarily predetermine one's stance on the gendered trope of Black tenant irresponsibility. The professional training and political exposure of appointees served as an effective measure of whether they would embrace conservative interpretations of this stereotype. Indeed, with conservative leadership at the federal level, local Black officials readily adapted and adopted an alarmist discourse that claimed that low-wage Black families hurt their ability to govern and grow their cities. In the process, they helped reshape the category of "undesirables" for political purposes.

But in the nation's capital, where there was a strong tenant activist culture, certain Black officials and other conservative political actors knew that racial attacks no longer worked as a means of advancing conservative urban housing policies. By the mid-1970s, these officials embraced the socially constructed category of "the underclass" to wield their political attack on tenant activists who demanded rent relief due to rising inflation. In this shifting discourse about the city's "undesirable" element, real estate powerbrokers linked arms with Black political allies who shared their belief that rent control was both an economic drain on the city and had a negative impact on the residents who remained, including many of the city's honorable poor.

3 Black (Class) Chasms

DC's Rent Control Debates, Underclass Discourse, and the Marginalization of Black Women in the 1970s and 1980s

· ·

In the summer of 1974, Loretta Ross and her five-year-old son, Howard Michael Ross, were living in a "beautiful" studio apartment overlooking the Woodley Park Zoo in Adams-Morgan.[1] An upper Northwest neighborhood that secured its name after two local primary schools were desegregated, Adams-Morgan was considered a gateway neighborhood for Black and Brown immigrant families by the 1970s. Ross came home one afternoon to a ninety-day eviction notice. The owner's reason for eviction was simple: he wanted to turn the property into condominiums. Ross's building housed working-class Black residents almost exclusively, and she knew she had to take action. She attended a tenant association meeting that night, and to her surprise, she was nominated and elected as president of the association. As their campaign against condo conversion developed, Ross and her neighbors quickly learned that the renovation of their building was part of a fast-paced gentrification effort that was targeting primarily Black and Brown neighborhoods located near highly desirable recreational and government sites. Hoping for higher profits after evicting mainly working-class tenants of color, developers sought to re-create these neighborhoods with renovated luxury apartments and new entertainment sites, shopping centers, and eateries.

Black women tenant activists, exemplified by the likes of Ross, demonstrated remarkable resilience in the face of the city's foray into urban growth politics, which emerged during majority-black political leadership in the early 1970s. As Congress granted the city limited self-governance (local elections and legislative powers) in December 1973, DC was undergoing a significant shift in real estate and housing politics. Speculative capital flooded sections of the city like Adams-Morgan, while HUD supported disciplinary housing governance and urban growth efforts to accommodate private redevelopment.

In the context of neighborhood gentrification, low-wage Black people were no longer useful to landlords interested in quick speculative profits. Redevelopment projects such as the one at Ross's building increased the exposure of working-class Black residents to forced displacement. In addition, state-driven development of affordable housing subjected many low-wage Black women and their families to disciplinary housing governance that emphasized punitive character oversight. The federal government condoned this turn toward punitive management by appointing a top-ranking Black HUD official who used such practices in his own properties. Organized tenants of affordable housing in the nation's capital challenged what they believed were disrespectful undercurrents of this punitive management style. Families living in the city's privately owned rental housing demanded that the majority-Black local government prioritize tenants over profits. Black women led the city's tenant base, demanding rent control. Establishing influential tenant-led organizations, Black women and other DC residents pushed Congress and the DC city council to pass a local rent control law in 1974.

The law infuriated the real estate industry, and its staunchest opponents waged a multiyear campaign to repeal it. However, the real estate industry's campaign occurred within a revamped national conservative movement that gained more traction in the 1970s. Within this context, the real estate industry launched its local campaign to abolish rent control in cities. This political endeavor became more significant in the nation's capital after leadership transitions in the city's tenant activist community in the early 1980s. Right-leaning think tanks and the press added to the public legitimacy of rent control abolition through its reframing of rent control as an undeserved welfare entitlement that benefited the wrong recipients—namely, the middle class and the Black "underclass." They argued that the former should pay higher rents and that the latter tanked property values and destroyed residential properties. Proponents of rent control fiercely challenged this claim, insisting that it was a necessary defense against the speculative tendencies of real estate that left most income-dependent renters vulnerable to price gouging during economic downturns.

While rent control advocacy essentially took place in the private rental market, residents within public and private housing understood that the battle for affordable rents resulted from cities' natural impulse to grow demographically and economically. This context inspired officials across the political spectrum to pose urban growth policy questions about who the city should attract and why. As such, the local battle over rent control devolved into cultural questions about the demographic future of the city. Many local Black politicians and business owners believed that if rent control remained unchanged, DC would fall into the metaphorical hands of the "underclass," a socially undesirable group that they viewed as a repellant to middle-class households and private capital. This gendered, racial, and class-based argument grew in strength as the city battled over revisions to rent control policy in the early 1980s. The debate revealed the productive force of the gendered trope of Black tenant irresponsibility and the role the racial uplift goals of the Black middle class played in rent control and urban growth politics. The consequences of this framing would unfold over the next several decades, but its immediate result was the passage of major reforms to the city's rent control law in 1985. After this fierce debate, many urban officials turned away from rent control. They embraced the idea of limited and means-tested housing vouchers, an approach that, by design, condoned the logic of conditional access to improved housing.

Local Government and the Urban Growth Impulse

The postwar middle-class exodus of mainly white Washingtonians worried public officials in the early 1970s. Census data showed that the city's population dropped from its apex of 802,178 in 1950 to 756,668 in 1970.[2] White flight accounted for much of the city's population dip, with over 330,000 white Washingtonians leaving the District of Columbia during this time.[3] Black migration to the city continued well into the 1960s and sustained the city's growth.[4] This relocation wave slowed by 1970, leaving the city's growth rate in the red. It was a downtrend local housing officials predicted would continue as the adverse effects of white flight compounded with Black middle-class professionals' pursuit of more reasonably priced homes in the city's suburbs.[5] This demographic transition turned DC into an overwhelmingly Black city. Joining a few other cities with this distinction, DC's new demographic status was enshrined in the funk band Parliament's popular song "Chocolate City." Black Washingtonians constituted over 70 percent of the city's population, white residents represented 28 percent, and other groups rounded out the rest.[6] However, housing administrators contended that urban growth initiatives were needed to attract white and Black middle-class families back to cities like Washington, DC, to expand the city's tax base and offset its rising expenses. At the time, several development initiatives were underway in DC, including urban renewal projects in areas that had weakened economically in the wake of the city's 1968 rebellion. In addition to urban renewal programs, the city's chief housing executive, James G. Banks, was actively recruiting middle-class homeowners to majority-Black neighborhoods, including those located east of the Anacostia

River.[7] The impact of Banks's growth initiatives was limited for bureaucratic and political reasons. It was not until the city received an infusion of private capital that primarily targeted majority-Black neighborhoods west of the river that these urban growth endeavors incited tenant protest.

The city's influx of private capital and subsequent tenant protest were indirect outgrowths of President Nixon's monetary policy. The beginning of Nixon's first presidential term in 1969 coincided with a national recession that ended almost a decade of economic growth and reduced poverty. Although the country routinely experienced recessions, this one inspired particular concern, as economists and politicians identified its roots in increasing domestic inflation and a crumbling international monetary system. With mounting budget deficits due to the costly Vietnam War and rising welfare state expenditures, the federal government struggled to maintain enough gold-backed dollars in the Federal Reserve to pay its bills. Hoping to stimulate growth and curb inflation, Nixon initially doubled down on public spending. However, he changed course in August 1971 and eventually shifted the country's monetary system from a fixed exchange rate tied to gold reserves to a free-floating exchange rate.[8] To ensure market stability after this "Nixon shock," the president implemented price and wage controls on essential goods and services, including caps on rent increases.[9]

This financial move had cascading effects on real estate. Rising inflation kept home prices and rents high, and the Federal Reserve hiked interest rates, making it more costly to buy a home. This economic slowdown would have typically stalled the growth of the real estate sector, but legal and financial changes soon opened up new revenue prospects. Namely, as financiers invested more money in the secondary mortgage market in the early 1970s, urban growth became a possibility worth exploring by developers in urban housing markets like DC.

Innovations in housing finance underwrote this market relationship between financiers and local developers. At the tail end of the 1960s, the American residential housing market showed signs of trouble as housing finance declined. This funding crisis was partly rooted in the federal government's response to the Great Depression. In 1934, Congress established the Federal Housing Administration, which standardized and insured self-amortizing mortgages, enabling millions to gain access to government-insured and relatively affordable loans. Notably, this funding strategy produced and perpetuated race (and gender) inequities since the underwriting process enshrined residential segregation through redlining and funding discrimination.[10] From the 1930s to the 1960s, a government-sponsored organization, the Federal National Mortgage Association (known as Fannie Mae), encouraged high-end investors to buy bundled mortgages from savings and loan associations, credit unions, and mutual savings banks so that these financial institutions could have more money to lend. However, by the 1960s, the limitations of this finance model were widely felt. The leading funding source for these mortgages came from depository institutions, including savings and loan banks. With rising inflation in the 1960s and congressional limits on interest paid on bank deposits, investors became bearish, helping to dry up funds in housing finance.

In response, Congress and HUD decided to infuse more capital into the secondary mortgage market. In 1968, HUD established a government-owned corporation, the Government National Mortgage Association (Ginnie Mae), to guarantee the mortgage-backed securities issued by private entities on federally insured mortgages. In 1970, Congress expanded the secondary mortgage market again with another government-sponsored organization, the Federal Home Loan Mortgage Corporation (Freddie Mac), to complement Fannie Mae. Freddie Mac bundled and sold mortgage-backed securities that were typically sourced from smaller banks or credit unions.[11] These financial moves were significant. As one real estate investor put it, "The GNMA [Ginnie Mae] mortgage-backed security gives us at the very least an entrée to corporate pension funds, state and local retirement funds, trust funds, endowment funds, foundations, investment bankers and many other diversified investment groups."[12] By 1970, financiers planned to introduce much of the $30 billion sitting in the country's pension funds into a secondary mortgage market. This vision would forever link workers (via institutional managers of their pensions and retirement plans) and investors in an endless pursuit of higher home prices and new buyers. Both were needed to ensure lucrative returns for retirement and other wealth portfolios.

In the wake of Nixon's price controls and these other financial reforms, the DC real estate industry scrambled to recalibrate its profit-making strategies. Investors' expansion of mortgages ultimately facilitated greater demand for homeownership in urban areas. In the city, developers built condominiums to grow the homeownership market. A form of common-interest ownership popularized in the postwar era, condominiums diversified ownership by restricting it to airspace within individual units while owners shared the upkeep costs of common areas. Developers liked this structure in cities because condominiums created dense, apartment-like communities that attracted wealthier white residents, who by the 1970s included young adults from the baby boomer generation.[13] They also considered it an effective profit-making strategy because the country's economic downturn tempered other real estate developments like schools and hospitals.[14]

Real estate interests capitalized on these structural shifts by targeting specific neighborhoods for gentrification. The concept of gentrification grew in popularity after sociologist Ruth Glass coined the term to explain the demographic turnover in a 1960s London neighborhood. Gentrification refers to the neighborhood transformation that results from increased investment in certain areas, which leads to rising property values, higher-yielding land usage, and more economic development. However, when this phenomenon hit DC in the early 1970s, tenant activists and public officials did not use the term "gentrification" to explain their residential change. Instead, they used the familiar term "speculation." Tenant activists noticed that nearly 70 percent of the city's speculation was concentrated in five neighborhoods, including Adams-Morgan, Mount Pleasant, and Capitol Hill.[15] The proximity of these walkable neighborhoods to employment opportunities, entertainment, and historic architecture made them ripe for speculative redevelopment. Developers and speculative buyers targeted the most vulnerable in existing units: elderly homeowners and low-wage renters. They harassed elderly homeowners with offers to purchase their single-family homes while they gave low-wage Black renters in subdivided homes thirty-day eviction notices.[16] A 1969 legal ruling may have incentivized this move in properties where landlords typically failed to comply with the DC housing code: the DC Court of Appeals clarified that landlords could issue thirty-day eviction notices if they could not bring non-compliant units up to code.[17] Meanwhile, developers built expensive condominiums on vacant land to serve wealthier clientele instead of multifamily rental units.

Outside these neighborhoods, real estate interests understood that limited land and the developers' preference for homeownership increased price pressures on remaining rental units. They also understood that federal policy affected profit margins, and responded accordingly. Landlords increased rents every time Nixon phased out wage-price controls that his administration had issued in the period from August 1971 to early 1973.[18] In the first four months of 1973 and on the heels of one of the Nixon administration's last wage-price controls, landlords raised rents for 65 percent of all DC residents.[19] City officials attempted to counter rising rents by working with real estate interest groups to implement a voluntary agreement among landlords to keep rent hikes to the industry's standard of 6 percent.[20] That attempt failed. With little relief in sight, tenants did what they knew best: they organized.

By 1973, the organizational infrastructure of tenant activism had grown locally and nationally. This organizational strength enabled tenants to organize quickly to challenge the city's inflationary real estate market. The National Tenants Organization (NTO) created a far-reaching network of tenant leaders who demanded increased state investment and protections for low-rent housing. The NTO supported local chapters, which consisted of tenant associations and tenant unions. DC's chapter, the Washington Area Federation of Tenants Association (WAFTA), organized tenants to maintain rent control once the Nixon administration's wage-price controls expired. Ernest Withers Jr., son of famed civil rights photographer Ernest Withers Sr., was the DC chapter's cofounder and chair. He also worked as an assistant to the dean of Federal City College (later renamed the University of the District of Columbia). Under Withers's leadership, WAFTA represented "150 tenant groups from throughout the metropolitan Washington area" whose members ran "the gamut of income levels, race, creed, and local geography."[21] WAFTA kick-started its campaign with a daylong meeting at the progressive All Souls Church in Columbia Heights on February 11, 1973. The result of that meeting was sending petitions to Nixon and to Walter Fauntroy, DC's first congressional delegate, asking them to support rent control.[22] Nixon was unmoved by the group's arguments, but Fauntroy responded strongly to WAFTA's call. He convinced Congress to grant the city council the power to pass rent control legislation in the summer of 1973. After WAFTA's success with Fauntroy, local groups grew or sprouted up, adding more infrastructural advocacy for rent control. Local service providers like the Adams-Morgan Organization, the Capitol East Housing Coalition, and Housing Counseling Services supported the growing tenant movement for rent control, viewing the campaign as an economic relief measure and an institutional tool to counter what they believed to be price gouging during an economic downturn.

Although there was widespread tenant support for rent control, there was less agreement about how to define it. Perhaps hoping to ease fears in Congress and among business leaders that rent control would terrify real estate investors, WAFTA backed market-friendly rent control, which stabilized rents but allowed owners to profit.[23] How much profit remained a perennial source of contention among tenant activists, politicians, and landlords. For example, the City Wide Housing Coalition (CWHC) wanted a profit margin closer to the industry standard of 6 percent. Launched in May 1974, the CWHC brought together forty member organizations from all parts of the city; Black and Latinx people were the largest demographics in these organizations. The CWHC also linked rent control to broader struggles for housing affordability, including campaigns for an anti-speculation tax, for tax relief for elderly homeowners, and for a citywide freeze on condo conversions.[24] For the CWHC, rent control provided a way of making profit contingent on compliance with the city's housing code. The CWHC believed that once owners were compliant with the code, landlords should receive a profit allowance (or rate of return) of no more than 7 percent to ensure that DC tenants did not "carry the full burden" of not only "an economic system of guaranteed inflation and unemployment, but also of this landlord-oriented system of guaranteed profit."[25]

Landlords were incensed at the possibility of rent regulation. But, unlike previous years, when real estate representatives defended their business interests with racist tropes about Black tenants' undesirability, they foregrounded colorblind economic arguments that contained racially coded undertones. For example, John O'Neill, who represented DC's largest real estate lobby group, the Building Owners and Managers Association, suggested that the city already had a default form of rent control because certain demographics "in certain sections of the city can only pay so much rent; so, if you raise an apartment $150 from $100, there are not very many takers to speak of."[26] O'Neill emphasized that with tenant-initiated litigation still high, "inner city property costs more to maintain, there is a higher rent loss and a bad debt loss factor." Without mentioning race, O'Neill's reference to neighborhood location and tenant litigation was indirectly racially coded, as both correlated strongly with Black people who were living in disinvested buildings. This marked an essential turn in the discursive tactics of the real estate industry: its defenses were no longer explicitly tied to racial messages. Instead, O'Neill warned, the economic distress resulting from rent control would incentivize landlords to double down on condominiums to ensure that they earned profits.[27]

With opposing battle lines drawn, city officials reluctantly supported rent control. Housing official James Banks initially downplayed the inflationary rents in the city but later admitted that rent control could be a beneficial temporary measure since rents still exceeded projected estimates at the beginning of 1974. Others shared a similar perspective, hoping that rent control could be fine-tuned because, in the words of one official, "We don't want to take a snow plow to swat a gnat."[28] Congress agreed, granting DC the power to pass a rent control ordinance in December 1973 (the same month that Congress approved limited home rule government for the city, which empowered its popularly elected mayor and city council to pass laws and govern its local affairs with congressional oversight).[29] But Congress also curbed the city's legislative reach, stipulating that the rent control measure should last only a year if such a law were passed.[30] In July 1974, after deliberations, the city council passed DC's first rent control law in over thirty years. The 1974 law set limits on rent increases for DC's 190,000 rental units.[31] Landlords were entitled to a 4 percent rent increase the first year and another 8 percent the following year but were required to provide tenants with a thirty-day written notice when they increased rents. The law also mandated that all landlords comply with DC's housing code, outlawed retaliatory evictions, protected the right of tenants to organize, ensured tenant access to landlords' financial records, and offered tenants the option of the first right of refusal if a landlord chose to sell. Lastly, if landlords claimed financial hardship or if tenants alleged that a landlord did not comply with the code, both parties could petition a rent control commission appointed by the mayor to administer the law.[32]

The 1974 law was historic, but the city's early stumbles with enforcement exposed political divides within the newly elected local government regarding the impact of rent control on urban growth and economic development. Shortly after the rent control law passed, Mayor Walter Washington implemented a freeze on new condominiums, giving the city's strong tenant activist community another victory. The real estate community vowed war against these new regulations. Its representative lobby group, the Apartment and Office Building Association of Metropolitan Washington (AOBA), won a court injunction to halt the full enforcement of the rent control ordinance, citing the city's failure to adequately establish the law's enforcement infrastructure.[33] Mayor Washington's support for the law eventually waned despite his initial eagerness to comply with the law. He appointed WAFTA members Ernest Withers and Betty Briscoe, housing lawyer Florence Roisman, and landlord representatives Edward J. Walsh and Irving Kriegsfeld to the rent control commission.[34] But the rent control appointees soon began to publicly decry the city's sluggish approach to rent control enforcement. The public's intensifying criticism of administrative missteps started to affect Mayor Washington's support. For example, the Rent Control Commission's capacity to hear and adjudicate rent cases was significantly hobbled due to inadequate city assistance and limited funds. Congress was crucial to the latter problem; it allocated only $85,000 to monitor nearly 200,000 rental units.[35]

As rent control fell into an administrative and legal quagmire, city officials started to openly question the efficacy of the law, especially as landlords and business owners threatened to withdraw capital.[36] After Banks transitioned into the real estate industry as a lobbyist, Lorenzo Jacobs, DC's new housing director, sought reforms to the rent control law to keep the city attractive to developers.[37] The law was modified in the summer of 1975, but the rent control issue continued to pressure officials to take sides. On one side, tenants argued that speculative real estate activity should be regulated; on the other side, developers claimed that their work engendered growth and brought much-needed taxpayers back to the city.

Rent Control Exemption and the Urban Growth Politics of Rent-Assisted Housing

As tenant activism around rent control and its enforcement intensified, public housing and rent-assisted residents encountered a political landscape that accommodated urban growth and economic development. Following several scandals at HUD in the early 1970s, Nixon issued an eighteen-month moratorium on most housing programs. When the moratorium was lifted in the summer of 1974, a new Housing and Community Development Act placed greater emphasis on the private sector leading the production and management of affordable housing.[38] The city's rent control ordinance exempted housing subsidized by federal and district governments on the logic that property usage should be unencumbered after an affordability contract ends. During this time, HUD supported a changing management paradigm that tacitly criticized rent control and dissuaded tenant activism in specific affordable housing communities.

H. R. Crawford best represents HUD's new management paradigm. Crawford was born in North Carolina in 1939 but was raised in the nation's capital. He began managing properties in DC's overwhelmingly Black Southeast neighborhoods in his mid-twenties. He became one of the city's first certified Black property managers in 1968.[39] As a property manager, Crawford quickly gained a reputation as a blunt, gun-toting disciplinarian who knew how to keep majority-Black affordable housing profitable and crime free.[40] His punitive management style eventually gained the praise of business leaders, and in March 1973, Nixon appointed him as assistant secretary for housing management at HUD. Crawford's rise from local affairs to HUD was an example of national conservative leaders embracing punitive responses to poor people accused of running afoul of the law.[41]

Crawford's management style blended features of a punitive mode of disciplinary housing governance—punishment and humiliation—with behavioral management tactics that had become popular in the urban renewal era. He selected tenants "with meticulous care," probing applicants about their personal affairs. He scrutinized the character of single Black mothers particularly, brazenly asking them how many more children they intended to have.[42] If tenants did not provide desirable answers, Crawford took that as a sign that they were not working to "improve their lives" and denied them access to the new or improved housing under his management. Crawford's intrusive focus on applicants' domestic and private lives extended beyond standard vetting practices like credit and employment checks to questions about housekeeping.

Crawford's management style did more than name "undesirables." In order to keep low-rent housing profitable and trouble-free, Crawford implemented a demographic quota system. Only 10 percent of tenants in a low-rent building should be white, he stipulated, unless the building was in a "Southeast ghetto." In that case, no whites should be allowed at all, as he believed that they wouldn't "be happy there."[43] Students and single persons accounted for another 10 percent of tenants. Significantly, Crawford only allowed for 10 percent of people he called "undesirables," such as former public housing residents, single mothers, and others with allegedly inappropriate domestic habits. Because the units he managed had three or fewer bedrooms, Crawford excluded large families as tenants, claiming that they were the responsibility of public housing. The final demographic in Crawford's acceptable tenant population consisted of low-wage (Black) families with only a few children.[44]

Crawford argued that diligent surveillance of his tenants was necessary to maintain order in his properties. He tracked tenants' behavior, including potential criminality and allegedly troublesome household configurations, on "problem boards." Crawford placed green pins on these boards to indicate the presence of children in the unit, orange for tenants who paid market value, yellow for "problem" tenants, gold for single tenants, and red for vacant units. Former public housing residents were usually earmarked as potential "problem" tenants when they first moved in. However, Crawford claimed that he provided them with paternalistic guidance, such as teaching them "how to use appliances and how to conform to building rules."[45] He labeled families with "uncontrollable boys, too many children, [and] low incomes" as problem tenants, as well as "single women" because "they have boyfriends."[46] Crawford's managerial attempt to fuse judgment of behavior with the demographic composition of rent-assisted buildings exemplified discriminatory practices in the private rental market. As one housing specialist confirmed, "He's no different than any other professional manager in the city, except that he's Black. He uses all the well-tried techniques that property managers have used in housing to make it work."[47]

Crawford's management style unnerved some Black residents, who accused him of being condescending and intrusive. But tenant activists who challenged Crawford experienced harassment and backlash. At Park Southern Apartments, a federally assisted 350-unit high-rise development located in the Southeast neighborhood of Washington Highlands, Crawford asked residents to spy on tenant activists who raised concerns about management. When the activists teamed up with the NTO, Crawford quickly swooped in; he attended tenant meetings, ordered an aide to take photos of activists, and threatened to report activists to the FBI.[48]

In his capacity at HUD, Crawford directed resources toward training property managers in his management style. He led site visits for HUD staff to demonstrate the importance of his tough approach.[49] Crawford's management style perpetuated gender stereotypes about Black irresponsibility and subtly suggested that Black men were best suited for disciplinary roles in public and rent-assisted housing. Crawford once said, "It's time for our [Black] kids to be presented with something other than Superfly. I tried to provide a strong male image."[50] However, his masculinist interpretation of racial uplift rested on compelling low-wage Black families to accept his authority as the gatekeeper and judge of which tenants deserved improved housing. Moreover, Crawford's self-perception seemingly obscured his ability to see that he validated using state resources to mark rental communities of low-wage Black families as undesirable and to make way for middle-class revanchism.

In his HUD leadership role, Crawford also pursued public housing demolition initiatives that suggested that low-wage Black families were not the desirable demographic that majority-Black cities should retain or recruit as they sought urban growth projects. The nationally televised 1972 demolition of the Pruitt-Igoe public housing community in St. Louis, Missouri, inspired Crawford to implement the same tactic in DC. He found his opportunity with the privately owned but poorly performing High Point-Barnaby, a 330-plus multifamily apartment complex located at the city's southeast border.[51] In 1973, after he was allegedly unable to purchase the property himself, Crawford argued that it was better to tear down the majority-Black working-class complex and build townhouses on the site. He pursued the same outcome with Sky Tower Apartments, a rental community with sixty families in the Anacostia neighborhood. Despite the potential for acquiring new funds via the Housing and Community

Development Act of 1974, Crawford chose not to access money for rehabilitation, explaining that preserving Sky Tower conflicted with his vision of urban growth in Southeast: "We have too many large low-income families concentrated in these types of buildings. At some point, you have to make hard decisions and try to relieve the overcrowding."[52] Crawford and local housing officials suggested that rental communities like Sky Tower contributed to the neighborhood's decline and should be displaced to make space for a more desirable urban demographic, such as middle-class homeowners.[53] Instead of acknowledging the implicit revanchism of his endeavor, Crawford shifted attention from the dispossession of Black working-class residents to the topic of inequity in the distribution of poor residents in the region—a position that white business leaders and planners used to justify urban renewal projects. Crawford asked, "At some point, don't you think that every city has to take inventory and ask itself how many units of low-income housing do we have? The district must have a tax base. . . . The outlying areas must take on some of the responsibility. Isn't the entire metropolitan area supposed to share in the responsibility for the poor?"[54]

The actions of public housing and rent-assisted tenant activists needed to become more consistent and effective in the face of Crawford's punitive management style and his vision of urban demographics. Although local and national groups raised concerns about Crawford's paternalism and his mistreatment of tenant activists, they rarely publicly criticized the racial, class, and gendered implications of his behavior—and, by extension, the stance of HUD officials on the distribution of poor Black residents. As a result, Crawford often used his social position as a Black man and avoided discussions about his class to argue that his urban growth initiatives were compatible with racial uplift. Crawford's influence on national housing politics was short-lived, however. Like many HUD officials in the 1970s, Crawford's tenure ended in scandal. Crawford resigned in January 1976 while the Department of Justice investigated allegations that he had used his HUD networks to negotiate employment terms in the private sector.

Yet during Crawford's time as a HUD official, he legitimized the time-worn and gendered trope of Black tenant irresponsibility in the post–civil rights era. The civil rights movement culminated in several federal laws that were intended to destroy the institutional vestiges of the Jim Crow segregationist era, including in residential housing. The Civil Rights Act of 1968 (also known as the Fair Housing Act of 1968) outlawed housing discrimination based on race, color, religion, and national origin (sex, disabled people, and families with children were added later) and other inequitable treatment, including differential maintenance. The law enabled many marginalized groups to enter historically segregated white neighborhoods. However, as assistant secretary of housing and urban development for housing management at HUD, Crawford paid particular attention to the law's exemptions. Notably, the law did not require landlords to rent to every tenant who applied for a property; they had to have "objective business criteria" for excluding tenants. These criteria included tenant screening that assessed whether a tenant could pay rent or take care of the property. These exemptions often meant exclusions of those with poor credit histories or with criminal records.[55] As the previous chapters demonstrate, the gendered trope of Black tenant irresponsibility motivated scores of real estate officials to avoid housing much of the Black working class in new units because they presumed that they could not take care of the property or pay market rents. As a Black male property manager, Crawford legitimized this stereotype by assuming that specific household compositions were proxies for troublesome tenants and that such tenants should be rejected.[56]

But Crawford's positions did more than validate the persistent attempts of some landlords to exclude or mistreat the poor in the post–civil rights era. He also helped elevate Black conservatism to mainstream political discourse. In the wake of the successes of the civil rights movement, Nixon and other white Republican elites understood that in the post–civil rights era it was necessary to distance themselves from the racist discourse that had been socially acceptable during the nation's segregationist era.[57] Instead, racial appeals became more coded. Political appointments of conservative Black leaders like Crawford enabled white conservatives to include Black leaders in government positions while expecting them to enact conservative colorblind policies designed to disproportionally punish undesirable segments of the electorate, including the urban Black poor.[58] In the District of Columbia, however, Black conservatism could not simply rely on white conservative elites; it would also have to appeal to the city's Black middle class, a growing and increasingly important demographic in the city's politics. DC's rent control battle of the 1980s is one of the prominent political examples of this historically contingent relationship.

Black Women: Vanguard Defenders of Rent Control Enforcement

As HUD continued to act as a shadow participant in DC's urban growth politics, tenant activists focused on local authorities. After all, rent control and urban growth politics were technically local matters.[59] In city council hearings, Black women continued to provide compelling testimonies about why market regulations like rent control were more important than the behavioral regulations long championed by landlords and real estate interests. They shared their disappointment that real estate capitalists saw low-wage Black families as undesirable and disposable. Consider the experience of Rosetta Byrd, a block captain of Linden Place (close to the disinvested business district on H Street NE). In 1974, Byrd's block suddenly became a "speculator's market." She explained, "Sixteen homes were brought up by . . . Capitol Hill real estate agents."[60] Byrd understood that the threat of displacement derived from "private ownership and private property," but she hoped the city would act as a mediator to protect the rights of renters to remain in gentrifying neighborhoods. Byrd expressed distress that her renter-dominated, working-class Black neighborhood must now accept that they were considered disposable in the context of gentrification.[61]

The majority-Black city council was packed with civil rights activists turned politicians such as Marion Barry, Sterling Tucker, Douglass Moore, Julius Hobson, and John A. Wilson. Black working-class tenant activists like Byrd must have believed that this left-leaning council would address their interests. Nevertheless, they were willing to engage in confrontational political acts that pressured officials to take action. For example, Betty Briscoe, a federal employee and WAFTA leader, was a member of the rent control commission who did not hesitate to speak up and demand accountability from Mayor Washington.[62] When he did not adequately address her concerns, Briscoe joined the CWHC and other direct-action tenant groups whose efforts sometimes included surprise protests at city council meetings. Even though WAFTA tenant leaders gained more representation on the rent control commission, Black women tenant activists did not abandon the political tactics that had helped them secure legislative victories. Activists' appeals for redress were rarely just about race. They also cultivated citywide tenant solidarity. In their pursuit of this ideal, Black women tenant activists gained political confidence, strengthened their communities, and sharpened their political analyses of the structural forces that left them susceptible to dispossession.

Access to leadership positions in civic organizations was key in enabling Black women to develop political experience and confidence. However, their role in creating and anchoring the numerous tenant associations that emerged in the wake of rent control truly showcased their contributions.[63] The CWHC best demonstrates this. Shortly after the city passed its rent control law, the CWHC broadened its operational focus from battles for legislation to supporting the development of tenant associations. The group launched over one hundred tenant associations throughout the city in its first five years. It also established a tenant hotline and a tenant rights guide and organized assemblies, rallies, and forums for political candidates it favored. One founding member estimated that close to 12,000 DC tenants participated in CWHC activities.[64]

Black women such as Yvonne Christopher extended their historical practice of placemaking through tenant activism as members of the CWHC. In 1975, Christopher was a young mother and social work student at Federal City College living in the Fort Greble Apartments in Southwest's Bellevue neighborhood. After her landlord notified tenants about an upcoming rent hike of up to 43 percent—an increase that Christopher knew that she and many of her neighbors could not afford—she chose to advocate for rent control to protect the long-term affordability of their homes.[65] Christopher quickly began to organize. She studied the rent control law, solicited advice from the CWHC, and recruited other tenants to conduct a building-wide survey of housing conditions to ascertain if the rent increase was justified. After learning that a rent hike required the landlord to comply with the housing code, they researched similar campaigns and, with CWHC support, decided to present their case to the Rental Accommodations Office. Christopher helped her neighbors prepare to testify about poor housing conditions to stop the landlord's petition to raise rents higher than the law allowed. Christopher's organizing story was one of hundreds; it was part of a powerful trend among Black women to defend their homes from external threats. Black feminists later theorized that mothers such as Christopher engaged in this resistance because they had an expansive understanding of cooperative survival.[66]

The perennial threat of rising rents and poor housing conditions emboldened Black women to establish organizing practices that embraced tenets of participatory democracy. The collective investment of women such as Christopher in rent control encouraged them to politicize their relationships with friends and neighbors, cultivate political interdependence, and form effective tenant associations. As they held regular meetings and elected tenant officers, Black women engaged in political discussions, accommodated competing concerns, developed collective commitments, and sustained multiple relationships. These activities anchored tenant associations. Black women modeled leadership skills such as reliability, emotional responsiveness, problem-solving, conflict management, flexibility, and active listening.

Their dedication to ongoing study and political development was the distinguishing factor that enabled these activists to challenge local and national politicians who advanced urban growth policies that would undermine tenant solidarity and threaten long-term affordability. In 1976, CWHC volunteers were invited to deepen their commitment to tenant rights and learn valuable leadership skills through an all-Black study group on Marxist-Leninist thought. Led by Jimmy Garrett, a former SNCC organizer and a political science professor at Howard University, the meetings took place every Sunday morning at St. Steven's Episcopal Church in Northwest DC's Mount Pleasant neighborhood. While any Black person involved in the CWHC was welcome to join, most of the attendees were women. Each week, the study group—which typically numbered no more than twelve at a time—committed to reading a book, listening to a lecture by Garrett about the book, and engaging in discussion on how to apply its lessons to the CWHC's political work. According to participant and CWHC leader Loretta Ross, the study group introduced members to "radical economics" to help them better understand "not just condo conversions . . . but the whole capitalist structure."[67]

These study sessions enabled CWHC members to assess the city's changing political climate and devise campaign interventions. From 1974 to 1977, the AOBA repeatedly threatened that real estate interests, including financial institutions, would abandon the city if officials continued rent control. One financial institution did just that in the summer of 1976, when Perpetual Savings and Loan Bank, DC's largest thrift institution, announced that it would stop funding apartment construction and rehabilitation in the city.[68] Perpetual's disinvestment aligned with the position of other financial institutions that insisted that rent control was why "no financer in Washington, New York or anywhere else will even talk about apartment properties."[69] This strike of capital providers seemed to motivate city officials to accept several reforms in 1977, including exempting new construction from rent control, transferring utility costs to renters, and ending rent control for housing units that required substantial rehabilitation.[70]

For the CWHC, these reforms registered as major defeats. However, as a multiracial organization with a working-class tenant base, the organization saw these legislative setbacks as an opportunity to strengthen cross-racial collaboration, particularly between white and Black leadership. In 1978, the CWHC held a community learning series for more than twenty of its strongest tenant leaders. Over the ten-week series, the CWHC presented a materialist analysis of the city's racialized housing market. Participants learned why politicians embraced urban growth policies that raised rents and con-

Yulanda Ward, a Black feminist organizer who served as co-chair of the Citywide Housing Coalition in 1978. Ward also was a leader in a number of other community organizations, including DC Rape Crisis. Loretta J. Ross Papers, Sophia Smith Collection, Smith College, Northampton, MA.

doned tenant displacement. Because the (Black working-class) renter was historically and structurally undervalued in a market geared toward (single-family) homeownership, series facilitators argued that enforcement of rent control was a necessary challenge to property rights. Facilitators also argued that rent control was essential for collective tenant stewardship. This analysis enabled tenant leaders to better situate their rent control enforcement campaign in a framework of housing justice. In addition, the CWHC insisted that the finance industry ideally could fund this vision for housing justice through more vigorous federal enforcement of the 1977 Community Reinvestment Act, which required banks to proactively reinvest in historically disinvested neighborhoods. The CWHC believed that the combination of rent control and collective stewardship would materialize their vision of transforming housing into a public good, not a speculative investment.[71] In this way, the organization's commitment to collective study strengthened tenant investment in rent control and the CWHC's broader affordability platform.

Black women were central to realizing this housing justice vision, and CWHC co-chair Yulanda Ward best represents this practice. Born in 1958 and raised in Texas, Ward moved to Washington, DC, in 1976 to attend Howard University. Ward became politicized at Howard, where she engaged in

Loretta Ross, circa 1987. Ross joined the Citywide Housing Coalition in 1974 and served as an officer until 1980. She later became an internationally recognized scholar-organizer who helped shape the concept of reproductive justice. Photo by Charlene Eldridge Wheeler. Courtesy of Smith College Special Collections.

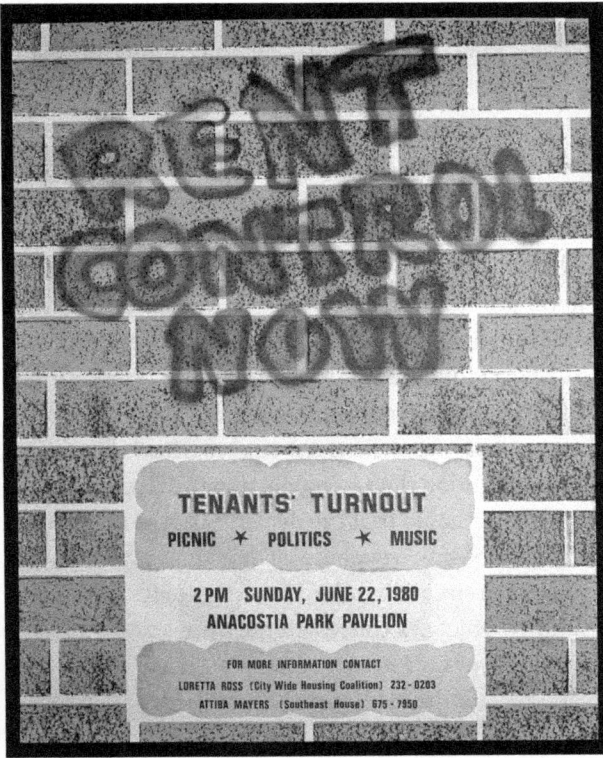

A rent control flyer produced by the Citywide Housing Coalition to recruit community participation. Courtesy of Smith College Special Collections.

TENANTS' TURNOUT
PICNIC ✳ POLITICS ✳ MUSIC

2 PM SUNDAY, JUNE 22, 1980
ANACOSTIA PARK PAVILION

FOR MORE INFORMATION CONTACT
LORETTA ROSS (City Wide Housing Coalition) 232-0203
ATTIBA MAYERS (Southeast House) 675-7950

community activism and served in leadership roles in the DC Rape Crisis Center, the National United Black Front, and the CWHC.[72] Ward eventually took a leave of absence from Howard to focus on activism full time. She became the co-chair of the CWHC in 1978. That year, known in the local press as the "Year of Tenant Rebellion," the CWHC and similar groups led several successful campaigns for a broader affordability platform. Tenant groups convinced the city council to pass an anti-speculation law, the Columbia Heights Community Ownership Project established a land trust to renovate and sustain affordable housing, tenant associations picketed to demand rent rollbacks for residents of buildings with housing code violations, and the CWHC led a "Stop People Removal" campaign to exact "stronger controls of evictions and rent levels."[73] The CWHC hoped that by the following year, more working-class tenants would own and manage their buildings. (This goal became achievable after tenant activists won the passage of the Rental Housing Conversion and Sale Act in the summer of 1980. The law, popularly known as TOPA, enforced tenant activists' long-championed goal of tenants' first opportunity to purchase in the event of an owner's building sale.) Ward played a crucial role in planning and executing the CWHC's goals, including assisting tenant leaders like Yvonne Christopher and shaping campaign strategies.

While Ward modeled a commitment to broad tenant solidarity, she also demonstrated that Black women tenant activists were willing to sharpen their political analyses through investigative and grassroots research. In the late 1970s, Ward researched and coauthored a piece on the evolving tactics of rent control opponents in an article entitled "Spatial Deconcentration." The article postulated that public officials approved rent control rollbacks because cities were invested in urban growth and capital recruitment.[74] Ward argued that this impulse toward growth persisted even in majority-Black cities with Black leaders with civil rights histories, whom she suggested were more invested in protecting their class position than in supporting the interests of the working class. The article also intimated that the dispersal of the Black poor, which was achieved through housing vouchers or housing mobility programs, obscured the revanchist desires of landlords and city officials.[75] It also charged that these institutional practices concealed intentions to undermine Black working-class political power and weaken tenant activism since Black families that were relocated to suburbs via housing mobility programs were less likely to engage in activism. Ward's article raised important questions about alternative motivations for state support of Black poverty dispersal.

Organizing Setbacks: Grassroots Black Leadership Withers

In nearly seven years, Black women made an indelible mark on the city's organizing infrastructure and on the campaign for rent control enforcement. However, by 1980, the face of the rent control enforcement battle had become technocratic, less confrontational, and led by white professionals. The demographic shift in public leadership was both accidental and foreseeable. On November 2, 1980, Ward and two other movement organizers were walking home in Southeast DC when three men accosted them. Even though Ward and her friends attempted to comply with the assailants' demands, one of them shot Ward in the back of the neck, killing her instantly.[76] Ward's death shocked and terrified her allies. DC organizers like Loretta Ross and Nkenge Toure later shared that the timing of the murder of Ward was particularly unsettling because, around the same time, several CWHC organizers were robbed or received anonymous phone calls telling them to quit their housing activism.[77] According to Ross, Ward's death weakened the resolve of many Black tenant activists, some of whom endured intrusive police searches in its aftermath.[78] However, there were other faults within the city's Black tenant activist network. It was well-known that organizer turned professor Jimmy Garrett regularly engaged in inappropriate sexual relationships with his female students at Howard University, some of whom attended the CWHC's all-Black study group.[79] The emotional distress women felt due to Garrett's sexual impropriety undermined their ability to advance within the organization.

As the CWHC was losing Black leaders, the group suffered from other internal weaknesses, including its own anti-Black bias. Organizer David Reed recalled that as the CWHC continued campaigning for rent control enforcement, it moved away from its original constituency of Black and Latinx families and toward (white) middle-income households threatened by condo conversions. White members of the CWHC were sometimes oblivious about their racial blind spots. They would say things like, "We've got to get more Blacks into City Wide," but were increasingly resistant to supporting more Black leaders within the organization.[80]

As the CWHC fell into disarray, policy experts, lawyers, and other nonprofit organizations filled the vacuum in DC's affordable housing advocacy. In 1979 and 1980, the CWHC joined a coalition of over thirty housing advocacy groups to promote the People's Rent Control Bill of 1980. The ambitious bill hoped to win back lost rent control protections and included a provision to allow tenants to deduct personally funded repairs from their rent. Unlike in years past, when tenant-based groups led legislative negotiations, housing policy experts and lawyers now controlled them. According to Reed, these self-appointed campaign leaders were more self-interested and less collectively minded. They used insider status to negotiate for more organizational funding instead of securing tenant-focused goals like better eviction controls.[81] The coalition's relationships and trust frayed as groups like the CWHC had to lobby their own allies to keep their focus on initial campaign goals, such as including working-class tenants. As the campaign progressed, more of these lawyers and policy experts began to question the utility of including tenants in the campaign. When there was a small turnout at a CWHC campaign protest, the experts and other nonprofit leaders took it as proof that grassroots tenant leadership was no longer effective. As Reed put it, their mindset seemed to be, "See, trying to mobilize the community doesn't work anymore. Good thing we didn't waste time on that."[82]

The coalition's weakening dynamics left housing advocates vulnerable to Mayor Marion Barry's shrewd political practices. Hailing from rural

Mississippi, Barry had attended LeMoyne-Owen College in Memphis and had earned a master's degree in organic chemistry from Fisk University in Nashville. While at Fisk, Barry participated in the Nashville sit-ins and secured the respect of fellow young civil rights activists, who elected him as the first chair of SNCC. His work with SNCC ultimately relocated him to DC in 1965, where he quickly became a household name in local politics for his work to organize young Black men and to establish PRIDE, a youth workforce program. He entered city electoral politics and won an at-large council seat in 1974. He was elected mayor in November 1978. Barry's political experience as a civil rights organizer and public official made him particularly adept at talking to different stakeholders and making them feel heard. However, as the rent control bill made its way through negotiations, tenant activists began to worry that Barry would exclude them from the details of final agreements. The rent control coalition's internal disagreements and limited tenant participation most certainly made it easier for Barry to marshal the necessary support for a bill he hoped would appease both landlords and tenants. However, many tenant organizers were dissatisfied with the new law: it kept the 1980 rent law in place for five years, it permitted landlords to increase rent each year by up to 10 percent (with an additional 10 percent for vacancies), and it introduced a new profitability formula that made it easier for landlords to claim financial hardship. To appease tenant coalitions, the law prohibited landlords from converting rental units into condominiums or hotels.[83]

Conservative Cultural Politics and Anti-Rent Control Discourse

The disappointing conclusion to the campaign for the People's Rent Control Bill in the fall of 1980 corresponded with a shifting cultural context that depicted the urban Black poor as a threat to the country's economic revitalization and moral progress. The 1980s began with doggedly high interest and unemployment rates. The economic downturn that had triggered local rent control movements paralleled a national rise in urban Black poverty, and the nation's capital was no exception. While the metropolitan region's economic strength remained sound compared to the hard-hit Midwest, DC's unemployment rate hovered around 7 percent (the metropolitan area's rate was close to 5 percent).[84] Black manual laborers and youth were most likely to be unemployed because the region's job sector primarily consisted of knowledge-based industries that required formal education.[85] Welfare-assisted Black mothers also suffered. By 1980, over 60 percent of the region's public assistance recipients lived in the District of Columbia.[86] Despite increased local investments, welfare payments never kept pace with inflation, and as a result, recipients' poverty deepened. These urban subpopulations of the Black poor did not engender sympathy among politicians, businesspeople, and journalists. Instead, the Black poor generated disgust and frustration in social welfare debates, including those about rent control.

In addition, by the 1980s, conservative political discourse had begun to link the gendered trope of Black (poor) irresponsibility to the concept of entitlement. President Ronald Reagan best typifies this trend. A few years earlier, in his campaign speeches, Reagan had lambasted the mythical "Cadillac-driving welfare queen" whose alleged entitlement to scarce welfare resources drove her to lie and scam the government—and, indirectly, white suburban taxpayers.[87] The cultural discourse of entitlement served as a powerful emotive frame that directed rage and disgust at welfare-assisted families of color. Reagan continued to remind audiences about undeserved entitlement on the campaign trail, sharing another fictitious story about Black and Brown rent-assisted families living at Taino Towers, a rental community with more than 600 units in New York's East Harlem neighborhood. "If you are a slum dweller," he claimed, "you can get an apartment with 11-foot ceilings, with a 20-foot balcony, a swimming pool and gymnasium, laundry room and playroom, and the rent begins at $113.20, and that includes utilities."[88] The story's takeaway was not subtle: welfare-assisted urban families were costly, parasitic, morally irresponsible, and unaware that their alleged welfare entitlement harmed those who adhered to an unspoken "contractual understanding of citizenship."[89] Reagan used these narratives to convey the belief that welfare entitlement bred weak citizens who "add[ed] nothing to our economy" and failed to perform civic obligations such as military service, wage work, and paying taxes.[90]

Liberals who shared the same foundational logic as conservatives promoted "the underclass" as an explanatory framework for Black urban poverty. In the 1980s, the number of academic studies and journalistic depictions of the Black urban poor increased. Black male academics like Douglas Glasgow and William Julius Wilson published widely cited studies about the "Black underclass"—typically individuals who were dislocated from the formal labor market or poor people engaged in nonnormative reproductive behavior. Journalists like Ken Auletta then wrote about academic findings for popular audiences by highlighting the lives of the so-called underclass. Sensationalized in the press, articles about the "underclass" focused on the alarming rise in single Black mothers who relied on welfare or youth accused of criminal activity.[91] Liberals often held unmarried mothers, particularly single Black mothers, personally responsible for condoning undesirable domestic practices. *Washington Post* columnist Juan Williams—a socially conservative Black Democrat—drew a direct line from "illegitimacy" to youth detention centers. This womb-to-prison pipeline could be disrupted, he argued, only if low-wage Black mothers changed their cultural frame of entitlement to parenthood, which then fostered entitlement to welfare. Williams claimed that "uneducated" Black women were opposed to abortion on moral grounds: "[They] persuade their daughters to give birth, rather than have an abortion, even if it means bringing a child into an unstable family without a father and with no income except welfare."[92] Williams's comments reflected a growing anxiety among the city's Black middle class, who believed that the Black poor failed to embrace traditional family values and fulfill their citizenship obligations.[93]

Williams's comments were evidence of a growing social and spatial distance between the city's Black middle class and female-headed Black poor households—a class dynamic that was a direct outcome of post–civil rights gains. Until the end of the civil rights movement, Black economic success was largely defined by access to top federal appointments in the nation's capital.[94] After the civil rights movement toppled many institutional barriers to postsecondary institutions and private employment, DC's Black middle class exploded, ballooning from percentages in the teens in 1960 to nearly 40 percent by 1980.[95] The federal government was key to the expansion of the Black middle class in the city. By the end of the 1970s, Black people occupied close to half of the federal government's highest-grade positions. The result was greater income parity; as journalist Jacob Eisen reported in 1978, the "typical black earn[s] 81 percent as much as a white on the city payroll."[96] Black people's entry into the middle class continued in the 1980s, as DC became home to one of the country's highest concentrations of Black professionals who worked not only in government jobs but also in other high-earning, knowledge-based industries, including law, finance, medicine, and telecommunications.[97]

This historic level of Black economic success eventually ignited panic politically. Journalists and government officials in the District of Columbia openly worried about the growing loss of middle-class heterosexual Black families to the city's suburbs. As an increasing number of single Black mothers and their children stayed in the city, local officials complained that the remaining Black families were tax burdens that weakened the public image of the city and of Black people generally.[98] Local journalists suggested that the political concerns of the Black middle class that remained in urban centers were less about structural discrimination and more about addressing the alleged cultural failings of the Black poor, evidenced by "Black female-headed households, teenage pregnancy, high Black youth crime rate, illiteracy, and drug abuse."[99]

The deepening investment of Black middle-class residents in the social reform of the Black poor provided an opportunity for them to form an ideological alliance with white social conservatives who also blamed single mothers for poor parenting and rising crime. A white social conservative who believed politics should promote and preserve moral fundamentalism on social issues ranging from marriage to school prayer, journalist Michael Novak singled out Black single mothers for disproportionally raising children who lacked respect for traditional family values and institutional norms. In an *Evening Star* op-ed piece, Novak wrote, "If children are born out of wedlock, their chances of complete parental advice, care and discipline are much diminished. Little schooling is likely to take place in the home. . . . Marketable skills and attitudes are not likely to be fostered. The pressure of childhood and adolescent peers is likely to be far stronger than that of the single parent. Peer pressure leads too often to predatory crime."[100]

This socially conservative and gendered discourse about welfare entitlement soon permeated challenges to rent control. However, this linkage only developed after the conservative movement transformed in the 1970s. Before this time, conservative leaders typically released pamphlets and research decrying rent control as a free-market blasphemy, an unfair encroachment on private property rights, and a disincentive for developers.[101] This perspective often failed to reach a broad audience. But after progressive social movements, including consumer rights activism, secured more legislative victories like rent control, conservative-minded businessmen demanded greater coordination and more visibility in local and national politics to counter these left-leaning movements.

One such example was Lewis Powell, a corporate lawyer for the Phillip Morris tobacco company whom President Nixon appointed to the Supreme Court. In August 1971 (shortly after Nixon's price controls measures), Powell penned a rousing memo demanding that corporate America get organized. He charged that the "extremists of the left are far more numerous, better financed, and increasingly are more welcomed and encouraged by other elements of society, than ever before in our history."[102] To counter this small but mighty "socialist cadre," Powell called on business leaders to combine resources and sharpen political strategies to dramatically influence media, politics, jurisprudence, academia, and popular opinion. His memo influenced wealthy conservative donors. Heeding Powell's call, in the 1970s these donors and business groups poured money into activist think tanks like the Manhattan Institute, the Cato Institute, and the Heritage Foundation.[103] Conservative activists soon deepened their inroads into public life after one of the Heritage Foundation's co-founders, Paul Weyrich, co-founded the Moral Majority with conservative Baptist minister Jerry Falwell in 1979. This organization joined other socially conservative evangelical groups, interweaving probusiness ideals of privatization and free market with moral virtue. These conservative ministers promised millions of their members that they would defeat the "left-wing, social welfare bills that will further erode our precious freedom."[104]

With this expanded base of support, business leaders successfully lobbied the Reagan administration to threaten to end federal aid to localities with rent control.[105] However, this symbolic measure was ineffective for cities such as Washington, DC, which had councils packed with officials who saw rent control measures as market-friendly. Organized real estate in DC sought more than this accommodation; they wanted rent control abolition. To that end, business groups increasingly commissioned reports to illustrate the disastrous effects of rent control on DC's housing market. For example, *Rental Housing in the Washington Area*, which was funded by businesses and private foundations, concluded that rent control introduced a "sickness" that impacted middle-class and poor households differently. The authors argued that rent control indirectly encouraged undesirable tenant behavior. They added that the poor exhibited troublesome behavior like rent strikes and vandalism because tenants were less likely to maintain their buildings when they lived in rent-controlled units and that middle-class tenants had an unhealthy dependence on rent control even though the latter group could pay higher rents.[106] As a result, rent-controlled localities like DC attracted more Section 8 affordable housing development instead of new unsubsidized units whose tenants paid rent at market values. This move, the report implied, had negative effects on property values and capital recruitment. Reminiscent of Crawford's criticisms of affordable housing, the report portrayed this outcome as undesirable because more affordable housing would discourage wealthier and middle-class residents from remaining in the city.

Landlords, developers, and politicians used reports like *Rental Housing in the Washington Area* to reframe rent control as a problem of welfare entitlement, and the local press circulated the message that irresponsible rent-assisted Black families destroyed rent-controlled buildings. In January 1985,

Washington Post journalist Michel Marriott published a piece about Rhode Island Plaza in Northeast DC's Brentwood neighborhood, home to a wide array of working-class families and to Gallaudet University, a premier institution for deaf and hard of hearing communities. Painting a dystopian narrative of Rhode Island Plaza's "decline" over the previous ten years—symbolized by the "angry graffiti" on its walls—Marriott depicted a once-storied development that had housed "the nation's proudest . . . upwardly mobile blacks during the waning years of segregation."[107] The implementation of rent control, he argued, fostered an influx of poor and destructive Black tenants, prompting "affluent blacks" with middle-class jobs like "nurses, doctors, lawyers, educators, and government workers" to flee the property. With a sensationalistic flourish, Marriott wrote, "Some tenants, such as mail carrier Leroy Fisher, conclude that [building] conditions will never improve unless something is done to halt the influx of publicly assisted families moving into the Plaza." Rent-assisted families, Fisher said, "have a different attitude" and "tear up" the community. In highlighting this perspective, Marriott reiterated an argument long touted by landlords and supported by *Rental Housing in the Washington Area*: rent control attracted uncooperative tenants who would "tolerate . . . poor living conditions" because their choices were limited.[108]

These anti-rent control stories are evidence that cultural arguments about the Black poor were still a powerful discursive tactic that diverted attention away from the structural critiques of speculation and displacement that tenants made. These stories exploited intraracial class politics within the Black community, suggesting that rent control undermined middle-class Blacks' pursuit of social prestige and forced them to live with rent-assisted families whose entitlement to welfare condoned irresponsibility. That frame implied that within the working class, social distinctions mattered more than the long-term affordability of rental properties. This discursive framing was significant. It meant that middle-class tenants would have to accept paying more rent and, as *Rental Housing in the Washington Area* noted, upward of $400 for new rental units to accommodate profits and higher building costs.[109] This narrative reinscribed the belief that low-wage households were more responsible for their housing conditions than middle-class ones because their cultural practices reinforced tendencies that led to disinvestment and property devaluation. This discourse of the "Black underclass" gave conservative Black politicians an updated cultural frame for repackaging the gendered trope of tenant irresponsibility and for advocating for structural reform to shift from rent control to the free-market ideology of unregulated rents.

New Alliances, Old Rifts: Black Politicians, Landlords, and the Evolving Opposition to Rent Control

These differences in perspectives between the Black middle class and the Black working class played out in the 1985 debate over rent control legislation. The election of Ronald Reagan as president and the gendered backlash against the urban Black poor provided the cultural backdrop that enabled critiques of rent control to gain more ground in political discourse. The economic decline of Washington, DC, coincided with this cultural backlash, giving local real estate interests an incentive to challenge rent control with legislation. Local real estate leaders were ready to seize the political opening because they had backed business-friendly candidates for the city council since the early 1980s.[110] This probusiness political strategy would not bear notable fruit until 1985, when the AOBA, the Board of Trade, and other real estate interest groups found a city council member who was willing to push for the abolition of rent control in the District of Columbia. Their man was John Ray. For some, however, Ray's biography would suggest he had more politically in common with Black working-class tenant activists than real estate developers. John Ray, who was born in rural Georgia in 1943, understood the cramped conditions that many postwar working-class Black families experienced, having lived in a two-bedroom apartment with fifteen family members.[111] He was raised by a single mother and never met his father. Ray eventually moved to DC to attend George Washington University, earning undergraduate and law degrees.[112] After his initial foray into electoral politics ended in defeat when Marion Barry won the mayoral race in 1978, Ray was elected to the city council in 1979, taking Barry's vacated seat (with Barry's blessing).[113]

In his first term, Ray made a name for himself as a hardline social conservative when he championed and won harsher and longer mandatory minimum and maximum sentencing for gun and drug offenses.[114] Ray was ready to tackle rent control the year it was set to expire. In January 1985, council chair David Clarke (D-At Large), a rent control advocate, introduced a bill to extend the 1980 rent control law to 1989. Clarke, a member of DC's inaugural city council, was a politician who, like Barry, had a history as a civil rights activist. He tied his support for rent control to the fact that the city's tenants vigorously championed it. Ray countered Clarke's move by introducing a rent control bill with key recommendations from *Rental Housing in the Washington Area*. Ray's bill proposed increasing rents to a new base level until rent control was phased out over six years. The bill also called for the abolition of rent control for vacant units. Only elderly tenants would be exempted from vacancy decontrol. Everyone else, including low-wage Black families, would need to survive in the rental market. Some low-wage families would be assisted with a new city voucher program for local housing that would enable them to rent in the private market. To defend his bill, Ray cited the state of the city's real estate economy, which had once thrived because of new construction and housing sales but now was stalled because developers were more focused on commercial business districts and luxury condominiums. He also noted familiar points from *Rental Housing in the Washington Area*: "Despite our years of rent control, we have seen the supply of rental units dwindle by the thousands. Today, there are at least 5,000 wasted apartments in vacant and boarded-up buildings and many more that are unsafe and unfit to live in."[115] Ray argued that rent control was more than just an economic and political problem of capital flight; it was a cultural and political issue of crime, and the best solution was a return to an unregulated housing market.

Unsurprisingly, Ray's bill infuriated many DC residents who had come to see rent control as the city's protection and as an investment in long-term working-class tenancy. By 1985, the city's affordable housing advocacy community had shifted to nonprofits specializing in affordable housing finance and development. Some groups, such as Washington Inner-City Self-Help (WISH) and Ministries United to Support Community Life Endeavors (MUSCLE), continued the CWHC's tradition of protest and direct action. These groups joined the Ward 1 Coalition and the Emergency Committee to Save Rental Housing in organizing against Ray's bill. They helped organize DC residents, including Black women. Many groups held press conferences and mass meetings to denounce Ray's bill. One community meeting was held at St. Augustine Church, a Catholic church close to 14th and U Street NW, one of the city's historic Black entertainment hubs. By the 1980s, the church had well-known clerical leaders like Father Raymond Kemp, who engaged in community service and supported several active community groups, such as WISH. Council member Ray agreed to attend a community meeting in February 1985 to defend his bill. Black mothers confronted Ray about what they saw as his insensitivity to their families' economic strain. As one mother said, "My mother and I need a new apartment but cannot afford the high cost. . . . You are going to give the landlords the ability to raise rents again. Where do you propose we go? The streets?"[116] They wanted Ray to focus on tenant rights, such as enforcement of the housing code. Rosa Foster, a Black mother of four, said that inconsistent code enforcement had forced her to leave her children with friends to "shield them from the lice and mice in her efficiency apartment."

Tenant activists produced grassroots research to identify why many community groups opposed Ray's bill. They contended that the bill was a smokescreen for rent hikes and would make it easier for landlords to evict tenants. Activists tracked the higher rents that followed vacancy decontrol in other northeastern cities. Their research noted that Ray's bill included some troublesome provisions regarding eviction. Unlike the eviction protections in the 1980 rent control law, Ray's bill incorporated "six more grounds for eviction ranging from being a nuisance to damaging the rental unit."[117] However, the bill did not define what constituted "nuisance behavior," and tenant activists feared that landlords would be the ones to determine what that definition was. Those who had a history with DC landlords' discriminatory and punitive treatment toward low-wage Black families understood that this provision would disproportionally affect families that were already labeled (racially and economically) undesirable.

After several large demonstrations and a strong turnout at council hearings on the two rent control bills, it became clear that Ray's side was outnumbered. Three of the city council's five members of the Consumer and Regulatory Affairs Committee sided with Clarke. Despite signs that Ray's bill was approaching defeat, Clarke worked hard to get seven council members to back his proposal to extend rent control. John Wilson (D-Ward 2), Polly Shackleton (D-Ward 3), Wilhelmina J. Rolark (D-Ward 8), Hilda Mason (Statehood, At-Large), and Carol Schwartz (R-At-Large) supported Clarke's bill. Only H. R. Crawford (D-Ward 7) (who after his ouster from HUD resurfaced in DC's local politics when he won the Ward 7 seat in 1980) publicly supported Ray's bill. However, in early March 1985, five council members still had not publicly stated their position, and Ray continued his campaign throughout the city.

His defense of the bill extended beyond rhetoric about crime to incorporate cultural discourse about being a progressive defender of the Black middle class. In community meetings, for instance, he reportedly became emotional as he shared his feeling of helplessness when he saw Black children living in rent-controlled homes that were infested with rats. For Ray, the humane policy response was to change how the state assisted people experiencing poverty. He preferred housing vouchers over rent control because vouchers gave specific populations access to rental assistance within the private market. The elderly and mothers with children would be privileged beneficiaries of that strategy, he said. He did not depict men as deserving recipients because of the long history of the gendered expectation that men would secure their social reproduction needs through wages.[118] Ray argued that income-based housing vouchers best aligned with a deregulated housing market and would entice developers to return and rebuild in a city that needed to attract and retain middle-class households, mainly middle-class Black families. The latter point was significant to him as a Black political leader. To defend his position, Ray quoted Black conservative Andrew Corley's testimony at one of the city's hearings on rent control legislation: "The housing conditions in the District are driving middle-class renters—particularly the young, educated Black renter—into Maryland and Virginia. We are losing a whole generation of middle-class Blacks to Prince George's County. If they remained here, they would be the future taxpayers, civic leaders, homeowners, and voters of our city. We are losing them because they will not live in drug-infested buildings."[119] This stance was promoted by well-known Black journalists such as William Raspberry. In a *Washington Post* editorial, Raspberry wrote, "Black ghettoes used to provide positive role models even for the children of the most problem-afflicted families. But the mobility afforded by racial integration has drained the ghettos of their middle-class role models."[120] Ray warned that if his bill did not pass, the flight to the suburbs would continue, leaving poor Black families in the city without the moral and behavioral guidance of the Black middle class.

Although Ray and other opponents of rent control used the possibility of Black middle-class revanchism to support their position, other policy advisors and national politicians were not as sophisticated. In New York City, which had the nation's longest history of rent control, conservatives struggled to articulate a defense beyond the familiar argument that rent control unfairly benefited the middle class. As one conservative policy advisor with the Hudson Institute opined,

> Rent-control abolition will probably help the more stable areas of New York for a very crude reason: the increased rents will make it more difficult for the poor to penetrate. Since the landlords will have to compete for tenants, more money will certainly be spent on maintenance. . . . More important, higher rents in New York City will certainly encourage some families to leave the city and others will not move in. This out-migration is probably desirable. . . . Quite bluntly, we can do without those elements of the middle classes who have demanded endless subsidies and other "social programs" that ultimately benefit them.[121]

In Los Angeles, the city with the second largest population in the country, the debate about rent control devolved into acrimonious personal attacks and proxy debates about race. The Los Angeles City Council eventually embraced rent control in the late 1970s, albeit reluctantly, as inflation and sluggish development drove real estate prices and rents to historic highs because of demand for housing driven by the entertainment, aerospace, and defense contracting industries. The intensity of rent hikes was unevenly distributed, though. Areas such as West Hollywood and Santa Monica experienced higher rent spikes, while East Los Angeles and South Los Angeles saw declines in population and capital investment.

Instead of discussing these complex matters, Black members of the Los Angeles City Council bickered with advocates of rent control. Dave Cunningham, a Black council member who represented Southwest Los Angeles, dismissed rent control as an issue "where you could get 60% of the vote just by running against the niggers. It's the same thing here, with people trying to out-rent-control each other."[122] Robert Farrell, another Black council member who represented South Central Los Angeles, derided both rent control advocates and housing industry leaders, contending that "both screw my constituents. None of the people organizing for controls have bothered to come into my district or to acknowledge us . . . and the building industry kissed off my area for new construction a long time ago. There's a reason why there's no real action south of Adams Boulevard. . . . It's because of the institutional racism in our society and the fact that 85% of my constituents are black."[123]

Greater demographic and geographical polarization in Los Angeles and New York City paralyzed rent control debates in the 1980s. At the same time, politicians like Ray leveraged the growing class division among Black residents in Washington to advance his pro-market argument. What made DC's rent control debate different was that business-savvy Black politicians like Ray focused on a narrative about a future DC that was a testament to Black excellence in urban governance. He once said, "Blacks, a minority in this country, are a majority here. They control the legislative process, the executive branch. . . . We have a chance to make Washington, DC, the model for what Blacks can accomplish, and I intend to be a part of that."[124]

Ray's vision of Black excellence in urban governance meant that he needed to align with members of the business community who linked opposition to rent control to the gendered trope of Black tenant irresponsibility. Some Black conservatives made these cultural arguments explicit in their arguments against rent control. In his testimony at the rent control hearings, for example, Andrew Corley condemned the tenant vandalism that he believed was condoned in rent-controlled buildings: "A tenant can literally get by with paying two to three months' rent per year. Here's how. He moves in and pays the first month's rent, then he creates a few code violations, gets the inspector out and gets the violations cited and uses them as a defense against non-payment of rent."[125] Corley's defense of market logic included a devaluation of urban Black domestic life—a ubiquitous undercurrent in these discussions. Moreover, while the duplicitous Black tenant he described was ostensibly gender-blind—he used the neutral pronoun *he*—the tenant who was deserving of assistance was generally imagined as the impoverished but law-abiding Black mother. However, that was where conservatives' deployment of Black underclass discourse was contradictory. Corley denounced the underclass as scourges on DC real estate, but he had sympathy for some low-wage Black families, those he felt aspired to class and household configurations he preferred. For (social) conservatives like him and Ray, the deserving poor were a better population for the state to support. However, he believed it was up to the Black elite to determine which subpopulations should be protected and why. Seen in this way, the demographic and political category of the honorable poor was flexible in part because those who used it needed it to adapt to the evolving needs of a racialized and uneven housing market. In the context of this rent control debate, Ray suggested that the deserving poor—in this case, single mothers and the elderly—would welcome the leadership and example of the Black middle class and adapt their lives accordingly. Although Ray was silent about *how* middle-class Black adults would shape the behavior of poor Black people, his stance discursively linked the access of poorer Black families to better housing with the condition that the Black middle class provide moral oversight and models of respectability.

Ray's framing helped divert analytical attention away from several flaws in this policy agenda. A return to market rents without explicit attention to housing conditions, (dis)investment patterns, labor markets, and access to formal education would inevitably reproduce the same tiered rental market that tenant activists had long condemned. In addition, although rent control incentivized tenants to stay put, the mortgage market's persistently high interest rates and down payments meant that middle-class homeowners were more desirable urban residents than low-wage Black tenants. Therefore, vacancy decontrol would hypothetically push the city's poorest families to its edges or into poorer suburbs, especially if the city could not subsidize their tenancy in gentrifying neighborhoods. Finally, Ray and other pro-market advocates failed to realize that many Black middle-class Washingtonians remained in the city and understood rent control as a political project of broader working-class solidarity. These

Black residents believed that access to rent-controlled housing should be grounded in economic justice, not individual achievement.

Although Ray's cultural reasons for opposition to rent control differentiated him from many white conservatives, those people were his closest political allies. Ray invited Peter D. Salins, a white professor of urban affairs at Hunter College and a fellow at the conservative Manhattan Institute, to the city's rent control hearings so he could share New York City's complex history of rent control and compare it with the experience in Washington. Salins suggested that if DC continued its rent control policy, the city's economic future would be as dark as it was in New York. Anthony Downs, a white political moderate and an advocate of the fast-growing and right-leaning field of public choice theory, was also invited to the hearings to defend Ray's bill. Downs backed vacancy decontrol because it protected "two elements: a free market in housing without rent controls and universally available income supplements for poor households so they can pay the costs of decent housing."[126] Unlike Salins, Downs, believed that the federal government should pay for a housing voucher program for all poor renters. Moreover, like Ray, his vision for the program included middle-class civic oversight of low-wage Black residents, whom Downs hoped would relocate to the suburbs and decrease the potential for urban rebellion and the concentration of Black poverty in urban centers.[127]

Despite having strong support from conservatives and real estate interests, Ray initially lacked council backing—until the political tide shifted in his favor in April 1985, just as the rent control law was about to expire. With no clear majority, the council convened to discuss the forty-plus amendments that members had drafted for the bill. During these closed meetings, representatives from the Washington Board of Realtors, the AOBA, and the Greater Washington Board of Trade effectively lobbied for their preferred amendments. Suddenly, the pendulum swung in Ray's direction. By late April, seven council members, including Republican Carol Schwartz and Democrat Charlene Drew Jarvis, voted for a bill that incorporated the amendments desired by the anti-rent control faction.[128]

As a result of this backroom negotiating, the council voted for vacancy decontrol on the condition that DC's rent control administrator could exempt buildings with 80 percent vacancy on a case-by-case basis. This change would go into effect in four years instead of six, provided that DC's overall vacancy rate remained higher than 6 percent and that the city implemented a locally funded $15 million housing voucher program. In addition to vacancy decontrol, tenants could face 12 percent rent increases on vacant apartments instead of the current rate of 10 percent. Barry publicly supported Clarke's bill when tenants turned out in great numbers but was noticeably silent during negotiations. After vacancy decontrol passed, Barry chose to defend it.

Rent control advocates were surprised when Clarke's bill died while many of Ray's provisions passed. Tenant activists and journalists saw the vote as a signal that this council fundamentally differed from the inaugural council that had supported rent control in response to tenant power. This time, tenant power was muted by the organized money that had funded the rise of the politicians who voted against Clarke's bill. It was a now a business-friendly council that, according to one tenant activist, was "more conservative, not as open and shows less of a willingness to be honest with constituents and their concerns. This is big-city politics now."[129]

Tenant activists refused to concede and mobilized their networks in an effort to reverse the decision. While Ray published an op-ed piece in May 1985 that boasted about the forthcoming success of vacancy decontrol and his housing voucher program, tenant activists launched a referendum campaign to reverse the new law. However, although Black tenants had led the campaign that led to the rent control law in 1974, that was not the case with the referendum campaign. They were undoubtedly present among tenant participants, but most of the campaign's leaders were in certain Northwest and Southwest DC neighborhoods, where the city's non-Black presence was the highest. Nevertheless, the Emergency Committee to Save Rental Housing recruited hundreds of tenants to pass out leaflets and knock on doors in all wards. Like the CWHC's methods, this outreach strategy centered on establishing tenant associations and politicizing tenants through their involvement.

Advocates' outreach proved successful. They collected the signatures of over 25,000 registered DC voters in less than two months, in time to get the referendum on the ballot in November 1985. The referendum asked tenants to consider rejecting four provisions in the new law:

Single-family homes owned by four or fewer persons, rather than corporations, would be exempted from controls once they are vacated.

Buildings that were at least 80 percent vacant as of April 30 [1985] would be exempted from controls on a case-by-case basis at the owner's request, provided that tenants are properly relocated.

Buildings that were declared "distressed" properties could be decontrolled under a new city program in which landlords could receive tax breaks, loans, and grants to restore them.

Starting in 1989, all rental units would be exempted from controls as they became vacant, but only if the city's rental vacancy rate was 6 percent or more and only if a newly authorized rent subsidy program of up to $15 million was operating to assist low-income tenants.[130]

The referendum campaign led to a confrontation with the city's leaders. Council members Ray, Schwartz, and Nadine Winter stood with Mayor Barry and landlords in defending the new law, claiming that their vote was for the poor. To temper the fear of low-wage Black families about displacement via vacancy decontrol, Barry said that he was still a rent control supporter but "did not want a city of extremes, of the very poor and the very rich," prioritizing Black middle-class revanchism as a benefit of the law.[131] Clarke, Shackleton, Wilson, Rolark, Mason, and Frank Smith disagreed, insisting that Barry and the seven council members who voted for rent control rollbacks had voted in service of their moneyed interests, not tenants.

Victory may have been possible for the referendum, as it was an off-year election, but it was certainly not guaranteed. Again, the real estate industry funded the anti-rent control faction: Barry and other council members outspent the tenant groups seven to one. As the vote drew near, the likelihood that the referendum would succeed decreased as Barry went to his campaign stomping grounds in far Southeast DC, insisting that he cared about the housing needs of Southeast residents more than the referendum's supporters did. The stark contrast in leadership on the referendum led *Washington Post* columnist Courtland Milloy to comment that referendum supporters were white and educated yuppies while opponents were resource-rich landlords.[132] The referendum secured a narrow victory. With fewer than 1,000 more votes, DC voters successfully challenged big business, Ray, and Mayor Barry and reversed the new rent control law.

The victory signaled that the Black poor and middle class in DC valued working-class solidarity enough to vote to protect rent control. Data on voter breakdown is scarce, but it is clear that gentrified and wealthy neighborhoods with a high percentage of homeowners, such as Chevy Chase, Glover Park, and Capitol Hill, voted against rent control protections. Wards with renter-heavy neighborhoods such as Columbia Heights, Anacostia, Adams Morgan, and Congress Heights voted for the measure.[133] This class breakdown revealed that even if they were not the referendum's leading strategists, low-wage Black tenants largely voted to protect affordability for all.

Resident Hierarchies Reinforced: DC's Voucher Program and the Marginalization of Black Women

Despite the referendum's success, Ray chose to press forward with a housing voucher program. He emphasized that the elderly and single Black mothers were the deserving poor who should be given priority as eligible recipients. The council agreed, and in August 1985, it initiated the city's first housing voucher program: the Tenant Assistance Program (TAP), which was administered by DC's Department of Housing and Community Development (DHCD). Housing bureaucrats developed the rules of the program, and landlords and tenant activists associated with the Emergency Committee to Save Rental Housing reviewed them.

TAP was modeled after the federal government's rental subsidy program. During the Reagan administration, HUD shifted its focus to assisting individual tenants through housing vouchers instead of place-based assistance such as public housing, project-based Section 8 assistance, and rental supplement programs, all of which had been severely cut during the Reagan years.[134] HUD's experimental voucher program granted more geographic flexibility than some earlier ones but maintained sunset eligibility provisions that required recipients to secure housing within a restricted window. TAP also instituted sunset eligibility in DC, giving voucher recipients three months to find an apartment. If they failed to do so, they had to relinquish the voucher so the agency could provide it to another family in need of housing. As was the case with HUD's experimental voucher program, officials who promoted TAP claimed that these reforms made housing assistance more efficient, administratively straightforward, and responsive to consumers. In other words, vouchers were better for low-wage tenants.

HUD's experimental housing voucher program continued the federal government's commitment to disciplinary housing governance. This commitment was underscored by the Reagan administration's creation of a new federal housing voucher that emphasized work obligations in exchange for housing or welfare assistance, aligning with conservative political scientist Lawrence Mead's call to link welfare assistance to work. This context is crucial for understanding the broader policy landscape in which TAP was implemented.[135] Washington, DC, was selected as one of seventy-eight locations nationwide to participate in the Reagan administration's $25 million demonstration program to test the efficacy of workfare. Mayor Barry announced, "Our goal is to . . . do all we can with job training, with education, with stimulation, with anything else we can do to get people off the treadmill of poverty, to get them off of government assistance into 'workfare.'"[136] Barry also hoped to use federal monies to convert the city's more than 5,000 vacant rental units into renovated homes for low-wage and middle-class families. However, HUD refused to increase funding for project-based rehabilitation. From 1980 to 1984, HUD granted only 151 vouchers to DC, in stark contrast to the 503 vouchers the city had received during the Carter administration. The 1984 demonstration grant provided one hundred new vouchers, and since the program focused on single parents aged twenty-one to twenty-five with one or two children under ten years old, most of the vouchers went to Black mothers. Social workers would vet and select families and help them create self-sufficiency plans to ensure that young parents learned how to sustain their families on wages they earned in the formal labor market. But HUD's focus on behavioral regulation ignored the structural factors that shaped Black poverty, including rising rents and sluggish local economies still entrenched in gendered, racial, and skill-based hierarchies. With vouchers, Black mothers in DC paid more for housing because landlords retained the right to increase rents as they saw fit.[137]

Notably, however, the city's TAP vouchers did not place behavioral conditionalities on recipients. Like HUD's housing vouchers, DC's TAP was income-restricted and not universally accessible. Instead of universal aid, the city used a lottery to ensure fairness and transparency because officials could not guarantee assistance to the more than 30,000 eligible DC residents. Thus, tenants had to apply for vouchers in the hope that they would be selected. Over 10,000 tenants applied for the 200 TAP certificates in the first round of applications. The DHCD chose to issue only several hundred vouchers in each round to minimize tenant competition, partly because landlords did not flock to the program despite their years-long insistence that vouchers were better than rent control.

Only twenty-five landlords agreed to participate when TAP launched in August 1986, even though the DHCD hoped that vouchers would enable tenants to rent 5,000 units. According to AOBA executive vice president Donald Slatton, the reason for low landlord participation was simple: DC still enforced a form of rent stabilization. The TAP program adjusted rents every two years instead of the annual rent hikes in HUD's voucher program. Why participate when the rent control law, as loathed as it was by landlords, continued to permit annual rent hikes?

Landlords' tolerance of rent control over TAP suggests that the gendered trope of Black tenant irresponsibility still underwrote their sluggish acceptance of DC's voucher program. When voucher-assisted single mothers disclosed that they had young children, landlords frequently rejected them for two main reasons: they preferred not to go through the additional administrative hurdles to enroll in TAP and many landlords still believed that low-wage Black families were representative of the undesirable many who depressed property values and threatened a building's social prestige. By the fall of 1987, less than two years after TAP started, the city was struggling to overcome these challenges. After the city issued over 2,000 TAP vouchers, only 700 recipients were able to find apartments they could lease as TAP recipients. The rest were left to navigate the rental market without state assistance.[138] The inability of tenants to lease apartments within the allocated time meant that the city spent only $3 million of the $15 million allotment during its first year.

To ease landlords' fears and generate broader appeal, DC officials agreed to lift tax liens on landlords' properties to convince them to accept rent-assisted low-income families. This strategy cost millions but yielded only about 250 new landlord participants by 1988, leaving qualified TAP tenants still struggling to find housing. Landlords retained the authority to choose which families or individuals got to live in TAP-approved units. The result was that single Black mothers with more than three children, individuals with disabilities, and unhoused people experienced the most difficulty finding landlords who would rent to them.

The lucky few voucher recipients who found TAP housing were likely subjected to landlords' varying eligibility standards. This practice increased as the city pursued gentrification as a primary mode of economic revitalization in the 1990s and beyond. Moreover, inclusion in the program did not necessarily facilitate economic stability. In many cases, the exact opposite happened. Cleo E. Harris, a disabled resident, complained that she spent half her welfare check on housing even though she had a TAP voucher. Like HUD's voucher program, TAP guaranteed rental assistance, not stabilized rent levels. Harris struggled to find another landlord who would accept lower rent so that her contribution to her housing expense could decrease. Harris explained, "I get a monthly check of $229 and I spend $150 for rent. I have to borrow from all the friends I have. I'm not surviving. I'm existing."[139] If she wanted to pay less in rent, she would most likely have had to have relocated to an area with higher vacancy rates and lower levels of code compliance because those were the areas where landlords were mostly likely to lower rents to attract tenants. Even though these experiences were widespread, the city refused to mandate universal acceptance of TAP certificates, preferring to entice landlords to buy property in DC. AOBA representatives preached patience, even in the face of a growing crisis of homelessness that was made worse by rising local poverty.

DC's choice not to include disciplinary housing governance experiments with TAP vouchers did not necessarily prevent landlords from enforcing their own practices. Some landlords who participated in the project-based Section 8 housing program implemented their versions of disciplinary housing governance. Patricia Penny, a longtime ONE DC member, recalled that the landlord assessed her housekeeping before she was approved to move into a project-based Section 8 apartment in DC's Shaw neighborhood in the early 1980s.[140] Archival evidence also shows that landlords were as likely to exclude tenants they found undesirable as they were to vet potential renters' housekeeping or personal lives, a practice that required personnel and a property management infrastructure to perform character oversight and behavioral regulation, including a willingness to evict for noncompliance. The default exclusion of low-wage Black tenants is an example of rampant discrimination. HUD confirmed these persistent forms of discrimination against low-income Black families in the 1980s. Some of these discriminatory examples included landlords refusing rent to families with children under a certain age or forcing families to rent ground or second floor units because "their children are noisy and will disturb tenants who live below them."[141]

· · · · · ·

The city's rent control debate in the 1970s and 1980s revealed the centrality of the cultural discourse about the Black urban poor. The gendered cultural discourse that politicians, journalists, and real estate representatives used about the city's Black underclass activated and exposed intraracial class tensions. In that class divide, some Black city officials aligned with those who opposed rent control. Discourse about the Black underclass provided a legitimating frame for Black politicians like Ray to back rent control opposition because they imagined Black middle-class revanchism to be a racial uplift project that would complement urban growth goals.

The nearly ten-year debate over rent control presented several powerful lessons about tenant activism. First, this historical moment showed that Black working-class families, particularly Black women, challenged the market and political forces that contributed to the city's social reproduction crisis of dispossession via gentrification. This moment revealed how central Black tenants, particularly Black women, were in leading political action that generated the public will and political pressure needed to secure the passage of the city's rent control law. This legislative victory resulted in the growth of nonprofit advocacy professionals who then led negotiations with politicians during battles of rent control enforcement.

Even after the demographic and political focus of the city's rent control organizing infrastructure changed, Black women and their families continued to participate in such efforts. Tenant activists working across racial and class lines challenged John Ray's third mayoral campaign, pooling their funds to distribute fliers that denounced his failure to champion tenant rights and rent control.[142] For these activists, Ray's campaign to overturn the city's rent control law threatened a vision of long-term affordability that they were determined to defend, even when the internal dynamics of community organizations became challenging or officials equivocated and championed market-friendly reforms to the law.

Second, this historical moment revealed the continued salience of Black feminist materialism. The persistence of the gendered trope of Black tenant irresponsibility made it possible for opponents of rent control to frame their arguments with narratives about the so-called Black underclass. Black politicians like Ray tied racial uplift ideology to Black middle-class revanchism, making the latter a potential solution to the city's interconnected crises of capital flight and rising urban Black poverty.

The gendered trope of Black tenant irresponsibility continued to shape debates about public housing in the 1980s, when public housing was widely assumed to be the "dumping ground" for US society's most undesirable tenants. During this period, conservative federal officials justified disciplinary housing governance and updated experiments to include it. As real estate interests did with Ray, federal officials teamed up with a select group of Black public housing tenants to defend this practice. The political stakes of this short-lived alliance between conservatives and Black women living in public housing would be massive because the federal government would contend that the new honorable poor should be those who desired homeownership—and that the rest deserved (more) punishment.

4 I Want to Own the Plantations

Tenant Management, Conservative Populism, and Austerity Politics in the 1980s

· ·

After leading a historic multiyear rent strike in the 1970s, DC public housing residents entered the 1980s with little evidence that their actions had improved housing conditions. With the Department of Housing and Urban Development's (HUD) shift to providing privately managed, rent-assisted housing, public housing became synonymous with disinvestment, crime, poverty, and despair. However, against the backdrop of this federal retreat, low-wage Black mothers fought to make public housing safe and fit for family life.[1]

If this battle for decent public housing had a captain, it was Kimi Gray. Born in 1945 in Washington, DC, Gray was the oldest of four. She and her family experienced public housing as a saving grace. Until the age of five, her family lived in a rooming house in Northwest, and "everybody [at the Northwest house] had to use one bathroom and one kitchen." When her family gained entry into Frederick Douglass Public Housing in DC's Anacostia neighborhood, Gray "was happy as I could be. We had a front yard, a back porch, and a nice backyard to play in. I thought we had just bought a new house. I didn't know my mother was on public assistance."[2] Gray carried the belief that public housing was and could be a safe place for raising children when she created a family of her own. At the age of nineteen and in 1965, Gray, who was divorced and had five children, moved into Kenilworth Courts, a 422-unit public housing community in Kenilworth, a Far Northeast neighborhood next to the boundary between DC and Prince George's County, Maryland. By the time she moved into Kenilworth Courts, much had changed from her childhood. Public housing had deteriorated as the result of mounting maintenance costs, increased poverty, and fewer resources.

Unwilling to let her new community fall further into disrepair, Gray turned to her neighbors to ask them to help transform their community. One night in the early 1970s, they assessed the failure of the local rent strike that Gray and others had participated in and decided to try another approach.

Director of DC's Department of Housing and Community Development Robert "Bob" L. Moore (*center*) spoke to public housing residents during a meeting of the Residents Advisory Council in Washington, DC, June 12, 1981. Carolyn Lilly (*left*) served as the council's secretary and council chair Kimi Gray (*right*) presided over the meeting. Photo courtesy of *The Washington Post.*

They wanted to turn public housing into a powerful force for positive youth development and tenant engagement. That night, Gray joined neighbors Ms. Roy, Mr. Harris, and Mr. Carsons at Gwendolyn Gordon's house to create a "plan of action."[3] They agreed to focus on building community power through participation in electoral politics and civic life. By the late 1970s, they had created youth education programs, had conducted voter registration drives, and had selected court captains, who typically represented building concerns at tenant association meetings.

With an expanded tenant network, Gray and her neighbors began to demand community control. When Gray spoke, others listened. By her own admission, she was a magnetic force. A plus-size woman standing almost six feet tall, she had "rapid-fire speech" and an infectious smile. Gray acknowledged, "Whenever I walk into a room, all attention is on me because I'm so big."[4] With charisma and clarity of purpose, she worked with fellow tenants to call for tenant management and, ultimately, tenant ownership of public housing. As Gray publicly mused, "I want to own the plantations. Yes, the plantations. That's what public housing communities are, aren't they?"[5] She reasoned, "When our children reach the age of fourteen and get their first summer job, and they buy their first pair of new, name-brand tennis shoes, they take care of them tennis shoes. But when Mama buy them, the strings are always unloosed; they walking on the back of them; their pants hanging off their hips. But if you buy them, you take care of them. You maintain it better."[6]

Gray's philosophy of public housing ownership eventually garnered the attention of conservative elites who longed to turn public housing's disinvestment crisis into a solution that only the private market could provide.[7] As the nation grappled with high unemployment and low economic growth, Republican president Ronald Reagan introduced a politics of austerity that emphasized lower taxes and less government spending on welfare (notably excluding military spending). In the post–civil rights shift to colorblind political rhetoric, conservatives increasingly coded the racial and gendered implications of their welfare reforms. Toward this end, conservative leaders increasingly relied on performances of racial inclusion to repackage and defend the gendered trope of Black tenant irresponsibility.

This chapter examines the short-lived but complex political history of tenant ownership of public housing in the 1980s. Floundering under Reagan's edict of welfare austerity, HUD left policy innovation to conservative think tanks that applied neoliberal principles like deregulation and privatization to public housing. In this context, Black neoconservatives supported Gray's concept of tenant management of public housing, arguing that privatization was more cost-efficient and more effective in regulating poor Black residents than existing welfare measures were. White conservative elites like Jack Kemp reinforced this position when he decided to champion the Heritage Foundation's privatization goal for public housing. If public housing tenants proved that they could collectively manage (and discipline) their neighbors, Kemp argued, they could earn the opportunity to purchase the property and achieve the status of homeowners. To defend his proposal, he employed a racially inclusive performance of neoliberal populism, calling upon Black neoconservatives and Black public housing tenants like Gray to back his policy goals. While Kemp garnered a public image as a compassionate Republican, Republican leaders fiercely disagreed with Kemp's reform bill. More specifically, Reagan's top advisors pushed back on Kemp's privatization proposal, countering that since only a fraction of public housing residents could afford the high interest rates and other contingency costs of homeownership, its effects would be minimal. The policy would be more symbolic than fiscally sound.

The debate over public housing ownership became a critical inflection point in the country's welfare history. By presenting these activists as representatives of the honorable poor, political leaders could legitimize more robust punishments for the remaining tenants who allegedly embodied the stereotype of the irresponsible tenant. While it is possible that tenant activists were unaware of politicians' interest in punitive policies, Gray endorsed critical tenets of conservative ideology, including the belief that traditional gendered and heterosexual scripts should govern domestic life and influence real estate management practices. Ultimately, Gray's brief alliance with conservative leaders served as a cautionary tale for Black public housing activists who learned the painful lesson that alignment with the Republican Party meant punitive forms of disciplinary housing governance, welfare austerity, and more police.

Public Housing Activism in the Shadow of State Disinvestment

Reagan rightly represents the face of welfare reform in the post–civil rights era. His role as a national advocate for welfare reform was part of a post–1960s transformation of the Republican Party into one that played on many white citizens' fear of integration while publicizing the belief that welfare undermined the country's moral and cultural values.[8] Shortly after the civil rights movement ended, Republican leaders executed the electoral plan known as the Southern Strategy. Republican strategists encouraged conservative candidates like Reagan to embrace racially coded issues like public housing and integrated busing to turn white southerners' anger into Republican votes. However, in their political speeches and in the press, Republicans used colorblind moral language, arguing that they were advocating economic policy stances that benefited the middle class and defended socially conservative family values.[9] This coded discourse became a hallmark of conservative welfare politics. Republican leaders often deployed one narrative in public to curry electoral favor, even among urban Black voters, while privately harboring different concerns or goals. This coded ideological context enabled Republicans to enact their federal retrenchment of the welfare state in the 1980s.

After Reagan won the presidency in 1980 with strong middle-class and southern support, his administration vigorously pursued welfare austerity despite the racial implications of such priorities.[10] To defend these cuts, Reagan's top budget advisor, David Stockman, focused on terminating government programs, citing a "reevaluation of housing subsidy programs" as a primary way to reduce federal spending.[11] To achieve more significant federal cuts, Reagan's budget and policy advisors later argued that welfare reform—a far-reaching initiative that would affect all means-tested welfare spending—was necessary to both curb domestic spending and resituate private domestic labor as the appropriate means to address a family's social reproduction needs.[12] To deflect accusations that these cuts were examples of racial bias, Republican leaders repeatedly relied on Black representatives to articulate and defend these economic policies as beneficial to Black people. By the end of Reagan's first term, Black Republican leaders had identified Kimi Gray as a captivating but unlikely spokesperson for their cause.

Gray's rise to national housing politics paradoxically emerged after she and her neighbors tried to quietly address the consequences of federal disinvestment in their public housing community. When Kenilworth Courts opened in 1959, few of its residents would have predicted that the property would slide into disinvestment less than a decade later. A 400-plus multifamily rental community that primarily consisted of three-, four- and five-bedroom units, Kenilworth Courts was built for Black families displaced by urban renewal. Nestled in a working-class neighborhood, the community contained garden-style, two- to three-story townhomes fitted with new appliances. The community initially flourished because it hosted fun, family-friendly events, including gardening shows that were well-known in the area.[13] But by the late 1960s, the area had begun to show signs of disinvestment. In the next decade, the budgetary challenges of the National Capital Housing Authority and HUD's refusal to enforce the Brooke Amendment forced public housing communities like Kenilworth Courts to manage the fallout of rising crime rates and inconsistent maintenance.[14]

Environmental racism, capital flight, and state neglect compounded the disinvestment at Kenilworth Courts. The buildings were near a local highway that was adjacent to one of the city's largest dumps. Kenilworth Dump, which opened in 1942, was a municipal waste site where garbage burned in open air and spewed ash at nearby residents.[15] Debris reportedly traveled up to two miles away, even after an incinerator was installed to reduce smog pollution in the early 1960s.[16] Kenilworth residents complained of health challenges and property damage. If they hung clean laundry outside, dump debris would spread so fast that their clothes were "suddenly black with soot."[17] Although a multiyear campaign to close the dump ended in victory in 1970, Kenilworth residents faced the adverse effects of capital flight.[18] As early as the mid-1960s, local merchants began complaining that Black youth stole goods and vandalized their properties. For their part, young Black people complained of poor treatment and discrimination.[19] The city's April 1968 rebellion ultimately validated the fears of banks and local merchants that crime was increasing. Businesses had abandoned the area by the early 1970s, leaving only a liquor store and a Chinese restaurant within walking distance of Kenilworth Courts.[20] To make matters worse, the closest park to the neighborhood, the fourteen-acre federally funded Kenilworth Aquatic Gardens, had sustained federal cuts and was operating with limited staff.[21]

Despite federal disinvestment, the local commitment to youth services gave Kimi Gray a platform for community organizing. Gray focused on youth development after participating in the city's public housing rent strike. Under Mayor Marion Barry's leadership, the city maintained its investment in youth recreational services provided through the DC Department of Recreation. Adults served as roving leaders to respond to community needs. As a roving leader, Gray typically worked the 1:30 to 10:30 P.M. shift, assisting youth in finding legal help, summer employment, prenatal care, and afterschool programs.[22] Through this work, local youth saw Gray as a trusted and supportive figure, so it was no surprise when three Kenilworth Courts highschoolers asked her to help them raise funds to attend college in 1974. As Gray recalled later:

> I, myself, had not been fortunate enough to attend college, therefore, I had no idea of which route to take. I went to the social service agencies in our community and asked for support and advice. I then went to the HEW [the Department of Health, Education and Welfare] and began doing my own research to find out ways to receive financial aid which would assist my students. . . . "College Here We Come" is the name the students voted on. . . . We met religiously every Tuesday at 7 P.M. with new ideas and support for each other. Our main concern was that nothing was going to get in the way of our students going to college.[23]

College Here We Come emphasized community organizing practices like leadership development and participatory decision-making. Through the program, youth learned that Kenilworth's resilience was only as strong as its residents' linked faith—the belief that the neighborhood's progress required young people to acquire an education, then return to teach and mentor younger students.[24] Within a year, the program was considered a success. Seventeen students enrolled in college in 1975, and four years later, eight students graduated at the top of their class and four entered graduate school. All of them returned to support the neighborhood's collective uplift.

College Here We Come proved to be a gateway for mobilizing parents as activists. Gray and her neighbors created the Parent Booster Club to support the college prep program.[25] They held fundraisers like car washes, raffles, and food sales and soon expanded their focus to educational reform. Gray publicly condemned inadequate support in public schools for Black academic development.[26] She built relationships with civic-minded principals and teachers to counter these inequities and recruited some of them to provide after-school tutoring for student members of College Here We Come. Parents also planned summer internships, scheduled campus visits, and hosted an annual college day at Kenilworth Courts that introduced public housing youth to representatives from colleges.

By the late 1970s, Kimi Gray's organizing talents had earned accolades from DC neighbors and politicians. Native Black Washingtonian Vickey Nelson fondly remembers Gray as "a very sweet lady," recalling that "she would always look out for people in Kenilworth."[27] Gray's neighbors described her as a "dedicated soul . . . [who] goes all out for anybody in need of help."[28] Her supporters extended well beyond her neighborhood; private donors, local colleges, welfare officials, and Mayor Barry praised Gray for turning a socially isolated and disinvested public housing community into a local model for positive Black youth development and parental involvement.

Advocacy regarding their children's education eventually led parents back to public housing activism. The Parents Booster Club was a leadership pipeline for the Kenilworth-Parkside tenant advisory board. This body combined Kenilworth Courts with its sister property, Parkside, located in the same neighborhood (hereafter Kenilworth-Parkside). With Kimi Gray at the helm, Kenilworth-Parkside tenants saw how federal and local disinvestment impacted their quality of life and began questioning the city's approach to public housing management.

National publicity surrounding tenant management shaped the context in which Kenilworth-Parkside residents considered their options. Tenant management of public housing had emerged as a key demand in a nine-month rent strike in St. Louis, Missouri, in 1968. The St. Louis Housing Authority and HUD eventually agreed to adopt the model after tenants completed management training and benefactors like the Ford Foundation aided in its expansion in the 1970s.[29] Growing federal support for this tenant management model likely inspired Gray and her neighbors at Kenilworth-Parkside.

The opportunity to work toward tenant management at Kenilworth-Parkside came when the city considered extending its contract with a private management team. According to Kenilworth-Parkside tenant leaders, DC's approach to public housing management had been failing since the city began contracting private management firms in the wake of the public housing rent strike. At Kenilworth-Parkside, housing officials installed a Black-owned private management company, Central City Property Management (CCPM), without tenant approval. CCPM's contract was set to expire in 1975, and Gray and her fellow board members demanded tenant inclusion or else. As Gray later recounted, "When it came time to renegotiate the second contract, we participated and made sure that they fully understood that residents must participate or there will be no rent paid again. . . . Or we would do a lot of bad other things that would make it very uncomfortable for them."[30] Their threat convinced the city's housing officials and CCPM to concede. Soon after, Gray and the tenant advisory board met with CCPM's executives to negotiate. The management company ultimately agreed that public housing residents would be first in line for available property management jobs. The resident council created a job bank to assist with this change and surveyed residents to identify their skills and job experience.

The advisory board's partnership with CCPM yielded positive results for Kenilworth-Parkside tenants but also exposed class tensions between CCPM and residents. By 1979, activists' persistent enforcement of the resident-first hiring policy had filled over 80 percent of the community's management positions with public housing residents. However, this achievement required Gray and her neighbors to push back against CCPM's subtly expressed assumption that Black public housing residents were best suited for low-wage and unskilled labor. Gray remembered that on several occasions, she had to remind CCPM leaders that public housing residents "do not only clean streets, mop hallways. They can be reexamination clerks. They can become assistant managers. And they can take tests and become managers."[31] As tenants became more involved in staff and management matters, CCPM eventually grew tired of fielding input from the tenant advisory board. CCPM's manager for Kenilworth-Parkside declared that he would no longer accept tenants "telling him what to do."[32] Kenilworth-Parkside tenants refused to tolerate another bout of disrespect and took their concerns to CCPM's chair. Shortly after the meeting with CCPM, tenant leaders became convinced that community control through tenant management was the only solution to their multiyear struggle to improve their public housing community.

Capitalizing on her rising popularity in Washington, Kimi Gray contacted Mayor Barry's office in 1979 to request city funds for two years of tenant management training for Kenilworth-Parkside residents. Barry administration officials were initially reluctant but agreed to keep the conversation open. However, an incident at Kenilworth-Parkside soon changed their perspective. Gray recounted:

> On December 30, 1980. I will never forget it . . . we were having a New Year's Eve party and the [CCPM] project management firm had walked off and left us and we did not know it. . . . Pipes began to burst all over our property. The worst weather we had since 1949, the weather forecast said. I have never seen radiators splitting and pipes bursting like that. And we immediately began calling downtown. But then we realized, if we are ever going to take charge, we will take charge right now. We called on some of the fathers who were former engineers and plumbers. And they knew exactly what to do. We went down to the boiling room and we found the plumbing blueprints; learned where all the pits were on the property and where all the gate vales were to know where to cut the water off. . . . We went down to the alley where there are these abandoned cars and got the old radiator hose off them and put them around the pipes and put clamps on them to stop the water from running so folks could at least have heat until daylight came. The next day, we went to Pep Boys and bought more heating hose. . . . We really did not know how much we could accomplish if we really, truly worked together. We worked all night long and we brought the New Year in, working together. Women were out there fixing the men hot beans and bread to feed them. And the men were out there soaking wet, some of the men were out there with suits on. We did not care. This was ours and we were going to save it and make it better for all of the residents.[33]

The willingness of tenants to step in and pool their private resources to address this breakdown in infrastructure finally proved to DC housing officials that Kimi Gray and her neighbors were ready and willing to manage their community. Where CCPM had exhibited indifference, Kenilworth-

Parkside tenants had demonstrated their dedication. In January 1981, the tenant association received a $78,000 grant with the condition that Kenilworth-Parkside would not receive rehabilitation funds, as other public housing communities had more severe infrastructure issues. Gray accepted the stipulation, and the resident council agreed to raise funds privately. Consequently, Gray and her neighbors could run Kenilworth-Parkside's community center with full autonomy while using city funds to learn how to manage public housing.

Popularizing Austerity: New Political Alliances and the National Stage for Black Tenant Managers

After Reagan was elected, Black neoconservatives who were asserting their influence in Republican policy circles brought Kimi Gray's leadership successes to the attention of party elites.[34] As historian Manning Marable notes, Black conservatism had different variants, including the philosophical conservatism of public intellectual Thomas Sowell, who backed laissez-faire capitalism; the neoconservatism of Robert Woodson and Charles V. Hamilton, former leftists who rebuked liberalism and protest as ineffective tools for Black progress; and business leaders like Samuel Pierce and William T. Coleman who were dedicated to the Republican Party platform of lower taxes, (Black) entrepreneurialism, and corporate growth. Despite this ideological breadth, Black conservatives were united in what they wanted from Reagan's administration. According to Dan Smith, a California State Commission for Economic Development member, "The past 20 years have been the civil rights era. Now we're in the era of economic rights. We want to see the development of independent black wealth in the black community."[35] To achieve this vision, Smith and other Black conservatives supported tax and finance reform to stimulate Black entrepreneurship and an end to school busing, rent control, affirmative action, minimum wage laws, and a "host of 'dependency-encouraging' social programs."[36] They also called for high-profile appointments to the Reagan administration because, as one Black Republican insisted, "If we're going to build a Republican presence in the Black community, the people who work in the trenches have to gain recognition."[37]

Although Reagan's top advisors engaged with Black conservatives during his first term, there was little evidence that they had much influence, particularly regarding their call for high-profile appointments. The only Black appointment to Reagan's cabinet was Samuel Pierce, a lifelong

Republican and successful New York lawyer that Reagan selected as HUD's secretary in January 1981. Pierce defended Reagan's call for welfare austerity: "Inflation is public enemy No. 1. . . . I am certain there is going to be some substantial cut . . . in HUD expenditures."[38] Besides offering HUD funding cuts, Pierce provided little in terms of visionary housing policy. This later earned him the nickname "Silent Sam" in the press and among political insiders.[39]

Black neoconservatives continued trying to fill roles in policy leadership. Robert Woodson was one of the most prominent Black conservative advocates of changes in housing policy. Born in Philadelphia in April 1937, Woodson dropped out of high school to join the Air Force, earning his GED as he served. Woodson became involved in civil rights organizing while he studied mathematics at Cheyney University and earned a master's degree in social work from the University of Pennsylvania. Until the 1970s, he did a variety of service jobs: he worked for several years as a corrections officer, for seven as a social worker, and over a decade in neighborhood groups. In 1976, Woodson abandoned his civil rights roots and agreed to join the American Enterprise Institute (AEI), a conservative think tank founded in 1938 by elite New York businessmen, as its first Black fellow. His job there was to steward the organization's Neighborhood Revitalization Project.

AEI gave Woodson an institutional platform to push his agenda for conservative welfare reform. AEI produced scholarship on free enterprise, limited government, and market democracy. Until the late 1960s, it was a relatively small and politically timid entity. Following the conservative resurgence in the early 1970s, the institute rose from political obscurity and rebranded itself as an activist policymaking enterprise. William Baroody Sr., an AEI executive for nearly twenty-five years, decided to recruit disillusioned leftists who questioned the utility and limitations of the US welfare state. This community eventually became known as neoconservatives. They publicly rebuked what they saw as the left's insufficient faith in American exceptionalism. They also tended to be anticommunist interventionists who aggressively imposed their policy priorities on other countries. Baroody Sr. (and his son Baroody Jr., after he took over AEI in 1980) recruited neoconservatives such as Irving Kristol, Jeane Kirkpatrick, and Michael Novak to influence policy and public opinion in the highest levels of government.[40] Alongside fellows like Woodson, these neoconservatives were tasked with popularizing the organization's vision of welfare reform, which called for a return to "mediating structures"—the family, churches, neighborhood groups, and charity organizations.[41] Welfare regulations, AEI members argued, hobbled the ability of these mediating structures to adequately address poverty and other welfare issues.[42] In May 1981, Woodson converted this political philosophy into a two-day AEI-sponsored conference entitled "Urban Crisis: Can Grassroots Groups Succeed Where Government Has Failed?" which promoted the idea that Black grassroots leaders were failing to obtain welfare resources like community development grants because regulatory procedures discouraged community access.

At the conference and in the local press, Woodson spoke of the need for welfare reform, highlighting what he believed to be the inability of liberal officials to recognize and value Black community leaders who provided self-help programs for the Black poor. According to Woodson, the Black community had distinct mediating structures in the form of churches, lodges, fraternal organizations, and barbershops. He added that community leaders in these spaces were more effective than the state in dealing with poverty, community violence, and disinvestment. Woodson frequently showcased "neighborhood activists who work with youth gangs in Philadelphia, Puerto Rico, and Los Angeles, train unemployed adults in Hawaii to become business people and spearhead successful efforts to rebuild and renovate a blighted neighborhood in St. Louis."[43] He wanted the federal government to divert resources to these neighborhood activists. Woodson's message of redistribution of welfare services dovetailed with Reagan's austerity platform. He contended that local activists did not need as much money as state-funded welfare programs, which he condemned as paternal, wasteful, and ineffective. Instead, he emphasized that the community groups he spotlighted achieved poverty reduction or economic development by avoiding government funding and resisting "the lure of new grants to expand" when they were ill-equipped to do so.[44]

Woodson's message that cost-saving deregulation would benefit deserving Black welfare providers resonated with Republican members of Congress. Congressman David Durenberger (R-MN) held a hearing in Congress in the summer of 1981 on what he called "alternative service delivery." He intended to highlight local examples of where the federal government could transfer welfare services "back to people—not just to governments closer to people, or to other providers who are more efficient, but to the people themselves."[45] Conservative populist rhetoric was a strong feature of the congressional hearing. Durenberger wanted such rhetoric to portray traditional welfare institutions as undeserving beneficiaries of government resources. Woodson and Kimi Gray were invited to testify at this hearing, and the two most likely met there. Gray's testimony detailed her success with the College Here We Come youth program. She concluded her moving statement by asking the program's college graduates to stand while the audience applauded. Woodson's testimony rehashed his message from AEI's "Urban Crisis" conference, adding more teeth to his criticism of the "social welfare elite," which he noted, "not only fail to reach their intended recipients but in some cases exacerbate the very problem they are intended to solve."[46]

Woodson soon began to promote Gray as a national example of Black grassroots leaders' cost-effective success at poverty reduction and youth development. In other congressional hearings, Woodson praised "Miss Kimi Gray" as a "woman living in a public housing project who has been able, through the use of volunteers there, to motivate 274 children living in public housing to go on to postsecondary education. This she did without any outside support for the first 4 years, using volunteers."[47] His narrative was meant to dramatize the welfare state's ineffectiveness, but his message overlooked a complicated truth. Woodson neglected to mention that Gray was a government employee who eventually used state funds for her projects. For example, she took advantage of Comprehensive Employment and Training, a federally funded program, to pay for youth internships. The program was terminated during Reagan's first wave of massive social welfare cuts, a decision that must have hurt Gray's youth development community work.[48] But in Woodson's conservative framework, Gray's first four years were more significant because she had relied on private sources—particularly unpaid volunteer labor—to make her program work. He praised her fiscal resourcefulness as akin to small-scale entrepreneurs using wages, savings, and unremunerated labor to fund their startup costs.[49]

Unlike white neoconservatives like Michael Novak who unapologetically blamed single Black mothers for various problems, including urban poverty, Woodson highlighted the positive aspects of single Black motherhood. He argued that households led by Black women were not inherently pathological and insisted that they could create productive families. He portrayed them as innovators of poverty reduction measures. This was a bold assertion since conservatives typically prioritized respect for "hierarchical, often private regimes of rule" sanctioned by monotheistic customs and the laws of nation-states.[50] Perhaps Woodson's experience of being raised by a widowed mother of five helped him view single Black motherhood through the lens of respect and admiration rather than contempt or pity. In one congressional hearing, he said, "Households without a resident adult male are not necessarily lacking some way to fulfill the economic or socialization functions allocated to the male head in the model nuclear family. Nor is it true that the mother's death or absence indicates that children lack mothering. Cooperative economic activity, physical maintenance of the household, role modeling, socialization, and physical caring for the children may be tasks distributed over a number of homes that share responsibility on a mutually supportive, reciprocal basis."[51]

Respect for single mothers was a point that feminist scholars and welfare rights activists had long emphasized. Black feminist scholars, in particular, regularly challenged conservatives' negative depiction of single Black mothers.[52] But their social capital was no match for Woodson's, who, as a neoconservative Black man, had access to political spaces where it was accepted as truth that (welfare-assisted) single Black mothers were problems that needed to be managed.[53]

Woodson's readiness to see single Black mothers as innovators, community protectors, and capable parents enabled those spearheading community programs like College Here We Come to view him as a partner. As a political pragmatist, Woodson contended that Black conservatism must exhibit flexibility to resonate with the broader Black community. He once remarked that his interpretation of conservatism departed from restrictive "definitions of the past" and encompassed "[aspects] of liberalism, conservatism, Black nationalism, and American patriotism."[54] Kimi Gray seemed to support Woodson because he was a power broker who backed grassroots leaders like her. She valued Woodson's acknowledgment of her community's autonomy in decision-making: "The reason we respect Bob Woodson is he lets us dream our own dreams. He has helped us. Everything you see out here, the residents did it. But he will assist me in getting a lot of doors that I could otherwise not open."[55]

Although Woodson and Gray's political partnership garnered much public visibility, it yielded few gains during Reagan's first term. The Reagan administration ultimately slashed HUD's budget by 60 percent after cutting domestic spending and prioritizing anticommunist foreign policy in his first term. This meant public housing communities like Kenilworth Courts had to do more with less.[56] Yet given Reagan's openness to the policy recommendations of Black conservatives and Republican Party leaders' embrace of Woodson's claim that Black community leaders did not need substantial government funding for their community work, the administration's lack of follow-through on Woodson's policy recommendations is surprising. However, archival evidence suggests that some of Reagan's advisors believed that courting urban Black voters was a lost cause. In an internal memo to Reagan's chief of staff about building a winning coalition for Reagan's 1984 reelection campaign, political strategists categorized urban public housing renters as an "Inner City Streets" voter bloc with "almost 70 percent of its households being black." They characterized these communities as "represent[ing] the South Bronxes of America," adding that this voting bloc "ranks second in percentage of Hispanics, mostly Puerto Ricans" and "has been [an] urban renewal target for three decades; consists of large families living in rented public housing. These people are almost all completely dependent on the government for everything. They are hardcore Democrats." Reagan's advisors proposed "a strategy that will entail doing the minimum, in terms of policy, symbolism, or both, so that it will not look like we are purposely ignoring them; but that does not require us to squander our political capital on 'hostiles.'"[57]

However, during Reagan's second term, he eventually backed tenant management and private ownership of public housing. Woodson and Gray garnered bipartisan support from Republican and Democratic leaders, who then persuaded Reagan and his advisors to endorse the passage of the Housing and Community Development Act of 1987, a law that encouraged tenants to manage and purchase their public housing residences.

Bipartisan Support for Tenant Management and Disciplinary Housing Governance

Woodson and Gray's decision to cultivate bipartisan support resulted in a broader coalition of policy influencers who pressured the Reagan administration to back public housing reform. In 1984, Woodson continued his relationship with AEI but launched his own organization, the Center for Neighborhood Enterprise (CNE), which offered assistance and advocacy support to "self-help" community groups. He also started a political advocacy group called the Council for a Black Economic Agenda (CBEA). It encouraged Black entrepreneurs and grassroots leaders like Kimi Gray to lobby federal officials to back their policy proposals. Woodson partnered with Representative Walter Fauntroy (D-DC) through this work. Early in Reagan's second term, Fauntroy agreed to support the CBEA's bill that sought to grant higher operating subsidies to tenant-run businesses and public housing communities managed by tenants.[58] Although Fauntroy's willingness to align with Black conservatives may seem incongruous given his civil rights background and liberal roots, his working relationship with Woodson reinforced a trend among Black members of Congress at the time, who increasingly measured their political strength by their capacity to broker legislative deals, gain committee leadership posts, or siphon off private or federal funds for their political priorities.[59]

White conservative policy activists eventually collaborated with Woodson and the CBEA to promote a neoliberal approach to public housing reform. By 1984, conservative scholar Stuart Butler advocated for the inclusion of tenant management and public housing ownership. Born in 1947 in the United Kingdom, Butler immigrated to the United States in 1974 and established a political foothold as a young policy analyst at the Heritage Foundation. Like AEI, the Heritage Foundation supported probusiness and anticommunist policies. Its scholars crafted policies committed to incorporating marketplace logic into almost all aspects of social policy.[60] Neoliberalism underpinned these policy proposals. A postwar political philosophy that gained greater wider acceptance during the conservative resurgence of the 1970s, neoliberalism promoted variants of market fundamentalism that favored limited government, deregulation, privatization (of state services), and a conservative moral order.[61] A neoliberal advocate, Reagan embraced the Heritage Foundation's policy recommendations and adopted most of the legislative reforms in its *Mandate for Leadership* report, which outlined numerous ways his administration could shrink the federal government and advance a conservative agenda.

Conservative policy entrepreneur Stuart Butler needed a congressional ally to champion his ideas in Congress. He found his champion in Jack Kemp. Born in 1935, Kemp gained early fame as a quarterback; he played professionally for nearly thirteen years in the National Football League, the Canadian Football League, and the American Football League. During this time, he dabbled in electoral politics, volunteering for Republican Barry Goldwater's presidential campaign and Ronald Reagan's campaign for California governor. After retiring from football, Kemp was elected to the House of Representatives and became a powerhouse in Republican politics. He served as chair of the House Republican Conference from 1981 to 1987 and even ran for president. Kemp embraced Butler's policy proposal for housing reform because he was an acolyte of the neoliberal theory known as supply-side economics. This macroeconomics theory posited that lower tax rates would generate more government revenue because businesses would use the lower taxes to stimulate economic growth.

The neoliberal housing policy in the United Kingdom inspired Butler and Kemp's proposal for public housing ownership. Butler and Kemp were influenced by UK Prime Minister Margaret Thatcher, who championed a similar policy.[62] However, Thatcher was not the first to champion the idea of public housing ownership. As political scientist Chloe Thurston has uncovered, in 1967, the National Council of Negro Women (NCNW), a Black women's civil rights group, met with Black women in rural Oxford, Mississippi, where both groups agreed that public housing ownership could help improve dismal housing conditions in rural areas.[63] In September 1968, the NCNW worked with community leaders and HUD to implement the country's first public housing ownership program in North Gulfport, Mississippi, a program that soon expanded to urban areas. It is unclear if Butler and Kemp knew of HUD's previous attempts to privatize public housing. Nevertheless, Butler, as the head of Heritage Foundation's domestic policy division, proposed that HUD secretary Samuel Pierce abandon the agency's bifurcated approach to tenant management and public housing ownership and combine the two policies in 1984.

Butler and Kemp most likely pressed for the privatization of public housing because it was one of the few policy research areas that HUD had agreed to explore during Reagan's first term. In the early 1980s, HUD launched a small-scale demonstration program in public housing homeownership in response to growing pressure in Congress from Democrats for a policy other than budget cuts. However, internal research at HUD showed that public housing homeownership was unlikely to adequately address the affordability crisis confronting many low-income families in urban areas. In the study that contributed to HUD's small demonstration program, the department's Office of Policy and Research found that public housing ownership had been inconsistently applied since 1974, when Section 5(h), meant to help low-income families purchase public housing units, had been approved as an amendment to the 1937 Housing Act. In the decade that Section 5(h) had been in effect, fewer than 550 units had been sold to public housing residents.[64] However, Secretary Pierce hoped that HUD's demonstration program would have a different result because it gave local public housing authorities more autonomy to choose eligible tenants and neighborhoods, set sale prices, and determine the levels of assistance that potential homeowners needed. The program stipulated that local authorities had to certify that residents could assume the total cost of homeownership because no subsidies would be granted after the sale. Only rental units that met local housing codes could be sold to tenants in order to minimize their future maintenance costs. To that end, HUD used some of its limited modernization funds to ensure that the 1,455 public housing units it had approved for sale had been rehabilitated.[65] However, HUD's public housing demonstration program barely affected federal policy. Out of the country's 3,400 local public housing authorities, only thirty-four applied to participate during the first year, and HUD selected only sixteen to implement the program.[66]

Unlike HUD's demonstration program, Butler wanted HUD to sell directly to tenant management associations, eliminating the middlemen of local public housing authorities. To demonstrate their readiness to become owners, public housing tenant associations would need to prove that they could efficiently manage public housing. His proposal sought to eliminate both the waste and corruption he charged was widespread in public housing authorities and evidenced in the allegedly immoral behavior of public housing residents. Once tenant associations demonstrated their financial and behavioral management proficiency, tenants could apply directly to HUD for authorization to purchase their public housing units. If they were approved, tenants could buy at a selling price of 30 percent of a unit's market value.[67] To keep subsidy costs low, Butler proposed that HUD exempt public housing associations from the Davis-Bacon Act of 1931, which required the federal government to pay a prevailing wage to construction workers, which typically translated into union wages. He also called for changes in public housing finance to realize his goal of privatization for public housing.[68] Kemp wholeheartedly supported Butler's proposal and introduced the Urban Homestead Act in 1984 to create a broader path toward tenant ownership of public housing. Kemp's bill stipulated that housing authorities assume the mortgages for public housing tenant management associations and only transfer them after the associations provided sweat equity, reduced operating costs, and transformed tenant behavior. If associations could meet these standards, the tenants who did not want to buy would be permitted to rent or receive a housing voucher to move elsewhere.[69]

While Butler and Kemp's proposal seemed innovative at the time, it was a clever way to repackage conservative ideas about the gendered trope of Black tenant irresponsibility.[70] Unlike former conservatives who had long claimed that the personal and cultural choices of low-wage Black families were the reason for their poor living conditions, neoliberal conservatives like Kemp and Butler blamed the state. They criticized housing authorities and their employees for establishing the expectation that social welfare recipients—in this case, public housing residents—were victims taught to depend on the state for their housing. As Kemp said when he introduced the Urban Homestead Act, "Public housing discourages work and savings. . . . Tenants have little incentive to conserve utilities or properly maintain projects, and public housing authorities have just as little incentive to upgrade projects or fill vacant units since they get paid whether the unit is vacant or filled."[71] Kemp reasoned, "The mere act of homeownership transforms tenants, giving them a new sense of belonging and self-reliance. Homeownership encourages stable and intact families, creates a longer outlook on life and the future, and gives the poor new reasons to work and save. Homeownership can help give new life to the inner-city poor by promoting human dignity, personal achievement, and social stability."[72]

Kemp seemed to understand that this policy platform required a grassroots populist approach that included Black conservatives and public housing tenant activists like Kimi Gray. In his speeches to promote the Urban Homestead Act, Kemp characterized public housing managers as ineffective employees who benefited from an allegedly ineffective welfare state. In contrast, he identified public housing residents such as Kimi Gray as ideal frontline disciplinarians, people who were best positioned to implement the stringent management tactics needed to motivate tenants to behave responsibly. Kemp cited Kenilworth-Parkside as a shining example of the ability of public housing residents to reduce costs and transform resident behavior. Kemp rarely (if ever) shared the details of how Gray and her neighbors accomplished these outcomes. He left the policy defense work to Black conservatives and tenant leaders. In the congressional hearing for Kemp's bill, Cicero Wilson, a Black fellow at AEI, who, like Woodson, had a civil rights activist past, testified that in its first two years of operation, Kenilworth-Parkside's tenant management had increased rent collection and reduced crime, the number of teenage pregnancies, and the number of welfare recipients in the two public housing communities. The leaders had also established several tenant-run businesses on site. Wilson attributed their entrepreneurialism and poverty amelioration to their commitment to cultivating a work ethic that was presumed to be absent in the Black urban poor: "Residents were educated about their responsibilities to respect their neighbors, to keep the units and grounds clean, to reduce damage due to vandalism, and to pay their rent on time. Part of the residents' social responsibility included helping themselves and their children improve their skills and earning capacities. It is not acceptable to collect welfare and watch soap operas all day. There is a strong improvement ethic at work in Kenilworth-Parkside."[73] According to Wilson, Kenilworth-Parkside tenant leaders' approach to property management included behavior modification incentives like peer pressure alongside punishment tactics like fear and humiliation. Wilson explained,

In most apartment buildings, when an appliance has been destroyed by not being cared for properly, it is replaced with a new appliance. At Kenilworth the resident who destroys her stove by not cleaning it and letting fires burn in it is not rewarded with a new stove. That resident gets a used stove that once belonged to someone who took good care of it. Kimi will roll the new stove up to the poor house-keeper's door. She will then replace it with the well-maintained stove from a good housekeeper's apartment and the good house-keeper gets the new stove. That's an embarrassment for the poor housekeeper and it puts a lot of pressure on her to demonstrate that she, too, can take care of property.[74]

Wilson's remarks made plain the central role of psychological manipulation, shame, and conditional praise in Kenilworth-Parkside's "successful" management practices. That tenants expressed their resentment toward these invasive management tactics in other spaces seemed to matter little.[75]

Wilson and the Black public housing tenant activists invited to testify in support of the Urban Homestead Act believed that disciplinary housing governance was a necessary but unspoken provision in public housing policy. In the congressional hearing for Kemp's bill, witnesses presented Kenilworth-Parkside tenant leaders as bold practitioners of disciplinary housing governance. These tenants seemingly updated their version of disciplinary housing governance by blending management tactics used in private and public housing communities. For example, Kenilworth-Parkside tenants were issued fines similar to those found in suburban homeowner's associations. Building and court captains and management staff penalized tenants for littering, loitering in hallways, sitting on fences, and not cutting their grass. They also used the postwar public housing management model that used tenant screening protocols like personal interviews. Gray described the interview protocol: "We do a screening process. We come to your home. You're not accepted readily because you're making x amount of dollars. You're not accepted readily because you wear a three-piece suit and you come up here just saying, 'I can afford to live here.' No, that's not so."[76] Tenant leaders also implemented mandatory Sunday classes on housekeeping, budgeting, home repair, and parenting.[77]

Because these conditional measures were considered legal and objective business practices, few questioned their racial, gendered, and class implications. Moreover, the advocacy of Black political figures like Gray and Wilson gave the impression that Black people believed that discipline through punishment was the best mode of governance for the city's Black poor. Gray's social capital as a Black woman and valued community leader in urban public housing also helped legitimize the assumption that Black welfare-assisted families needed paternal oversight to contain their presumably unruly domestic spaces.

Gray's support of the Urban Homestead Act burnished Kemp's populist image too. Typically, conservative populists were known as defenders of economic nationalism, nativism, and segregation.[78] However, Kemp's alliance with Black leaders like Gray presented the Republican Party as a racially inclusive site of neoliberal populism. Notably, this political performance appropriated the leftist argument that lived experience was an important political factor in policymaking. In political alliance with Gray, white conservatives like Kemp and Butler could claim that tenant leaders knew their housing conditions best and were in the best position to identify the irresponsible tenants among them and administer reform and discipline. While these conservatives rightly chose to listen to Black tenant leaders, it was a selective hearing that only acknowledged the Kenilworth-Parkside management practices that were not different from those of landlords, property managers, and housing officials who insisted that Black poor people were the most undesirable tenant demographic. One wonders what nonpaternalistic management tactics could have been used if political leaders had not begun from a belief that residents of majority-Black public housing communities were deviant.

Yet Gray's independent political thinking was evident even as she partnered with conservative leaders. In another congressional testimony, Gray rejected conservative calls for more workfare. She also challenged the Reagan administration's slashing of social welfare programs. She stressed that government funding was crucial to Kenilworth-Parkside's early success with tenant management, insisting that her programs had been feasible only because she and her fellow leaders had negotiated to have the city cover utility expenses. She defended the welfare state and argued for a guaranteed employment model for the entire family. With a subtle nod to the Black worker justice campaigns of the late 1960s, Gray insisted the state should provide funds and employment opportunities in order to reduce Black poverty.

Although Gray expressed strong but qualified support for a welfare state, she still embraced a socially conservative perspective that linked access to public housing with heteropatriarchal domesticity. She emphasized that the owners of tenant-run businesses at Kenilworth-Parkside were required to train and hire other residents. She saw this model as a way to ensure that unemployed Black men, particularly, gained access to work. Sometimes referring to the program as "Bring the Fathers Out of the Closet," Gray believed that once unemployed Black men had jobs, they would regain their pride, choose to formally join a lease, and publicly partner with or marry the mothers of their children. Like some postwar sociologists who studied Black poverty, such as Daniel P. Moynihan and William Julius Wilson, Gray believed that the employment of Black men should be a prerequisite for marriage. Gray may have thought that marriage would strengthen heterosexual Black families. However, like these sociologists, Gray failed to recognize that changing cultural expectations about coupling meant that male unemployment was not the primary or sole reason why marriage rates declined among the Black poor and the working class generally.[79] Nevertheless, Gray seemed to believe that it was her role to reestablish an earlier management model that emphasized the honorable poor and treated public housing as a site of prestige and upward mobility.

Gray's valorization of heteropatriarchal households also signified a departure from the ideology of earlier welfare rights activists such as DC native Etta Horn. Where Horn rejected state intervention in Black domestic life, Gray believed that two-parent, heteronormative homes were essential for healthy children and communities.[80] Her version of welfare rights was more closely aligned with Black cultural nationalism, a movement that emerged in the late nineteenth century that celebrated Black pride and self-determination.[81] The movement's latest iteration in the 1960s experienced renewed popularity after Black-owned press and political leaders stressed that Black pride and collective uplift would best be achieved by adhering to strict gender ideologies. This, they argued, would empower Black men to reclaim their public role as leaders and financial providers and encourage Black women to anchor the domestic sphere appropriately.[82] Whether or not Gray subscribed to Black cultural nationalism, her perspective undermined welfare and tenant rights activism by suggesting that private domestic choices—for example, nuclear families—were enough to address the rising poverty Reagan's austerity policies caused.

The symbolic capital Gray provided in the conservative-driven debate on public housing reform ultimately garnered the support of many Democratic politicians. In 1984, Walter Fauntroy introduced HR 4026, a bill to amend the Housing Act of 1937. Fauntroy argued that it would incentivize the creation of more Kimi Grays in public housing. It specified that if a public housing community established a resident council, identified a management specialist to administer feasibility studies and/or tenant management training, and launched a resident management corporation, it would gain access to additional operating subsidies. The tenant management team could use any unspent subsidies for social services or other initiatives that resident leaders wanted to implement.[83] Soon after Fauntroy introduced his bill, he agreed to cosponsor a bill with Kemp to merge their legislative goals.[84]

The "Compassion" Issue: Conservative Optics, Market Logic, and Black Urban Poverty

Unlike members of Congress, Reagan's administration officials expressed significant concerns about Kemp and Fauntroy's legislative proposals. As early as 1981, HUD staff communicated their reservations about public housing homeownership. In the spring of 1984, a cabinet-level task force on housing that included HUD Secretary Pierce, Secretary of the Treasury Donald T. Regan, and Office of Management and Budget (OMB) director David Stockman met to discuss public housing ownership. While the task force supported the policy idea, participants agreed that its impact would be minimal. They based this opinion on the assumption that any public housing ownership program would need to adopt the same metrics used in private finance. The proposed public housing ownership program would use the Federal Housing Administration's (FHA) interest rate for mortgage loans (which in fiscal year 1985 oscillated between 9.5 and 10.52 percent) and would set sale prices based on the "current operating cost of the unit, plus property taxes and an allowance for replacements."[85] But according to the Section 5(h) provision that regulated public housing ownership, HUD agreed to pay the debt service while the tenant paid all operating costs. This led to a lower sale price. However, Reagan's budget advisors urged direct sales to public housing tenants, a calculation that meant only 1 percent of public housing residents could afford to purchase their homes, while another 1 percent could afford to purchase if HUD agreed to cover operating costs. Reagan's advisors also insisted that any presale expenses for modernizing housing units would have to be folded into a higher selling price.[86] Thus, in theory, no more than 2 percent of public housing residents would be eligible to participate in the homeownership program.

HUD's own research substantiated Reagan advisors' lukewarm response to Kemp and Fauntroy's proposal.[87] Research on HUD's 1984 public housing ownership demonstration program showed that only nine families had purchased their homes. There was plenty of evidence in DC to explain why the numbers were so low. Wylie Court, a twenty-eight-unit multifamily public housing community that had participated in the demonstration program, had opened in 1980 with the expectation that accepted tenants would purchase their homes. Although the District of Columbia set aside a portion of tenants' rent for future down payments, housing official Sidney Glee wanted potential homeowners to prove their readiness. To that end, Glee required applicants to undergo credit checks, and city workers inspected their prior residences and interviewed their current neighbors as well as personnel from their children's schools.[88] Applicants were also expected to attend counseling sessions and classes in homeownership and money management. Finally, applicants needed an annual income of at least $20,000—far more than the median income of public housing renters—and credit scores that were high enough to secure financing from local banks.[89] However, these requirements did not close the gap between applicants' wages and the contingency costs of homeownership. According to one journalist, the incomes of DC public housing residents were so low that many struggled to pay rent, let alone a down payment or fluctuating insurance premiums, property taxes, and maintenance costs.[90] An uncertain labor market and low wages meant that the city would have to cover the rent when accepted tenants lost their jobs before they had saved enough for a down payment.[91]

The limited feasibility of Kemp and Fauntroy's bill was not the only problem. Reagan's advisors wanted conservative policies that shrunk the size of the welfare state, not ones that created new constituents to defend its reproduction. They claimed that the successful passage of the bill would aid in "the development of unrealistic expectations about the program's potential" and intensify "pressures for deeper and deeper subsidies to expand the benefits not only for public housing tenants but for up to 11 million other low-income homeowners as well." Their apprehension was fueled by the realization that low-wage earners, the most likely to be in precarious work, would be unable to keep up with mortgage payments in an economic downturn, which would lead to a "probable high default rate of public housing tenants/homebuyers."[92] The advisors' concerns were not unfounded, as Kemp and Fauntroy's legislative proposal did call for more federal funding. Most likely as a bipartisan compromise, Kemp agreed to back Fauntroy's goal of supporting more tenant management associations by allocating more funds for unit modernization and operating subsidies to tenant management associations.

Reagan administration officials also believed that Kemp and Fauntroy's proposal ran counter to the administration's policy preference for public housing disinvestment. In Reagan's second term, HUD was tasked with further reducing federal funds for public housing by allocating money only to communities considered "economically and socially viable."[93] Viability would, in part, be determined by "comparing the cost of modernizing and operating the project as public housing" with the cost of housing vouchers.[94] The Office of Management and Budget estimated that executing this austerity strategy could save up to $300 million by 1989. If this austerity plan went into effect, Kemp and Fauntroy's proposal would have been promptly shelved because the OMB wanted HUD to only sell properties that were in good or excellent condition, a designation that applied to only 36 percent of the country's public housing; namely, newer communities built in the period 1974 to 1979. Without additional HUD funding, this stipulation would have excluded postwar public housing communities like Kenilworth-Parkside because years of deferred maintenance would have to be addressed first to qualify these properties for privatization.

It remains a mystery if Kimi Gray knew about these backroom debates about public housing ownership. However, because Gray and other advocates focused more on a tenant's character and behavior than on the market, their support for tenant management and public housing ownership ultimately represented their investment in the homeownership model. This stance did little to change the perpetuation of racial segregation, discrimination, and uneven development within the real estate industry.

Nevertheless, the symbolism of making the Republican Party appear responsive to Black urban poverty resonated with some of Reagan's top advisors. In February 1987, Jack Kemp penned a message to Donald Regan, the president's chief of staff, expressing disappointment that the administration had not endorsed the Fauntroy-Kemp bill. Noting that "President Reagan was right on target when he said in 1985 that 'It's time that all public housing residents have the opportunity of homeownership,'" Kemp argued that in order to realize Reagan's vision, the administration needed to publicly endorse the bill in a show of support for privatization.[95]

In contrast to Reagan officials who opposed the Urban Homestead Act, Gary Bauer, Reagan's domestic policy advisor and director of the Office of Policy Development, saw Kemp's bill as a political opportunity to make Reagan more appealing to a broader voter base. Bauer, a "staunch conservative and abortion foe," wanted the Republican Party to project a conservative populist image—one that was responsive to the urban poor. He once explained, "We as conservatives have so far failed to show that our philosophy is the most relevant to poor and working-class people."[96] Prominent Democrats and civil rights leaders agreed, charging that the Reagan administration lacked sympathy toward the poor.[97] In response, advisors like Bauer advised Chief of Staff Regan to view the Urban Homestead Act as an opportunity to "address the 'compassion' issue."[98] Bauer saw tenant management and tenant ownership of public housing as a way to cater to a broader voter base of neoconservatives, the Christian right, and moderates who were sensitive to social issues. He also believed that community self-help initiatives such as tenant management and public housing ownership were the perfect conservative antidote to welfare and rising urban crime. He said, "Experiments allowing public housing tenants to buy or manage their own units show that that alone improves the lives of those families—the upkeep is better, there is less crime."[99] Bauer also hoped that if the Kemp-Fauntroy bill passed, Reagan could have a "great media event" in which he could "visit a new 'homeowner' as a result of our policies."[100] Chief of Staff Regan agreed with Bauer and directed his staff to work with Kemp to get the bill passed.

After several rounds of intense negotiations, the 100th Congress and the president passed the Housing and Community Development Act of 1987. Although Reagan and his advisors balked at the bill's high price tag and its provision of new federal housing programs, they supported it because it bolstered Reagan's image as a compassionate and racially inclusive populist leader.[101] Much of the original Kemp-Fauntroy bill made it into the final law, which gave resident councils the opportunity to manage their communities and offered the possibility of sale after three years of successful self-management. Eligible resident councils would also receive preferential access to renovation funds. However, the law required tenants who wanted to purchase their public housing units to turn to the private sector, not housing authorities, for financing.

The law rewrote HUD's public housing formula to still include austerity, another policy tenet of neoliberalism. It stipulated that HUD determine public housing funding based on the number of units the agency believed to be viable (e.g., cost-efficient) and in use rather than on the number of existing units.[102] The law also gave the federal government stronger powers to reprimand ineffective public housing authorities by reducing funds or enforcing other punitive measures. At first glance, these inclusions were uncontroversial and reasonable. However, when examined in the context of the fact that 98 percent of public housing residents were ineligible to purchase their homes, it becomes clear that the provisions made it almost impossible to broadly sustain public housing in the 1980s.

The Other 98 Percent: Austerity, Carcerality, and the Continued Decline of Public Housing

A management crisis lay at the core of conservatives' successful push for tenant management and public housing ownership. Across the country, scandals about public housing mismanagement kept hitting the airwaves. They included gut-wrenching stories of young children dying in public housing elevators that had been left inoperable, daytime shoot-outs, and Republican-appointed HUD officials issuing government contracts in exchange for kickbacks. These stories told a narrative that public housing was a cesspool of domestic turmoil and bureaucratic incompetence.[103]

The mismanagement of public housing was also present in the nation's capital. Even though 10 percent of the city's population lived in public housing, public housing governance fell into the proverbial backwaters of DC government. Static HUD funding, rising operating costs, and the limited income of tenants made it difficult to attract talented leaders to DC's public housing department. No longer was this position considered a steppingstone to political power, as it once was for Walter Washington and James Banks. By the 1980s, public housing leadership positions were viewed as jobs few wanted. DC's public housing executive had to haggle with HUD for limited funds to oversee the city's fifty-two public housing communities and deal with the fact that at least 25 percent of the city's public housing buildings were so badly deteriorated that it would cost the city $60 million to bring them up to code. With elderly women and single mothers and their children as the city's principal tenants, the public housing executive could not charge rents high enough to pay that $60 million maintenance price tag due to low incomes and flatlined welfare subsidies. In addition, it was an open secret that this public housing workforce had a troubling reputation of deceit. At least 40 percent of the city's public housing staff were known to be dishonest and corrupt because "they drink, steal, or are insensitive" to public housing residents.[104] The city's public housing culture of extraction and mistreatment also seemed to extend to some tenants. Some residents stole plumbing from vacant units to sell on the black market, while others stole from their neighbors.

In the wake of state disinvestment and chronic mismanagement, the underground economy deepened its hold on many public housing communities. Because of postwar segregationist politics, many of the city's majority-Black multifamily public housing communities had been placed near highways or jurisdictional boundaries, locations that later offered benefits to small-time drug dealers. For example, East Capitol Dwellings suffered from rising crime because its closest intersection at Southern Avenue and Fifty-Seventh Street SE was one of the city's largest open-air drug markets. Because it was next to the city's boundary line, sellers who needed to flee had an escape route; local reporters noted that the market's location enabled sellers to easily elude the police. Some drug dealers built markets next to public housing that sold to the market's poorest clientele. Local reporters explained that sellers would "stand on the corner and brazenly shout 'get that wacky weed' [marijuana sprayed with PCP, an animal tranquilizer]; 'Nickle bags of heroin'; and 'loose joints, grab some smoke.' . . . to lure passersby."[105]

Public housing's sizeable youth population also made public housing an attractive site for illicit drug distribution. Even though Mayor Marion Barry amassed a great deal of public support because of his popular summer youth employment program, at least half of the city's youth remained unemployed. Most of the city's unemployed youth did have access to positive recreational outlets like attending go-go concerts, school-related activities, and student-led community groups like College Here We Come. Some young people, however, were enticed by the potential status, profits, and leadership opportunities in the illicit drug economy.[106] Political scientist Clarence Lusane notes that DC's illicit drug trade expanded during the Vietnam War. After the war, illicit drug sales and use were mainly covert, often taking place in private residences. When such transactions happened in public, they were limited to locales near popular entertainment districts like U Street. However, by the end of the 1970s, crews of neighborhood youth—who had turned away from their brief involvement in organizations like Black Power and community defense groups—had begun to embrace and expand drug distribution.[107] Because the underground drug economy was inherently illegal, organized drug cartels increasingly saw youth as a replenishable yet disposable labor force with a short shelf life due to the likelihood of arrest, death, or other forms of labor attrition.[108]

Notably, in congressional discourses about the need for public housing reform, Black mothers in public housing were often blamed for their children's involvement in the underground economy. Some even charged that it was single Black mothers who made it possible for the illicit economy to expand because, according to one public housing executive, single (Black) mothers are a "very fragile base on which to build a community."[109] However, this blame-deflecting narrative about single Black motherhood ignored how public housing residents, including single Black mothers and their families, were often victims of the extractive business tactics of the underground economy.

Glo, a native Washingtonian born in the 1950s, shared how this was the case. In the 1970s, Glo became a successful hustler, at first distributing high-end cocaine and marijuana to wealthy clients. Glo joked, "My husband called himself a hustler, but he was using drugs. I would just sit back and be fly and go to the go-gos, then I got a connect."[110] This connection sold her cocaine, which allegedly was 98 percent pure. Once she met this supplier, Glo set out to become a better drug dealer than her partner. Glo preferred the wealthier clients she had access to through contacts she established while working in local and federal government jobs as a typist. In order to elude detection, Glo enlisted friends and trusted aides who moved the drugs from different homes, usually private residences. In public housing, however, dealers forced their way in. Glo explained, "Most of them [dealers in public housing] were hustlers who came in from out of town. We had the Jamaicans in the 80s and 90s. People coming down from New York." To get access to public housing, Glo said, dealers would find "a girl that is strung out." The dealers would typically find a woman who was on the drug that dealers preferred to sell and use her addiction as a means to move into the unit and distribute drugs on site or nearby. Dealers would sometimes treat these substance users as testers for new or cheaper drugs in order to keep them addicted. Once inside certain public housing communities, Glo elaborated, "you really [didn't] give your product to a junkie"; instead, "you [gave] your products to lieutenants, and most of them came from middle-class areas [not public housing]."

To support her argument, Glo cited Rayful Edmond, a young Black man who gained fame and fortune from his growing drug empire in Washington, DC, in the 1980s.[111] Based in DC's northeast quadrant and raised in a two-parent household with parents who also had a history in the illicit drug trade, Edmond used his lieutenants to get a foothold in the city's public and assisted housing and on major thoroughfares such as New York Avenue. These lieutenants frequently deployed low-grade entrapments like addicting residents to certain drugs or selecting young Black women in public housing to be their sexual partners and used those relationships to distribute drugs near or in public housing.[112]

Glo's commentary on the spatial and hierarchical networks of drug distribution suggests that women in public housing were seen as malleable, exploitable, and disposable pawns in the expansion of the illicit drug economy and were sometimes treated this way by Black people in relatively better economic circumstances. Yet even as Black women and their families were unable to control drug distribution, they bore the weight of the public's rage and fear at the expansion of the illicit drug economy in the United States.

The public's frustration with visible drug use in public housing made it ripe for punitive backlash in the 1980s. HUD Secretary Pierce argued that many urban public housing authorities mismanaged public housing and failed to curb crime and irresponsible behavior like illicit drug use. In the spring of 1984, HUD's inspector general indicted the country's seventy-one largest public housing authorities, claiming that they had underreported tenants' incomes in order to secure more federal subsidies.[113] In September 1984, HUD released an audit of DC's public housing authority and found that officials had been lax about rent collection and that buildings had fallen into such disrepair that over 1,400 units were left vacant. Moreover, some of these units were used to conduct illegal activities while over 13,000 applicants waited years to gain entry to public housing.

HUD threatened cuts if the city did not improve its public housing management and curb the poor behavior of troublesome tenants. HUD's threat felt real to DC officials since the department provided almost half of their public housing budget. Hoping to halt further HUD intrusion, Mayor Barry shuffled DC's public housing leadership for the fourth time. In 1980 to 1984, Barry had appointed at least three different heads to the Department of Housing and Community Development (DHCD), the housing agency that included public housing. Barry hoped that appointing Madeline M. Petty as the DHCD's first Black woman director would appease HUD. It had the opposite effect. In March 1986, Pierce sent HUD's public housing official James Baugh to work with DC administrators to correct the seventy infractions HUD had found in its audit of DC's public housing.[114]

HUD's disciplinary moves prompted Barry to respond with a conservative move of his own—he threatened mass evictions for lease infractions. In June 1986, Barry held two press conferences to announce the city's corrective responses, including a plan to evict public housing tenants behind in their rent and tenants who opened their homes to family members and friends not added to their leases. Barry claimed that up to 40,000 individuals in public housing were living off the lease. Housing officials insisted that this stunning number was partially to blame for the rapid decline in the conditions of public housing buildings since these unapproved tenants resulted in higher utility and operating costs. Barry said, "I sympathize with people who need housing, but the District cannot do it all," adding that most cities cannot afford to house their entire poor population.[115] He added after the city evicted these unofficial public housing residents, the city would not help them find housing.

Barry invited Kimi Gray to join him at his second press conference about his plan for mass evictions. There, he averred, "I think it is only proper and fair that we take them [tenants with rent arrears and individuals not on the lease] to court and evict them. Evict them. Now, that may sound kind of harsh, but how do you break this cycle of dependency—of drugs, crime, and poverty—unless you have this kind of self-help direction?"[116] He pointed to Gray, noting that she agreed with him and castigated those "mushy-headed" liberals who refused to accept the seriousness of the problems in public housing, which included welfare dependence and illegal activities. According to Gray, Barry's proposal offered hope because "public housing should not be treated as the last resort." Gray believed that Barry's plan would impact few since only "5 to 10 percent" of public housing residents "do not adhere to their lease."[117] According to Gray and Barry, these undesirable few were not victims but perpetrators. Barry suggested that they were drug dealers, squatters, and thieves. These lease-breakers, Barry said, represented the undesirable Black underclass. He asserted, "If we don't turn this around—particularly in the Black community—we are going to have nothing but chaos in the next 40 years."[118]

Barry's threat of mass eviction was evidence of a turn among Black liberal politicians toward an embrace of a carceral response to the urban Black poor. Barry's civil rights past, which had been shaped by campaigns in which he criticized the racist American government and advocated more welfare state investment, was now complicated by his adoption of punishment and police as preferred state responses to the city's economic and social inequities. Local Black politicians like Barry pushed progressive challenges to market failure and state neglect to the margins of political debate in favor of neoliberal arguments for withholding government assistance and meting out punishment.

While it remains unclear if Barry would have chosen a different policy response if Reagan's administration did not enforce austerity and punishment as its default policy stance, it is clear that residents felt helpless about the city's descent into disinvestment and crime. Former Black public defender James Forman Jr. captured this sentiment in his work on the embrace of carceral solutions in the 1980s among Black residents of DC.[119] Fear, anger, and disillusionment pushed many residents like Gray to support calls of police and local officials for carceral solutions to the underground economy. For these community leaders, carcerality—a valorization of surveillance, punishment, and prisons—became an essential means of compelling the behavioral compliance of the urban Black poor.

Nevertheless, this shifting governance focus toward punishment downplayed the structural realities of urban poverty. While Barry characterized structural explanations for rule breaking as naiveté, liberal critics of his proposal countered that there were degrees of rule breaking. For example, *Washington Post* columnist Dorothy Gilliam argued, "The fact is, many of these illegal tenants fall into special categories that deserve consideration. Some are teen-age or young adult mothers who, with their babies, are residing with their parents. Others are young unemployed men living with their mothers. While an additional baby or a son forced back to his mother's home might constitute additional people in a given home, and while their names may not be on any official lease, they certainly do not fit the description of people defrauding the city by living in public housing."[120] Gilliam did not address two other categories of rule breakers: families who opened their units to boarders and residents who used drugs. In the context of federal cuts to means-tested welfare, it is not surprising that some families commodified access to public housing. Because poverty engenders intergenerational cohabitation and often requires families to pool resources, cash-strapped families frequently took in boarders, a long-accepted practice in the private housing market. For some families in public housing, their homes were one of the few assets they could exchange for resources.

Barry's call for mass eviction soon came to an anticlimactic end. His proposal collapsed under the weight of federal austerity and political resistance. The city's top US marshal said that his office could not carry out the number of estimated evictions because of federal cuts. Other city leaders challenged the feasibility of the measure, with some city council members contending that Barry's proposal was poorly conceived. Housing advocates criticized Barry for his insensitivity, given that the city was undergoing a growing homelessness crisis. As a result, the city said it would mail warning letters to 4,000 tenants, the new number of potential lease breakers.[121]

Black Women Tenant Managers and the Conservative Carceral Agenda

Even though Barry's attempt to enact a punitive response to public housing residents did not succeed, the federal government intensified its carceral response in public housing communities. Reagan administration officials wanted to make it easier to evict public housing households accused or convicted of illicit drug use. However, they had to challenge the legacy of tenant victories in the 1960s and 1970s. During this time, tenants had succeeded in winning legal protections, such as grievance hearings to ensure due process. For Reagan officials, this was another example of a flawed judicial system that protected rule breakers.[122] As conservative elites had done with public housing homeownership reform, Reagan officials and other Republican leaders looked for Black-led local models that backed easier evictions.

Republican leaders soon found Vincent Lane, a Black public housing executive who defended easier evictions. A Chicago native who had once lived in public housing, Lane eventually headed one of the country's largest Black-owned real estate firms. In 1988, he was appointed to run the Chicago Housing Authority (CHA), where he pioneered aggressive policing tactics in public housing.[123] One of the CHA's most well-known policing initiatives was Operation Clean Sweep, which was described as an aggressive program that often included warrantless and unannounced inspections of every public housing unit, blocking access to common areas, evicting households where any drug-related activities were suspected, requiring government-issued photo identification for entry, and tenant-led security patrols. It also included beautification and youth programs directed by tenants.[124]

Kemp eventually tapped Lane to advocate a similar enforcement program for all public housing communities. After President George H. W. Bush was elected in the fall of 1987, he appointed Jack Kemp as HUD secretary. Once in office, Kemp added Lane's program as another example of his neoliberal populism. He praised Lane and considered Operation Clean Sweep a "progressive" and "innovative" policy.[125] After he identified Chicago's anti-drug initiative (which soon was ruled unconstitutional) as ideal, Kemp presented a ten-point plan to "drive out the drug dealers" and users from public housing in a 1989 congressional hearing. His plan blended aspects of the crime-reduction strategies of Vincent Lane and Kimi Gray. It called for "tightening security by quickly evicting illegal tenants, furnishing legitimate residents with I.D. cards, repairing public areas, and training guards."[126] It also included waiving "unnecessary Federal Lease and Grievance Rules to evict tenants engaged in illegal drug activities" since HUD no longer required "duplicative administrative lease and grievance proceedings when due process protections are fully afforded by State or local law." "Kemp's plan invited "US Attorneys to seize apartments of drug dealers and users and return them to legitimate law-abiding tenants," and "encourage[ed] resident management and homeownership efforts."[127] Kemp added, "I am asking Kimi Gray of the Kenilworth-Parkside project and other tenant management leaders to tour with me and teach residents how to remove drug dealers and manage projects."[128] With this statement, Kemp gave his initiatives a populist imprint and once again, Kimi Gray served as the ideal grassroots defender of uncompromising rule enforcement. Kemp added that he hoped that Black women public housing leaders would develop partnerships with youth groups like Boys and Girls Clubs to provide recreational alternatives to the illicit drug trade.

Kemp's carceral policy proposal for public housing existed in a national context where many urban local officials like Barry willingly increased police presence in working-class neighborhoods with illicit drug use. For example, in the summer of 1986, DC launched an anti-drug initiative.[129] DC's assistant police chief, Isaac Fulwood Jr., admitted that arrests and seizures of assets often targeted the poorest consumers of illicit drugs.[130] As he said in September 1986, "If you come into the District and buy a nickel bag of marijuana, and we see you and stop you and you are the owner of that car, we are going to seize that vehicle. We have to make [drug dealing] unprofitable, and when you take people's cars, you're telling them you're turning the volume up and increasing the risks."[131] Fulwood's comments were not unique and reflected a national trend toward urban officials expanding police powers in response to the recreational use of illicit drugs among the Black poor.[132]

Nevertheless, Kemp's legislative plan for easier public housing eviction and increased police presence affirmed the federal government's fusion of disciplinary housing governance with carcerality. But austerity once again tempered Kemp's plan. He was unable to increase HUD's budget because of President Bush's hardline stance on continued welfare austerity. With no forthcoming funding, Kemp recommended reallocating modernization and operating funds to support the anti-drug priorities in his plan. If localities were torn between spending money on maintenance or on anti-drug initiatives, Kemp wanted them to prioritize anti-drug policing.

Black women like Kimi Gray served the symbolic purpose of legitimizing HUD's austerity while furthering the government's carceral reach. What was ironically telling about Kemp elevating Gray was that she took pride in Kenilworth-Parkside's low eviction rate, especially since she and her team put so much emphasis on character vetting.[133] However, when someone at Kenilworth-Parkside was accused of selling or using drugs, Gray and her fellow tenant leaders gave thirty-day eviction notices. But before issuing the writ of eviction, Kenilworth-Parkside leaders usually met with the leaseholder (usually a mother or grandmother) and advised them that they should tell the accused family member to leave their unit or take the risk that tenant leaders would use their legal connections to make sure that the eviction case for their household was given priority.[134] For Kenilworth-Parkside's tenant management, peer pressure and contacts in the legal system were the preferred and most effective crime-reduction tactics.

Once again, it is unclear if Kenilworth-Parkside tenant leaders understood the emotional and financial toll the expanding carceral state would take on their public housing community. With each arrest, public housing families experienced aspects of a social reproduction crisis. Numerous families were separated, saddled with debt, pulled into a complex legal system, and evicted. Low-wage Black women often were expected to provide the emotional and domestic labor (and sometimes resources) their families needed to negotiate and navigate the painful experience of entanglement in the carceral system.

DC and Beyond: Tenant Management Falls out of Political Favor

Kimi Gray's golden girl status in Republican-driven public housing reform had dimmed by the 1990s. Eventually, Gray's public housing ownership plan encountered the political realities of austerity. Kenilworth-Parkside residents had long envisioned a housing cooperative for their community and hoped that the Housing and Community Development Act of 1987 would finally provide the means. The Republican stance on limiting operating expenditures meant that tenants had to get private financing, which meant higher costs and other hurdles.[135] As Gray wrestled with these challenges, the press began questioning the favoritism bestowed upon Kimi Gray and Kenilworth-Parkside, especially as other public housing communities were languishing. In 1991, the community fell under the scrutiny of investigative journalists who began asking questions about the cost of Kenilworth-Parkside's redevelopment, which they estimated ran over $60 million. This was a steep price tag under any circumstances, but the fact that both Reagan and Bush had discouraged new public housing construction—which, while not cheap, would have cost $50,000 to $75,000 per unit compared to the $130,000 spent on those at Kenilworth-Parkside—made it especially noteworthy.[136]

In the political context of federal austerity, the high cost of redevelopment at Kenilworth-Parkside eventually pushed even the staunchest conservative allies away from tenant management. David L. Caprara,

HUD's deputy assistant secretary for resident initiatives, acknowledged that "Kimi Gray is a national hero." But, he added, "Kenilworth is not a prototype," arguing that HUD could rehabilitate public housing for far less money.[137] What remained unsaid but was implied was that the community's tenant leaders did not have the income or the technical expertise to negotiate the private housing industry efficiently. Specifically, neoconservative Robert Woodson's advocacy group, the Center for Neighborhood Enterprise, knew that Kenilworth-Parkside's move to tenant ownership via a limited equity cooperative would work only if each tenant owner earned $12,500 annually, if the building was 95 percent occupied, and if a nearly $5 million operating reserve was established.[138] To keep up with the rising costs of maintenance, tenants' incomes would have to increase by 6 percent each year and every tenant would need to buy their apartment. But conservatives who supported the project glossed over these inconvenient facts when Republican leaders held a press conference in 1988 about the possibility that tenants at Kenilworth-Parkside could eventually earn incomes high enough to turn their community into a limited-equity cooperative.[139]

Tenant participation in public housing policy was not a priority for Democratic President Bill Clinton in the 1990s. His administration preferred professional bureaucrats over community leaders. Notably, HUD secretary Henry Cisneros distanced himself from public housing ownership and tenant management, preferring the concept of "tenant participation" and only "where it is voluntary, wanted and appropriate."[140] The Clinton administration valued the technical expertise of public housing executives like Vincent Lane over the grassroots experience of tenant leaders like Kimi Gray.

The Democrats' turn away from grassroots leaders was aided by an increase in investigative reports about tenant managers' mismanagement and corruption. In 1996, St. Louis unfortunately earned a national spotlight when two of the city's remaining public housing tenant management groups, at the Carr Square and Cochran Gardens communities, were reprimanded for improper bookkeeping and misconduct. The tenant management group at Carr Square was caught not paying private contractors. The situation at Cochran Gardens proved more scandalous. Investigative journalists discovered that tenant management board chair Bertha Gilkey had used the board's credit cards to purchase goods for personal use and for the consulting firm she had established to teach other public housing residents about tenant management.[141]

The fall of Bertha Gilkey was symbolic of the decline in political support for tenant management. Gilkey, who was born in 1949 in Round Pound,

Arkansas, moved with her family to St. Louis in 1960. They were one of the first Black families to integrate Cochran Gardens. By the late 1960s, the tenants were primarily elderly residents and single Black mothers with children. Gilkey felt that the St. Louis housing authority was ignoring the public housing community. At the time of the 1969 rent strike, Gilkey described herself as a Black Panther. She was practicing Black power by procuring grants to run daycare centers at Cochran Gardens. When the city finally delegated management responsibilities to tenants in 1976, Gilkey was elected as the management team's unpaid chair. Her team's responsibilities slowly grew until the St. Louis Housing Authority approved a management transfer in 1992. At that time, Gilkey, as chair, presided over a paid staff of forty-seven and a five-member tenant board of directors. Unlike at Kenilworth-Parkside, not all the staff resided at Cochran Gardens; the manager, accountant, and engineer were outside hires.[142]

As he did with Kimi Gray at Kenilworth-Parkside, Jack Kemp pointed to Bertha Gilkey and her work at Cochran Gardens as examples of neoliberal populism. Kemp was fond of saying, "Bertha Gilkey is living testimony to the idea that when people have access to power and control over their own lives—and some assets to go with it—that changes attitudes, alters behavior."[143] In the public spotlight and at congressional hearings, Gilkey, like Gray, embraced disciplinary and carceral responses to irresponsible Black tenants. When Cochran Gardens acquired additional funding for updated blinds, Gilkey promptly stated, "Poor housekeepers ain't getting no window blinds. They got to go through a housekeeping course." If tenants broke the rules by selling or using drugs, Gilkey unabashedly enforced evictions, even when it was her brother or her mother's best friend, noting, "It wasn't personal. They knew the rules."[144] Her uncompromising stance notwithstanding, Gilkey's dedication to Cochran Gardens endeared her to her neighbors. Gilkey's decades-long tenure as management team chair and tenant leader earned the respect of her neighbors for her commitment to living there despite her rising economic and political status.

However, in a sad and ironic twist of fate, Gilkey was subjected to the carceral reach she had willingly subjected her fellow tenants to. In addition to her work at Cochran Gardens, Gilkey had established a tenant management consulting firm and earned around $30,000 annually (equivalent to $63,351 in 2025). In 1998, she was discovered using credit cards that had been issued to the Cochran Gardens tenant board to purchase over $33,000 of goods for herself and her consulting firm. Gilkey pleaded guilty to embezzlement in 2002, and after a lengthy investigation, US attorneys found that she had misused HUD funds too.[145] Despite her protests, Gilkey was forced to move out of Cochran Gardens and resign from her positions on the tenant boards at both Cochran Gardens and the St. Louis Housing Authority. In response to her mismanagement, the city's public housing authority terminated its management contract with the Cochran Gardens Tenant Management Corporation and fired the remainder of its employees.[146]

During the same time as Gilkey's ordeal in St. Louis, a high-profile tenant management group, Bromley-Heath, suffered a similar fate in Boston. Bromley-Heath was established in 1973 in Boston's Jamaica Plain neighborhood as the country's first tenant management corporation. Like Gray and Gilkey, Bromley-Heath's chair, Mildred Hailey, was a beloved tenant activist who took charge. Over the years, she helped her community negotiate rents, hire their security force, and establish an onsite health care clinic and drug treatment program. She also conducted beautification campaigns and demanded that management responsibility be transferred to residents.[147] However, for years, residents and some workers had complained that the illicit drug trade operated in the community with little pushback from the tenant management board. In 1998, after two years of undercover surveillance, police raided the 1,200-unit public housing community and arrested thirty-eight people, including two of Hailey's grandsons. Shortly after the raid, the Boston Housing Authority said that the decision to end its contract with the tenant management corporation was overdue.

Although these high-profile scandals did not spell the end of tenant management, they certainly tempered enthusiasm for the concept. By the late 1990s, HUD officials rarely spoke about tenant management and public housing ownership, even if they publicly embraced the ideas. Important aspects of tenant management and public housing ownership had been enshrined in HUD's Homeownership and Opportunity for People Everywhere (HOPE) program. But these measures took a backseat in HOPE VI, which called for the demolition of public housing and the redevelopment of these communities into mixed-income neighborhoods.

· · · · · ·

As feminist and urban studies scholars have pointed out, liberals who have supported the expansion of carceral responses and welfare reform have relied on curated or exploited optics of Black consent.[148] Likewise, conservative advocates for public housing ownership and tenant management in the 1980s employed an explicit strategy of racial and gendered imagery. A Black feminist materialist analysis reveals the importance of a racialized analysis of social reproduction and its tendency to blame the poorest Black families for social reproduction crises. During the 1980s, the bipartisan consensus was that social reproduction crises should ideally be dealt with by individuals. Racialized carceral responses made the social reproduction crises of public housing disinvestment, welfare austerity, and illicit drug markets worse for poor Black people. Representational politics obscured this racialized analysis of social reproduction crises because political elites selected and highlighted "exceptional" models of Black respectability among the Black working class to contrast them with the undesirable "welfare queen" caricatures who were blamed for the continued decline of public housing. Symbolically, Gray was portrayed as an honorable and thus exceptional low-wage Black woman—a position that political elites conferred on her only because they saw her as a grassroots defender of carcerality and disciplinary housing governance. However, her actual politics were often far more complicated, and at Kenilworth-Parkside, Gray remains a beacon of enduring inspiration. Significantly, her family and friends have maintained the community as one of the country's only operating tenant management teams.

Despite the constraints that political realities imposed on Gray and other Black women tenant leaders, their hope and determination to improve their communities deserve respect. The country's practice of uneven racialized development produced the negative consequences of the illicit drug market and disinvestment in public housing. It is impressive that tenant leaders such as Gray believed that community self-determination via tenant management could counter these structural forces. This belief in the power of community self-determination is a testament to their resilience and empowerment. Sadly, federal austerity undermined their ability to fully realize their vision. In the wake of their political defeat, Black women in public and assisted housing faced another structural force: capital recapture. In the decade when tenant management faded into political obscurity, Black women public housing tenant leaders in DC would have to fight not just to contribute to low-rent housing politics but also to remain in a city that was economically under siege.

5 Like Middle-Class People without Money

Urban Growth Politics and the Return of the "Honorable Poor" at the Turn of the Twenty-First Century

. . . .

Jacqueline Williams, who had dreamed of becoming a nurse in childhood, probably never thought she would come to symbolize the growing support for punitive welfare reform in Washington, DC. Williams emerged as a central figure in DC's battle to control its spiraling welfare costs in the late 1980s. In March 1987, Mayor Marion Barry met her while visiting the Capitol City Inn, a motel his administration paid hefty fees to to house the swelling number of homeless families in the District of Columbia. A pregnant Williams approached Barry and told him that she and her husband were struggling to find an affordable home that was large enough for their household of sixteen. According to Williams, Barry replied with the admonishment, "Why don't you stop having all these babies?" Stunned, Williams dismissed Barry's loutish comment, responding "I don't intend to stop until God stops me."[1] She saw her decision to give birth to fourteen children as her business and that his decision to become mayor made it his responsibility to help all residents find affordable shelter. Their encounter was brief and Williams considered the matter closed. Barry saw it differently. A few months later, the mayor casually brought up the story during a press conference, depicting Williams as the epitome of what was wrong with DC's growing Black poor: they turned to the government to subsidize irresponsible personal choices, like having fourteen children.

For the next several months, local media had a field day questioning Jacqueline Williams's reproductive choices and condemning her view that the city should help her find affordable housing. The debate reopened class fissures in DC's Black community. Some agreed with Barry that Williams was just another example of welfare-dependent Black women "who can't take care of themselves and their children."[2] For William Raspberry, the socially conservative Black columnist for the *Washington Post*, Jacqueline Williams represented the problem with DC's approach to welfare. "Public welfare and public housing," Raspberry wrote, "conceived as emergency assistance for those temporarily out of luck, become rewards for indigence. The only eligibility requirement for the prize is economic failure." He added, "We keep pretending that we expect public housing or welfare clients to behave more or less like middle-class people without money, and yet we almost deliberately disconnect them from the reward/punishment assumptions that guide middle-class decisions."[3] His argument deployed a conservative interpretation of economic disparity that posited that class was shaped not by state or capital but by a series of personal decisions that justified the hierarchical sorting of Americans based on social expectations—in this case, middle-class ideologies of reproductive morality. By Raspberry's logic, people become middle class by making correct choices, such as maximizing tax code benefits or earning more income, not by taking advantage of options that should come as a last resort, like welfare.[4]

Finding common cause, white Washingtonians seized the opportunity to portray Williams as a prime example of the "gimme mentality" that presumably ran rampant among (Black) welfare recipients.[5] White feminist *Washington Post* columnist Judy Mann claimed that it was ignorant of Williams to expect "taxpayers to take care of her" after choosing to have fourteen children.[6] Mann's position contrasted starkly with radical Black feminist arguments that reject corporate and public policies that "deny people the right to control their bodies, interfere with their reproductive decision making, and, ultimately, prevent many people from being able to live with dignity in safe and healthy communities."[7] Mann characterized Williams's demand for safe, affordable housing as simply another burden on taxpayers who took the more socially appropriate route of using birth control and engaging in paid labor.

This local debate died down after Williams appeared on Phil Donahue's popular talk show in July 1987 alongside Mayor Barry and poverty sociologist Mary Jo Bane. While the episode was more or less a public confessional in which Donahue asked Barry to apologize to Williams for his insulting comments, it also served as a referendum on welfare. Barry and others argued that reform was necessary to prevent the creation of a permanent (Black) underclass.[8] Despite Barry's position, his administration upheld its duty to serve residents in need and eventually found a seven-bedroom home for the Williams family in a Northeast neighborhood. Williams received a Tenant Assistance Program (TAP) voucher and was expected to pay for utilities and part of the rent.[9]

In March 1990, Williams was thrust back into the public spotlight when the family was ordered to vacate their rent-assisted home. DC's housing department had deemed the property unfit for habitation due to unpaid utilities, unsanitary living conditions, and numerous housing code violations. Most of Williams's children were placed in foster care. Once again, the press shined an unfavorable light on Williams, portraying her as an undeserving welfare recipient and making a tabloid spectacle of her eviction and the loss of ten of her children. Mayor Barry was noticeably absent from the second round of media attention, as he was standing trial for narcotics use. Ward 7 councilmember and longtime affordable housing developer H. R. Crawford stepped in to lead the call for punitive welfare reform. Crawford demanded a welfare fraud investigation, arguing that Williams represented the worst type of welfare cheat—someone who was receiving public funds for food, housing, medical care, and childcare but had chosen not to pay her portion of the last three months' rent. Even though Williams maintained that she had withheld rent after her requests for maintenance fell on deaf ears, Crawford insisted that families like hers should not receive any more welfare assistance. He depicted Williams as the opposite of Kimi Gray, whom he depicted as an exemplar of the "deserving poor" who embodied "discipline, responsibility, cleanliness and hard work." Crawford claimed that "people all over the country are laughing at us" because of welfare recipients in DC like Williams.[10]

For Crawford and many others, Williams was both the modern embodiment of the gendered trope of Black tenant irresponsibility and the face of the undesirable Black poor. The media stories about Williams's wasteful expenditure of welfare resources generated shock and disgust, a reaction that left little room for critical discussion about Williams's poverty or the inadequacy of the stereotypical trope of a welfare queen. Jacqueline Williams was not a single mother. She was married. However, her first husband's unexpected passing had plunged the family into unplanned debt and her second husband was struggling to make ends meet as a restaurant cook. Her family's limited wages, unplanned life expenses, and rising household costs had pushed the family into deeper poverty.

The media did not spend much time analyzing the reasons for the social reproduction crisis Williams and her family were experiencing. The press mentioned only briefly that she had been married twice and that her current husband was unemployed. This indirect attempt to name Williams's husband as partially responsible for their family's poverty did not preclude placing the burden of the family's welfare scandal and punitive consequences squarely on Williams's shoulders. In the media's narrow social script, Williams was a "marked woman," seen only through the negative frames of welfare queen, Jezebel, and ineffective Black matriarch.[11]

Forced to carry the public humiliation of the family's social reproduction crisis, Williams was also expected to endure the psychological pain of the public's disgust.[12] Williams later stated that the scandal and the backlash she experienced threw her into a severe depression: "I have walked into the Safeway and people who don't even know me low-rated me. I stay in the house. I have no friends."[13] Those who mocked Williams publicly may have thought that discipline through social isolation and shame was a valid response to a woman whom they believed had exercised inappropriate entitlement to welfare.[14]

Williams's embarrassment and pain had indirect political consequences. The scandal helped silence other welfare-assisted families, demonstrating that those who unapologetically embraced a welfare rights stance rooted in (Black) reproductive autonomy would have few political allies. The backlash against Williams also illustrated growing public interest in reforming the city's welfare system to benefit the so-called honorable poor, a position that was expressed most prominently in the 1990s and early 2000s when the city simultaneously pursued urban growth and welfare reform.

This chapter traces DC's shift back to prioritizing welfare for the "honorable poor" during the city's federal receivership and subsequent economic resurgence. Under the federal government's watchful eye, city officials embraced urban growth policies, targeting public and assisted housing for demolition and redevelopment in order to concentrate wealth and disperse Black poverty. This relatively swift remaking of DC's demographic landscape relied on long-circulated dystopic renderings of welfare-assisted Black women and their families, which were contrasted with heroic renderings of middle-class households as desirable residential anchors and ideal welfare beneficiaries. In this context of economic revival, the city updated its model of disciplinary housing governance to demand that low-wage families mimic middle-class financial practices. This included high(er) credit scores, clean rental records, no criminal records, and consistent work histories alongside subjective assessments like proper housekeeping and appropriate parental practices. The result was unsurprising: welfare-assisted families struggled to remain in gentrifying areas where new affordable housing developments often privileged the "honorable poor," who were increasingly characterized as upwardly mobile, single young professionals and senior citizens. The city's affordable housing advocacy network failed to mobilize with the zeal of the 1960s and 1970s. Instead, affordable housing advocates grew more fragmented and silent about the racial and gendered ramifications of a gentrifying housing market and a political culture that normalized the exclusion of the "undesirable" welfare-assisted Black poor.

Budget Battles: Attacks on DC's Welfare State in the Early 1990s

The public's response to Williams's claim to rent-assisted housing took place within the national context of an intensifying attack against means-tested welfare and the welfare state. In the late 1980s, the world's geopolitical order changed, producing political cleavages for conservatives to push the national conversation about means-tested welfare and the welfare state further to the right. The revolutions of 1989 within the Soviet Union and its satellite states capped a decade of democratic revolutions and ended a nearly fifty-year Cold War with the United States and its allies. The Soviet Union's demise left the United States as the world's only superpower. Its military capability and economic force as the world's reserve currency buoyed the United States' hegemonic authority.

Many Americans might have felt the country's Cold War victory was more pyrrhic than triumphant.[15] In 1989, the country was heading toward another recession. The Federal Reserve's decade-long restrictive monetary policy eventually reduced American consumers' confidence in the economy.[16] Employers flatlined American workers' wages, prompting many to take on more personal debt to keep up with the rising costs of living. Meanwhile, Americans witnessed Reagan profess a politics of welfare austerity in order to balance the budget, only to watch him double the country's budget deficit while funding defense spending to safeguard US global dominance. To make matters worse, Reagan oversaw the deregulation of the savings and loans (S&L) industry by allowing it to participate in riskier speculative financial investments like commercial real estate to shore up profits. The move proved catastrophic, since many of these thrift institutions overindexed their funds in commercial real estate. This directly contributed to overbuilding, a profit dip, and a historic wave of S&L closures. The result was predictable: bankers reduced lending, employers laid off workers, unemployment grew, and the recession of 1990 set in.[17] In response to these economic struggles, President George H. W. Bush and Congress bailed out the industry with close to $124 billion of taxpayers' dollars to prevent the national collapse of the S&L industry.[18]

With a rising national debt and a weakened economy, conservative populists saw an opportunity to link the nation's hobbled condition to another debate about its priorities, including its commitment to welfare. Business-man and third-party presidential candidate Ross Perot politicized the country's trade deficit as un-American. He advocated taxes, budget cuts, and trade reform to ensure that the country maintained a balanced budget.[19] White supremacist turned Louisiana representative David Duke (R-LA) charged that the existing political establishment supported a welfare state that unfairly benefited Black Americans and immigrants of color instead of white Americans—the allegedly forgotten and deserving recipients.[20] While in office, Duke railed against welfare-assisted families, demanding massive welfare cuts and advocating drug tests programs for not only welfare recipients but also beneficiaries of food stamps and Medicaid.[21] Similar to Duke, conservative pundit Pat Buchanan accused certain conservatives of colluding with liberal elites. A former speechwriter for Nixon and communications director under Reagan, Buchanan embraced an older variant of conservatism called paleoconservatism. In contrast to neoconservatives' bullish calls for free trade and foreign intervention, paleoconservatives like Buchanan were seen as ultranationalists who promoted isolationism, economic protectionism, restrictive immigration reform, social conservatism, and the abolition of the welfare state.[22] Buchanan foresaw a battle within the Republican Party to make these policies its default agenda. He explained, "The first task of genuine conservatism is to throw off the neocon [neoconservative] control."[23] Then, Buchanan said, the Republicans could "roll back the New Deal" and "dismantle the welfare-warfare state of FDR [Franklin D. Roosevelt].[24]

This right-leaning debate about the welfare state and needs-based entitlements directly influenced the 1992 presidential election.[25] Hoping to regain Democratic control of the White House for the first time in twelve years, New Democrats, a centrist faction in the Democratic Party that began in 1985, insisted there was a "Third Way" to reform the welfare state.[26] This faction of ambitious young Democrats called for a governance model that moved away from New Deal liberalism. Rather than supporting welfare state expenditures as a way of reducing poverty and bolstering consumer spending, as Democratic Party primary nominee Jesse Jackson did in the 1980s, New Democrats adopted the negative and racially coded sentiment that conservatives long touted about welfare. Consistent with this perspective, New Democrats argued that welfare recipients needed to work or acquire formal education in exchange for state assistance. New Democrat and 1992 presidential candidate Bill Clinton became this governance model's most prominent proponent, promising voters nationwide that he would "end welfare as we know it."[27] Not only did Clinton embrace welfare reform, he also argued that the government could become more efficient and less costly if Democrats adopted market principles like growth and competition while implementing liberal principles of fairness and opportunity. New Democrats believed that in order to reduce the size of the welfare state, localities, particularly cities, needed to become engines of economic growth and compete for growing industries. Like Republicans, New Democrats argued that the return of the middle class to urban centers would bolster local economies and attract knowledge-based industries.[28] Lower taxes and fiscal conservatism would encourage these particular stakeholders to remain in select locales.

Once Clinton was elected to the White House in 1992, New Democrats sought to make their view the new governance standard of the Democratic Party. Relatedly, Republicans continued to press their policy stances on the welfare state—austerity, privatization, and punishment—but this time, in response to the welfare struggles of urban centers. New Democrats grew adept at reframing these welfare reform measures as colorblind and morally conscious, often using select Black officials or public housing property managers to champion their pro-market welfare reform measures.[29] This backdrop of changing views within the federal government about welfare reform shaped how local politicians in the nation's capital responded to its welfare state troubles.

The political autonomy of the District of Columbia was always fragile and contingent, leaving DC vulnerable to federal intervention. In exchange for limited home rule, DC was required to secure congressional approval for its annual budget and federal payments. Because of this, both Congress and the White House had an outsized role in the city's politics and management of its finances. Until 1990, the District had balanced its budget through higher taxes and municipal bonds that funded infrastructure and other public services. DC managed to balance its budget even though the federal government's payment stalled at the same amount for five years straight in the late 1980s. In 1990, two of the nation's leading bond rating firms, Moody's and Standard & Poor's (S&P), lowered DC's municipal bond ratings for the first time since the city began issuing them in 1984. S&P's and Moody's bond ratings gave investors information about the city's financial standing. To justify the lower rating, S&P pointed to DC's rising welfare costs, including an increase in funding for police and the city's failure to generate new revenue streams to offset the federal government's limited payments.[30] The implicit message was clear: DC officials needed to curb welfare spending or risk further lowered bond ratings and higher debt repayments.

Given mounting criticism from investors, Mayor Barry knew he could not continue to rely on deficit spending that could make the city insolvent by 1991.[31] Yet because of his trial for drug possession and perjury, which lasted from January to August 1990, he had few political allies, and Congress refused to provide additional funds to the city. Congress agreed to an emergency $100 million supplement and an increase of $200 million to the 1991 and 1992 federal payments only after Sharon Pratt Kelly, a Black DC native and a politically connected former Pepco executive, became mayor in 1991. Congress hoped that the new mayor would use these funds to restructure the city's welfare system by eliminating wasteful spending and administering services more efficiently.[32]

Even though Kelly agreed in theory with slashing welfare spending, she quickly learned that welfare politics required deft negotiation with multiple stakeholders, particularly city personnel. Personnel costs accounted for half of DC's $3 billion budget in 1991. Kelly believed that employee cuts were inevitable and proposed terminating 2,000 midlevel management jobs. Organized labor and its allies on the city council criticized Kelly's plan, asserting that the proposed cuts lacked a racial understanding of DC's economy, as they would disproportionally affect Black middle-class employees.[33] Black middle-class families were leaving DC at record levels due to high taxes, persistent street crime, and poor service delivery, and officials insisted that in that context, Kelly's proposed cuts sent the wrong message about whom the majority-Black government wanted to remain in the city. In the debate over personnel cuts, some city council members demonstrated that they understood the racial implications of these policy decisions, particularly when they impacted the middle class. In defending jobs related to the administration of the welfare state, officials effectively argued that the Black middle class was DC's desired core demographic and thus most deserving of the welfare state's largesse.

In the hierarchy of deservingness that emerged, welfare-assisted families like Jacqueline Williams's did not have state protection or public sympathy. Politicians and increasing numbers of middle-class residents complained that they were growing tired of the rising costs associated with caring for the social reproduction of low-wage families, an attitude described as "compassion fatigue."[34] As one *Washington Post* writer opined in February 1990, "Help people, and they may come back for second helpings. For many of us, there is a slow process by which a gift can begin to feel like an obligation, generosity can turn into resentment and sympathy can turn hard. How many have turned angry at problems that wouldn't stay solved, at people who wouldn't be cured?"[35] Under the weight of compassion fatigue, DC residents increasingly supported political calls for needs-based welfare cuts. This shift in public sentiment had profound consequences for the city's most vulnerable populations.

Unhoused people and those who received public assistance bore the brunt of the city's compassion fatigue. Black women and children were overrepresented in both groups. In the fall of 1990, DC residents first showed the limits of their compassion when they voted to abolish Initiative 17, a law that granted unhoused people the right to overnight shelter. After Initiative 17 was defeated, the city council pursued steep cuts to other homeless services, for example, by contracting out shelters to private companies and granting local institutions like schools the power to block new shelters from opening in their neighborhoods. DC could not cut the federally mandated programs of welfare provision, such as Medicaid and Aid to Families with Dependent Children (AFDC). Still, it aimed to balance its budget by slashing local welfare services, such as drug treatment programs, AIDS treatment programs, and assistance with the cost of daycare.[36] The city also discontinued cost-of-living adjustments for over 56,000 ADFC families.[37]

Steep cuts to means-tested welfare were not enough for the city to balance its budget. By early 1994, DC's debt had soared to over $500 million. Congress and municipal bond investors believed that the city's continued deficit spending was evidence of weak governance and Kelly's unwillingness to take the aggressive steps necessary to enforce welfare austerity and practice fiscal soundness. In an ill-fated attempt to find new revenue sources, Mayor Kelly tried to gain political support for tax-generated proceeds like a sewage tax and a commuter tax. Congress rejected both measures and demanded that the city focus on budget cuts. In the fall of 1994, Congress instituted a federal appropriations clause that required the city to slash $140 million from its budget and cut 2,000 full-time jobs.[38]

Local judges joined Congress in expressing a lack of confidence in Mayor Kelly's leadership. In the early 1990s, citizens filed lawsuits against welfare agencies for chronic mismanagement and poor service delivery. One example is a 1992 class action lawsuit filed by a legal team from the corporate firm Covington & Burling and the nonprofit organizations Neighborhood Legal Services and the Washington Legal Clinic for the Homeless against the District of Columbia Department of Public and Assisted Housing on behalf of 12,000 families on the city's waiting list. The suit stated that the average wait time for public housing was seven years and that public housing officials had failed to renovate DC's 2,000 vacant public housing units.[39]

Superior Court judge Steffen Graae appointed a special master in April 1993 to observe the attempts of the public housing department to correct its violations.[40] Over the next year, the special master watched the agency fall deeper into chaos. In the summer of 1994, a federally prosecuted case exposed a scheme in which DC housing staff accepted cash bribes in exchange for distributing housing vouchers to families willing to pay.[41] The case revealed that in 1990–1993, only ten of 400 federal housing vouchers were given to families who had gone through the proper channels.[42] This massive mismanagement scandal made the city's failure to reduce the vacancy rate in public housing, which was nearly 20 percent, even more galling. Judge Graae ultimately placed the Department of Public and Assisted Housing in receivership in August 1994.[43] That gave a court-appointed receiver sweeping authority, including the power to hire, fire, and evaluate staff; revamp service delivery; and ensure financial solvency. The receiver reported only to the court, which effectively removed the city's authority over the agency until Graae believed that DC could be successfully reinstated as a governing body.[44]

The judge's decision to impose external leadership on city governance signaled another shift in welfare politics. In the early 1990s, federal and local housing officials began to install a small group of court-appointed receivers for public housing authorities into public housing leadership positions.[45] This shift in leadership reflected the belief that transplanted agency specialists could take the politics out of governance and administer city services more efficiently. Following this trend, Judge Graae tapped David I. Gilmore to reform DC's Department of Public and Assisted Housing. Gilmore was a Boston native who had gained a national reputation after successfully removing public housing authorities in Boston, San Francisco, and Seattle from HUD's list of problem agencies.

In response to the possibility of court receivership, city officials tried to revive past experiments in disciplinary housing governance. Several months before Judge Graae issued his ruling, Mayor Kelly created a five-member executive board that consisted of HUD officials and local housing specialists, including former DC housing authority executive James Banks. She tasked the board with revamping public housing operations.[46] The board recommended behavioral management protocols that had been used in the past, such as a more stringent screening method for admission to public housing rather than needs-based eligibility protocols. The board also proposed that the public housing department contact landlords or staff at the previous residences of applicants (including homeless shelters) to evaluate applicants' housekeeping habits, to search for past evictions, and to check their criminal and credit records. Lastly, the board suggested that the department select suitable tenants to screen their potential neighbors.[47] It defended these recommendations by citing the city's past experience with such methods and the fact that public housing authorities in neighboring locales had implemented similar measures. For example, Prince George's County, Maryland, used evaluation of housekeeping as a precondition for access to public and assisted housing.[48]

Once again, DC's rehabilitative efforts seemingly relied on the cultural narrative that Black tenant irresponsibility was to blame for the city's mismanagement. Although the board refrained from citing specific cases, it agreed that domestic irresponsibility among public housing tenants exacerbated the department's problems. This discursive choice locked in certain outcomes. Instead of identifying potential signs of unstable tenant behavior to justify limited oversight in *specific* cases, the board presented a unilateral management mandate. The board recommended that most—if not all—public housing tenants prove their domestic management skills before accessing public housing. Gone were the days when tenant activists like Precious Smith and Etta Horn demanded tenant-responsive management practices that did not mandate domestic oversight.

Mayor Kelly's hasty attempt at public housing reform failed to sway local judges or public opinion about her leadership. In the fall of 1994, she lost the mayoral seat to Marion Barry, who had mounted a successful campaign that emphasized his rehabilitation. However, although many DC residents embraced Barry's return, Congress did not. Around the same time that Barry became mayor for the fourth time, city officials learned that DC's debt had jumped to $722 million as the costs of Medicaid and corrections facilities ballooned beyond expectations. Congress hesitated to give additional aid to a city that seemed to be in financial crisis.[49]

To complicate matters, in 1994, changes in leadership at the federal level meant a more uncompromising stance in Congress toward city officials. Republicans won majority status in both congressional chambers in that election. House speaker Newt Gingrich (R-GA), who was hailed as the leader of the "Revolution of '94," vowed to implement the Contract with America, an extensive list of Republican policy goals that ranged from welfare reform and anti-crime measures to the reform of government operations.[50] Shortly after their electoral victory, House Republicans began promoting a measure that would remove DC's ability to borrow from the US Treasury in emergencies.[51] This federal intrusion in local matters compelled Barry to negotiate for local autonomy.[52] Barry attempted to build bipartisan connections in Congress, hoping to receive support for more federal aid. However, members of Congress rebuffed him, insisting that DC's core problem was mismanagement and threatening to revoke the city's home rule entirely if it did not make cuts to its welfare agencies. To forestall a complete withdrawal of local authority, DC representative Eleanor Holmes Norton proposed a financial control board that would consist of five members appointed by President Clinton. On April 7, 1995, the 104th Congress voted to establish the board, giving it the power to reorganize city government, slash spending, and reject union contracts. It also had the power to veto Mayor Barry's nominations for chief financial officer, who was responsible for enforcing budget control, and inspector general, who conducted an annual audit of the city's finances.[53] Congress stated that it would not end its financial receivership until after the city had passed a balanced budget for four consecutive years, maintained a sizeable reserve, stabilized its credit, repaid all loans, and obtained the approval of the financial board.

After HUD secretary Henry Cisneros urged Barry to stop his campaign to prevent court receivership, David Gilmore took the helm of DC's beleaguered Department of Public and Assisted Housing in May 1995.[54] The combination of federal oversight and financial receivership meant that the city was now beholden to unelected officials who imposed their own agendas for welfare reform. Gilmore championed HUD's public housing reform priorities and Republicans executed their welfare reform agenda. For example, in the fall of 1995, the Republican-controlled Congress attempted to bully DC into ending rent control as a way of accelerating capital reinvestment.[55] The financial board also advocated for privatization of and sizeable cuts in personnel and government services. The board terminated the TAP voucher program because it was considered too costly, even though local officials and Republicans had once touted it as the preferred alternative to rent control.[56]

DC's Receivership Era: Disciplinary Housing Governance and the "Undesirable Poor"

Federal priorities became the city's default political agenda during its receivership era. This was especially true in public housing reform. In the early 1990s, HUD embraced a new approach: demolishing and redeveloping disinvested multifamily public housing. In 1992, Congress and HUD secretary Jack Kemp released a report published by the National Commission on Severely Distressed Public Housing. Public housing executive Vincent Lane and Representative Bill Green (R-NY) co-chaired the commission, which included Black women public housing tenant managers alongside business leaders and public housing executives like Gilmore.[57] The report ambitiously proposed a national action plan to demolish 86,000 "severely distressed" public housing units and turn the sites into mixed-income communities by 2000.[58] The Clinton administration accepted the report's findings, which outlined support for Homeownership and Opportunity for People Everywhere (HOPE) initiatives, including tenant management, extensive social services, and mixed-income redevelopment of public housing (the latter known as HOPE VI). In 1992, Congress allocated $50 million for HOPE VI grants.[59]

Gilmore implemented this federal agenda as the court-appointed receiver overseeing DC's public housing. But before he led HOPE VI redevelopment projects in the nation's capital, he shored up the department's infrastructure so it could deliver better service. Early in his tenure, Gilmore disbursed millions of dollars in modernization funds that the city had failed to distribute. Numerous public housing communities received upgraded appliances and renovated units. This move generated a great deal of good will and support from residents.[60] However, Gilmore's infrastructure upgrades were accompanied by a more significant investment in carceral measures. Following the passage of the Violent Crime Control and Law Enforcement Act of 1994 (popularly known as the Crime Bill of 1994), Gilmore enacted carceral initiatives in public housing that upheld the federal preference for being "tough on crime."[61] One of the most notable programs under his purview was Operation Safehome, an initiative that surveilled and arrested gang members who used public housing units as drug distribution sites.[62] He also evicted undocumented tenants and those who were delinquent with rent. The agency issued photo IDs to all building residents over the age of ten, reevaluated the eligibility of existing tenants, inspected every unit, installed No Trespassing signs on the premises, and established a local community group to dissuade future illicit activities.[63]

Gilmore's carceral measures helped expand the category of the undesirable poor. More specifically, Gilmore revived discussions about the demographics of preferred tenants as he promoted his eligibility reform initiative. In October 1997, Gilmore called for a new screening policy that banned anyone who had been convicted of any crime (including misdemeanors) and reduced access for nonworking families, whom he suggested should be counted among public housing's "undesirables." According to this new eligibility proposal, half of the vacant public housing in the city would go to "working families," 45 percent to nonworking families, and 5 percent to homeless people. Following the policy trend set by the federal welfare reform agenda, Gilmore and his staff argued that their proposal adhered to changes HUD had made in its regulations about desirable tenants in 1996. That year, Congress passed the Personal Responsibility and Work Opportunity Reconciliation Act, and HUD implemented a "one strike, you're out" policy.[64] The former limited the period a family could receive public assistance and linked that income to workfare, which required welfare recipients to work or participate in job training programs.[65] The "one strike" policy allowed localities to ban evicted tenants from future public or assisted housing residences. HUD encouraged localities to revise their tenant preference regulations to reflect these laws. Because less than 15 percent of the city's public housing residents earned taxable income, Gilmore believed it was poor management policy to prioritize unhoused or unemployed tenants over employed ones. He opined, "When you change the definition of who you admit, you get down to the most fundamental change that affects the agency."[66]

Discussions about tenant preference presented an institutional way to justify racialized and gendered class biases. Gilmore's "colorblind" proposal minimized consideration of the measure's disproportionate impact on low-wage Black women and their families. Instead, the proposal implied that DC might need to foster a higher tolerance for displacing poor (Black) and homeless people, as cuts in tenant assistance made it unlikely that the private housing market would reabsorb these families. Gilmore's proposal also suggested that individuals entangled in the carceral state had to be excluded from the city's reformed welfare state. That prospect did not sit well with some local tenant activists. Jacqueline Massey, a Black woman tenant activist who lived in the Valley Green public housing community in DC's southeast quadrant, disagreed with the proposal's outright ban on anyone convicted of a crime: "If you're going to re-try people for something they did in the past, that's not good business. All should be forgiven, and they should go on the [public housing] waiting list."[67]

HOPE VI and the "Undesirable Poor"

Battles about who preferred tenants should be had racial and gendered consequences for HOPE VI redevelopment projects. In 1993, HUD selected the 134-unit Ellen Wilson Dwellings as the first HOPE VI redevelopment site in

DC.[68] Located in Capitol Hill, where gentrification had brought more white professionals and homeowners back to the neighborhood years earlier, Ellen Wilson was one of the city's first public housing communities that was open to white families. However, Ellen Wilson became majority Black in the 1960s, shortly before HUD decreased operating support in the 1970s. Maintenance on the building declined, and officials were forced to close the property in 1988. The city initially planned to demolish the site, replace it with modern buildings and security, and implement stringent tenant-screening measures. However, DC's Department of Public and Assisted Housing did little to move redevelopment forward, and the property remained vacant until HUD stepped in with a HOPE VI grant in 1992.[69]

The prospect of HOPE VI funds emboldened local tenant groups to promote their differing visions for the redevelopment of Ellen Wilson. One group lobbied for a limited-equity cooperative for unhoused veterans. The short-lived campaign gained national attention in the fall of 1992, when activists—all homeless veterans themselves—squatted in the community's abandoned buildings for five days. They demanded inclusion in the redevelopment process and a guarantee that the new property would provide deep affordability and prioritize directly impacted individuals.[70] However, their attempt was unsuccessful. City officials wanted Ellen Wilson to be mixed-income, not an exclusively affordable project. That vision was shared by the Ellen Wilson Neighborhood Redevelopment Corporation—a politically influential, probusiness organization composed of local business executives, religious leaders, residents, and two former Ellen Wilson tenants.

Debates about the preferred tenants for a redeveloped Ellen Wilson perpetuated the gendered trope of Black tenant irresponsibility. From the earliest meetings of the Ellen Wilson Neighborhood Redevelopment Corporation, participants battled over who deserved to live there. Building on the belief that the demise of the property was partly due to the former concentration of poor (Black) tenants, the group argued that the new development needed the "right" mix of residents to avoid a repeat of Ellen Wilson's past. Local business executive James M. Didden insisted that at least half the new units be designated as market rate and for single-family homeowners. Didden claimed that "there naturally tends to be more crime and more single-parent families who are less capable of controlling their circumstances in these low-income communities."[71] Didden's comment suggested that single Black mothers were more likely to be irresponsible tenants and therefore undesirable neighbors. He wanted homeowners and middle-class families to be the anchoring residents of the redeveloped property.

The debate over who should live in the new community, which would be renamed the Townhomes on Capitol Hill, took on renewed intensity when the neighborhood redevelopment group joined forces with the Telesis Corporation, a Georgetown-based developer, and Corcoran-Jennison, a Massachusetts-based real estate firm. This team agreed to design a mixed-income, limited-equity cooperative. Unlike a fee-simple model, which ties homeownership to a sole proprietor, a limited-equity cooperative requires residents to purchase individual units and collectively share the cost of building upkeep. To preserve long-term affordability, limited-equity cooperatives also impose restrictions on how much profit a resident can earn if they decide to sell.[72] Tenant activists had long championed this model of collective ownership, but in the political context of HOPE VI, which prized privatization over deep affordability, it was used as a tool of exclusion.[73]

The marginalization of low-wage Black women and their families grew as the project progressed. In the redevelopment plans initially submitted in 1994 for a HOPE VI planning grant, the team committed to allocating at least half of the units to families that acquired their income from Social Security or public assistance.[74] However, as HUD increased funding for the project, the designated income mix changed. In 1995, the redevelopment team agreed on the following breakdown for the Townhomes on Capitol Hill: thirty-three units assigned to households earning up to 25 percent of the region's annual area median income (AMI; in 1995, that was $14,487, or $30,542 in 2025 dollars); thirty-four units to those earning up to 50 percent of the AMI; forty-seven units for those earning up to 80 percent; twenty units for those earning up to 115 percent ($68,453, or $144,316 in 2025 dollars); and thirteen units to be sold for private ownership. The team's decision about who would inhabit the renovated property was clear: very few of Ellen Wilson's former residents, whose median income was 12 percent of the AMI.[75]

Tenant screening protocols and eligibility standards also severely limited the access of public housing residents to the Townhomes on Capitol Hill. In addition to saving up three to four months' carrying costs (5 percent of a household's annual income), prospective occupants were required to undergo home visits at their current residence, submit satisfactory employment references, have at least one line of credit, pass criminal and credit checks, and provide evidence that they had "not intentionally damaged property or caused disturbances to neighbors."[76] Applicants who proved their eligibility still had to participate in a lottery to win a spot in the new community.

For supporters of the Townhomes on Capitol Hill, these tenant screening measures were the most effective way to exclude the "undesirable poor." Defending these conditions, Gilmore later said, "No, we don't want violent criminals. And we are excluding people who aren't credit-worthy and who don't pay their bills."[77] Gilmore's conflation of poor credit scores and violent crime demonstrates a finetuning of disciplinary housing governance and the category of the undesirable poor. Affordable housing officials and developers used the malleable category to justify multiple classifications to suit their purpose (e.g., violent tenants, neglectful parents, or troublesome youth). In the context of HOPE VI, the category of undesirable poor expanded to include most welfare-assisted families and those who could not navigate housing insecurity privately and legally (i.e., without lapses in debt repayment).

Like the category of the "undesirable poor," the category of the "honorable poor" could be adapted to a specific political and economic context. Gilmore agreed with previous public housing executive James Banks that credit scores should be used to vet tenants' character. But Gilmore's behavioral mode of governance identified the honorable poor by developing admission standards that emphasized the ability of low-wage Black families to follow middle-class financial practices, such as maintaining good credit. The colorblind aspect of credit scores enabled officials such as Gilmore to go beyond the invasive character screenings of the past that questioned single Black mothers about their personal lives. Instead, following HUD secretary Jack Kemp's valorization of market principles in public housing reform, credit scores emphasized market logic as a guiding principle in evaluations of the behavior of public housing tenants. Low-wage Black families were expected to save their money and submit their financial information to banks to gauge their trustworthiness as potential occupants of public housing communities, just as middle-class households were as potential owners of single-family homes.

In the context of HOPE VI redevelopment politics, the political and cultural investment of HUD and local housing officials in middle-class revanchism enabled local homeowners and business leaders to have an outsized role in shaping the categories of the honorable and undesirable poor. The HOPE VI project sought to return homeownership and capital to disinvested urban communities. This institutional preference for homeownership is one reason why homeowners and business leaders attempted to dictate how to attract more middle-class families to these redevelopment sites. Sociologist Johanna Bockman has shown that DC's business elite treated the Ellen

Wilson Dwellings project as a site of revanchist recapture. Business leaders often used HOPE VI's discourse of poverty deconcentration in ways that concealed their racial and class bias. Poverty dispersal, according to them, would reduce their fears of having to live near public housing residents, whom they suspected would host "crack parties," steal from unsuspecting homeowners, and most likely, reduce property values.[78]

These homeowners were operating in a cultural context that repeatedly demonized the Black urban poor. The press played a decisive role in fueling public panic and dystopic renderings of Black welfare-assisted women and their families. Rosa Lee Cunningham provides an illustrative example. In the fall of 1994, as the Townhomes on Capitol Hill project was underway and the city was wrestling with the dual threats of bankruptcy and federal receivership, Black *Washington Post* journalist Leon Dash published an eight-part series covering Rosa Lee Cunningham's life. Dash used the story of Cunningham and her family to shine a light on the crisis of the intergenerational Black underclass—families that, according to Dash, constituted close to 60 percent of this so-called class.[79] Dash portrayed a series of life events to dramatize "the choices [Rosa Lee] had and the choices she made" and illustrate the "interconnections of racism, poverty, illiteracy, drug abuse, and crime, and why these conditions persist."[80] Born during the Great Depression in 1932, Rosa Lee Cunningham relocated with her family from North Carolina to rural Maryland and then to DC after World War II. There, Cunningham became a welfare-assisted single mother of eight, living in public housing and struggling with heroin dependency and eventually with AIDS.

The series emphasized Cunningham's mothering to underscore how maternal practices perpetuated social norms of intergenerational poverty. One of the stories described how Cunningham raised her six children in an overcrowded apartment and shared a bed with her daughter Patty. Cunningham's bouts of unemployment led her to engage in sex work, which she sometimes conducted at home. Readers learned that Rosa Lee introduced sex work and illicit drugs to her children, including Patty. She also did not send Patty to school until she was seven or eight. "Change the name and go backward 20 years," one article noted, "and it's hard to tell the difference between Patty's school record and Rosa Lee's. Both fell behind at an early age. Both began skipping school regularly. Neither one had a parent who believed education was important. Neither one learned to read by the time she dropped out."[81] Other articles described maternal practices that read as a confusing maze of obligation, loyalty, inconsistency, and hypocrisy.

When one of Cunningham's teenage sons became addicted to crack, she glibly told him, "You got to take care of your own habits."[82] When Patty struggled with the same addiction, Cunningham expressed shame, disappointment, and guilt. During long stretches of unemployment, Cunningham helped sustain her family by subsisting on welfare, selling drugs, engaging in sex work, or shoplifting. As a result, jail and public housing served as her two alternating but stable residences.[83]

Dash hoped that his series would elicit sympathy, sensitivity, and support for Black uplift and liberal policy goals, like investment in public education.[84] Some readers certainly had that response. Others responded with disgust and outrage. For white columnist Richard Cohen, Dash's colleague at the *Post*, Cunningham personified the allegedly parasitic tendency of the "criminal and dysfunctional underclass."[85] He wrote,

> Among other things, she lives in publicly subsidized housing ($120 a month in rent) and has dipped in and out of various public assistance programs—welfare, food stamps, Medicaid, emergency grants of one sort or another and a Social Security program for the disabled that now gives her $437 a month. Much of her money has gone to illegal drugs for her or her children. . . . It's hard to know what to do with Cunningham and, by implication, others like her. But I do know that Cunningham has been a thief—she says she no longer steals—and the money she took is ours.[86]

Cohen saw Cunningham as a modern-day personification of deviance and immorality. It was up to the public to push the government to enforce the law, punish "thieves" like her, and compel a morality standard among the poor. In 1996, Cohen argued in favor of a time-restricted workfare law because it would have removed the welfare "oxygen" that allowed Cunningham to perpetuate intergenerational poverty.[87]

Cohen's remarks demonstrate the power of linking voyeuristic media coverage of the so-called Black underclass to the gendered trope of Black tenant irresponsibility. These stories give more weight to personal choices, pushing the audience to prioritize personal responsibility and retribution. Indeed, for many readers, because of the choices Cunningham and her family made, they deserved neither compassion nor support. Black feminist scholars Cathy Cohen and Beth Richie have pointed out that this type of selective media depiction helps readers ignore the gendered and racialized preconditions of urban poverty.[88] Rosa Lee Cunningham and her family had to navigate a postwar city that refused to properly include poor Black migrants in the labor market and in the housing market. This structural dislocation produced a social reproduction crisis that many Black families were required to address on their own. Marriage or sex work were two of the tactics young women like Cunningham used to mitigate this crisis.[89] For Cunningham, she certainly experienced misogynoir as a result of these structural challenges, including domestic abuse, sexual assault, and teenage pregnancies. Enduring these challenges on her own, Cunningham reacted negatively to Dash's persistent questions about the (im)morality of her life choices, retorting, "You keep talking about prostitution. . . . I saw it as survival."[90]

Dystopic stories about Black mothers such as Cunningham and Williams certainly informed homeowners' perceptions of welfare-assisted families and discouraged them from supporting the rehousing of such families in HOPE VI developments. Cunningham's story confirmed the worst fears of many middle-class homeowners and public officials about welfare-assisted Black women and their assumed propensity to engage in destructive behavior. While it was true that Cunningham's substance use undermined her ability to give nurturing and protective care to her children, her story also reinforced political support for public housing reform that sought to root out and punish undeserving mothers and vindicated activists like Kimi Gray who were unhappy that law-abiding and therefore "honorable" public housing residents had to live alongside troubled families like Cunningham's. In this way, her story demonstrated the need for public housing reforms such as HOPE VI.[91] However, HOPE VI and initiatives like it marked most welfare-assisted families as the undesirable poor, an identification that had wide-ranging personal and political consequences.

Gilmore, HUD officials, and the development team explicitly treated welfare-assisted families as undesirable by deeming them ineligible for residence at the Townhomes on Capitol Hill. They determined that cash assistance was a "non-dependable income source"—a view that presumed that welfare-assisted families could not afford to live there, especially if they were denied state assistance under the Personal Responsibility and Work Opportunity Reconciliation Act of 1996. Because the law ended lifetime entitlement, welfare recipients faced a higher likelihood of income instability if they were subjected to sanctions or when the time for their participation in a program expired.[92] These decision makers probably thought they were making a colorblind market calculation that had little to do with the cultural and political context that produced a negative, racialized perception of welfare and welfare-assisted families. But that context mattered. Their decisions contributed to a series of outcomes that made it easier to use state resources to justify exclusionary tenant preferences.

The structural marginalization of welfare-assisted Black women and their families persisted in later HOPE VI developments. The Townhomes on Capitol Hill opened in 1998 with a great deal of media and political fanfare. The press focused primarily on the building's impressive architectural design and strict eligibility protocols. Some local newspapers briefly mentioned that fewer than eleven of the original Ellen Wilson Dwellings tenants were rehoused in the redeveloped community.[93] Critical urbanists would later criticize private developers and the state's willingness to exclude the poorest residents in favor of housing upwardly mobile families, pointing out that HOPE VI centered a pro-market, entrepreneurial approach to the redevelopment, finance, and management of public housing.[94]

What critics often missed was the local press's depiction of HOPE VI's developers as visionary heroes. After he served as a Ward 7 council member for three terms, Crawford enjoyed a brief public resurgence as a local developer. In 1996, he won a $24 million HUD grant to demolish the publicly subsidized Ridgecrest community (located in the city's Southeast neighborhood, Washington Highlands) and build 140 townhomes. The local press applauded Crawford for his decades-long commitment to displacing the Black poor and attracting middle-class homeowners: "Ridgecrest residents were disproportionately unemployed welfare moms, [but] Walter Washington Estates [the new development] hosts a doctor, police officers, and a handful of teachers. The project is now hosting busloads of tourists and potential investors who come to see the urban miracle under way in a neighborhood that isn't even on the tourist maps."[95] In the story the media told, such projects were a vital way to launch the economic and social resurgence of the city. The return of doctors, teachers, and police officers as residents, according to the press, confirmed a definitive shift in who the city preferred to assist with welfare state resources: members of middle-class households who not only demonstrated domestic respectability but also paid higher housing costs that helped reduce HUD's operating expenses for public housing.

As revelatory and impactful as HOPE VI developments were, they were only one aspect of a structural shift in DC's real estate market. Although HOPE VI redevelopment projects constituted only a small part of the District of Columbia's public housing topography (the city won only seven HOPE VI grants but managed over fifty public housing communities), those projects provided a powerful discursive and political road map for legitimizing mass dispossession and displacement.[96] By condemning the residences of welfare-assisted families as sites of domestic dysfunction and obsolescence, housing officials and developers across the racial spectrum could justify demolition and revanchism elsewhere in the city.

Economic Resurgence: Gentrification and DC's Real Estate Boom

In the late 1990s, after years of financial distress, DC finally showed signs of an economic resurgence, partly due to Clinton administration policies that encouraged economic growth through gentrification as a means of revitalizing urban centers. Few federal officials admitted this aim publicly, but local officials embraced the goal of gentrification as they implemented the Clinton administration's policy recommendations. In exchange, the federal government agreed to share the costs of DC's spiraling welfare state.

In 1997, Clinton signed three bills that set the stage for DC's economic recovery. Clinton signed the Balanced Budget Act in August 1997, after taking the advice of Republicans, certain Democratic economists, and business leaders who wanted cuts in welfare entitlements to reduce the country's budget deficit.[97] The law slashed federal spending on Medicaid but increased the federal contribution to the city's Medicaid costs from 50 to 70 percent. In the same month, Clinton approved the Taxpayer Relief Act, which contained important provisions that were relevant to DC: a $5,000 credit for first-time homebuyers purchasing a residence in the city; the creation of federal enterprise zones, a special tax designation that incentivized investment in urban centers; and the creation of empowerment zones, which offered generous tax breaks to communities in exchange for their greater investment in local labor and social services.[98] DC's designation as a federal enterprise zone granted sizable tax benefits to businesses and developers who owned property located in census tracts with federal poverty levels of at least 10 percent (instead of the typical poverty threshold of 35 percent) as well as an exemption from a capital gains tax.[99] These provisions made the entire city (with the exception of the wealthiest areas) attractive to both developers and financiers. In September, Clinton signed the National Capital Revitalization and Self-Government Improvement Act, which transferred several of DC's biggest financial responsibilities to the federal government. The federal government agreed to take over the cost of pensions for certain city workers, including teachers, firefighters, police, and judges. It also agreed to pay to improve the city's transportation infrastructure and to take over the imprisonment of DC residents convicted of a felony. In exchange for taking on these responsibilities, the federal government amended its annual payment to a reduced contribution that the city was required to use to pay down its debt, invest in key welfare reforms, and implement a citywide strategy for economic revitalization.[100]

Local officials matched this federal move to attract capital back to DC with targeted economic development projects and other business-friendly reforms. In 1997, for example, the city council established business improvement districts, designed to kickstart neighborhood boosterism and development.[101] That same year, after years of insider lobbying from the Federal City Council (a DC business lobby group that started in 1954), local developer and professional sports team owner Abe Pollin opened the MCI Center, a state-of-the-art sports complex that was one of the city's most consequential economic development projects. The MCI Center (now known as the Capital One Arena) was located on city land next to the Gallery Place–Chinatown metro stop in a neighborhood not far from downtown.[102] Despite public outcry that the project's favorable tax, leasing, and other public benefits reeked of corporate welfare, political and business leaders saw the MCI Center as a critical launchpad for DC's economic resurgence. They argued that it would entice suburban consumers to spend their disposable income in the city, which would lead to higher revenue for the district via parking fees and taxes on sales and income.[103] That perspective resonated with city officials, who not only backed the sports complex but also fast-tracked plans to build a convention center nearby as well as new metro stops in anticipation of the high-density retail and residential districts to come.

Although the Clinton administration supported these moves to increase city revenues, it wanted DC to revise its approach to the economic development of public lands. To that end, a provision added to the National Capital Revitalization and Self-Government Improvement Act required the city to create a quasi-public corporation governed by presidential and mayoral appointees to execute the district's economic development strategy. DC business leaders cheered the provision, having long championed the tactic. In 1998, the city launched the National Capital Revitalization Corporation (NCRC), which replaced the Redevelopment Land Agency (RLA) as the overseer of the district's urban renewal and public land policies. The NCRC was given broad powers to issue bonds and sell public lands and buildings to private developers to maximize density and city revenues. Put bluntly, the NCRC was an entrepreneurial and undemocratic arm of the city's government that sought to turn DC's public land into a cash cow for a revenue-hungry city.

The aggressive push for urban development and capital recruitment solidified during Anthony D. Williams's tenure as mayor. A Los Angeles native who eventually relocated to DC, Williams had been a fiscal bureaucrat for a number of government agencies. Barry nominated Williams to serve as the city's chief financial officer (CFO) during its fiscal crisis in September 1995. Barry's nomination seemed to be the extent of his control over Williams as CFO. The fact that the financial control board was the only entity that was legally able to fire him gave Williams political space for disagreeing with Barry, which he repeatedly did.[104] During his three years as CFO, Williams was widely credited as the person responsible for the city's swift financial rebound. In each of those three years, the city had a budget surplus.

When Barry decided not to run for a fifth term, Williams was elected mayor in the fall of 1998. His campaign platform focused on the practices that had garnered him praise from Congress, Clinton, and the financial control board. He committed to run DC with the same fiscal toughness he had demonstrated as the city's CFO. He promised a government with balanced budgets and large revenue reserves and strategies to recruit capital in order to ensure that the city could pay its debts promptly and deliver services efficiently. Williams's record as the implementer of fiscal austerity policies gave the financial control board enough confidence to begin transferring control of the city's finances back to the mayor's office shortly after his victory.[105]

Williams became mayor just as the stock market rallied to historic heights during the tech boom of the late 1990s. Partly because of a strong economy, generous tax incentives, and an increase in mortgage-backed securities, DC's residential real estate market emerged from its years-long recession. By 1998, the nation's capital was leading the country in the number of building permits issued.[106] But even though the DC metropolitan area led the country in construction, it did not have enough homes to meet buyer demand. Following free-market logic, developer interest skewed toward the wealthy, and the luxury housing market exploded while the construction of housing for buyers with low to moderate incomes stalled.[107] DC's thriving luxury housing market soon pushed investors beyond typically wealthy areas like Upper Northwest. By the early 2000s, gentrification had moved into centrally located, majority-Black neighborhoods, aided by Fannie Mae and Freddie Mae's expansion of mortgage-backed securities, which increasingly included subprime loans. As one real estate agent noted at the time, "We're starting to see investors, speculators, and renovators moving into areas they hadn't considered before: the area north of H Street, for instance . . . and Shaw is on fire."[108] However, unlike the speculation-driven gentrification of the 1970s, the wave of gentrification at the turn of the twenty-first century took place during an economic boom that drove developers and home sellers to set record-setting prices. This buying frenzy resulted in the structural decoupling of homebuying from household income and forced purchasers to pay more than ever to live in gentrifying cities like DC.[109]

DC's hot real estate market eventually pushed developers and landlords to turn the city's rental housing stock into sources of higher revenue and incentivized more challenges to rent control. Despite federal and local attacks on DC's rent control law, it remained one of the toughest in the nation. According to that law, conversions to condominiums required the approval of at least 50 percent of the tenants, and landlords' requests to sell triggered tenants' first right of refusal. These tenant protections made tenants, particularly organized tenant associations, a powerful stakeholder in DC's real estate market. Landlords and developers devised redevelopment plans that addressed this institutional factor. Given the long-standing class fissures in DC's housing politics, it is not surprising that landlords generally chose to include wealthier tenants in their redevelopment projects and offer benefits like insider discounts. For example, to secure tenant approval for condominium conversions in Upper Northwest neighborhoods, many landlords offered affordability protections to seniors, having learned their lesson from tenant resistance in the 1970s. In addition, developers and landlords often engaged in deceptive tactics to sideline poorer and usually Black residents in gentrifying neighborhoods.

Many working-class Black residents living in gentrifying neighborhoods like Shaw, H Street, Logan Circle, or Columbia Heights once again found themselves treated as disposable and undesirable by moneyed interests. As the 1990s drew to a close, landlords grew more adept at exploiting the pro-capital concessions in DC's rent control law. In neighborhoods with increasing rents, landlords fought hard for rent ceilings that ensured a 12 percent return, blindsiding working-class tenants who learned that their annual lease renewals came with bigger rent hikes. Other landlords tried to block tenant involvement in building sales by selling majority interest in the buildings in covert deals that became known as the 95/5 loophole. By selling 95 percent of their ownership interest and retaining only 5 percent, these landlords exploited the rent control law that said that only 100 percent sales triggered the right to refusal.[110]

The 95/5 loophole increasingly affected rent-assisted developments. In the late 1990s, landlords in over 5 percent of the city's rent-assisted buildings chose to end their affordability contracts and transition their buildings to market-rate housing. As an increasing number of project-based affordability covenants expired, HUD could do little to stop the loss of these communities, since the Republicans painted HUD as an ineffective agency that should be abolished.[111] Congressional pressure ultimately shrank HUD's budget and its programs were streamlined. Notably, one of the few commitments HUD followed through on was ensuring that families living in project-based communities with expiring contracts received federally funded housing vouchers to assist them in either staying in their current residence or relocating elsewhere. However, HUD cuts meant that low-income tenants who were not undergoing displacement but were in need of housing assistance often had to wait longer for housing assistance. HUD's shift away from project-based rental assistance and its demand for fair rents and better management also incentivized sales.

With several institutional forces pushing gentrification, voucher discrimination became more prominent. Landlords became craftier about implementing their preference for non-assisted, wealthier tenants. Property managers were known to tell voucher-assisted applicants that the building's quota for voucher holders had been exceeded. They also told voucher-assisted applicants that their income needed to be high enough to qualify without the federal subsidy. Some even stated that voucher-assisted individuals need not apply. Since over 95 percent of all DC voucher holders were Black (and most of that 95 percent consisted of women with children), these tactics amounted to widespread racial and gender housing discrimination. As a result, more and more low-wage Black women and their families were pushed out of gentrifying housing markets they could not afford.[112]

A "Colorblind" Market: Liberal Growth Politics and the Housing Production Trust Fund

In a climate of economic recovery and aggressive urban redevelopment, DC's local politicians and economists began to fuse urban growth goals with redirecting the city's limited welfare to middle-class families. In summer 2001, Alice M. Rivlin, chair of DC's financial control board, and economist Carol O'Cleireacain of the Brookings Institution think tank presented a report that argued that DC's best defense against future budget crises was to focus on population growth. Their report called for "accelerating economic development of middle-income and upscale housing" as the best way to attract 100,000 new residents to the city. Half of these, Rivlin and O'Cleireacain hoped, would be middle-class families with children and the other half adult professionals without children. According to the report, this wave of growth would reduce poverty to 14 percent because a strengthened DC economy would enable the city's poorest to enjoy the benefits of new jobs, rising real estate values, improved schools, and better city services.[113]

The Rivlin-O'Cleireacain report included few policy details to substantiate the argument that a real estate market oriented toward the wealthy would translate to poverty reduction. This was an adaptation of a popular postwar theory that economic growth reduces poverty; only now, economic development and urban planning would ostensibly help the poor.[114] The report validated the gentrification schemes already in place in neighborhoods like Shaw and called for "faster development of market-rate housing by streamlining the zoning processes; assisting developers in assembling packages of land for multiunit housing; implementing aggressive efforts to clean up the Anacostia River and to build housing along the waterfront; and requiring the inclusion of housing as well as commercial development in plans for downtown and areas around Metro stations." Rivlin and O'Cleireacain contended that in a post-receivership climate with fewer federal resources, this strategy for growth was DC's way out of the city's historic financial calamity. They estimated that if DC properly executed their recommendations, it would earn $300 million in added tax revenue.[115]

To underscore their argument, Rivlin and O'Cleireacain itemized the positive and negative impacts of different household configurations on the city's budget and services. Even though middle-class families were a costly demographic because the city would have to invest extensively in schools and recreational spaces, the report claimed that those families created better neighborhoods and contributed to a stronger economy.[116] Left unsaid was the presumption that low-wage (Black) families were cost burdens to the state and were unable to sustain decent neighborhoods. This conspicuous omission of discussion of the needs of poor families in the context of a gentrifying city implicitly valorized middle-class households as the deserving beneficiaries of DC's welfare state.

To help make this political goal of middle-class revanchism palatable to the public, Rivlin and O'Cleireacain emphasized that middle-class families of color would return to the city too. Seemingly sensitive to the city's racial politics, they attempted to make this urban growth agenda compatible with the political investment of some Black politicians in Black middle-class revanchism as a racial uplift tactic for assisting the Black poor. However, there was little evidence that the city or the financial board were willing to give

Estimated Impact on the District's FY2003 Own-Funds Operating Budget for a
New Resident Household by Household Type

	Estimated Cost	Estimated Revenue	Net Impact
Single Person	$1,502	$5,847	$4,345
Childless Couple (2 earners)	$3,004	$15,954	$12,950
Four-Person Family (2 earners)	$21,993	$15,740	−$6,253
Three-person family (1 earner)	$20,491	$3,908	−$16,583
Two-Person Family (1 earner)	$10,260	$3,968	−$6,292

Source: O'Cleireacain and Rivlin, "Envisioning a Future Washington," B3.

more resources to ensure that Black poor and middle-class families could compete with white middle-class families in the city's gentrifying housing markets.

Nevertheless, policy influencers and urban officials embraced the perspective that growth was the only solution for the city's perennial budget woes. Mayor Williams endorsed the Rivlin and O'Cleireacain report and eventually made its recommendations his signature policy goals for his second mayoral term. He soon championed and signed the Housing Act of 2001, which included a key provision that came to define DC's affordable housing politics for the foreseeable future: funding for the Housing Production Trust Fund (HPTF). The fund had been established in 1988 to provide gap financing so developers could afford to purchase or rehabilitate housing for low- to moderate-income tenants facing displacement. But by 2000, the fund was rarely used. Seeing an opportunity to pressure Mayor Williams to earmark additional monies for the preservation and construction of affordable housing, a coalition of bureaucrats and nonprofit service providers led a campaign to revive the trust fund, calling for a tax transfer from commercial developments to provide baseline funding for the trust of $20 million.[117]

As he introduced the 2001 act to the DC council, Williams assured city council members that the HPTF would invest in affordable housing developments: "In our city, we have to bring back the middle class. We need to expand our tax base in order to fund services."[118] He continued, "I propose committing 15 percent of the recordation and real estate transfer taxes to the trust fund—linking downtown economic successes to our neighborhood. That means we'll deposit $15 million into the Housing Production Trust every year."[119] Williams's argument ultimately swayed the council, resulting in legislation that created tiered eligibility for qualified buildings with incomes up to 80 percent of DC's AMI for access to HPTF resources. The law also granted tax abatements for apartment construction in downtown and gentrifying neighborhoods, gave special tax considerations to low-income homeowners, and banned discrimination against Section 8 renters.

Most of DC's affordable housing advocates were thrilled with the legislation, hoping the HPTF would be a pragmatic instrument that would ensure that equitable development became a core principle of DC's real estate boom. Their joy quickly evaporated, though, when they saw that Williams treated the fund as a way to finance the city's rapid growth agenda. Only five months after signing the most comprehensive housing law since the 1985 rent control legislation, Williams convinced the city council to divert some of the HPTF's funds to tax abatements for luxury developments and other line items in the budget.[120] Williams argued that cuts in the trust fund could not be helped. As long as DC was facing the perennial threat of budget shortfalls, the tax revenue from real estate transactions would have to serve as one of the city's essential financial resources.

After two years of failing to keep his promise to fully fund the HPTF, Mayor Williams introduced another structural limitation to the trust fund: the New Communities program. Following Rivlin and O'Cleireacain's policy recommendation of targeted redevelopment, Williams selected nine public and rent-assisted housing communities in or near thirteen neighborhoods the city viewed as desirable for building new mixed-use, highly dense communities that would contain a mix of market-rate and affordable options. In speeches defending the program, Williams argued, the increasingly unpopular HOPE VI federal program, New Communities would be a local effort that minimized the displacement of poor Black families by guaranteeing one-to-one replacement of demolished units. Williams explained that the city would raise most of the $200 million the program needed through bonds and private capital, but that the remainder must come from the Housing Production Trust Fund.

Williams considered New Communities to be a concession to the irate affordable housing advocates who regularly criticized him in the press and in city council hearings for failing to fund the HPTF and cutting other services that directly benefited the city's poorest residents. He said, "We were criticized for displacing the poor when we first started creating mixed-income communities, but we have learned from our mistakes."[121] Giving a subtle nod to the city's reforms in public housing eligibility in the 1990s, Williams continued, "Through our New Communities initiatives, new housing complexes maintain the same level of low-income units as the old housing complexes. If people don't come back, it won't be because of income.

It'll be because of behavior." Explaining that those with "a history of bad credit" and convictions for crimes would most likely be ineligible, Williams, like his predecessors, left the door open for conditional measures that would prevent DC's poorest from accessing redeveloped communities.[122]

The city's colorblind approach to disciplinary housing governance obscured how city officials like Williams continued to target poor Black women and regulate their lives indirectly. With colorblind metrics like credit scores and criminal background checks, the state and developers could exclude those who did not make what officials considered to be behavioral choices that proved that they would not be a problem in new developments. But the conditions such policies mandated were not exclusively about behavioral choices. Because low-wage Black families were structurally vulnerable to precarious employment, greater police surveillance, and prosecution, they were more likely to have lower credit scores and thus be marked as undesirable tenants.[123] Longtime tenant activist Debbie, a DC native who was a single Black mother of four, explained how housing that was conditional on a good credit rating disproportionally hurt low-wage Black mothers: "That bad credit score could be back from years. And you are still trying to clear it. . . . It's discrimination because [landlords] know the majority of low-income Black people's credit [isn't great]. I won't say all because you got a good third [with good credit]—because I got some family members with the bomb credit! But [landlords] know one of the advantages they can get. Because you got all these Black females, who gotta raise kids. They are single parents and they are making [ends meet] day to day."[124] Credit scores could have additional impacts on a person's eligibility for housing. If a low-wage tenant fell behind on their rent and their landlord took them to court, the court case could appear on their credit history, even if it was decided in the tenant's favor. It took time and tenant activism to reform this measure so that tenants could eventually have these rent delinquency notices removed from their credit reports.[125]

Advocacy of Affordable Housing in a Fragmented Landscape

Despite the mixed victories for affordable housing in the 1990s, the city's affordable housing advocacy community continued to fight for tenant rights. However, by 2000, the affordable housing advocacy landscape had changed dramatically. For one thing, the city's leading affordable housing advocates had died.[126] For example, Kimi Gray passed away in March 2000. In addition, the influence of homeless-led organizing and church-led tenant advocacy groups like Washington Inner-City Self-Help (WISH) and Ministries United to Support Community Life Endeavors (MUSCLE) had decreased, and some groups closed their doors. Several new community organizing groups had emerged in their wake, including the Washington Interfaith Network (WIN), EMPOWER DC (founded by WISH's last two employees, Parisa Norouzi and Linda Leaks), the Shaw neighborhood tenant group Manna CDC (once a subsidiary of Manna Inc., renamed ONE DC in 2006), and the DC chapter of the Association of Community Organizations for Reform Now (ACORN).

Although these community groups engaged in neighborhood campaigns to improve and expand the housing stock for low-wage (Black) families, their political reach was often limited in the growth-oriented city. Instead, it was policy think tanks and professional housing coalitions that increasingly shaped the context for affordable housing advocacy in the 1990s and into the 2000s. Groups such as the DC Fiscal Policy Institute worked to make affordable housing more politically attractive to officials and legislators, and a timely merger between housing and economic developers provided critical organizational support for advocates seeking ways to influence local government officials. For example, the Coalition for Nonprofit Housing and Economic Development (CNHED), which was established in 2000, led the campaign to convince DC officials to reactivate the Housing Production Trust Fund. However, these advocates tacitly accepted the city's pro-growth agenda. They and their proposed strategies implicitly accepted a real estate market whose land prices and property values would spike. In 2000–2004, DC's rents jumped from a median of $693 to $799. At the same time, DC's stock of affordable homes plummeted to its lowest point.[127] DC's gentrification wave would continue to make it harder for advocates to balance their pro-growth concessions with the economic reality that made it difficult for low-wage residents to afford to stay in the city without massive infusions of welfare support for the city's poorest residents.

Community organizer Dominic Moulden, the cofounder of ONE DC, understood the economic reality that in order to ensure more affordable housing in the city's competitive real estate market, the HPTF would have to increase its funds, and fast. Moulden believed that if DC's affordable housing advocates were serious about ensuring equitable inclusion of the city's poorest residents, they needed to demand an annual $1 billion set-aside for the trust fund. But many members of the CNHED would have dismissed this number as politically unrealistic, even if it was truly necessary to provide low-wage (Black) families with the resources to access affordable housing in a real estate market flooded with new capital.[128]

Because much of DC's organized advocacy community accepted the city's growth-oriented mission, rent control continued to suffer. The trust fund was arguably established to help rent-controlled tenants exercise their right to purchase their unit if their building was sold. The Tenant Opportunity to Purchase Act, a victory that resulted from the rent control battles in the 1970s and 1980s, requires landowners to offer tenants the first right of refusal and allows tenants to pay the building's sale price. However, the HPTF's limited funds and complex development protocols often prevented many cash-strapped tenants from receiving timely assistance. Predictably, in 2000, the number of the city's rent-controlled units dropped to 101,500 from over 160,000 in 1975.

Rent control did not seem to factor strongly in the affordable housing debates of the early 2000s. Because market logic shaped the implementation of the trust fund, it was understandable that rent control faded as a prominent reform initiative. However, Moulden recalls this shift happening even earlier, sharing, "You know, [ever since] I showed up in DC [in 1985], it [is] interesting how little rent control is talked about as a daily strategy for the future."[129] As a community organizer who assisted working-class Black tenants to create limited-equity cooperatives, he frequently encountered the capitalist maxim that rent control was deflationary and discouraged capital investment and that it was more pragmatic to subsidize consumer transactions than to regulate builders through rent control. Moulden suggested that the entrenchment of nonprofits in the private housing market may have created an ideological blind spot that prevented affordable housing advocates from promoting rent control as a structural solution to the city's affordability crisis.

In the context of the decreasing prominence of rent control as a campaign issue, many affordable housing advocates chose to also quietly disavow public housing. Mayor Williams's call for the demolition of public housing in his New Communities initiative did not elicit the same outcry as his initial cuts to the trust fund did. Hannah, a white affordable housing organizer in her thirties, suggested that liberal optimism may have initially blinded affordable housing advocates in nonprofit housing organizations: "A lot of [nonprofit housing providers] thought New Communities was promising because of the city's promise to build first. I think they thought they were signing on to something better than what was done in other places."[130]

Liberal optimism tells only a fraction of the story. It obscures the ways that nonprofit housing providers, which were primarily staffed by white professionals, benefited from public housing reform. During Gilmore's tenure as the city's public housing receiver, nonprofit organizations were awarded city contracts to provide "counseling" to public housing residents facing displacement and favorable deals for turning hundreds of rental units into market-rate homes for middle-class buyers. Through such private-public partnerships with the city, some nonprofits acquired material benefits and greater political relevance, a development that most likely fragmented the city's affordable housing advocacy community even more. Some affordable housing advocates even used anti-Black tropes about public housing and low-wage tenants. When Daisy, another white affordable housing advocate, reflected on these biases, she said, "When I was previously employed [with a DC nonprofit developer], the nonprofit tried very hard in their role as the intermediary. I don't think they would ever say, 'Public housing is dangerous.' But they gave vague and veiled threats about what would happen if the city just left residents in public housing."[131] She added, "Case management is required . . . in most nonprofit housing. The assumption behind that is [tenants] don't have [their] shit together. So, we are going to hold your hand and navigate the big bad world out there." What made the political position of nonprofit housing developers different, Daisy suggested, was that they often paired assumptions of Black tenant irresponsibility with critiques of government incompetence and asserted that they could provide better character rehabilitation services in public housing. The sad irony was that it was not Black tenant activists, whose tenant management campaign had advanced similar arguments, that profited from the state's devolution of public housing to private actors. This shift primarily benefited the white-led affordable housing advocacy community.

Many advocacy professionals in the city's nonprofit housing development groups continued to keep low-income Black women tenant activists in nominal roles in debates about affordable housing reform. Although these tenant activists rarely shaped policy priorities directly, they were still considered essential to the campaigns of DC's many nonprofit developers and service advocates. One nonprofit leader insisted that low-wage tenant activists were "extremely effective spokespeople" that had the ability to appeal to politicians' emotions with their personal experiences.[132] And while there was certainly truth in this argument, these comments lacked a historical perspective that recognized that the political involvement of low-wage Black women extended far beyond the role of spokesperson. Seen in this historical light, low-wage Black women's testimonies of victimization in a gentrifying housing market or of their successes in nonprofit programs seemed to have more value to affordable housing advocates than developing campaigns rooted in a structural analysis of the city's racially tiered, growth-oriented real estate market. Black women tenants recognized that they were asked to provide their stories only as leverage for campaigns that did not meet their needs and did not address the structural factors that were contributing to the city's affordability crisis. As Charlene, a Black mother of one, observed, their heartfelt testimonies were often used to "beg politicians" for "15 dollars and [get] 50 cents."[133]

The social capital of the testimonies of low-wage Black women about their struggles to access affordable housing did little to counter the gendered trope of Black tenant irresponsibility they had to continue to navigate privately. Some Black women tenant activists understood that the public stigma of irresponsibility was theirs to bear and challenge in their own way. For example, Dawn, a Black mother of four, lived in the Arthur Capper and Carrollsburg public housing community (known colloquially as Cappers), located in the city's Southwest Navy Yard neighborhood. Cappers was one of the last HOPE VI redevelopments in DC. In the early 2000s, city officials decided to demolish it as part of their vision for a new waterfront district. Tenant organizers jumped into action to ensure that the city fulfilled the right of Cappers tenants to return to the redeveloped site, a welfare rights claim organizers had revitalized in the era of HOPE VI and urban growth. Dawn was initially reluctant to join them. She recalled rebuffing the initial attempts of organizers to recruit her: "HOPE VI? I don't care! I looked at them, and told them, 'Let them take it. I'm sick of the drugs. I am sick of these kids running around tearing our stuff up.'"[134] It was only after Dawn observed what she considered to be deceptive tactics on the part of city officials (such as holding meetings during the day and not keeping up-to-date records on tenants' residences) that she saw the value of joining tenant organizing efforts.

Alongside activists like Debra Frasier of the Friends and Residents of Arthur Capper and Carrollsburg group, Dawn witnessed the many ways urban officials and private developers invalidated tenants' claims of the right to return.[135] For instance, Cappers residents had to dispute the idea of using unpaid hospital bills as a potential disqualification for reentry—a metric that disproportionately hurt single mothers and elderly citizens who fell further into debt because of medical expenses.[136] Tenants were also required to have a certain credit score in order to be eligible for a right to return. When I asked her about the minimum credit score needed for entry, Dawn admitted she did not remember but declared, "I didn't care. Mines was good. I was working two jobs. And I didn't have no bills. And I didn't have no bad nothing." Dawn's comment reveals a keen understanding of the political context in which she had to defend her right to return to public housing. With two jobs and no debt or criminal record, she knew she met the updated behavioral metrics for a deserving tenant that officials and private developers used.

Dawn's remarks hide hurt and frustration. She resented that she had to prove her deservingness in a gentrifying city even though families like hers had endured bureaucratic neglect and the abandonment of private capital investors and had had to watch as the city willingly spent resources for middle-class resettlement. She asserted, "I knew I was coming back 'cuz I told them, 'If I don't come back, I'll burn it down.' Nobody is going back down there, 'cuz if it had not been for us, they would not have been down there because this was all swamp land. And y'all came down here and put public housing down here for poor people to live in here. And y'all chase us out. Nah, I don't think so."[137] In the end, all Cappers residents were displaced and most were unable to return to the redeveloped site, even though the city claimed that its provisions for the right to return were generous. Dawn's experience with the right to return campaign at Cappers proved that low-wage Black women and their families would have to learn how to traverse the complexities of evolving disciplinary housing governance tactics in a growth-oriented city.

In this changing context, low-wage Black women became vocal critics of the city's new affordable housing programs. In 2006, for example, a law granting inclusionary zoning (IZ) in new developments seemed like a win for affordable housing advocates. When developers sought to build for a greater density than their lot allowed, inclusionary zoning mandated that they set aside a certain percentage of units for the city's poorest. In 2001, some sympathetic DC officials had hoped to pass IZ legislation, proposing that 10 percent of developments requesting approval for increased density be set aside for those who earned less than 30 percent of the city's AMI. A 2006 law, in contrast, made a provision for set-asides for tenants earning up to 80 percent AMI for IZ rentals and up to 120 percent AMI for IZ homeownership. Sensitive to developers' interests, city officials initially dragged their feet rolling out the program. According to one administrator, "We need to be very careful so we don't stifle the sort of development that might happen [without IZ]."[138]

As a result, during the first few years of IZ, new IZ housing production was slow. But for city officials, IZ and the HPTF were clear evidence of the city's commitment to affordable housing. For low-wage Black mothers, these affordable housing programs were neither affordable nor friendly to families. For one thing, IZ incentivized developers to overproduce smaller units (studios and one- and two-bedroom units) and pegged affordable rents to the highest income percentiles permissible by law. Monica, a mother of four who was displaced from public housing to make way for a New Communities mixed-income development, said, "These new 'affordable' units just ain't affordable for us."[139] Other Black mothers criticized the regulatory hurdles they had jump through in order to qualify for IZ units. Applicants for such units had to apply with the city, attend a two-hour IZ orientation, meet the income requirement of 50 to 80 percent of DC's AMI, and provide financial evidence with eight pay stubs, tax returns, and other assorted financial documentation. Some IZ units, especially those in luxury-market developments, required applicants to earn enough to cover amenity fees. And after these extensive procedures, applicants still had to participate in a lottery to access specific units, with no guarantee that they would win.[140]

These affordable housing programs cemented the city's return to the middle class as the welfare state's most deserving beneficiaries. The individuals most likely to qualify for the city's affordable housing programs were typically upwardly mobile, young, and single professionals. For the long-time, low-wage Black families who wanted to enjoy these programs, it must have felt like IZ and similar programs actualized the punitive welfare reform mantra that officials had loudly touted in the 1990s: "Public housing is something you qualify for. It is not a right."[141] These market-oriented affordable housing programs conveyed the implicit message that the middle-class behavior that low-wage families imitated meant little if they lacked the funds to keep pace with rising rents in a gentrifying DC.

· · · · · ·

Negative discourse about low-wage Black women and their families opened up the political and cultural space to attack welfare and support gentrification. While the priorities of the Clinton administration provided a major impulse for DC's intense gentrification in the late 1990s, it was the cultural depiction of welfare-assisted Black women and their families that made this political agenda seem like common sense in the nation's capital. The Black feminist materialist analysis applied here shows how this cultural depiction influenced city policies and market forces. Negative discourse about specific Black mothers allowed officials and moneyed interests to continue to use tactics that excluded certain types of tenants. Low-wage Black women and their families who wanted to remain in a gentrifying city had to adapt to the updated experiments in disciplinary housing governance that increasingly demanded that they mimic the financial and cultural practices of middle-class families. Structural discrimination against the poor continued, since few low-wage Black family members were willing to publicly and consistently challenge the cultural context of their structural marginalization. Moreover, such discrimination against the Black urban poor contributed to the systematic undermining of rent control.

A fragmented affordable housing advocacy community varied in its commitment to protecting and expanding the tenant protections that Black women tenant activists had long defended. But despite pro-growth politics and fragmentation among affordable housing advocacy groups, an inventive impulse remains that continues to aminate tenant organizing in the city. As the 2000s entered its second decade, more affordable housing professionals began to embrace a structural critique and challenge the rollbacks of rent control and welfare. Groups like ONE DC and EMPOWER DC were willing to challenge the racial, class, and gender bias implicit in these political projects. Yet no matter the what the structure of tenant organizing and advocacy was, the Black women tenant activists featured here proved that they were ready to keep fighting to remain in a city that continually adapts to the market and political demands of urban growth.

Conclusion

Like We Don't Belong

· ·

If you were to walk through DC's Shaw neighborhood, you might marvel at the number of rent-assisted affordable housing communities still standing on Seventh Street. These rent-assisted developments are now adjacent to million-dollar rowhouses that have been renovated in the last three decades. What is left unspoken—unless you are a neighbor who is in the know—is that many of these rent-assisted developments are constantly threatened by gentrification. ONE DC has been an important community advocate that has prevented additional loss and worked to generate new production of deeply affordable housing. In July 2010, a year after ONE DC engaged in failed negotiations with city officials to enforce a community benefits agreement, we collectively decided to liberate the land known as Parcel 42. Always ready to throw a celebration for a worthy cause, the organization held a block party on Sixth Street, a block away from Parcel 42. After several hours of festivities, we took the bullhorn and led over 200 dancing residents and supporters to Parcel 42, unlocked the gate, and made our way onto the site. Black mothers led the charge, with some chanting, "If we cannot live here, no one should!" It was a powerful and symbolic show of force. Hundreds of ONE DC members and allies stewarded the land for seven days, holding political discussions and breaking bread. Black mothers brought their children to play as police stood watch, surprisingly and rightly making no arrests. Community residents and ONE DC members then took over the area and maintained it for thirty days, creating makeshift homes and providing security for the site.

After the protest concluded, it took the DC government another thirteen years to finally build the deeply affordable housing outlined in ONE DC's 2006 deal. Although ONE DC occasionally reminded city officials of their original promise of funding support, they instead welcomed private capital to provide gap financing for the project. In 2022, Amazon, a multinational tech corporation, stepped in and loaned the politically connected developer the necessary gap funding to develop Parcel 42. After years of inaction, almost 100 of the new units would become affordable for those earning under $60,000 a year.

Considering the need, this victory was long overdue but underwhelming for many longtime DC residents. Long-term low-wage residents recognize that newer affordable developments, like the one now at Parcel 42, still engage in deceptive tactics to sort tenants and minimize access to lower-income applicants of color. In addition, some Black women tenant activists worry that the lucky few who can gain entry into truly affordable units will still be seen or treated as undesirable in these developments.

That was Sonya's experience when she moved into a new affordable housing development. A Black mother of three in her sixties, Sonya had watched her native city transform from the country's first majority-Black city to its "most intensely gentrified city."[1] Indeed, by 2018, DC had realized former Mayor Washington's goal of welcoming 100,000 new residents and boasted 40,000 new rental units that had been built since 2000. Of course, this outcome came at the cost of 20,000 Black Washingtonians who were displaced to make way for this historic surge in development.[2] Sonya was not necessarily opposed to development; she strongly believed that DC had enough space to recruit new residents and accommodate native working-class Black Washingtonians like her. For years, Sonya had worked in nonprofits committed to affordable housing to organize Black tenants who faced displacement just like she did. She supported those tenants as they negotiated deals to protect rent-controlled or rent-assisted communities over the long term. She also helped those who fought for deeply affordable set-asides in primarily market-rate, luxury apartments. Equitable inclusion in the city's economic resurgence was a goal Sonya supported.

Yet she was troubled by the insidious ways that working-class Black women and their children were seen and treated as a threat to the city's renaissance. "I've noticed some subtle changes," she admitted in the 2010s after moving into a new multifamily residential community located east of DC's Anacostia River. Local officials praised the development's accessibility and affordability due to inclusionary zoning requirements that stipulated that a minimum of 10 percent of developed units be set aside as affordable for households earning under 80 percent of the DC metropolitan area median income. Even so, Sonya noticed that only three of the development's twenty-plus units were available for voucher-assisted families like hers; single white professionals mostly occupied the rest. Sonya understood that tenant relationships and the cultural milieu were in flux in a new building. However, she learned quite quickly that her presence as a dark-skinned Black foster mother of two young children caused discomfort for a predominantly white middle-class tenant demographic. She recalled, "A couple of months after I moved in here, I hadn't seen all of my neighbors. And this white woman got on the elevator. And me [and Sonya's two toddlers] were there and this white woman clutched her purse, as if the three of us were going to mug her! And she averted her eyes. It was so subtle. But I had become attuned to that kinda stuff."[3] Sonya realized that the white newcomers did not welcome her family: "I also noticed, even when I walk down the street, these white folks walk down the street like I don't belong there. . . . And if I am pushing [my daughter] in the stroller and [a white person] is coming down the sidewalk, they expect me to move! I kept pushing it straight—I am gonna hit your shins if you don't move!" She lightheartedly confessed, "I don't even let it bug me most of the time, but there are sometimes when I am having a bad day, I might utter 'ass.'"[4]

Sonya's feelings of rejection and marginalization in a gentrifying city are not new. *The Undesirable Many* has shone an analytical light on the multiple institutional and structural forces that enable the persistence of interpersonal interactions like the ones Sonya recently experienced. Since the early decades of urbanization in the District of Columbia, Black working-class families have been treated as a threat to residential property values. As middle-class (Black) families gained greater access to homeownership and the country's housing stock, Black welfare-assisted families continued to occupy the lowest rung of residential property value as institutional actors ranging from banks and the press to politicians refined their rationales for treating the homes of Black welfare-assisted families as undesirable sites that were nonetheless worthy of recapture.

The Undesirable Many shows that single and welfare-assisted Black women and their families play a powerful yet unenviable position in affordable housing politics. Historically, politicians have made a spectacle of the assumed moral failings of poor Black women and their families to justify swift and sweeping institutional action, such as austerity or a more significant police presence. These families were also used to help justify the real estate industry's pursuit of profit maximization. In the case of rent control, local politicians and real estate industry actors painted these families as a drag on property values. They lobbied for and won drastic measures such as rollbacks in rent control protections or wholesale demolition and redevelopment. The routine and cyclical cultural devaluation of welfare-assisted Black families later opened up space for capital recapture and dispossession of those families.[5]

This book has showcased the importance of cultural narratives in producing and valorizing socioeconomic inequities in urban real estate. In DC's real estate market, cultural narratives about welfare-assisted Black women and their families justified conditional access to new or improved housing stock. Disciplinary housing governance has validated differential treatment of housing consumers, including a discretionary and selective approach toward the honorable and undesirable poor—categories created through such practices. Historical iterations of disciplinary housing governance from the Progressive Era to the present have helped state and private actors justify the redirection of welfare resources away from cities' poorest and back to residents deemed to be upwardly mobile and morally normative. Disciplinary housing governance has also naturalized the belief that the poorest people deserve to live in the worst housing conditions because they do not demonstrate a commitment to character transformation (e.g., middle-class behavior). Political investment in disciplinary housing governance and its adoption of character oversight has enabled numerous institutional actors to defend the mass displacement of tenants and property redevelopment.

Ultimately, conditional access to housing led to housing scarcity for low-income families through the dispossession process. Although politicians such as H. R. Crawford publicly embrace poverty dispersal, acting as if it is the ethical duty of neighboring suburbs to absorb people experiencing poverty, in the history of racialized housing in the United States, this political stance has also served to conceal the ways that cities have use negative discourse about the poor to minimize their responsibility to the poor. Meanwhile, suburban and rural politicians in the post–civil rights era have compounded welfare retrenchment in cities by continuing the practice of exclusion by failing to make the welfare investment needed to house low-income families properly.[6]

This book has also uncovered the evolving ways localities such as DC have privileged the housing needs of certain demographics. For example, politicians and real estate interests have often spoken of the needs of the middle class as they promoted cuts to other means-tested welfare programs. This divisive strategy is not new in US welfare state politics. However, this book underscores how different political interest groups have leveraged competing interests of both the Black middle class and the Black poor for affordable housing to achieve various political ends, including gentrification.

In recent years, DC's local government, led by Muriel Bowser (D-DC), has recognized that access to affordable housing continues to fail along racial and class lines.[7] Notably, the city's aggressive growth strategy in the late 1990s contributed to normalizing housing unaffordability for most low-wage and middle-class Black families. By 2022, the city's population skyrocketed to over 700,000 residents, up from its fifty-year low of 572,059 in 2000.[8] Single middle-class professionals continue to dominate the city's demography. Close to half of DC's population are single adults, and the median household income is $104,110.[9] This economic and demographic growth contained racial disparities. In 2022, the average income for white households was $160,690, while the average Black household income was $75,473.[10] And despite the city's notable presence of Black middle-class households (approximately 40 percent), a considerable number of these households are unable to afford housing.[11] According to one local study, only 8 percent of home sales in DC were affordable for the first-time Black homebuyer. Another study confirmed a similar dynamic for low-wage Black renters. From 2019 to 2023, nearly 30 percent of Black DC renters were extremely rent-burdened (meaning they spend more than 50 percent of their income on housing costs), in contrast to 13.8 percent of white renters.[12]

Reminiscent of the New Democrats' policy recommendations for urban governance in the 1990s, current city officials in DC argue that more growth is the best remedy for this racial and class inequity in the housing market. Bowser and housing officials have emphasized the need for more housing construction. They contend that encouraging more density on city land will eventually result in lower rents citywide. Bowser and city housing officials understand that more housing construction is a long-term strategy. Still, as Democrats who continue the New Democrat governance tradition of liberal inclusion, they also believe that marginalized housing consumers deserve the opportunity to gain access to the current housing market. Toward that end, Bowser has increased affordable housing funding to help Black homeowners with down payment costs and has earmarked more production funds for deeply affordable housing.[13] Bowser also ensured that there were local housing vouchers and protective measures to make sure voucher-holders could access an array of rental options. These moves were widely praised as bold because other cities have continued to enforce the post–welfare reform tenets of fiscal conservativism, lower taxes, and limited investments in affordable housing.

Bowser's moves are indeed commendable. But Black women tenant activists with ONE DC and similar groups have repeatedly argued that Bowser's progressive measures still fail to meet the need for deeply affordable housing because the city's housing construction is still skewed toward the wealthy. They also contend that the city's lack of attention to this matter meant that over 20,000 Black residents were displaced from the city in

2000–2013.[14] Affordable housing proponents who care about the historical harm of displacement argue that the city should consider reparative measures and not simply focus on subsidizing transactions in the housing market (e.g., vouchers and assistance with down payments).

These activists' criticism is particularly relevant since Bowser recently introduced changes to a crucial affordability measure. On February 12, 2025, Bowser recommended that the DC council adopt significant changes to the Tenant Opportunity to Purchase Act (TOPA). Bowser recommended exemptions for certain multifamily properties from TOPA to support landlords and developers' desire for quicker building sales in order to facilitate more real estate development. Bowser's proposal also calls for accelerated evictions. With historically familiar arguments, real estate and business interests are lauding the measure because "TOPA has been exploited by tenants who often negotiate thousands of dollars from their landlords in order to waive their TOPA rights."[15] As has been the case for much of the post–civil rights era, the argument about irresponsible tenants is colorblind, but given that the city's disproportionate impact of displacement has been on Black families, this accusation has racial and gendered implications.

The narrative of unfair tenant practices in TOPA transactions distracts and sidelines a needed conversation about the structural changes in DC's real estate market. Federal politics still impact DC's real estate market. Since the conservative populist and Republican president Donald J. Trump won the White House again in the fall of 2024, DC's real estate market is currently undergoing the shock of the Trump administration's extensive personnel firings.[16] This book has also demonstrated that less federal spending on affordable housing has pressured local economies to submit to capitalistic market demands like growth. However, local growth imperatives can often leave officials at the political mercy of business interests who would rather control the entire market instead of debating the terms of market behavior, as tenant activists continue to do with their demands for rent control and TOPA rights. Yet even with these consumer protective measures, business interests continue to maximize their command over real estate. For many affordable housing advocates, various real estate interest groups, including private equity and other rental companies, seek higher rents and more regulatory control while enacting deceptive tactics to undermine tenants' demands for affordable rents, quality maintenance, and responsive customer service.[17]

The Undesirable Many provides important evidence about the historical harm localities have inflicted on working-class Black families, particularly low-wage Black women and their families. Since this history impacts the present, city officials must grapple with the legacy and current practices of racial and gendered extraction. However, redressing this historical harm requires a methodological framework that moves beyond just analyzing the market. Black feminist materialism provides the necessary analytical framework because it identifies numerous institutional actors who shape policy outcomes and social expectations about social reproduction. Suppose city officials and researchers want to provide structural solutions to the long-standing affordability crisis of low-wage Black families. In that case, they must consider how cultural expectations impact policy outcomes to identify and achieve more equitable corrective market and societal reform measures.

Changing cultural expectations requires seeing historically undermet social reproduction needs of marginalized populations as a politically urgent issue and meeting those needs as an economically viable possibility. Black feminists have long argued that an ethic of care should guide our economy and govern measures to provide care.[18] Black feminists have historically infused this ethic of care into the community institutions they have established to meet the social reproduction needs of marginalized populations, including gender-expansive health clinics, cooperative farms, and housing cooperatives.[19] This cultural value must be extended beyond small-scale community organizations. Black feminists and other social justice groups must advocate for more cultural changes in state and market practices. Organizing and advocacy groups must continue to champion institutional changes that challenge profitability schemes tied to marginalizing Black working-class households in the housing market. The national group Right to the City, an affordable housing alliance committed to solving the nation's affordability crisis, provides an instructive example of how to challenge inequitable market norms and unfair state policies.[20] To supplement such efforts and to ensure that this cultural shift in our affordable housing politics is comprehensive, I offer a Black feminist materialist care ethic that has three interconnected components—reparative care, restorative care, and sustainable care.

Reparative care refers to the institutional and economic responses that address the structural and historical causes of harm. Financial and real estate markets have long benefited from inequitable and speculative valuations of land and housing, and race continues to underwrite unequal valuations of Black working-class housing in particular. Reparative care requires the institutions responsible for this structural harm, including finance institutions, real estate entities, and governments, to implement race-conscious structural solutions oriented toward housing affordability.

Restorative care increases the capacity of the welfare state to address the social reproduction needs of working-class families adequately. Historically, the welfare state has attempted to reduce the population it assists based on subjective assessments of deservingness. Restorative care rejects these socially constructed moral hierarchies and aims to help all working-class families with their social reproduction needs. As part of this goal, grassroots and community-responsive social work and community organizing should be important in generating nonpunitive restorative care approaches to poverty amelioration.[21] These groups would continue to interrogate and reinvent existing welfare initiatives, such as job training and workfare programs, to ensure that they no longer perpetuate the humiliation and isolation of the poor but rather encourage labor and community collaborations as well as guaranteed employment.[22]

Lastly, sustainable care addresses the environmental consequences of commodified housing. Speculative building accelerates ecological degradation and perpetuates privatization. Sustainable care recognizes Indigenous people's call for Americans to reorient their relationship to the land.[23] Sustainable care centers redistribute access to the existing housing supply while advancing efforts to minimize future ecological destruction and housing commodification through alternative and collective stewardship models, such as cooperatives.[24]

This multidimensional approach to care broadens the political scope that local activists, scholars, and policymakers will need to redress social reproduction crises such as housing unaffordability and homelessness. Implementing it would encourage us to collectively recognize the dignity and respect of all people, a stance Black women tenant activists have historically asked for in their local housing campaigns. It is also a message that recognizes and rejects the culture's mistreatment and punishment of those who are not quite middle class. Monica, a Black woman tenant activist living in DC's public housing, best captured this sentiment. She shared, "For me, I am God's property. My life has not been all the way perfect. But I still care about people. And I feel very strongly that God created this earth to provide for all of our needs. . . . I think people put too much judgment on other people. . . . We do so much segregating, discriminating, labeling, judging."[25]

For Monica, this judgment of Black families' domestic lives enables housing officials and landlords to ignore the fact that everyone needs shelter.

When politicians and other elites advocate punitive disciplinary measures to ensure conditional access for the so-called honorable poor, it only perpetuates housing scarcity. Such measures carry the racialized message that the poorest segments of the (Black) population should accept external surveillance of their lives, even if it does not result in upward mobility. This is painful and paradoxical for Monica because, as she sees it, Black working-class families are forced to prove their deservingness of new or improved housing. At the same time, the legacies of white supremacy are left unchallenged. Monica aptly noted: "Look at all those white people who done hung people. They did not have not one jail time or have a record. So why you wanna get to us and start putting all of this that and the third? Throughout their history, you did not lock their asses up for tar feathering, raping, for stealing. You hear me? So you feel it is ok, just because a person made a fuckup in their life. . . . How you do you feel it is ok to say this person cannot have a place to stay?"[26] Monica's comments issue a powerful call to action for those of us who believe that societies should always strive for the inclusion of all, not just those who can afford to dominate them.

Notes

Introduction

1. ONE DC pairs direct-action work with community learning and local alternatives such as worker cooperatives and limited equity cooperatives.

2. Hyra, *Race, Class, and Politics in the Cappuccino City*; Sam Gringlas, "Old Confronts New in a Gentrifying DC Neighborhood," *NPR*, January 16, 2017, https://www.npr.org/2017/01/16/505606317/d-c-s-gentrifying-neighborhoods-a-careful-mix-of-newcomers-and-old-timers; "An Oral History of Gentrification in Shaw and U Street NW," *Washington City Paper*, August 28, 2019, https://washingtoncitypaper.com/article/1820/an-oral-history-of-gentrification-in-shaw-and-u-street-nw/; Summers, *Black in Place*.

3. To learn about Williams's recruitment goal, see chapter 5 of this book and Cole-Smith and Muhammad, *The Impact of an Increasing Housing Supply on Housing Prices*.

4. DC minister, civil rights activist, and politician Walter Fauntroy worked with the Model Inner City Community Organization to champion urban renewal funds to benefit local Black residents. For the history of this campaign, see Summers, "La douleur exquise"; Asch and Musgrove, *Chocolate City*, 349–51; Eugene L. Meyer, "MICCO Cutoff Ends Citizen Control of Urban Renewal," *Washington Post*, January 22, 1973; Claudia Levy, "Shaw Groups Divided on Apartment Plans," *Washington Post*, August 10, 1971; Ronald Taylor, "2d Apartment Project Starts in Shaw Area," *Washington Post*, November 22, 1971.

5. Scarcity is already baked into urban real estate markets. Economists consider land to be a nonproducible good and thus in limited supply. Land scarcity drives up housing prices and as a limited commodity incentivizes landowners to charge higher rents ("super-profits" in economic parlance). Affordable housing necessarily exists within an urban real estate climate prone to inflation and speculation. In my work, I stress that discourse about who occupies housing and land plays an important role in urban real estate markets, helping to justify prices, depreciation, and state support (or lack thereof) for affordable housing. For more about land as a nonproducible good in urban real estate markets, see Stanford, *Economics for Everyone*, 73.

6. Taylor Candiloro, "Home Prices vs. Inflation: Why Millennials Can't Afford Homes (2022 Data)," Anytime Estimate, September 12, 2022, https://anytimeestimate.com/research/housing-prices-vs-inflation/.

7. For a historical examination of this trend, see Taylor, *Race to Profit*. For a contemporary examination of this trend, see Kevin Schaul and Jonathan O'Connell, "Investors Bought a Record Share of Homes in 2021: See Where," *Washington Post*,

February 16, 2022, https://www.washingtonpost.com/business/interactive/2022/housing-market-investors/.

8. See, for example, Desmond, *Evicted*.

9. See Williams, *The Politics of Public Housing*; Taylor, *Race to Profit*; and Rodriguez, *Diverging Space for Deviants*.

10. See, for example, Sugrue, *The Origins of the Urban Crisis*; Glotzer, *How the Suburbs Were Segregated*; Contreras, *Latinos and the Liberal City*; Taylor, *Race to Profit*; Rothstein, *The Color of Law*; Baradaran, *The Color of Money*, 101–33; Satter, *Family Properties*; Jackson, *Crabgrass Frontier*; Slater, *Freedom to Discriminate*; Connolly, *A World More Concrete*; and Hirsch, *Making the Second Ghetto*.

11. Vale, *From the Puritans to the Projects*; Hunt, *Blueprint for Disaster*; Vale, *Purging the Poorest*.

12. Hirsch, *Making the Second Ghetto*; Taylor, *Race to Profit*; Rothstein, *The Color of Law*.

13. See Rodriguez, *Diverging Space for Deviants*; Golash-Boza, *Before Gentrification*; and Moskowitz, *How to Kill a City*.

14. I thank Howard University sociologist and community activist Walda Katz-Fishman for the term Black feminist materialism. She recommended the term when we were discussing a succinct way to describe my research methodology when I was in graduate school.

15. While I name this tradition of Black feminism, I understand that there are multiple variants and that some have political aims that are different than mine. Here, I embrace a radical Black feminist tradition that challenges the intersecting structures of capitalism, racism, patriarchy, and imperialism. For an excellent review of Black feminist typology, see James, *Shadowboxing*.

16. Collins, *Black Feminist Thought*, 5.

17. Jones, "An End to the Neglect of the Problems of the Negro Woman!"

18. Combahee River Collective, "(1977) The Combahee River Collective Statement," BlackPast, https://www.Blackpast.org/african-american-history/combahee-river-collective-statement-1977/.

19. I understand that Black feminist theory and Black feminist studies are expansive and interrogate many questions beyond culture and representation. However, many public debates related to Black feminist theory often attend to these questions. For a small sample, see Cooper et al., "On the Future of Black Feminism, Part 1," and "On the Future of Black Feminism, Part 2"; Brooks, *Liner Notes for the Revolution*; Harrison et al., "Black Love"; and Cottom, *Thick: And Other Essays*.

20. See, for example, Crenshaw, "Demarginalizing the Intersection of Race and Sex"; hooks, *Outlaw Culture*; and Jordan-Zachery and Alexander-Floyd, *Black Women in Politics*.

21. Taylor, *How We Get Free*; Davis, *Women, Race and Class*.

22. Stanford, *Economics for Everyone*, 20.

23. To learn more about racial capitalism as a historical and analytic frame, see Robinson, *Black Marxism*; Ransby, *Making All Black Lives Matter*; Robin D. G. Kelley, "What Did Cedric Robinson Mean By Racial Capitalism?" *Boston Review*, January 12, 2017, https://www.bostonreview.net/articles/robin-d-g-kelley-introduction

-race-capitalism-justice/; and Walter Johnson, "To Remake the World: Slavery, Racial Capitalism, and Justice," *Boston Review,* February 1, 2017, https://www .bostonreview.net/forum/walter-johnson-to-remake-the-world/.

24. Gilmore, *Golden Gulag.*

25. Haley, *No Mercy Here.*

26. Taylor, *Race to Profit.*

27. Brewer, "21st-Century Capitalism, Austerity, and Black Economic Dispossession."

28. Many feminist scholars have continued the Black feminist materialist tradition, including Angela Davis, bell hooks, Barbara Ransby, Mariame Kaba, M Adams, Jordanna Matlon, Donna Murch, and Premilla Nadasen.

29. See Mies, *Patriarchy and Accumulation on a World Scale*; Mohanty, *Feminism without Borders*; and Hennessy and Ingraham, *Materialist Feminism.* Social reproduction theory recognizes that there is an interlocking relationship between exploitation (often linked to class relations) and oppression (often linked to social relations and mediated by gender, race, [assumed] ability, etc.). For more about social reproduction theory, see Bhattacharya, *Social Reproduction Theory*; Briggs, *How All Politics Became Reproductive Politics*; Mohandesi and Teitelman, "Without Reserves"; Fraser, "Contradictions of Capital and Care"; and David Madden, "Housing and the Crisis of Social Reproduction," e-flux Architecture, June 2020, https://www.e-flux.com/architecture/housing/333718/housing-and-the-crisis-of -social-reproduction/.

30. Folbre et al., "Measuring Care Provision in the United States."

31. As many feminist and queer scholars have noted, sexuality is also always relevant in analyzing how gender works. See Wilchins, *Queer Theory, Gender Theory*; and Cohen, *The Boundaries of Blackness.*

32. For excellent historical and Black feminist analyses of Black women's complicated social reproduction, see Kelley, "On Violence and Carcerality"; Higginbotham, *Righteous Discontent*; Haley's *No Mercy Here*; and Hicks, *Talk with You Like a Woman.*

33. Omi and Winant, *Racial Formation in the United States,* 107.

34. To learn the difference between these forms of labor, see Nadasen, *Care: The Highest Stage of Capitalism;* Bhattacharya, *Social Reproduction Theory*; Briggs, *How All Politics Became Reproductive* Politics; and Dill, "Our Mothers' Grief."

35. Fraser, "Contradictions of Capital and Care." Premilla Nadasen offers an impressive account of the commodification of social reproduction in *Care: The Highest Stage of Capitalism.*

36. Standing, *The Precariat*; Agarwala and Chun, *Gendering Struggles against Informal and Precarious Work.*

37. Baker et al., "Recommending Toxicity."

38. Rachel Louise Snyder, "We Underestimate the Manosphere at Our Peril," *New York Times,* March 28, 2025; "Making Sense of the Gulf between Young Men and Women," *The Economist,* March 14, 2024; "Why Young Men and Women Are Drifting Apart," *The Economist,* March 13, 2024.

39. Conservatives and liberals engage in this type of behavior. See chapters 3 and 4 of this book.

40. Black feminists have long suggested that low-wage Black families endure social reproduction crises at higher rates than white households. This disparity is rooted in the long history of US racial capitalism. During enslavement, Black reproductive life was systematically undermined and exploited, particularly through the appropriation of Black women's reproductive bodies and labor. In the postbellum era, Black families were restricted to agricultural and low-wage service work and because of state support for segregation and exploitative labor relations were expected to furnish the costs for their own schooling, housing, and health care. Consequently, although even organized religion taught low-wage Black families to aspire to the gendered division of housework and wage labor, this ideal paradigm of social reproduction was difficult to replicate. Many low-wage Black families had to sustain different household compositions and experimented with different income-pooling strategies (e.g., taking in boarders). These social reproduction strategies are often invested in heteronormative gender norms. For a brief exploration of these social reproduction strategies and their intersection with wage labor see Collins, "Gender, Black Feminism, and Black Political Economy." For an example of Black male socialization under present-day racial capitalism, see Jordanna Matlon, "Black Masculinity Under Racial Capitalism," *Boston Review*, July 16, 2019, https://www.bostonreview.net/articles/jordanna-matlon-branded/.

41. Many Black queer feminists have illuminated alternative approaches to care and reproductive labor that do not reinscribe heteronormative hierarchies of power. See Cohen, "Punks, Bulldaggers, and Welfare Queens."

42. This research adds to welfare state studies offered by scholars such as Skocpol, *Protecting Soldiers and Mothers;* Frances Fox Piven and Richard Cloward, *Regulating the Poor.* These scholars present important literature reviews that theorize welfare state politics.

43. Black feminist political scientist Cathy Cohen expresses this perspective to remind social movements to create strategic yet broad alliances that include those seen as "deviant" or "unworthy." See Cohen, "Deviance as Resistance"; and Cohen, "Punks, Bulldaggers, and Welfare Queens."

Chapter 1

1. Patricia Penny, interview with the author, Washington, DC, February 6, 2022.

2. Like much of the country, DC eventually updated its housing code to follow the building model of the International Code Council. See *District of Columbia Building Code* (Washington, DC: Government of the District of Columbia, 2017), https://dob.dc.gov/sites/default/files/dc/sites/dob/publication/attachments/2017%20District%20of%20Columbia%20Building%20Code_Part%201.pdf.

3. "Washington in Transition: Racial Residential Patterns in the Nation's Capital, 1862–1900," n.d., Washingtoniana Periodicals Collection, People's Archive, DC Public Library, Washington, DC. For a comprehensive history of this political moment, see Asch and Musgrove, *Chocolate City*, 119–51.

4. For the history of Indigenous people in Georgetown, see Delany, *A Walk Through Georgetown*; and Robert Devaney, "Our Black History . . . in Georgetown,"

The Georgetowner, February 20, 2019, https://georgetowner.com/articles/2019/02/20/Black-history-georgetown-2/.

5. Lesko et al., *Black Georgetown Remembered.* For a history of Indigenous people in Washington, DC, see Jacob Steinhauer, "The Indians' Capital City: Native Histories of Washington, DC," Library of Congress Blogs, March 27, 2015, https://blogs.loc.gov/kluge/2015/03/the-indians-capital-city-native-histories-of-washington-d-c/. This post highlights Joseph Genetin-Pilawa's research.

6. "Washington in Transition," 20.

7. Gillette, *Between Justice and Beauty,* 109–29.

8. Alley home residents were notoriously undercounted; see Borchert, *Alley Life in Washington.*

9. For a history of building regulations in DC in the nineteenth century, see Hoagland, "Nineteenth-Century Building Regulations in Washington, D.C."

10. Jones, *The Housing of Negroes in Washington, D.C.,* 33.

11. "Housing of Negroes in Washington, D.C.," 14; Jones, *The Housing of Negroes in Washington, D.C.,* 30.

12. *Inhabited Alleys in the District of Columbia and Housing Unskilled Workingmen,* 11. Real estate interests and many white Washingtonians expressed similar beliefs about higher-earning Black residents. Black sociologist William Henry Jones found that while white developers such as Kite Realty and the Cafritz Company willingly built for wealthier Black residents, they often used inferior materials that led to substandard construction and higher maintenance costs—yet they still marked up their prices. Jones, *The Housing of Negroes in Washington, D.C.,* 91–93.

13. Riis, *How the Other Half Lives,* 117.

14. Weller, *Neglected Neighbors,* 28.

15. Weller, *Neglected Neighbors,* 29.

16. Weller, *Neglected Neighbors,* 47.

17. Weller, *Neglected Neighbors,* 32, 154.

18. Gillette, *Between Justice and Beauty,* 115.

19. Gillette, *Between Justice and Beauty,* 115.

20. Kober, *History and Development of the Housing Movement in the City of Washington,* 50.

21. Kober, *History and Development of the Housing Movement in the City of Washington,* 25.

22. Kober, *History and Development of the Housing Movement in the City of Washington,* 76.

23. George M. Sternberg, "Housing of the Poor," *Washington Evening Star,* December 8, 1906; Kober, *History and Development of the Housing Movement in the City of Washington,* 82.

24. Kober, *History and Development of the Housing Movement in the City of Washington,* 76.

25. "Attacks Alley Homes," *Washington Post,* February 28, 1915.

26. Hartman, *Scenes of Subjection,* 161.

27. "To Rid Capitol of Alley Houses," *Afro-American,* October 2, 1915.

28. Cooper, *Family Values*, 81.

29. Public Utilities Commission, *Rent and Housing Conditions*, 131.

30. Public Utilities Commission, *Rent and Housing Conditions*, 132.

31. *Antiprofiteering Rent Bill*, 114.

32. "Forbids 'Colored' Sale," *Washington Post*, May 8, 1918.

33. Newcomers were not protected under the resolution and had to wait for relief from the speculative trend until after labor and tenant groups pressured Congress to pass the Ball Rent Act. This act instated a three-person commission to "fix and determine fair and reasonable rates and rentals of dwellings, apartments, hotels and business properties in the District of Columbia upon complaint of either landlord or tenant, or upon its own initiative." See "Adopted by the Houses: Saulsbury Rent Moratorium Now for Senate to Accept," *Washington Post*, May 26, 1918; "Congress Dispute Aids Rent Gougers," *Evening Star*, July 14, 1918; "Tenants' Relief Nears," *Washington Post*, May 7, 1918; "Forbids 'Colored' Sale"; Huron, "Defending Tenants in the Midst of Plague," 43.

34. New York City tenants and settlement workers popularized the concept of rent control and eventually implemented rent control laws in 1920. See Huron, "Defending Tenants in the Midst of Plague," 41–43; and Lawson, *The Tenant Movement in New York City*.

35. In 1920, DC introduced zoning laws and in 1926 it established the National Capital Park and Planning Commission to coordinate city planning. For a history of racial covenants and other exclusionary zoning measures, see Glotzer, *How the Suburbs Were Segregated*; Sugrue, *The Origins of the Urban Crisis*; Jackson, *Crabgrass Frontier*; and Rothstein, *The Color of Law*. For DC's restrictive covenant practices, see "Covenants Map: Restricted Housing and Racial Change, 1940–1970," Mapping Segregation, accessed November 27, 2023, https://mappingsegregationdc.org/#maps.

36. Public Utilities Commission, *Rent and Housing Conditions*, 22–24.

37. Jones, *The Housing of Negroes in Washington, D.C.*, 73.

38. Jones, *The Housing of Negroes in Washington, D.C.*, 73.

39. Jones, *The Housing of Negroes in Washington, D.C.*, 60.

40. Jones, *The Housing of Negroes in Washington, D.C.*, 150. Grades were also applied to neighborhoods; see Glotzer, *How the Suburbs Were Segregated*.

41. *Antiprofiteering Rent Bill*, 105.

42. *Assessment and Taxation of Real Estate in the District of Columbia*, 26. Builders often identified "small houses" (which usually meant a home of 1,000 square feet) as the ideal starter home for immigrants and lower-income households. See Jon Gorey, "100 Years of Home Buying," *Apartment Therapy*, January 27, 2020, https://www.apartmenttherapy.com/1920s-real-estate-listings-36708482.

43. See Rothstein, *The Color of Law*, to learn how these negative impacts of property value assessments impacted Black Americans. To understand Black resistance to this mistreatment, see *Rent Commission in the District of Columbia*, 123–32 and 135–40; Masur, *An Example for All the Land*; and Masur, *Until Justice Be Done*.

44. *Assessment and Taxation of Real Estate in the District of Columbia*, 83.

45. For a map of DC's racial segregation by decade, see Chandler and Phillips, *Racial, Education and Income Segregation in the District of Columbia*, 12. Similar phenomena can be found throughout the country. One of the most prominent examples is in Baltimore; see Glotzer, *How the Suburbs Were Segregated*, 83–114.

46. National Housing Association, "House Betterment," 25–26.

47. The city passed an updated housing code for new properties in 1923.

48. Piven and Cloward, *Poor People's Movements*.

49. This report extensively cited William Henry Jones's prominent 1929 study of Black housing experiences in the nation's capital.

50. MacDonald and MacDonald, *Homemaking*, 15. For additional history on housewives, see Oakley, *Woman's Work*.

51. Johnson, *Negro Housing*, 39.

52. Johnson, *Negro Housing*, 77–79.

53. O'Conner, *Poverty Knowledge*, 45–54.

54. Johnson, *Negro Housing*, 245.

55. Vale, *From the Puritans to the Projects*, 168.

56. Liberty Square in Miami was the first Black public housing community in the United States. In DC, Hopkins Place was the first development to be constructed and funded through the Public Works Administration. However, Langston Terrace was the first public housing community to be leased back to DC's public housing authority to manage. Hopkins Place was also later managed under DC's public housing authority.

57. Friedman, "Public Housing and the Poor," 646. While this document was not specifically about DC's public housing policy, it cites Senator Robert F. Wagner's sentiments on the matter. Wagner was a key policy champion for public housing. A similar history can be found in Stanley and Dewa, *Public Housing in Hawaii*, 8; and *Investigation of the Program of the National Capital Housing Authority*.

58. Stanley and Dewa, *Public Housing in Hawaii*, 9.

59. National Capital Housing Authority, *Report of the National Capital Housing Authority for the Ten-Year Period 1934–1944*, 15.

60. National Capital Housing Authority, *Report of the National Capital Housing Authority for the Ten-Year Period 1934–1944*, 15.

61. Agnes M. Proctor to John Ihlder, October 12, 1939, "Applications for ADA Dwellings," box 1, Administrative History, 1935–1951, RG 302, Records of the National Capital Housing Authority, National Archives and Records Administration (hereafter NARA), Washington, DC.

62. For a comprehensive history of the complicated politics of public housing, see Vale, *From the Puritans to the Projects*.

63. John Ihlder to Sam Sirois, February 14, 1941, "Housing Management," box 6, RG 302, Administrative History, 1935–1951, Records of the National Capital Housing Authority, NARA.

64. Public Administration Service, *A Housing Program for the United States*, 26.

65. Internal correspondence between NCHA and RLA officials reveal that the RLA repeatedly gave cleared land formerly occupied by low-wage Black families to private developers, who built high-wage luxury homes. When the NCHA

challenged the RLA's pro-market practice, the RLA ignored the matter and advised the NCHA to rehouse more low-wage families. See William Simpson Jr. to Chester Smith, Chief Clerk for Committee for District of Columbia, January 4, 1960, "National Capital Housing Authority 1 of 2 ca. 1951–1966," box 45, collection 229, Walter A. Washington Papers, Moorland-Spingarn Research Center, Howard University, Washington, DC.

66. *Investigation of the Program of the National Capital Housing Authority*, 102.

67. Osbourne, *Public Versus Private Housing*, 4. A summary of the opposing viewpoints can be found in National Capital Housing Authority, *Report of the National Capital Housing Authority for the Ten-Year Period 1934–1944*, 3.

68. Phillips-Fein, *Invisible Hands*, 26–54.

69. Piven and Cloward, *Regulating the Poor*; Katznelson, *Fear Itself*; Fox, *Three Worlds of Relief*; Quadango, *The Color of Welfare*; Ervin, *Gateway to Equality*.

70. See Sugrue, *The Origins of the Urban Crisis*.

71. Griffith Stadium hosted many baseball games, including the Negro World Series. Eventually, the stadium became home to the Washington Football Team (then troublingly named the Washington Redskins). Martin Austermuhle, "When Blacks Fled the South, DC Became Home for Many From North Carolina," WAMU: American University Radio, September 23, 2016, https://wamu.org/story/16/09/23/when_Blacks_fled_the_south_dc_became_home_for_many_from_north_carolina/. There is also a Capital Classic that began hosting basketball games in 1974.

72. Osbourne, *Public Versus Private Housing*, 28.

73. "Housing Shortage for Defense Workers Shown in Survey," *Evening Star*, February 9, 1941; S. L. Fishbein, "Slum Clearance Critic, Property Owner Lays Blame for Conditions on Tenants," *Evening Star*, June 6, 1954.

74. This number increased with the Housing Act of 1954, which added federal funds for rehabilitation and conservation of deteriorating areas. Also, it should be noted that DC's powers of eminent domain were challenged in court in the 1954 case *Berman v. Parker*. The Supreme Court ruled in DC's favor.

75. Roger Young, "Basic Code for Housing Urged Anew," *Washington Post*, July 18, 1943.

76. National Capital Park and Planning Commission, *Housing and Redevelopment*, 13.

77. "Building Code Not Cure for Slums, He Says," *Evening Star*, July 31, 1939. Also see Bloom et al., *Public Housing Myths*.

78. "Building Code Not Cure for Slums, He Says."

79. Borchert, *Alley Life in Washington*, 57–99.

80. "Washington Memories: Petey Greene on His Childhood in Georgetown," *Washington Post*, January 18, 1984.

81. To learn more about the history of Black trickster tradition, see Kelley, *Hammer and Hoe*; Levine, *Black Culture and Black Consciousness*; and Ellison, *Invisible Man*.

82. For more about the complex motivations of low-wage young Black mothers who relied on extended family networks to raise their children before World War II, see Hartman, *Wayward Lives, Beautiful Experiments*.

83. "Washington Memories."

84. According to Greene, his grandfather had to work "eight straight hours of hoisting a hod—two sacks on either side of a solid bar—filled with bricks, up ladders to white bricklayers who completed the top stories of buildings for a contractor" because "no Black men were hired as bricklayers in Washington in the 1930s." Rackley, *Laugh If You Like*, 51.

85. Rackley, *Laugh If You Like*, 39.

86. There was eventually a great deal of organizing against the Southwest Urban Renewal Project. Marshall Heights residents living in a semi-rural Black settlement on the edge of the city also appeared before Congress to protest their inclusion in early urban renewal plans. Their protest halted redevelopment there and in Barry Farm and got their areas protected in a rider attached to the National Housing Act of 1949. See Asch and Musgrove, *Chocolate City*, 320–54; Derthick, *City Politics in Washington, DC*, 187–95.

87. Derthick, *City Politics in Washington, DC*, 187–95.

88. District of Columbia Redevelopment Land Agency, *Annual Report*, 9.

89. The "wickedest" quote is from Derthick, *City Politics in Washington, DC*, 192. Two other areas were not included in the Northwest Urban Renewal Project: Adams-Morgan, which was unique because it involved a citizen collaboration, and Foggy Bottom, where private rehabilitation (what some consider gentrification) replaced the renewal project. However, the RLA facilitated construction of the Watergate Hotel on unoccupied land in Foggy Bottom. See Asch and Musgrove, "'We Are Headed for Some Bad Trouble.'"

90. National Association of Housing and Redevelopment Officials, *The Present State of Housing Code Enforcement*, 46.

91. "Proposed D.C. Housing Law Ranks Favorably with Rules Elsewhere," *Evening Star*, December 3, 1954.

92. "Housing Association Backs Prentiss Plan on Enforcing Code," *Evening Star*, June 5, 1954.

93. Hector McLean, "Proposed Code for Housing Called 'Sham,'" *Evening Star*, December 1, 1954.

94. S. L. Fishbein, "Slum Clearance Critic, Property Owner Lays Blame for Conditions on Tenants," *Washington Post*, June 6, 1954.

95. "Proposed D.C Housing Code Called 'Too High' by Landlords' Association," Washington *Post*, March 27, 1955; S. L. Fishbein, "Slum Clearance Critic, Property Owner Lays Blame for Conditions on Tenants," *Washington Post*, June 6, 1954.

96. "Housing Code Strengthens D.C. for New Drive to Clean Up Slums," *Evening Star*, August 12, 1955.

97. Jean White, "Some Eyesores Are Gone, Others Transformed," *Washington Post*, August 7, 1956.

98. "Housing Code Strengthens D.C. for New Drive to Clean Up Slums."

99. *Washington Post* reporter Luther P. Jackson wrote a series on housing code enforcement in the summer of 1959, citing four years of checkered housing code enforcement. Luther P. Jackson, "Few Violators Punished in Struggle against Slums," *Washington Post*, August 23, 1959.

100. "NE Pilot Program Is Curbing Blight," *Washington Post*, April 27, 1957; Wes Barthelemes, "DC Moves to Stiffen Code Action on Housing," *Washington Post*, June 2, 1957.

101. "Slow Housing Law Action Scored by City Officials," *Washington Post*, May 5, 1957.

102. This point is complicated by two factors. Very few local banks were willing to offer loans to Black homeowners to repair their homes in Marshall Heights because they feared high default rates due to these homeowners' low-incomes. However, when a few capital institutions did consider lending, the FHA refused to approve the loans because their funding and demographic metrics considered them to be too high risk. Only after the 1961 Housing Act did the FHA agree to offer mortgage insurance for rehabilitation loans up to $20,000, but the FHA and local banks again refused, citing the same reasons. See Luther P. Jackson, "Marshall Heights View Offers Contrasts," *Washington Post*, November 12, 1961; Connie Feeley, "Gains Seen on War on DC Blight," *Washington Post*, January 28, 1959; John J. Lindsay, "Marshall Heights Renewal Effort Bogged Down by Poverty, Inertia," *Washington Post*, November 23, 1958; Eve Edstrom, "Marshall Heights Gaining in Campaign to Clean Up," *Washington Post*, January 14, 1958.

103. People with severe mental health issues also experience high rates of housing insecurity. However, during this time, institutionalization in state and local hospitals was seen as desirable. It was only after the national movement for deinstitutionalization in the 1960s that individuals with severe mental health challenges were reintegrated in the community. See Padgett, "Homelessness, Housing Instability and Mental Health."

104. Eve Edstrom, "Housing Code Limitations on Space Scored," *Washington Post*, October 15, 1957.

105. Wes Barthelemes, "DC Officials Uphold Housing Code, Oppose Exempting Large Families," *Washington Post*, October 16, 1957; Edstrom, "Housing Code Limitations on Space Scored."

106. Hirsch, "Containment on the Home Front"; Jackson, *Crabgrass Frontier*; Rothstein, *The Color of Law*.

107. McMichael, *McMichael's Appraising Manual*, 49–50.

108. Planning officials' investment in a majority-white city caused some leaders, such as RLA director William E. Finley, to advocate for regional planning of public housing to help localities outside the city take on a greater number of Black residents. Business leaders later supported this idea and advocated that it be included in the city's housing code. See Ndubuizu, "In the State's Shadow of Fair Housing." For a longer history of racist suburban development, see Jackson, *Crabgrass Frontier*.

109. Connie Feeley, "Official Agrees Renewal Area Rents Are High," *Washington Post*, August 12, 1959.

110. One can also consider this phenomenon within the economic context. Because typically a few suppliers eventually dominate the low-rent housing market, the negative consequences of competition are high. When housing quality and landlord accountability decline, landlords often seek to make renters responsible

for the costs of maintenance. This historical moment showed that landlords who dominated the low-rent housing sector were incentivized to minimize innovation because racial segregation gave them captive consumers. For a discussion of the impact of competition on capitalist production of goods and services, see Stanford, *Economics for Everyone*, 142–45.

111. Luther P. Jackson, "Few Violations Punished in Struggle Against Slums," *Washington Post*, August 23, 1959.

112. Luther P. Jackson, "Housing Need Aggravates Problems of Husbandless Mother of Five," *Washington Post*, February 7, 1960.

113. Luther P. Jackson, "Capital's Blight Hides in Its Dilapidated Byways," *Washington Post*, August 24, 1959.

114. Jackson, "Few Violations Punished in Struggle against Slums."

115. Taylor, *Race to Profit*.

116. Derthick, *City Politics in Washington, DC*, 190–97.

117. Derthick, *City Politics in Washington, DC*, 201–3.

118. Robert C. Albrook, "Drive to Avoid New Slums Set," *Washington Post*, December 2, 1955.

119. Ring's valorization of civic groups, particularly nonprofit charities, reflects a nationwide increase in public-private partnerships after World War II. For a history of this trend, see Dunning, *Nonprofit Neighborhoods*.

120. For other cities, see Vale, *From the Puritans to the Projects*, 283–332; and Stanley and Dewa, *Public Housing in Hawaii*.

121. Wood, foreword to *The Small Hard Core*.

122. Wood, *The Small Hard Core*, 3–4.

123. State Charities Aid Association, *"Multi-Problem Families,"* 3.

124. State Charities Aid Association, *"Multi-Problem Families,"* 4.

125. O'Conner, *Poverty Knowledge*, 20.

126. O'Conner, *Poverty Knowledge*, 20.

127. William Burden, "Family Therapy Plan Weighed," *Washington Post*, July 20, 1958.

128. Burden, "Family Therapy Plan Weighed."

129. Burt Hoffman, "5 Steps Proposed as Curb on Slums," *Evening Star*, May 16, 1958.

130. For further evidence of this pipeline, see Derthick, *City Politics in Washington, DC*, 129–43. Atlanta had a similar tendency; see Ferguson, *Black Politics in New Deal Atlanta*.

131. For more on Frazier's sociological study of Black families, see Geary, *Beyond Civil Rights*, 57–61; Ferguson, *Aberrations in Black*, 121; and Patterson, *Freedom Is Not Enough*, 29–38.

132. James Banks, "Washington's First Urban Renewal Demonstration Program," DC RLA D-1 Correspondence, container 7, RG 207, Records of Department of Housing and Urban Development, NARA.

133. "Table II: Distribution of 506 Family Data Cards by Family Type, Color, Income Level, Rating Score and Estimate of Need for Casework," DC RLA D-1 Correspondence, container 7, RG 207, Records of Department of Housing and Urban Development, NARA.

134. Southwest Urban Renewal Demonstration Project, "Report of Activities," DC RLA D-1 Correspondence, container 7, RG 207, Records of Department of Housing and Urban Development, NARA.

135. O'Conner makes a similar argument in the context of her critique of social disorganization theory in *Poverty Knowledge*, 75–98.

136. Southwest Urban Renewal Demonstration Project, "Report of Activities."

137. Luther P. Jackson, "5597 Families Still Seek NCHA Housing," *Washington Post*, February 21, 1960.

138. Luther P. Jackson, "How Officials Fight Slum-Breeding Habits," *Washington Post*, August 27, 1959.

139. Jackson, "How Officials Fight Slum-Breeding Habits."

140. Jackson, "How Officials Fight Slum-Breeding Habits." The citations were not issued until 1964.

141. Jackson, "5597 Families Still Seek NCHA Housing."

142. Charles D. Pierce, "Housing Officials Cloak Vandalism, Remon Declares," *Evening Star*, November 20, 1959.

Chapter 2

1. For a history of Wallace's segregationist politics and impact on civil rights organizing, see Carson, *In Struggle*; and Branch, *Pillar of Fire*.

2. King, *Letter from Birmingham Jail*.

3. Rasa Gustaitis, "Building Code Actions Fail to Halt Deterioration of Tenement House," *Washington Post*, April 14, 1963.

4. For an overview of the concept of misogynoir, see Bailey, "On Misogynoir"; and Bailey, *Misogynoir Transformed*.

5. United States Commission on Civil Rights, *Civil Rights USA*, 2.

6. United States Commission on Civil Rights, *Civil Rights USA*, 42.

7. *District of Columbia Urban Renewal Program*, 2.

8. "Adams-Morgan Plans Run into '61 D.C. Rules," *Evening Star*, July 26, 1961; "3 District Housing Code Cases Ended," *Evening Star*, November 14, 1964.

9. Rasa Gustaitis and Leslie H. Whitten, "Housing Code Is Virtually Suspended for Landlord in District Slum Areas," *Washington Post*, May 16, 1963.

10. Gustaitis and Whitten, "Housing Code Is Virtually Suspended."

11. Gustaitis and Whitten, "Housing Code Is Virtually Suspended."

12. Leslie Whitten, "Housing Violations Show Sharp Rise," *Washington Post*, May 18, 1963.

13. "Aide Admits Failure to Push for Repairs on Neumann Houses," *Washington Post*, June 12, 1963.

14. Rasa Gustaitis, "Housing Code Violations Uncovered," *Washington Post*, July 21, 1963.

15. Rasa Gustaitis, "Slum Owner Summoned on Defects," *Washington Post*, May 17, 1963; Rasa Gustaitis, "Deadline Set on Removing Housing Ills," *Washington Post*, May 23, 1963; Rasa Gustaitis, "Thorough Repairs Transform Once-Shabby Neumann Apartments," *Washington Post*, May 30, 1963; "Neumann Fixes 63 Build-

ings," *Washington Post*, June 23, 1963; "Way Cleared for Neumann Compliance," *Washington Post*, June 26, 1963.

16. "Neumann Officials Blame Tenants for Disrepairs in Slums," *Washington Post*, May 16, 1963.

17. Frank Caleara, "Housing Code Laxity," letter to the editor, *Evening Star*, May 24, 1963.

18. The same day that Caleara released his letter in defense of landlords, famed writers James Baldwin and Lorraine Hansberry, musician and actor Harry Belafonte, and other civil rights activists and supporters went to Attorney General Robert F. Kennedy's New York home to discuss race relations. The meeting yielded little, and someone from Kennedy's side leaked details to the *New York Times* about why they believed the meeting was not fruitful. Martin Luther King Jr.'s attorney, Clarence Jones, submitted a lengthy rebuttal to the Kennedy team's account. The negative fallout reportedly pushed President Kennedy's administration to take a more public stance on supporting civil rights for Black Americans. See Euchner, *Nobody Turn Me Around*, 120–21.

19. "Chilled Tenants Picket Rent Aide," *New York Times*, December 29, 1960.

20. "Harlem Housing Ills Laid to Landlords and Mayor," *New York Times*, August 4, 1963. In June 1963, civil rights organizers in Newark, New Jersey, also planned a rent strike to push landlords to invest in upkeep; James Clayton, "Negro Making Himself Heard Across the Land," *Washington Post*, June 9, 1963.

21. "Black Life in America," *San Francisco Chronicle*, June 30, 1963.

22. For a history of the march, see Branch, *Parting the Waters*; Carson, *In Struggle*; Lewis, *Walking in the Wind*; X and Haley, *Autobiography of Malcolm X*; and Asch and Musgrove, *Chocolate City*.

23. Transcript of John Lewis, "Speech at the March on Washington," August 28, 1963, Voices of Democracy: The US Oratory Project, https://voicesofdemocracy.umd.edu/lewis-speech-at-the-march-on-washington-speech-text/.

24. "Read Martin Luther King Jr.'s 'I Have a Dream' Speech in Its Entirety," Talk of the Nation, National Public Radio, January 16, 2023, https://www.npr.org/2010/01/18/122701268/i-have-a-dream-speech-in-its-entirety.

25. For a history of SNCC and Ella Jo Baker's critical role in generating the organization, see Ransby, *Ella Baker and the Black Freedom Movement*. For a history of Black women's contributions to the civil rights movement, see Holsaert et al., *Hands on the Freedom Plow*.

26. In its early years, NAG shaped public debate about civil rights by inviting organizer Bayard Rustin and Black nationalist Malcolm X to Howard University in October 1961.

27. Carmichael and Thelwell, *Ready for Revolution*, 136.

28. Carmichael and Thelwell, *Ready for Revolution*, 138.

29. Rasa Gustaitis, "Tenants Start First 'Rent Strike' in the District," *Washington Post*, January 25, 1964.

30. Gustaitis, "Tenants Start First 'Rent Strike.'"

31. Tom F. Ford, "Landlord Tenant Problems in Selected Cities and States: Some Recent Developments," 1966, quoted in *Housing in the District of Columbia*, 432–34.

32. Gustaitis, "Tenants Start First 'Rent Strike.'"

33. Donald Hirzel, "Holes in Leaking Apartment Roof Blamed on Rent Striker's Children," *Evening Star*, January 28, 1964.

34. Hirzel, "Holes in Leaking Apartment Roof Blamed on Rent Striker's Children."

35. "Rent Striker Denied Delay of Eviction," *Evening Star*, April 25, 1964.

36. "Court Rules Rent Strike Is Impractical Weapon," *Evening Star*, March 18, 1964.

37. "Rent-Striking Families Moved Out Just in Time to Beat Eviction," *Evening Star*, April 10, 1964.

38. David Braaten, "Church Report Blasts Slum Landlords, District Officials," *Evening Star*, April 21, 1965.

39. Benjamin Forgey, "Squalor in Slums: A Report on DC," *Evening Star*, October 3, 1965.

40. To learn more about this history, see Patterson, *Grand Expectations*, 524–92.

41. Valk, *Radical Sisters*, 28.

42. Quoted in Valk, *Radical Sisters*, 31.

43. Valk, *Radical Sisters*, 30.

44. Dorothy Gilliam, "DC Tenants Lose Their Fears and Learn to Mobilize for Action," *Washington Post*, May 29, 1966.

45. The Band of Angels had gained confidence before this press conference from their success in obtaining light bulbs, a crucial resource their community had lacked for years. They had contacted Walter Washington, who saw that they got them. See Gilliam, "DC Tenants Lose Their Fears and Learn to Mobilize for Action."

46. "'Angels' from Barry Farms War on Public Housing Unit," *Washington Post*, February 27, 1966.

47. John Carmody, "Band of Angels, Rebels with a Cause, Give Housing Chief Tough Afternoon," *Washington Post*, February 28, 1966.

48. SNCC established an official chapter in the District of Columbia in the mid-1960s. Marion Barry, Betty Garman (later Robinson), and others worked in that chapter. See Valk, *Radical Sisters*, 13–37.

49. "Barry Farm Tenants Ask 'Say' About Money Spent on Homes," *Washington Post*, March 1, 1966.

50. Michael Adams, "Tenants, DC Seek Solution," *Evening Star*, July 3, 1966.

51. "Tenant Grievances Against Management of NCHA," n.d., box 62, folder 29, Walter E. Washington Papers, Moorland-Spingarn Research Center, Howard University, Washington, DC (hereafter Walter E. Washington Papers). This document was also quoted in a housing hearing. The author was identified as John H. Stein. See *Housing in the District of Columbia*, 281.

52. Adams, "Tenants, DC Seek Solution."

53. Dan Morgan, "Irate DC Tenants Disrupt Unity Talk," *Washington Post*, May 17, 1966.

54. "DC Told to Curb Housing Violations," *Evening Star*, January 10, 1966.

55. "Bill Drafted for Reform of Landlord-Tenant Law," *Evening Star*, January 7, 1966.

56. S. Z. Fahnestock, "Tydings Hears of High Rents and Rats in Cardozo Area Tour," *Evening Star*, June 15, 1966.

57. *Housing in the District of Columbia*, 142.

58. Haynes Johnson, "Two-Price System Is Resented as an Economic Barrier," *Evening Star*, May 26, 1961.

59. *Housing in the District of Columbia*, 149.

60. *Housing in the District of Columbia*, 81–82.

61. *Housing in the District of Columbia*, 473. Critical urban geographers such as Neil Smith and David Harvey have historicized and theorized this business practice. See Smith, *Uneven Development*; and Harvey, *The Urbanization of Capital*.

62. *Housing in the District of Columbia*, 154.

63. *Housing in the District of Columbia*, 280.

64. *Housing in the District of Columbia*, 285.

65. For tenants' recounting of these events, see *Housing in the District of Columbia*, 281–88.

66. *Housing in the District of Columbia*, 206.

67. *Housing in the District of Columbia*, 207.

68. *Housing in the District of Columbia*, 405.

69. Kriston Capps, "How the 'Black Tax' Destroyed African-American Homeownership in Chicago," *The Atlantic's City Lab*, June 11, 2015, https://www.bloomberg.com/news/articles/2015-06-11/how-predatory-tax-lien-sales-destroyed-homeownership-for-african-americans-in-chicago.

70. There are numerous examples of this practice throughout the congressional hearing. For an illustrative one, see *Housing in the District of Columbia*, 208–11.

71. *Housing in the District of Columbia*, 97.

72. *Housing in the District of Columbia*, 104.

73. *Housing in the District of Columbia*, 105.

74. *Housing in the District of Columbia*, 350.

75. National Capital Housing Authority, *Report on Large Family-Rent Subsidy Demonstration Project*, 20.

76. *Housing in the District of Columbia*, 454–60.

77. For local examples of DC welfare rights activism, see Stuart Auerbach, "Tenants Block Welfare Agent in Car," *Washington Post*, May 20, 1966; "UPO Worker Arrested in Welfare Sit-Down," *Washington Post*, May 21, 1966; and Gilliam, "DC Tenants Lose Their Fears and Learn to Mobilize for Action." For a history of the DC welfare rights movement, see Valk, *Radical Sisters*, 38–59.

78. Carolyn Lewis, "She's Tenants' Ally: Florence Roisman Puts Law on Their Side," *Washington Post*, August 9, 1968.

79. Legal victories included increasing fines and imprisonment for landlords and clawed-back rent.

80. This victory resulted from Clifton Terrace's legal and organizing battle. For several years, Channing Phillips, NLSP lawyers, and public officials pressured the property's owner, Sidney Brown, to make code-compliant repairs. The impressive

campaign was eventually stymied because a number of community development groups, including Pride (cofounded by Marion Barry and his ex-wife Mary Treadwell), struggled with maintaining the property. See Carl Bernstein and Robert G. Kaiser, "City Sued by Tenants of Clifton Terrace," *Washington Post*, November 18, 1967; "Paying of Rent, Livability Tied by High Court," *Evening Star*, November 23, 1970.

81. "Paying of Rent, Livability Tied by High Court."

82. Patterson, *Grand Expectations*, 638.

83. See Bloom and Martin, *Black Against Empire*; and Kohler-Hausmann, *Getting Tough*.

84. Patterson, *Grand Expectations*, 638.

85. I am not suggesting that Lyndon Johnson always possessed a progressive vision or that his interests aligned with the left-leaning protesters who captured national attention. I share select historians' take that Johnson had different political considerations including fulfilling President John F. Kennedy's promise to address civil rights.

86. Carol Honsa, "While House Absolved in Slash of UPO Funds," *Washington Post*, December 13, 1966.

87. Michael Adams, "President Attacked on Poverty Slash," *Evening Star*, December 8, 1966; Carol Honsa, "Strong Poverty War Pushed," *Washington Post*, December 11, 1966.

88. Nikole Hannah-Jones, "Living Apart: How the Government Betrayed a Landmark Civil Rights Law," *ProPublica*, June 25, 2015, https://www.propublica .org/article/living-apart-how-the-government-betrayed-a-landmark-civil-rights -law. For histories of the uprising in DC, see Jaffe and Sherwood, *Dream City*; Asch and Musgrove, *Chocolate City*; and Pearlman, *Democracy's Capital*.

89. Colman McCarthy, "OEO and Poverty Are Still with Us," *Washington Post*, August 15, 1969.

90. Although the recession officially started in December 1969, signs of the downturn emerged in 1968.

91. Phineas Fiske, "DC Housing Unit Sees Fiscal Crisis," *Washington Post*, October 31, 1969.

92. "NCHA, Tenants Explain Their Positions in Rent Dispute," *Washington Post*, December 6, 1969.

93. Diner et al., *Housing Washington's People*, 107.

94. Eugene Meyer, "Public Housing: Evicting the Poor," *Washington Post*, December 10, 1972.

95. Peter Braestrup, "Public Housing Going Broke: Public Housing Beset by Financial Squeeze," *Washington Post*, September 1, 1972; Meyer, "Public Housing: Evicting the Poor."

96. Eugene Meyer, "HUD Renewal Chief Quit While under Investigation," *Washington Post*, July 29, 1970.

97. "UPO's Trustees Move to Guard Juvenile File," *Evening Star*, May 10, 1967.

98. Richard E. Prince, "Mayor's Aide to Head Housing Superagency," *Washington Post*, May 11, 1971.

99. William Raspberry, "The Need for Discipline," *Washington Post*, August 4, 1971.

100. Eugene Meyer, "District Aide Asks Reform on Housing," *Washington Post*, October 29, 1971.

101. Moynihan, *The Negro Family*, 11. For critical analyses of this report, see Ferguson, *Aberrations in Black*; Stack, *All Our Kin*; and Spillers, "Mama's Baby, Papa's Maybe." For a history of the political debate surrounding Moynihan's report, see Patterson, *Freedom Is Not Enough*.

102. Moynihan, *The Negro Family*, 42.

103. Kirk Scharfenberg, "Plan Devised to End Public Housing Ills," *Washington Post*, March 19, 1972.

104. For a representative example, see "Residents of Arthur Capper I," Arthur Capper (website), https://arthurcapper.omeka.net/residents1, accessed March 24, 2024.

105. "List of Tenant Council Officials by Area and Project," n.d., box 62, folder 29, Walter E. Washington Papers.

106. This point is especially salient when one considers historian Elizabeth Hinton's impressive research on the federal intervention into DC's police practices during the late 1960s and early 1970s. She cites the federal passage of District of Columbia Crime Control Bill of 1968 and the District of Columbia Court Reorganization Act of 1970. Both expanded the state's carceral reach, resulting in new categories of crime, greater police surveillance, longer sentences, and more arrests. See Hinton, *From the War on Poverty to the War on Crime*, 152–58.

107. See Orleck, *Storming Caesar's Palace*; and Nadasen, *Care: The Highest Stage of Capitalism*.

108. Carol Honsa, "Welfare Mothers Fighting for Dignity," *Washington Post*, February 5, 1967.

109. Winston Groom, "Rulings Bother Tenant Groups," *Evening Star*, March 15, 1971. There were similar findings in more than 700 lawsuits filed by Arthur Capper/Carrollsburg residents. See "Judge Says Rent Strike Can't be Settled in Court," *Evening Star*, January 8, 1970.

110. Harvey Kabaker, "New Court, Same Problem, Same Judge," *Evening Star*, February 1, 1971.

111. Harvey Kabaker, "Housing Code Applied to Public Housing," *Evening Star*, February 24, 1971.

112. "14 Tenants Win Cuts in Back Rent," *Evening Star*, February 27, 1971.

113. Harvey Kabaker, "Tenants' Rights Proposal Caught in Crossfire Here," *Evening Star*, March 15, 1970.

114. Stephen Green, "Revenue-Bill Rider Sanctions DC Welfare Rent Strikes," *Evening Star*, September 30, 1971.

115. Harvey Kabaker, "DC to Hold Welfare Rent," *Evening Star*, March 4, 1973.

116. Harvey Kabaker, "Firing of Rent Striker Upheld by Antipoverty Unit," *Evening Star*, February 19, 1970; Harvey Kabaker and Leon Coates, "2 Legal Services Aides Defy Transfers," *Evening Star*, June 3, 1970; Diner et al., *Housing Washington's People*, 107–8; "Rent Strike Leader Loses Job," *Washington Post*, January 31, 1970.

117. Diner et al., *Housing Washington's People*, 107–8.

Chapter 3

1. Lorretta Ross, interview with the author, Washington, DC, July 29, 2021.

2. United States Department of Commerce, *1990 Census of Population and Housing*; United States Census Bureau, "Resident Population in the District of Columbia."

3. Derrick, *City Politics in Washington, D.C.*, 4; Andrew Barnes, "Census Places D.C. Population at 71 Pct. Black," *Washington Post*, January 28, 1971.

4. Barnes, "Census Places D.C. Population at 71 Pct. Black."

5. Martin Weil, "Population Loss in D.C. Suspected," *Washington Post*, September 5, 1970. For cultural histories of the nation's capital, see Hunter and Robinson, *Chocolate Cites*; and Ruble, *Washington's U Street*.

6. Wells, "A Housing Crisis, a Failed Law, and a Property Conflict," 1050.

7. As an example, see *Washington Highlands*.

8. Jones, *Masters of the Universe*, 217–30; Richard Nixon, "Address to the Nation Outlining a New Economic Policy: "The Challenge of Peace," August 15, 1971, American Presidency Project, https://www.presidency.ucsb.edu/documents/address-the-nation-outlining-new-economic-policy-the-challenge-peace.

9. Ralph Blumenthal, "Most Housing Rent Rises Blocked by Nixon Order," *New York Times*, August 19, 1971.

10. Rothstein, *The Color of Law*; Sugrue, *The Origins of the Urban Crisis*; Baradaran, *The Color of Money*.

11. For a brief history of Fannie Mae and Freddie Mae, see Sorkin and Sorkin, *Too Big to Fail*, 183–84.

12. Daniel Poole, "New-Type Security Will Help Housing," *Evening Star*, April 24, 1970. Pension availability also declined as organized labor decreased and employers shifted to 401Ks as the primary financial vehicle for retirement. The principle of using retirement funds in real estate securities continued. See Aalbers, *Subprime Cities*.

13. McKenzie, *Privatopia*.

14. "Downtrend Seen in Housing," *Washington Post*, September 9, 1972.

15. District of Columbia Advisory Committee, *Neighborhood Renewal*, 18. For a more robust history, see Huron, *Carving Out the Commons*.

16. "Home Restorers Seen Displacing Poor," *Evening Star*, April 30, 1969.

17. Duncan Spencer, "Court Okays Eviction, Sets Re-Rental Terms," *Evening Star*, October 16, 1969.

18. The wage and price controls were mostly abolished by April 1974. However, housing controls had ended the year prior. Yergin and Stanislaw, *The Commanding Heights*, 60–64; Jack Kneece, "Area Rents Rise up to 38%," *Evening Star*, March 8, 1973.

19. *Rent Control Act of 1973*, 70.

20. *Rent Control Act of 1973*, 20.

21. *Rent Control Act of 1973*, 28.

22. William Elsen, "Tenants Ask Nixon to Cut Rent Rises," *Washington Post*, February 12, 1973.

23. Critical geographers have long argued that rent control is not an effective hedge against speculative real estate practices because it concedes profit accumulation. See Wells, "A Decent Place to Stay"; and *Rent Control Act of 1973*, 32.

24. Larry Weston, "Letter to Friend," "Housing & Urban Development: Correspondence File #3," Records of Federal City Council, Office of Public Records, Washington, DC, September 14, 1974.

25. Ted Overman, "The Need for Strong Rent Control," *Washington Post*, July 26, 1975.

26. *Rent Control Act of 1973*, 59.

27. O'Neill and his lobby organization originally backed a voluntary rent hike of no more than 6 percent. But as the rent control threat loomed larger, real estate leaders petitioned Nixon to exercise federal discretion in penalizing landlords who unjustifiably went beyond 6 percent in rent hikes. They thought it would be better for the federal government rather than localities to intervene in rent regulation. Jay Matthews, "Landlords Ask Probe of Raised Rents," *Washington Post*, February 28, 1973.

28. Lawrence Feinberg, "Rent Increases in Most DC Apartments," *Washington Post*, January 13, 1974.

29. Congress mandated certain legislative prohibitions on DC home rule, including lending public credit for private projects, imposing a tax on individuals who worked in the city but lived elsewhere, and submitting unbalanced budgets. See District of Columbia Home Rule Act, Pub L. 93-198, 87 Stat. 777 (1973).

30. Martha Hamilton, "DC Hill Unit Backs Rent Control Bill," *Washington Post*, June 5, 1973.

31. LaBarbara Bowman, "DC Rent Controls Passed," *Washington Post*, July 27, 1974; Linda Newton Jones, "District Mayor Signs Rent Control Measure," *Washington Post*, August 2, 1974; Thomas Lippman, "Backlog Waits DC Rent Panel," *Washington Post*, September 11, 1974.

32. Jones, "District Mayor Signs Rent Control Measure."

33. Leon Dash, "Enforcement Is Stopped on DC Rent Control Law," *Washington Post*, November 7, 1974.

34. LaBarbara Bowman, "Rent Control Panel Named," *Washington Post*, August 13, 1974.

35. *Rental Accommodations Act of 1975*, 27.

36. The city passed a permanent rent control bill in July 1975. This law also enabled tenants to request an audit of their landlords' books to ensure that rate of return was less than 8 percent. LaBarbara Bowman, "Council Votes Extension Bill on Rent Curbs," *Washington Post*, July 30, 1975.

37. John B. Willmann, "Anti-Development Concerns Tucker," *Washington Post*, November 23, 1974; "Officials Warned on Housing," *Washington Post*, November 8, 1975.

38. For more about the complexities of this law, see Hays, *The Federal Government and Urban Housing*.

39. Adrienne Manns, "The Future of Federal Housing for the Poor 'Looking for Something New,'" *Washington Post*, April 7, 1974; Hamil R. Harris, "Colleagues Remember Former DC Council Member," *Afro-American*, February 25, 2017.

40. Crawford often said that the media overstated his unyielding reputation. And while that may have been true, his methods harkened back to Booker T. Washington's well-known routine of surveilling Tuskegee on horseback. This image of a

Black male entrepreneur serving as protector, rule enforcer, and moral authoritarian has a long history, especially regarding the existing racial order. See Christian, *Booker T. Washington*.

41. Carceral scholars have noted the important role of national agencies in promoting and implementing punitive laws. See Hinton, *America on Fire*.

42. Claudia Levy, "SE's Model Manager," *Washington Post*, November 2, 1970.

43. Levy, "SE's Model Manager."

44. Levy, "SE's Model Manager."

45. Levy, "SE's Model Manager."

46. Levy, "SE's Model Manager."

47. Levy, "SE's Model Manager."

48. Eugene Meyer, "Tenants Divided on Strict Landlord," *Washington Post*, June 12, 1972.

49. Thomas Lippman, "HUD to Train Project Heads," *Washington Post*, March 21, 1974.

50. Eugene Meyer, "Black Nominee for HUD Backed," *Washington Post*, March 14, 1973.

51. Harvey Kabaker, "High Point Coming Down," *Evening Star*, June 22, 1973.

52. Michael Kiernan, "63 Families Get Sky Tower Reprieve until Feb. 1," *Evening Star*, October 11, 1974.

53. To see how poverty dispersal strategies relate to federal policy, see Hays, *The Federal Government and Urban Housing*.

54. Manns, "The Future of Federal Housing for the Poor 'Looking for Something New.'"

55. Daniels, *Fair Housing Compliance Guide*. Since the 2010s, there have been noteworthy advocacy efforts at the national level to combat certain forms of fair housing exemptions, including criminal background checks. In response to a Supreme Court ruling that recognized the racially disparate impact of universally applied exclusions of returning citizens, HUD updated its fair housing guidelines to encourage landlords to conduct case-by-case examinations of tenants with criminal records. See "Fair Housing for People with Criminal Records."

56. Meyer, "Tenants Divided on Strict Landlord."

57. To understand colorblind discourse in the post–civil rights era, see Omi and Winant, *Racial Formation in the United States*, 211–38.

58. For a close reading of Nixon's turn to colorblind politics, see Taylor, *Race to Profit*, 231–33. This dynamic became more pronounced in the 1980s; see the next chapter.

59. For a close reading of DC's tenant activist history regarding rent control and speculative real estate practices, see Wells, "A Decent Place to Stay"; and Wells, "A Housing Crisis, a Failed Law, and a Property Conflict."

60. *Hearings before the Committee on the District of Columbia*, 584.

61. *Hearings before the Committee on the District of Columbia*, 584.

62. Paul W. Valentine, "Mayor Hears Foes of Rent Bill Veto," *Washington Post*, July 2, 1975.

63. Diner et al., *Housing Washington's People*, 122. For examples of Black women's work with tenant associations, see Richard Cohen, "Tenants Learn Tactics to Fight Rent Increases," *Washington Post*, June 24, 1975; and Frances Sauve, "Apartment Rent Strikes Spread in the City," *Washington Post*, September 16, 1976.

64. Jimmy Garrett, "Statement from the SNCC Legacy Project: Celebrating the Life of James Hill," SNCC Legacy Project, January 12, 2017, https://www.crmvet.org/mem/hillj.htm.

65. Cohen, "Tenants Learn Tactics to Fight Rent Increases."

66. For thoughtful discussions of Black feminist theorizing on placemaking, see Chennault and Sutton, "At Home"; hooks, "Homeplace"; Rodriguez, *Diverging Space for Deviants*; and Winston, "Maroon Geographies."

67. Loretta Ross, interview with Joyce Follet, November 3–5, 2004, Northampton, Massachusetts, transcript in author's possession.

68. Charles Krause, "S&L Halts Apartment Loans," *Washington Post*, August 14, 1976.

69. Ned Scharff, "DC Rent Control, but Perilous to Oppose," *Evening Star*, September 6, 1977. During this period, New York City was also considered undesirable to invest in because its government was on the brink of bankruptcy. See Phillips-Fein, *Fear City*.

70. John B. Willmann, "Anti-Development Concerns Tucker," *Washington Post*, November 23, 1974; Charles Krause, "D.C. Panel Backs Eased Rent Curbs," *Washington Post*, May 6, 1976; Paul Valentine, "Mayor Reveals Plan to Spur New Housing," *Washington Post*, April 14, 1976; LaBarbara Bowman, "Council Eases Rent Control Bill," *Washington Post*, July 28, 1976.

71. Reed, *Education for Building a People's Movement*, 90–94.

72. "Yulanda Ward, Fatally Shot in Robbery, Howard Student," *Washington Post*, November 6, 1980.

73. Blair Gately, "Tenant Rebellion Fueled by Increases in Rent, Evictions," *Washington Post*, December 21, 1978.

74. Yulanda Ward Memorial Fund, "Spatial Deconcentration in DC."

75. Poverty dispersal measures were expanded in the wake of the Fair Housing Act of 1968 and local desegregation lawsuits. For this history, see Squires, *The Fight for Fair Housing*.

76. Thomas Morgan, "Robbers Kill DC Housing Unit Leader," *Washington Post*, November 3, 1980.

77. Athelia Knight, "Activists Seek Probe of Ward Murder," *Washington Post*, November 8, 1980; Kelly, "Yulanda Ward Investigation Continues"; Moira, "Grand Injury"; Loretta Ross, interview with Joyce Follet, November 5, 2004, University of Michigan, Ann Arbor, transcript available as "Global Feminisms: Comparative Case Studies of Women's Activism and Scholarship," https://findingaids.smith.edu/repositories/2/archival_objects/89289.

78. Ross, interview with the author.

79. Ross, interview with the author.

80. Reed, *Education for Building a People's Movement*, 69.

81. Reed, *Education for Building a People's Movement*, 111–12.

82. Reed, *Education for Building a People's Movement*, 113.

83. Keith Richburg, "Barry Signs Rent Control Legislation," *Washington Post*, January 8, 1981.

84. "Unemployment in District Slows Slight Increase," *Washington Post*, November 7, 1980.

85. Jane Seaberry, "Area's Jobs Will Grow—Not DC's," *Washington Post*, January 13, 1980.

86. Jack Eisen, "Welfare Families Said Hard-Hit in '70s," *Washington Post*, June 22, 1980.

87. For more about the myth of the welfare queen, see Hancock, *The Politics of Disgust*; and Levin, *The Queen*.

88. "'Welfare Queen' Becomes Issue in Reagan Campaign," *Washington Star*, February 15, 1976.

89. Kohler-Hausmann, *Getting Tough*, 125.

90. Kohler-Hausmann, *Getting Tough*, 125.

91. For a representative sample, see William Chapman, "The Welfare Enigma," *Washington Post*, May 8, 1977; Ken Auletta, "The Underclass," *The New Yorker*, November 8, 1981; David Treadwell and Gaylord Shaw, "Welfare in America," *Los Angeles Times*, July 5, 1981; and Richard Meyer and Mike Goodman, "Marauders from Inner City Prey on LA Suburbs," *Los Angeles Times*, July 12, 1981.

92. Juan Williams, "Illegitimacy," *Washington Post*, October 6, 1981.

93. For sociological examinations of Black middle-class thoughts about welfare, see Pattillo, *Black Picket Fences*; and Jackson, *Harlemworld*.

94. For a longer history of the cultural dynamics of upper-income Blacks in DC, see Gatewood, *Aristocrats of Color*, 38–66; and Frazier, *Black Bourgeoisie*.

95. Derthick, *City Politics in Washington, DC*, 26–29; Karen DeWitt, "Washington's Black Middle Class," *Washington Post*, January 26, 1975; Lawrence Feinberg, "Census Shows Loss of Middle-Income Blacks to Suburbs," *Washington Post*, February 2, 1984.

96. Jack Eisen, "Employment of Blacks in D.C. Continues to Rise," *Washington Post*, April 21, 1978.

97. Black wealth grew immensely in this period too. With affirmative action mandating minority contracting, a number of Black professionals became millionaires. These select individuals gained unprecedented access to the city and federal contracts in profitable industries such as telecommunications and defense. See Gerald Horne, "Taking Care of Black Business," *Philadelphia Tribune*, July 7, 1981; Dorothy Gilliam, "Fairness in Contracting," *Washington Post*, March 19, 1987; Lynne Duke, "Black MBAs Reflect on Affirmative Action and Hard Work," *Washington Post*, September 29, 1991; and "A Century of Black Economic Progress," *Philadelphia Tribune*, January 4, 2000.

98. Lawrence Feinberg, "Census Shows Loss of Middle-Income Blacks to Suburbs," *Washington Post*, February 2, 1984.

99. Gary Puckrein, "America's Black Middle Class," *Baltimore Sun*, April 8, 1984.

100. Michael Novak, "Racism Doesn't Explain Everything," *Evening Star*, February 22, 1977.

101. Jones, *Masters of the Universe*, 276.

102. Lewis F. Powell, Jr. to Mr. Eugene B. Sydnor, Jr., August 23, 1971, "Attack of American Free Enterprise System," US Chamber of Commerce, https://web.archive.org/web/20120104052451/http://www.pbs.org/wnet/supremecourt/personality/sources_document13.html.

103. Mayer, *Dark Money*, 94–110.

104. Phillips-Fien, *Invisible Hands*, 231.

105. William Raspberry, "Just What Is the Rent Control Question?" *Washington Post*, December 5, 1980; Sandra Evans Teeley, "Reagan Panel Targets Rent Controls," *Washington Post*, February 25, 1982.

106. Morton J. Schussheim and the Greater Washington Board of Trade, "Housing-Growth Forecasts for Housing Demands," in *Rental Housing in the Washington Area* (Washington, DC: Greater Washington Research Center, 1980), box 306, Special Collections, Research Center Collection, George Washington University Library, Washington, DC.

107. Michel Marriott, "Once-Proud Apartments Home of Despair, Frustration," *Washington Post*, January 7, 1985.

108. Schussheim and Greater Washington Board of Trade, "Housing-Growth Forecasts for Housing Demands."

109. Schussheim and Greater Washington Board of Trade, "Housing-Growth Forecasts for Housing Demands."

110. Michael Isikoff, "District Realtors Target 3 on Council," *Washington Post*, January 18, 1982. The Greater Washington Board of Trade followed a similar practice to endorse council candidates and recruited its business members for additional support. Marcia Slacum Greene, "5 of 6 Incumbents Endorsed for Council by Trade Group," *Washington Post*, August 22, 1984.

111. Forman, *Locking Up Our Own*, 130.

112. Milton Coleman, "Barry, Ray Take the Lead in Campaign Donations," *Washington Post*, February 2, 1978.

113. Edward Sargent, "Up from Georgia: Ray Sees Council Post as Opportunity to Advance Black Race," *Washington Post*, September 8, 1984.

114. Forman, *Locking Up Our Own*, 131.

115. Marcia Slacum Greene, "End to DC Rent Control Proposed," *Washington Post*, January 18, 1985.

116. Marcia Slacum Greene, "Tenants Voice Anger at Rent-Control Meeting," *Washington Post*, February 5, 1985.

117. Keary Kincannon, "City Sides: Why Tenants Oppose Decontrol," *Washington City Paper*, April 5, 1985.

118. However, the homeless movement gave many unemployed men a political platform for challenging this welfare state assumption. Kumfer, "Counter-Capital."

119. John Ray, "John Ray on Rent Control," *Washington Post*, May 6, 1985.

120. William Raspberry, "Will the Underclass Be Abandoned?" *Washington Post,* May 24, 1985.

121. B. Bruce-Briggs, "Rent Control Must Go," *New York Times*, April 18, 1976.

122. Josh Getlin, "Rich, Poor Caught in LA Rent Issue," *Los Angeles Times,* April 4, 1982.

123. Getlin, "Rich, Poor Caught in LA Rent Issue."

124. Sargent, "Up from Georgia."

125. Marcia Slacum Greene, "Council Gets an Earful on Rent Control," *Washington Post*, March 2, 1985.

126. Greene, "Council Gets an Earful on Rent Control."

127. Downs, *Opening Up the Suburbs.*

128. Marcia Slacum Greene, "Real Estate Industry Winner in Rent Control Vote," *Washington Post*, April 17, 1985.

129. Marcia Slacum Greene, "Rent Control Vote Puzzles Tenants," *Washington Post*, April 25, 1985.

130. Peter Perl, "Landlord, Tenant Panels Clash over Rent Control," *Washington Post*, October 7, 1985.

131. Joe Pichirallo, "Barry, Clarke Duel over Referendum," *Washington Post*, November 3, 1985.

132. Courtland Milloy, "In the Absence of Facts," *Washington Post*, November 3, 1985.

133. Marcia Slacum Greene, "Rent Fight to Go On: Tenant Activists Flex New Political Muscle," *Washington Post*, November 11, 1985; "DC Election Results," *Washington Post,* November 7, 1985.

134. To learn more about the longer history of housing vouchers in national politics, see Stedman, *Masters of the Universe*, 278–88.

135. For more on the history of punitive welfare reform, see Kohler-Hausmann, *Getting Tough*, 125–27; Chappell, *The War on Welfare.*

136. Sandra Evans, "New Rent Subsidy Plan to Be Tested," *Washington Post*, November 14, 1984.

137. Ann Mariano, "Variations Found in Housing Costs under 2 Programs," *Washington Post*, July 25, 1987; Ann Mariano, "The Voucher Controversy Drags On: Housing-Aid Plan Defended, Attacked," *Washington Post*, February 18, 1989.

138. Marcia Slacum Greene, "$12 Million Unspent in Rent Subsidy Plan," *Washington Post*, September 30, 1987.

139. Greene, "$12 Million Unspent in Rent Subsidy Plan."

140. Patricia Penny, interview with the author, Washington, DC, February 6, 2022.

141. Ann Mariano, "Reports of Bias against Families on Rise," *Washington Post*, September 22, 1990. For more on the design politics of housing large families, see Vale, *Purging the Poorest.*

142. Marcia Slacum Greene, "Attack on Rent Control Record Came as No Surprise to Ray," *Washington Post*, August 27, 1994.

Chapter 4

1. Robert Choflet uses the phase "fit for family life" in his dissertation, "'Unfit for Family Life.'"

2. Edward Sargent, "Kimi Gray's Dream Project," *Washington Post*, September 25, 1980.

3. "Life and Career of Kimi Gray," interview by Susan Swain, American Profiles, C-SPAN, January 11, 1990, video, 1:01, https://www.c-span.org/program/american-profile/life-and-career-of-kimi-gray/160086.

4. Sargent, "Kimi Gray's Dream Project."

5. Sargent, "Kimi Gray's Dream Project."

6. "Life and Career of Kimi Gray."

7. Taylor, *Race to Profit*.

8. This historical moment has been well studied. See Branch, *Pillar of Fire*; Lamis, *Southern Politics in the 1990s*; Rubin, *The Reactionary Mind*; and Rick Perlstein, "Exclusive: Lee Atwater's Infamous 1981 Interview on the Southern Strategy," *The Nation*, November 13, 2012.

9. Lou Cannon, "U.S. Housing Program Failure, Reagan Says," *Washington Post*, January 10, 1976; Harry Kelly, "Middle Class Bitterness: New Political Time Bomb," *Chicago Tribune*, November 27, 1977; John Averill and Paul Houston, "Conservative Ranks Grow in Congress," *Los Angeles Times*, June 24, 1979; William Raspberry, "Selling Reagan to Blacks," *Washington Post*, March 26, 1980.

10. Howell Raines, "Reagan Says His Drive Is Backed by New Coalition of Middle Class," *New York Times*, April 9, 1980; Richard Shogan, "Opportunity for Reagan," *Los Angeles Times*, November 6, 1980; E. J. Dionne Jr., "1980 Electorate Seen as Older, Whiter and More Inclined to Vote for Reagan," *New York Times*, November 5, 1980.

11. Kenneth Bacon, "Reagan Urges Speedy Action on Tax and Budget Cuts to Combat 'Economic Stagnation' and High Inflation," *Wall Street Journal*, March 11, 1981; Ndubuizu, "Reagan's Austerity Bureaucrats."

12. Stockman was also a bullish supporter of supply-side economics, emphasizing free trade, lower taxes, and deregulation. This political perspective underwrote his budgetary politics. See William Greider, "The Education of David Stockman," *The Atlantic*, December 1981, https://www.theatlantic.com/magazine/archive/1981/12/the-education-of-david-stockman/305760/.

13. Lapp, *Kenilworth*, 21.

14. Haynes Johnson, "The Merchants vs. the Young Destroyers," *Evening Star*, January 17, 1967; Bart Barnes, "'This Place Is Like a Reservation': Black Youths Hope to Quit Kenilworth," *Washington Post*, September 27, 1971.

15. Department of Energy and Environment, "Kenilworth Landfill Site," Government of the District of Columbia, accessed April 14, 2024, https://doee.dc.gov/service/kenilworth-landfill-site#:~:text=The%20Kenilworth%20Park%20Landfill%20Site,Kenilworth%20Park%20South%20(KPS). Maps of the site can also be found here at TheSandPeople, "Open Burning at Kenilworth Dump, 1966," Reddit, June 28, 2021, https://www.reddit.com/r/washingtondc/comments/o9ldab/open

_burning_at_kenilworth_dump_1966/#lightbox; and Justin Lini, "The Feds Made Kenilworth Park a Toxic Waste Site. Muriel Bowser Wants to Clean It Up," Greater Greater Washington, April 12, 2017, https://ggwash.org/view/63046/the-feds -made-kenilworth-park-a-toxic-waste-site-muriel-bowser-wants-to-clean-.

16. Elsie Carper, "Daily Dump Fire Clouds City's Skies," *Washington Post*, November 17, 1965.

17. Lapp, *Kenilworth*, 18.

18. Ivan C. Brandon, "Parkside Tenants 'Live in Fear,' Families Left in Project Want to Be Relocated," *Washington Post*, October 5, 1969; Martha M. Hamilton, "Kenilworth Dump Now Grassy Playing Field," *Washington Post*, December 31, 1972.

19. Johnson, "The Merchants vs. the Young Destroyers."

20. Barnes, "Like A Reservation."

21. Paul Hodge, "Aquatic Gardens—One of the City's 'Neglected' Paradises," *Washington Post*, August 11, 1977.

22. "Life and Career of Kimi Gray."

23. *Alternative Service Delivery*, 238.

24. *Alternative Service Delivery*, 238. For a review of the concept of linked faith, see Dawson, *Black Visions*.

25. *Alternative Service Delivery*, 238.

26. *Alternative Service Delivery*, 240.

27. Vickey Nelson, interview with the author, Washington, DC, March 27, 2022.

28. Sargent, "Kimi Gray's Dream Project."

29. Karp, "The St. Louis Rent Strike of 1969." The concept of tenant management was first proposed as early as 1961, when the suggestion was implementation in smaller units rather than high-rises. For a comprehensive history of tenant management in high-rise public housing, see Martin Arnold, "New Design, Managerial Ideas Sought in US Housing Projects," *New York Times*, November 26, 1961; "Ford Foundation, HUD Slate Program to Test Tenant-Run Housing," *Wall Street Journal*, July 1, 1976; "Cabrini-Green Has Its Own Version of St. Louis Plan," *Chicago Tribune*, August 1, 1976; Gary Washburn, "St. Louis Tries Self-Managed Public Housing," *Chicago Tribune*, August 1, 1976; Joan Cook, "Stella Wright Homes Seek Tenants Again," *New York Times*, December 17, 1975; Joan Cook, "Fresh Federal Aid and Tenant Gains Bring a New Era for Jersey Project," *New York Times*, July 28, 1975; Paul Delaney, "St. Louis Tests Housing Idea," *New York Times*, June 1, 1975; Rudy Johnson, "A 4-Year Rent Strike in Newark Ends," *New York Times*, July 18, 1974; "Tenant Protection Policy," *Baltimore Sun*, March 14, 1971; and Janelee Keidel, "Study Examines Feasibility of Housing Run by Tenants," *Baltimore Sun*, October 3, 1969.

30. "Life and Career of Kimi Gray."

31. "Life and Career of Kimi Gray."

32. "Life and Career of Kimi Gray."

33. "Life and Career of Kimi Gray."

34. Marable, *How Capitalism Underdeveloped Black America*; Guild et al., "Black 1980s."

35. William Endicott, "Black Conservatives See New Direction for Minorities," *Los Angeles Times*, December 15, 1980.

36. Endicott, "Black Conservatives See New Direction for Minorities."

37. Adam Clymer, "Black Republicans Want Reagan to Remember Them," *New York Times*, December 7, 1980.

38. "HUD Chief-Designate Pierce Favors Cuts in Spending, Leaner Housing Programs," *Wall Street Journal*, January 14, 1981.

39. For more on Samuel Pierce, see Riguer, *The Loneliness of the Black Republican.*

40. Reagan embraced AEI, appointing a number of its fellows to high-profile posts and quickly implementing a number of AEI policy recommendations. For example, following AEI senior fellow Murray Weidenbaum's defense of antiregulation, Reagan froze all new government regulations for sixty days during his first year as president. Moreover, AEI senior fellow Jeane Kirkpatrick's opinions about the increasing Soviet Union and Cuban presence in Latin America directly influenced Reagan's decision to expand the US military presence in El Salvador.

41. Peter Stone, "Conservative Brain Trust," *New York Times*, May 10, 1981.

42. Stone, "Conservative Brain Trust."

43. Herbert Denton, "Grassroots Activists Meet Conservatives," *Washington Post*, May 12, 1981.

44. Denton, "Grassroots Activists Meet Conservatives."

45. *Alternative Service Delivery*, 3.

46. *Alternative Service Delivery*, 103.

47. *Voluntarism and the Role of Action*, 127.

48. Danziger and Haveman, "The Reagan Administration's Budget Cuts"; Thomas Edsall, "Oct. 1, 1981, That Day Is Finally Here—Reagan's Budget Cuts Begin," *Washington Post*, October 1, 1981.

49. This entrepreneurial narrative has racial implications too. Since Black entrepreneurs typically encounter more capitalization hurdles, many struggle to immediately benefit from assumed best practices. This encourages business actors to secure debt from credit markets to fund startup costs. See Stanford, *Economics for Everyone*, 148–57.

50. Rubin, *The Reactionary Mind*, 24.

51. *The Extended Family: Society's Forgotten Resources*, 15.

52. Lorde, *Sister Outsider*; Walker, *In Search of Our Mothers' Gardens*; Guy-Sheftall, *Words of Fire*; hooks, *Ain't I a Woman*; Davis, *Women, Race, and Class*; Jordan, *Civil Wars*.

53. Stack, *All Our Kin*.

54. Lee Daniels, "The New Black Conservatives," *New York Times*, October 4, 1981.

55. Michel McQueen, "Robert Woodson May Have White House Access but the Conservative Infuriates Black Leaders," *Wall Street Journal*, June 2, 1987.

56. *Briefing Book: Department of Housing and Urban Development*, December 30, 1980, folder "Reports for Pres. Elect-Cabinet Briefings-HUD (1)," box 18 (OA 11261, 11263, 11264), Ronald Reagan Presidential Library and Museum, Simi Valley, CA (hereafter Reagan Library).

57. "A Conceptual Strategy for Assembling the Winning 1984 Reagan Coalition," n.d., folder "Tutwiler, Margaret: Files Series I: Chief of Staff Correspondence 1981–1982," box OA 10588 (cont.), 10589, Margaret Tutwiler Files, Reagan Library. Notwithstanding this purported intention to remain elusive, Black civil rights leaders publicly suspected that they were being snubbed, as Reagan either rebuffed their demands or refused to meet with them at all. See "NAACP Complains of Reagan 'Attacks,'" *Chicago Tribune*, February 17, 1985; "NAACP Head Calls Reagan 'Reactionary and Racist,'" *Washington Post*, May 18, 1985; Dorothy Gilliam, "Turning Back the Clock on Civil Rights Efforts," *Washington Post*, June 29, 1981.

58. William Raspberry, "A Black Unity Agenda," *Washington Post*, January 15, 1986.

59. Manning, *How Capitalism Underdeveloped Black America*; Reed, *The Jesse Jackson Phenomenon*; Reed, *Class Notes*; Taylor, *From #BlackLivesMatter to Black Liberation*.

60. Jones, *Masters of the Universe*, 85–133.

61. Mirowski, *Never Let A Serious Crisis Go to Waste*, 50–67.

62. Jones, *Masters of the Universe*, 308–13.

63. Thurston, *At the Boundaries of Homeownership*, 185–220.

64. Taylor, *Race to Profit*, 167–210.

65. *Homeownership Demonstration Program*.

66. *Homeownership Demonstration Program*.

67. John Cunniff, "Conservative Idea: Sell Tenants Public Housing," *Chicago Tribune*, June 17, 1984.

68. HUD implemented Butler's public housing finance reform in 1985, which later helped make public housing construction bonds less attractive to private investors and more costly for the federal government to build.

69. *Privatization of the Federal Government*.

70. Taylor, *Race to Profit*.

71. *Privatization of the Federal Government*, 27.

72. *Privatization of the Federal Government*, 28.

73. *Privatization of the Federal Government*, 28.

74. *Barriers to Self-Sufficiency for Single Female Heads of Families*, 518.

75. Arthur Brisbane, "Public Housing Tenants Experiment with Self-Government," *Washington Post*, May 20, 1985.

76. *Housing Act of 1985*, 750.

77. David Osborne, "They Can't Stop Us Now," *Washington Post*, July 30, 1989.

78. Ganz, *When the Clock Broke*.

79. While it is hard to pinpoint the origin of Gray's underlying political belief, her stance on marriage was not unusual, especially given the time period. While sociologists often dominated the popular discussion about Black poverty, Black psychologists also added to this discussion. Amos Wilson and Alvin Poussaint are two prominent examples. It is worth noting the powerful and outsized role (Black) heterosexual men played during the 1980s in shaping public discussion about Black marriages and family life.

80. "Life and Career of Kimi Gray."

81. For the complex history of Black cultural nationalism(s), see Floyd-Alexander, *Gender, Race, and Nationalism in Contemporary Black Politics*; Robinson, *Black Nationalism in American Politics and Thought*; and Taylor, *The Promise of Patriarchy*.

82. Allen, *Black Awakening in Capitalist America*; La Rue, "The Black Movement and Women's Liberation."

83. Interestingly enough, this amendment contained some troubling deregulation and antilabor provisions; namely, a rejection of organized labor and any other regulatory measures that members of Congress feared would raise the costs of public housing. Henry B. Gonzalez (D-TX) was one of the few representatives who resisted the turn toward deregulation that many Democrats wholeheartedly embraced in the 1980s. See *Tenant Management of Public Housing*, 1–3.

84. Marcia Slacum Greene, "Management by Tenants Promoted," *Washington Post*, March 26, 1986.

85. "Attachment III: Issue Paper on the Sale of Public Housing to Tenants," April 6, 1984, Public Housing Homeownership: 1981–1984, RD-F 54451, Records of the Office of Management and Budget, National Archives at College Park, College Park, MD (hereafter OMB Records).

86. Ann Mariano, "Transfer to Private Ownership the Issue," *Los Angeles Times*, July 22, 1985. They also worried about the constitutionality of Kemp's proposal. See "1986 Spring Planning Review: Public Housing Homeownership," n.d., Public and Indian Housing: 1981–1985, RD-F 54451, OMB Records.

87. Mariano, "Transfer to Private Ownership the Issue."

88. Judith Valente, "Housing Project Promising Home Ownership Opens," *Washington Post*, March 9, 1980.

89. Ann Mariano, "Kemp's Vision of Public Housing Ownership Hasn't Caught On," *Washington Post*, August 2, 1991.

90. Valente, "Housing Project Promising Home Ownership Opens."

91. It was almost a decade before Wylie Courts found enough prospective buyers to fill the community.

92. Memo from Susan Tanaka to Constance Horner, "Briefing Materials for the May 23 Meeting of the Cabinet Working Group on Housing Policy," n.d., Public Housing Homeownership: 1981–1984, RD-F 54451, OMB Records. Additional critique was recorded in Memo to David Stockman from Alan Rhinesmith (through Constance Horner), n.d., Public and Indian Housing: 1981–1985, RD-F 54451, OMB Records.

93. Constance Horner to Warren Lindquist, assistant secretary for Public and Indian Housing, March 6, 1985, Public and Indian Housing: 1981–1985, RD-F 54451, OMB Records.

94. Horner to Lindquist, March 6, 1985.

95. Jack Kemp to Donald Regan, February 4, 1987, box 11, "HS (Housing)," HS 47534–541052 (2 of 3), Reagan Library.

96. Spencer Rich, "Reagan Aid Decries 'Fixation' on Funding Levels," *Washington Post*, February 14, 1987.

97. National Urban League executive director Vernon Jordan once charged, "I do not challenge the conservatism of this Administration. I do challenge its failure

to exhibit a compassionate conservatism that adapts itself to the realities of a society ridden by class and race distinction." Sheila Rule, "At Urban League, Mondale Derides Reagan Values," *New York Times*, July 23, 1981. For an example of George H. W. Bush's use of "compassionate conservatism," see Jeffrey H. Birnbaum, "Bush's Speeches Are Moving Closer to the Middle in Bid to Broaden Base of Support among Voters," *Wall Street Journal*, October 11, 1988.

98. Memo from Gary L. Bauer to Donald T. Regan, February 10, 1987, box 11, "HS (Housing)," HS 47534–541052 (2 of 3), Reagan Library.

99. Rich, "Reagan Aid Decries 'Fixation' on Funding Levels."

100. Rich, "Reagan Aid Decries 'Fixation' on Funding Levels."

101. Memo from Benedict S. Cohen to Arthur B. Culvahouse Jr., February 3, 1988, box 11, HS 47534–541052 (2 of 3), Reagan Library.

102. Howard Kurtz, "Officials Delay Proposal on Public-Housing Cuts: Targeting of Vacancies Seen After Election," *Washington Post*, October 7, 1984.

103. "Bush Won't Assign Blame in HUD Influence Scandal," *Los Angeles Times*, June 27, 1989; Edward Pound and Jill Abramson, "Reagan Aides Overruled Their Advisers in Giving HUD Funds to Bush Associate," *Wall Street Journal*, June 16, 1989; Larry Green, "Elevators Out; Boy Dies After 16-Floor Climb," *Los Angeles Times*, March 7, 1981; Gene Blake, "Scandal Surfaces in City Rent Program," *Los Angeles Times*, February 9, 1982; Robert Boorstin, "Scandal Casts Shadow over Syracuse and Once-Powerful Man Who Led It," *New York Times*, June 11, 1987; Lisa Leff, "Trial of Ex-Official to Cast Spotlight on Public Housing," *Washington Post*, October 17, 1988.

104. LaBarbara Bowman, "District Officials Trying to Fill a Housing Job Nobody Wants," *Washington Post*, February 8, 1981. A lack of sensitivity among the maintenance staff was a long-standing resident complaint. They insisted that the staff expressed their disrespect with shoddy maintenance and delayed infrastructure upkeep. Throughout the city, public housing residents had to scramble to cope with the Black family tax that arose due to management's failure to invest in such maintenance. In 1980, when Kimi Gray and her neighbors pulled together to fix their frozen and broken pipes, another 5,000 public housing tenants endured the same infrastructure breakdown. But because many still wanted a management service that attended to maintenance, they chose to endure the Black family tax created by the backlog. These residents purchased blankets and heating goods and huddled near the kitchen stove to keep warm. Worse, some sent their children to live with family or friends while they battled the poor conditions. See LaBarbara Bowman, "Freeze Hits Tired Pipes in Projects," *Washington Post*, December 28, 1980.

105. "A Very Open Drug Market," *Washington Post*, January 13, 1980. To understand the ways public housing communities were seen as strategic distribution sites for illicit drug distributors, see Farber, *Crack*.

106. A musical genre native to the nation's capital, go-go became popular not only because of internationally recognized go-go artists like Chuck Brown but also because youth masterfully and creatively produced music "spiced with accentuated drum and bass playing and continuous rapping and chanting." And notably, many of go-go's top bands grew up in or near public housing; an example is

Backyard Band from Barry Farm. Weekends and summer months were packed with free or cheap go-go concerts where young people went to listen to bands such as Trouble Funk, Experience Unlimited, and Backyard Band. Edward Sargent, "Pumping Funk to Fans," *Washington Post*, February 26, 1981.

107. Lusane, *Pipe Dream Blues*, 41–44.

108. Yeager, "The Political Economy of Illicit Drugs."

109. *Drug Problem and Public Housing*, 117.

110. Glo, interview with the author, Washington, DC, August 28, 2022 (name changed for confidentiality).

111. See Lusane, *Pipe Dream Blues*, for more about Edmund.

112. For more on the business practices of illicit drug dealers, see Farber, *Crack*; and Murch, *Racist Logic*.

113. Howard Kurtz, "Public Housing Authorities Accused of Fudging on Income to Boost Aid," *Washington Post*, June 1, 1984.

114. Sandra Evans, "HUD Acts on DC Public Housing," *Washington Post*, March 12, 1986.

115. Arthur S. Brisbane, "Barry Defends Hard Line on Public Housing," *Washington Post*, June 14, 1986.

116. Brisbane, "Barry Defends Hard Line on Public Housing."

117. Brisbane, "Barry Defends Hard Line on Public Housing."

118. Brisbane, "Barry Defends Hard Line on Public Housing."

119. Forman, *Locking Up Our Own*.

120. Brisbane, "Barry Defends Hard Line on Public Housing."

121. Marcia Slacum Greene, "DC Eviction Plan Eased: Estimate of Illegal Tenants Called Too High," *Washington Post*, June 12, 1986.

122. For a history of Reagan's carceral policies, see Murakawa, *The First Civil Right*; and Kohler-Hausmann, *Getting Tough*.

123. Wagner and Vitullo-Martin, "New Hope for Old Projects." For histories of Chicago's public housing, see Vale, *Purging the Poorest*; Hirsch, *Making the Second Ghetto*; Hunt, *Blueprint for Disaster*; and Austen, *High-Risers*.

124. Jack Kemp, "Drug-Free Housing for the Nation's Poor," *Washington Post*, April 17, 1989.

125. Kemp, "Drug-Free Housing for the Nation's Poor."

126. *Drugs and Public Housing*, 88.

127. *Drugs and Public Housing*, 88.

128. *Drugs and Public Housing*, 88.

129. For a history of this policy initiative, see Forman, *Locking Up Our Own*.

130. Golash-Boza, *Before Gentrification*; Forman, *Locking Up Our Own*.

131. John Ward Anderson, "15 Vehicles Seized in DC Drug Cases," *Washington Post*, September 3, 1986. For a history of DC's War on Drugs initiatives, see Golash-Boza, *Before Gentrification*.

132. See Hinton, *America on Fire*.

133. *Tenant Management of Public Housing*.

134. Osborne, "They Can't Stop Us Now."

135. Roger Valdez, "Kenilworth: Why Didn't Tenant Purchase of Public Housing Work?" *Forbes*, March 6, 2024, https://www.forbes.com/sites/rogervaldez/2024 /03/06/kenilworth-why-didnt-tenant-purchase-of-public-housing-work/.

136. Robert Guskind and Carol F. Steinbach, "Kenilworth: Kemp's Costly Dream," *Washington Post*, April 21, 1991. Fauntroy eventually withdrew his support for this plan because, he said, the Republican Party was unwilling to provide more federal funding for public housing. He teamed up with Jesse Jackson to stage a counterprotest on the day Republican officials held a press conference that celebrated Kenilworth-Parkside's goal of becoming a housing cooperative. See "Kenilworth-Parkside and the Politics of Public Housing," *Washington Post*, July 30, 1989.

137. Guskind and Steinbach, "Kenilworth."

138. Guskind and Steinbach, "Kenilworth."

139. Guskind and Steinbach, "Kenilworth."

140. Jane H. Lehman, "Clinton Sympathetic about Housing Woes," *Los Angeles Times*, January 24, 1993.

141. "Time to Rein in Tenant Managers," *St. Louis Post-Dispatch*, January 16, 1998.

142. By the 1990s, Kenilworth-Parkside had also begun to hire outside applicants.

143. Jason Deparle, "Cultivating Their Own Gardens," *New York Times*, January 5, 1992.

144. Deparle, "Cultivating Their Own Gardens."

145. "Bertha Gilkey Pleads Guilty of Embezzling HUD Funds," *St. Louis Post-Dispatch*, January 26, 2002.

146. Norm Parish, "Housing Authority Takes over Cochran Complex," *St. Louis Post-Dispatch*, June 9, 1998.

147. Judy Radowsky and Tatsha Robertson, "City Seizes Control of Tenant-Run Complex," *Boston Globe*, October 31, 1998.

148. See Ndubuizu, "Faux Heads of Households and the Gendered and Racialized Politics of Housing Reform"; Táíwò, *Elite Capture*; and Taylor, *From #BlackLives Matter to Black Liberation*.

Chapter 5

1. Ed Bruske, "Mother of 14 Annoyed at Barry's Advice to Stop Having Babies," *Washington Post*, April 18, 1987.

2. Dorothy Gilliam, "The Scarlet Number 14," *Washington Post*, April 27, 1987.

3. William Raspberry, "Public Housing as a Reward," *Washington Post*, April 29, 1987.

4. While tax codes tend to benefit wealthier or middle-class families, race mediates their financial distribution. See Brown, *Whiteness of Wealth*.

5. Gilliam, "The Scarlet Number 14."

6. Judy Mann, "Paying for Ignorance and Too Many Children," *Washington Post*, April 22, 1987.

7. Ross and Solinger, *Reproductive Justice*.

8. Donahue and Barry seemingly understood the class, racial, and political implications of Barry's initial comments about Williams. On the television show, Donahue shared, "Barry's remarks in April encouraged the 'Archie Bunkers' of the nation" that would "get a standing ovation from the all-white Rotary Club." Barry responded, "I'd get a standing ovation from the all-Black Rotary Club, too." See Tom Sherwood, "Barry Helps Donahue Out on Welfare," *Washington Post*, July 23, 1987.

9. Sandra Gregg, "Family in Shelter Gets Own Home: City, Private Investors Join to Aid DC Couple, 14 Children," *Washington Post*, June 20, 1987.

10. Courtland Milloy, "Crawford Should Hang Tough on the Homeless," *Washington Post*, March 22, 1990.

11. Spillers, "Mama's Baby, Papa's Maybe," 64. I thank Derrais Carter for sharing this insight with me.

12. For a Black feminist analysis of the mobilization of affects like disgust in welfare reform discourse, see Hancock, *The Politics of Disgust*.

13. Patrice Gaines-Carter, "Expecting Her 15th, NE Woman Dreams of Independence," *Washington Post*, February 12, 1989.

14. Linda Wheeler, "Owners Feared Renting to City-Sponsored Family," *Washington Post*, March 13, 1990.

15. For a comprehensive history of the 1990s and its impact on national politics, see Ganz, *When the Clock Broke*.

16. Walsh, "What Caused the 1990–1991 Recession?"

17. The 1990 oil price shock was a decisive factor in the 1990 recession, too. To learn about how this recession resulted in a jobless recovery (i.e., the economy grew again but with fewer workers), see Nardone et al., "1992: Job Market in the Doldrums."

18. Robinson, "Savings and Loan Crisis."

19. Jack Nelson and Douglas Jehl, "Clinton and Perot Assail Bush Over Economy in First Debate," *Los Angeles Times*, October 12, 1992; Peter Passell, "Perot's Budget Cuts," *New York Times*, September 29, 1992.

20. Ganz, *When the Clock Broke*; Thomas B. Edsall, "In Louisiana, the Populist Coalition Splinters," *Washington Post*, August 30, 1995.

21. Thomas B. Edsall, "Gov. Roemer Struggles After Tax-Issue Defeat," *Washington Post*, May 14, 1989.

22. Ganz, *When the Clock Broke*; Allan Pell Crawford, "David Duke Meets His Peer," *Los Angeles Times*, November 17, 1991.

23. Charles Krauthammer, "Why Buchanan Runs: The Fight for the Right," *Washington Post*, November 24, 1991.

24. Krauthammer, "Why Buchanan Runs." Donald J. Trump would realize this goal decades later. Jeff Greenfield, "Trump Is Pat Buchanan with Better Timing," *Politico* (September/October 2016), https://www.politico.com/magazine/story/2016/09/donald-trump-pat-buchanan-republican-america-first-nativist-214221.

25. Alan Murray, "Presidential Candidates Tiptoe around Problem of Explosive Growth in Entitlement Spending," *Wall Street Journal*, June 29, 1992.

26. Michael Kelly, "The 1992 Campaign: The Democrats; Clinton Says He Is Not Leaning Left but Taking a 'New Third Way,'" *New York Times*, September 26, 1992.

To learn more about the origins of the "Third Way" political philosophy, see Giddens, *The Third Way*.

27. Clinton adopted this stance from conservative scholar Charles Murray. See Mayer, *Dark Money*, 136; and "Presidential Candidate Bill Clinton on Welfare Reform in 1991," *Washington Journal*, C-SPAN, October 1991, video, 1:18, https://www.c-span.org/video/?c5025152/presidential-candidate-bill-clinton-welfare-reform-1991.

28. See Geismer, *Don't Blame Us* for a close read of Michael Dukakis's enactment of this political strategy in Massachusetts, particularly in Boston.

29. See Ndubuizu, "Faux Heads of Households."

30. Michael Abramowitz, "Rating of DC Bonds Reduced," *Washington Post*, May 4, 1990. DC's general obligation bonds retained their AAA rating because companies agreed to financially back them. Traders claimed that without these provisions the bond rating would have been even lower. See Stan Hinden, "DC Municipal Bond Tax Has Some Residents Eyeing the Exits," *Washington Post*, August 5, 1991; and *District of Columbia Appropriations for 1991*, 29–30.

31. Michael Abramowitz, "District Expects to Double Size of Deferred Debt," *Washington Post*, September 30, 1990.

32. Nell Henderson, "Kelly Considers Cutting up to 3,500 City Jobs," *Washington Post*, January 15, 1992; "DC Bill Passed after Abortion Veto," *CQ Almanac*, 47th ed. (1991): 616–20.

33. Michael Abramowitz, "Vows to Cut DC Workforce Are Unrealistic, Experts Say," *Washington Post*, October 18, 1990; James Ragland and Alison Howard, "Workers File Lawsuit to Block DC Layoffs," *Washington Post*, October 21, 1991; Peter Perl, "The Mayor's Mystique," *Washington Post*, January 31, 1993.

34. Compassion fatigue is a psychological concept. *Psychology Today* offers this definition: "The experience of any empathetic individual who is acutely conscious of societal needs but feels helpless to solve them. People who actively engage in charity, or volunteering, may come to feel that they cannot commit any more energy, time, or money to the plight of others because they feel overwhelmed or paralyzed by pleas for support and that the world's challenges are never-ending." "Compassion Fatigue," n.d., *Psychology Today*, accessed July 18, 2024, https://www.psychologytoday.com/us/basics/compassion-fatigue.

35. Ellen Goodman, "Compassion Fatigue," *Washington Post*, February 3, 1990.

36. Nell Henderson, "Dixon Welfare Cuts Fell Hardest on Needy, Groups Say," *Washington Post*, March 7, 1991.

37. Nell Henderson and Kent Jenkins Jr., "DC Budget Clause Cuts Welfare Aid," *Washington Post*, April 19, 1991.

38. James Ragland, "Tax Proposal Puts Kelly, Hill on a Collison Course," *Washington Post*, February 5, 1993; Nell Henderson, "Kelly's Proposals for 2 New Taxes Still Hazy," *Washington Post*, February 12, 1993. Also see Nell Henderson, "District Work Force Dips," *Washington Post*, January 11, 1993; Kent Jenkins, "DC's Clout Dwindling on the Hill," *Washington Post*, July 5, 1993; "DC Statehood Initiative Dies in Committee," *CQ Almanac*, 48th ed. (1992): 223; Christine C. Lawrence "Where the Money Goes: District of Columbia—Fiscal Year 1994," *CQ Weekly*,

December 11, 1993, 60–61; and "House Rejects DC Statehood Bill, *CQ Almanac*, 49th ed. (1993): 208–9. During these budget battles in the early 1990s, Congress relentlessly treated DC as a policy laboratory for regressive welfare politics. See "DC Funding Clears at 11th Hour," *CQ Almanac*, 50th ed. (1994): 498–501.

39. Ruben Castaneda, "Court Asked to Force DC to Fix Housing," *Washington Post*, October 30, 1992.

40. Ruben Castaneda, "Court to Monitor's Management of Public Housing," *Washington Post*, April 24, 1993.

41. Serge Kovaleski, "Rent Voucher Revocations Still on Hold," *Washington Post*, June 6, 1994; Serge Kovaleski, "Illegal Rent Subsidy Vouchers Were Easy to Obtain," *Washington Post*, May 2, 1994; Cindy Loose, "Many Bribes Came from Wealthier Clients, Sources Say," *Washington Post*, April 16, 1994; Toni Lacy, "2 Former DC Officials Guilty in Scheme to Sell Housing Vouchers," *Washington Post*, January 20, 1995.

42. Serge Kovaleski, "DC Housing Agency Hustles to Avoid Receivership Order," *Washington Post*, August 8, 1994.

43. James Regland, "Housing Crisis Stirs More Doubts about Kelly's Management," *Washington Post*, March 25, 1994; Vernon Loeb, "Barry Asks Court to Overturn Receivership for Public Housing," *Washington Post*, January 11, 1995.

44. DC fought the transfer of city authority to the court for over seven months, until HUD pushed Mayor Barry to broker a compromise. See Vernon Loeb, "Barry Supports Respected Seattle Official to Be Receiver of DC Housing Agency," *Washington Post*, March 9, 1995; Vernon Loeb, "Cisneros Says DC Needs Receiver Now," *Washington Post*, April 26, 1995; Vernon Loeb, "Director Insists Future Is Bright for Housing Agency," *Washington Post*, May 4, 1995.

45. Serge Kovaleski, "Boston May Offer Model for DC Housing," *Washington Post*, September 4, 1994; Serge Kovaleski, "Hard Housing Lessons from the Deep South," *Washington Post*, April 17, 1994. Very few tenants organized in defense of a court receivership, but DC's famous public housing activist Kimi Gray rejected the idea and called for the city to create an independent public housing agency overseen by a strong resident advisory board. DeNeen Brown, "Residents Seek Role in Housing," *Washington Post*, June 21, 1994.

46. Serge Kovaleski, "New DC Housing Panel Holds 1st Public Meeting," *Washington Post*, May 17, 1994.

47. Serge Kovaleski, "Tougher Admission Standards Pushed for DC Public Housing," *Washington Post*, October 24, 1994.

48. Walt Harrington, "The Client and the Caseworker," *Washington Post*, May 26, 1991.

49. See Asch and Musgrove, *Chocolate City*, 425–57.

50. Like Kemp's policy agenda in the 1980s, much of the Contract with America policy goals were drafted by the Heritage Foundation. Jeffrey Gayner, "The Contract with America: Implementing New Ideas in the US," Heritage Foundation, October 12, 1995, https://www.heritage.org/political-process/report/the-contract -america-implementing-new-ideas-the-us.

51. David Vise, "House Republicans Seek to Strip DC of Treasury Borrowing Power," *Washington Post*, November 21, 1994.

52. "Who's in Charge?" *Washington Post*, December 17, 1995.

53. "Board to Oversee DC Finances," *CQ Almanac*, 51st ed. (1995): 3–25.

54. Loeb, "Cisneros Says DC Needs Receiver Now"; Vernon Loeb, "DC Cedes Control of Housing Agency: Takeover by Receiver to Last at Least 3 Years," *Washington Post*, May 5, 1995.

55. "DC Finances: The Hill's Turn," *Washington Post*, September 11, 1995.

56. David Vise and Howard Schneider, "Control Board Overrules DC on Worker Aid," *Washington Post*, November 23, 1995. From the onset of DC's financial crisis in the early 1990s, the city council grappled with how to reduce the costs associated with vouchers for TAP, the city's rental assistance program in the 1980s to early 1990s. By 1995, more than 1,500 TAP recipients had already suffered cuts, with the city capping assistance at 60 percent of contract rent. DC's financial control board came in after these cuts and recommended shutting down the program. For the history of TAP, see *District of Columbia Appropriations for 1997*, 545–48; David Vise, "DC Budget Battle to Go to Congress: City, Control Board Have Competing Plans," *Washington Post*, June 13, 1997; and Michael Powell, D'Vera Cohn, and Hamil R. Harris, "A Campaign Promise to Keep Very Busy," *Washington Post*, July 9, 1998. After the city's economic recovery, housing advocates successfully lobbied for another voucher program, Rapid Re-Housing. The program unfortunately perpetuated the racialized and gendered conditionality patterns of disciplinary housing governance. See Ndubuizu, "Where Shall the Monsters Live?" for a brief history and political analysis of the program.

57. Scandal eventually crushed Vincent Lane's political career. HUD took over Chicago's public housing authority in 1995, prompting Lane to resign. After his resignation, Lane went back into private development work. In 2001, he was charged with defrauding American National Bank by misleading investors about his private redevelopment deals. See Don Terry, "Ex-Chicago Housing Chief Says Bureaucrats Hindered His Efforts," *New York Times*, June 7, 1995; and "Ex-CHA Chief Gets Prison," *Chicago Tribune*, August 29, 2001.

58. National Commission on Severely Distressed Public Housing, *Final Report*.

59. Vale, *From the Puritans to the Projects*, 370. By 1999, Congress had significantly expanded the HOPE VI program, allocating nearly $3 billion to demolish and redevelop public housing communities.

60. Vernon Loeb, "DC Housing Chief Relishes His Role as Agency's Mr. Fix-It," *Washington Post*, June 26, 1995; Vernon Loeb, "A Miserable Place to Call Home," *Washington Post*, August 16, 1995; *Washington Post*, September 23, 1995; Vernon Loeb, "DC Housing Complex Becomes Showcase," *Washington Post*, November 5, 1995.

61. To understand Clinton's tough-on-crime rhetoric, see Gwen Ifill, "The 1992 Campaign: The Democrats; Clinton, in Houston Speech, Assails Bush on Crime Issue," *New York Times*, July 24, 1992; Hinton, *America on Fire*; and Donna Murch, "The Clintons' War on Drugs: When Black Lives Didn't Matter," *New Republic*, February 9, 2016, https://newrepublic.com/article/129433/clintons-war-drugs-Black-lives-didnt-matter.

62. "Drug Gang Swept Out of Housing Complex," *Washington Post*, May 26, 1995.

63. *DC Housing and Community Development Issues*, 62.

64. "No Second Chance: People with Criminal Records Denied Access to Public Housing," Human Rights Watch, November 17, 2004, https://www.hrw.org/report/2004/11/18/no-second-chance/people-criminal-records-denied-access-public -housing-0#:~:text=Access%20to%20public%20housing%20should,is%20of%20 scant%20public%20concern.

65. Technically, this legislation allowed states to define the parameters of workfare. Some of these parameters included education. Ultimately, the law incentivized welfare recipients to work instead of pursue educational advancement. See MacGregor Campbell, "Welfare Reform Has Led to More Work but Less Education," *NBER Digest* (January 2009), https://www.nber.org/digest/jan09/welfare-reform -has-led-more-work-less-education.

66. Vernon Loeb, "Public Housing Proposal Would Bar Criminals," *Washington Post*, October 28, 1997.

67. Loeb, "Public Housing Proposal Would Bar Criminals." There seems to have been no follow-up reporting on this proposal. However, anecdotal evidence suggests that the proposal was modified because DC public housing still accepts some households with members that have nonviolent felony convictions.

68. Bockman, "Removing the Public from Public Housing."

69. William Powers, "A Housing Complex DC Forgot: Group Seeks to Transform Abandoned Ellen Wilson Dwellings," *Washington Post*, August 22, 1992.

70. Linda Wheeler and Santiago O'Donnell, "Standoff with Squatters Is Broken," *Washington Post*, October 10, 1992; Linda Wheeler, "Kelly Fails to Satisfy Squatters," *Washington Post*, October 14, 1992.

71. Powers, "A Housing Complex DC Forgot."

72. See Huron, *Carving Out the Commons*.

73. To learn more about the history of DC tenant advocacy for limited-equity cooperatives, see Huron, *Carving Out the Commons*.

74. "District Notes: Ellen Wilson Grant Announced," *Washington Informer*, March 2, 1994; Maryann Haggerty, "Public Housing Renewal Plan Strikes a Nerve," *Washington Post*, September 23, 1995; Cindy Loose, "Abandoned Capitol Hill Complex to Be Site of Low-Income Housing," *Washington Post*, February 9, 1994.

75. For more on the history of the Ellen Wilson Redevelopment, see Laura Lang, "Ellen Wilson Projects," Arthur Capper(website), April 16, 1999, accessed May 4, 2024, https://arthurcapper.omeka.net/items/show/87#:~:text=Only%2033%20of %20the%20134,have%20homes%20in%20the%20neighborhood.

76. Linda Wheeler, "Wilson Housing Reborn," *Washington Post*, November 5, 1998.

77. Daniela Deane, "A New Face for Public Housing," *Washington Post*, May 8, 1999.

78. Bockman, "Removing the Public from Public Housing," 319.

79. Leon Dash, "Rosa Lee & Me: What One Family Told Me—and America— about the Urban Crisis," *Washington Post*, October 2, 1994, https://www .washingtonpost.com/wp-srv/local/longterm/library/rosalee/epilogue.htm. Notably, Dash won the Pulitzer Prize in 1995 for his coverage of Rosa Lee Cunningham and her family.

80. "Rosa Lee's Story: About The Series," *Washington Post*, September 21, 1994, https://www.washingtonpost.com/wp-srv/local/longterm/library/rosalee /backgrnd.htm.

81. Leon Dash, "Part Six: Daughter Travels the Same Troubled Path as Rosa Lee," *Washington Post*, September 23, 1994, https://www.washingtonpost.com/wp-srv /local/longterm/library/rosalee/part6.htm.

82. Leon Dash, "Part Four: Wrestling with Recovery in a Changing Drug Culture," *Washington Post*, September 21, 1994, https://www.washingtonpost.com/wp -srv/local/longterm/library/rosalee/part4.htm.

83. Leon Dash, "Part One: A Difficult Journey," *Washington Post*, September 18, 1994, https://www.washingtonpost.com/wp-srv/local/longterm/library/rosalee /part1.htm.

84. Dash, "Rosa Lee & Me."

85. Richard Cohen, "The Rosa Lee Story," *Washington Post*, October 4, 1994.

86. Cohen, "The Rosa Lee Story."

87. Richard Cohen, "Rosa Lee: The Case for Welfare Reform," *Washington Post*, September 10, 1996. Cunningham died in 1995 due to AIDS-related complications; Martin Weil, "Rosa Lee Cunningham, Subject of Series, Dies," *Washington Post*, July 8, 1995.

88. Cohen, *The Boundaries of Blackness*; Richie, *Arrested Justice*.

89. For a thoughtful reimagining of low-wage Black women's lives that does not justify public demonization, see Hartman, *Wayward Lives, Beautiful Experiments*.

90. Dash, "Part Six."

91. Not everyone in Cunningham's family was marked as "troubled." Two of her sons, Alvin and Eric, achieved economic and domestic security. Dash, "Part One."

92. Bockman, "Removing the Public from Public Housing," 320. For a history of the welfare program, Aid to Families with Dependent Children, see Collins and Mayor, *Both Hands Tied*; Nadasen, *Care: The Highest Stage of Capitalism*.

93. There is some dispute about the number of original residents who ultimately returned to the redevelopment. Bockman places the number at seven while journalists at the *Washington City Paper* put it at eleven. Bockman, "Removing the Public from Public Housing," 320; Laura Lang and David Morton, "Hood Winked," *Washington City Paper*, October 3, 2002.

94. Popkin et al., *Decade of HOPE VI*, 16. For scholarly critiques of HOPE VI policies, see Vale, *Purging the Poorest*; Goetz, *New Deal Ruins*; and Arena, *Driven from New Orleans*.

95. Stephanie Mencimer, "When Hell Freezes Over," *Washington City Paper*, November 5, 1999. For another positive rendering of the redeveloped property, see John W. Fountain, "After Long Slide, Hope Peeks from Ruins," *Washington Post*, May 27, 1998.

96. In addition, later HOPE VI redevelopments in DC emphasized a greater number of public housing units, even though the return rate for original tenants remained under 30 percent. See Gress et al., *HOPE VI Data Compilation and Analysis*.

97. David Stein, "The Deficit-Hawk Takeover: How Austerity Politics Constrained Democratic Policymaking," Roosevelt Institute, September 5, 2024, https://rooseveltinstitute.org/publications/the-deficit-hawk-takeover/.

98. "District of Columbia: Enact Capital Gains Exclusion, First-Time Homebuyer Credit." Urban scholar Lily Geismer provides an incisive historical and policy analysis of Clinton's empowerment zones in *Left Behind*.

99. This special designation resulted in part from Kemp's lobbying for DC to gain special tax preferences. Kemp saw DC's financial troubles as a perfect opportunity to champion a special tax designation through his nonprofit think tank Empower America. See Jack Kemp, "Okay, DC, Let's Get Radical," *Washington Post*, June 4, 1995. For the extension of the legislation, see "Norton Proposes Expanded Tax Breaks," *Washington Post*, April 18, 2002.

100. *The President's Proposal and Alternative Approaches for the District of Columbia*; *District of Columbia Appropriations for 1999*.

101. Schaller, "Situating Entrepreneurial Place Making in DC."

102. For a history of the development politics of the MCI Center, see Dave Sell, "Polling: Plan 'Interesting': Owner Noncommittal about Arena in DC," *Washington Post*, April 23, 1994; "Funding Set for DC Sports Arena," *Newark Star-Ledger*, July 20, 1994; and Peter Perl, "Full-Court Press," *Washington Post*, April 21, 1996. When the owners of the Washington Wizards and Capitals briefly considered relocating from the Capitol One Arena (formerly MCI Center) in 2024, the city crafted a sizeable deal that convinced them to remain in DC until 2050. See Josh Robbins, David Aldridge, and Ben Standig, "Capitals, Wizards to Remain at Capital One Arena as Potomac Yard Proposal Falls Through," *New York Times*, March 27, 2024.

103. Thomas Heath, "Business Leaders Say Arena Would Generate $108 Million in First Year," *Washington Post*, June 25, 1994.

104. David Vise and Howard Schneider, "Barry Ends Dispute with Finance Officer," *Washington Post*, November 15, 1995; David Vise, "Barry's Spending, Job Guts Fall Short, Fiscal Chief Says," *Washington Post*, December 18, 1996; R. H. Melton, "In Rough Waters, DC Fiscal Chief Remains Calm," *Washington Post*, December 26, 1996; Vernon Loeb, "Charting an Independent Course," *Washington Post*, August 27, 1998.

105. "DC Mayor Will Take Charge as Financial Authority Cedes Power," *Bond Buyer*, November 5, 1998.

106. Joint Center for Housing Studies of Harvard University, *The State of the Nation's Housing, 1999*, 6.

107. To learn more about the affordable housing market in light of DC's rise in luxury apartment construction in the 1990s and early 2000s, see *District of Columbia Appropriations for 2002*, 1106–7.

108. Sandra Fleishman, "What's Ahead for Housing," *Washington Post*, January 6, 2001.

109. See Nena Perry-Brown, "DC Home Prices Outpace Median Income at a Rate of 5 to 1," Urban Turf, May 31, 2017, https://dc.urbanturf.com/articles/blog/report_dc_home_prices_outpace_median_income_at_a_rate_of_5_to_1/12630. Also, it

should be noted that foreign capital increasingly got more access to real estate markets like DC during the 1990s, after certain countries' trade balances with the United States gave them more dollars to purchase assets like real estate. See Board of Governors of the Federal Reserve System, "Foreign Direct Investment in U.S. Real Estate Business," accessed April 16, 2025, *https://fred.stlouisfed.org/series/BOGZ1FR265014003A*.

110. Eric M. Weiss, "Renters Vent Anger over Housing Crunch," *Washington Post*, February 17, 2005.

111. James Gerstenzang, "Senate Passes Deep Spending Cuts for EPA, HUD," *Los Angeles Times*, September 28, 1995.

112. Debbi Wilgoren, "Landlords Accused of Rejecting Vouchers," *Washington Post*, April 11, 2005.

113. Carol O'Cleireacain and Alice M. Rivlin, "Families vs. Singles, Cost vs. Benefits," *Washington Post*, July 1, 2001. For an example of a similar policy agenda, see Stein, *Capital City*.

114. To learn more about the investment of liberals in growth metrics as the preferred policy solution for poverty after World War II, see O'Conner, *Poverty Knowledge*, 139–65.

115. O'Cleireacain and Rivlin, "Families vs. Singles, Cost vs. Benefits."

116. The report recommended setting aside 25 percent of the new apartments and homes for lower-income families. HUD's expansive definition of affordable housing identified "low-income" as up to 50 to 60 percent of DC's AMI. See Debbi Wilgoren, "Forum Offers Vision of Renewed and Inviting DC," *Washington Post*, June 15, 2001; O'Cleireacain and Rivlin, "Families vs. Singles, Cost vs. Benefits."

117. Robert Pohlman, "Priced Out of the City," *Washington Post*, April 15, 2001.

118. Debbi Wilgoren, "Council Passes Housing Act," *Washington Post*, January 9, 2002.

119. Anthony Williams, "A Place to Call Home," *Washington Post*, January 6, 2002.

120. Joseph Daniels and Robert Holum, "Reneging on a Promise to House the Poor," *Washington Post*, June 2, 2002.

121. Courtland Milloy, "What's Missing from the Mayor's Housing Record," *Washington Post*, June 15, 2005.

122. Milloy, "What's Missing from the Mayor's Housing Record."

123. Murch, *Assata Taught Me*.

124. Debbie, interview with the author, Washington, DC, July 2014 (name changed to protect confidentiality).

125. During the COVID-19 pandemic, DC reformed its tenant protections to include protections against lifetime bans for households with evictions or court appearances. Annemarie Cuccia, "DC's New Tenant Rights Bill Protects Voucher Holders, Seals Certain Eviction Records," DC Line, March 16, 2022, https://thedcline.org/2022/03/16/dcs-new-tenant-rights-bill-protects-voucher-holders-seals-certain-eviction-records/.

126. More specifically, homeless activist Mitch Snyder, who led widely publicized direct actions to successfully win federal and local resources for unhoused indi-

viduals, also gained national attention when he died in 1990. For a history of Synder's activism, see Kumfer, "Counter-Capital."

127. Lori Montgomery, "Number of Affordable Housing Units Plunge, *Washington Post*, September 13, 2005.

128. Dominic Moulden, interview with the author, Washington, DC, January 25, 2023.

129. Moulden, interview with the author.

130. Ndubuizu, "Where Shall the Monsters Live?" 226.

131. Quoted in Ndubuizu, "Where Shall the Monsters Live?" 227.

132. Ndubuizu, "Where Shall the Monsters Live?" 224.

133. Quoted in Ndubuizu, "Where Shall the Monsters Live?" 226.

134. Dawn, interview with the author, Washington, DC, October 31, 2022 (name changed to protect confidentiality).

135. Many other tenant activists and organizations were involved in this multiyear campaign.

136. Debra Frasier and Dushaw Hockett, "House Poor in the District," *Washington Post*, August 31, 2003.

137. Dawn, interview with the author.

138. Mike DeBonis, "Affordable Housing Not Inclusive," *Washington City Paper*, November 30, 2007. To be sure, IZ is not necessarily welcomed by all developers, but it has been viewed as a more desirable alternative given its flexibility in identifying affordability levels for developers. For a critique of IZ, see Scott Beyer, "Inclusionary Zoning Is Rent Control 2.0," *Forbes*, May 27, 2015, https://www.forbes.com/sites/scottbeyer/2015/05/27/inclusionary-zoning-is-rent-control-2-0/.

139. Monica, interview with the author, Washington, DC, July 7, 2022 (name changed to protect confidentiality).

140. "Inclusionary Zoning Program," Department of Housing and Community Development, accessed July 19, 2024, https://dhcd.dc.gov/service/inclusionary-zoning-iz-affordable-housing-program.

141. Kovaleski, "Tougher Admission Standards Pushed for DC Public Housing."

Conclusion

1. Katherine Shaver, "DC Has the Highest 'Intensity' of Gentrification of Any US City, Study Says," *Washington Post*, March 19, 2019, https://www.washingtonpost.com/transportation/2019/03/19/study-dc-has-had-highest-intensity-gentrification-any-us-city/; Martin Austermuhle, "DC No Longer the 'Most Intensely Gentrified City' in US, Ranking 13th in New Study," NPR, June 19, 2020, https://dcist.com/story/20/06/18/dc-is-the-13th-most-gentrified-us-city-study/.

2. Cole-Smith and Muhammad, *The Impact of an Increasing Housing Supply on Housing Prices*.

3. Sonya, interview with the author, Washington, DC, March 25, 2016 (name changed to protect confidentiality).

4. Sonya, interview with the author.

5. See Stein, *Capital City*.

6. There is a much longer and complicated racialized and gendered history of federal governance over fair housing and nonurban resistance to affordable housing. See Jackson, *Crabgrass Frontier*; and Rothstein, *The Color of Law*.

7. Jonathan O'Connell, "The Rent Is Too High in Big Cities," *Washington Post*, September 16, 2016.

8. Matthew B. Gilmore, "December 2024 update," Washington DC History Resources, December 2024, https://matthewbgilmore.wordpress.com/district-of -columbia-population-history/.

9. "Households/Income Data for City: District of Columbia," 2024 Demographics, DC Health Matters, https://www.dchealthmatters.org/demographicdata?id =130951&sectionId=936.

10. "Households/Income Data for City: District of Columbia."

11. Alaya Linton, "Places Where Black Americans Thrive the Most (and Least)," Lendingtree, August 28, 2023, https://www.lendingtree.com/debt-consolidation /thriving-black-americans-study/.

12. Charlene Crowell, "Harvard Report: Blacks, Latinos Hit Hardest by All-Time High Rental Costs," *Washington Informer*, February 1, 2024; Connor Zielinski and Mychal Cohen, "Nearly Half of All Renters and More Than Half of Black Renters in DC Struggle to Afford Rent," DC Fiscal Policy Institute, April 14, 2025, https://www .dcfpi.org/all/nearly-half-of-all-renters-and-more-than-half-of-black-renters-in-dc -struggle-to-afford-rent/.

13. Some of these housing units are allocated to Housing First, a policy approach to the homelessness crisis that underscores permanent housing options first and then supportive social services. While this model has existed since the early twentieth century, it gained greater recognition within the United States after the homebuying boom in the 1990s placed more significant displacement pressure on low-rent and older homes. This approach notably challenges disciplinary housing governance's foundational premise of conditional access tied to behavioral surveillance, and it has successfully reduced homelessness. Despite this approach's noteworthy success, competing national and local funding priorities limit its scope. Furthermore, Housing First programs rarely deal with the structural inequities that accelerate homelessness, including rising housing costs and limited or declining wages.

14. Cordilia James, "D.C. Has Had the Most Gentrifying Neighborhoods in the Country, Study Finds," DCist, March 19, 2019, https://dcist.com/story/19/03/19/d-c -has-had-the-most-gentrifying-neighborhoods-in-the-country-study-finds/.

15. Jennifer Jette, "Mayor Bowser's Rental Act: Impact on D.C. Real Estate," Friedlander Misler, February 2025, https://www.fmlaw.com/news-resources/mayor -bowsers-rental-act-impact-on-d-c-real-estate/.

16. Lesile Shaver, "How DOGE will Impact Washington, DC-Area Multifamily Owners," MultifamilyDive, March 11, 2025, https://www.multifamilydive.com /news/Doge-apartment-rents-multifamily-occupancy-job-cuts/742163/.

17. "Root Solutions for Housing and Land Justice," Race Forward, accessed April 5, 2025, https://www.raceforward.org/resources/briefs/root-solutions-housing-and -land-justice?utm_medium=email&utm_source=Act-On+Software&utm_content

=email&utm_term=Learn%20More&utm_campaign=RF%20April%20%2725%20 Newsletter; Dinyar Godrej, "How Private Equity Eroded the Right of Housing, August 9, 2019, New Internationalist, https://newint.org/features/2019/06/19 /unitednations-leilanifarha-housing.

18. Black Indigenous feminists (in the United States and abroad), Latinx feminists, cultural feminists, and others have also historically practiced a care ethic similar to that of Black feminists.

19. Premilla Nadasen offers an impressive survey of radical care initiatives that practice a feminist ethos of care; Nadasen, *Care: The Highest Stage of Capitalism.* Also see Ashanté Reese and Dara Cooper's excellent work on Black feminist care ethic and food justice, which argues that this care ethic is essential to Black liberation. Reese and Cooper, "Making Spaces Something Like Freedom."

20. Visit https://www.righttothecity.org/ for more information.

21. Social work has a complicated institutional history in the lives of working-class Black people. However, there are impressive counter-movements within the field of social work that may be useful; for example, a growing practice of restorative justice. See Van Wormer, "Restorative Justice as Social Justice for Victims of Gendered Violence"; and Nayak, "For Women of Colour in Social Work." For a critique of the history of institutional racism within social work, see Roberts, *Torn Apart.*

22. Ndubuizu, "Where Shall the Monsters Live?"

23. See Red Nation, *The Red Deal.*

24. Some scholars and practitioners are discussing how to make housing more environmentally sustainable, although they might not share my cultural analysis. For an example, see Gorlin and Newhouse, *Housing the Nation.*

25. Monica, interview with the author, Washington, DC, July 7, 2022 (name changed to protect confidentiality).

26. Monica, interview with the author.

Bibliography

Primary Sources

Archives

College Park, MD
    National Archives at College Park
        Records of the Office of Management and Budget
Simi Valley, CA
    Ronald Reagan Library
        Edwin L. Harper Files
        Margaret Tutwiler Files
        WHORM: Housing Files
Washington, DC
    DC Public Library
        The People's Archive
    George Washington University Library
        Research Center Collection, Special Collections
    Moorland-Spingarn Research Center, Howard University
        Walter E. Washington Papers
    National Archives and Records Administration
        Records of the Department of Housing and Urban Development
        Records of the National Capital Housing Authority
    Office of Public Records
        Records of Federal City Council

Newspapers and Magazines

Afro-American
Atlantic
Baltimore Sun
Bond Buyer
Boston Globe
Boston Review
Chicago Tribune
CQ Almanac
CQ Weekly
DCist
DC Line
e-flux Architecture
Evening Star

Forbes
Governing
Human Rights Watch
KTAL News
NBER Digest
Los Angeles Times
New Republic
New York Times
Newark Star-Ledger
NPR
off our backs
Politico
ProPublica

Psychology Today
PYMNTS
San Francisco Chronicle
St. Louis Post-Dispatch
Urban Turf
Wall Street Journal
*Washington City
Paper*
*Washington Evening
Star*
Washington Informer
Washington Post
Washington Star

Books and Reports

Carmichael, Stokely (Kwame Ture), and Ekuweme Michael Thelwell. *Ready for Revolution: The Life and Struggles of Stokely Carmichael*. New York: Scribner, 2005.

Chandler, Jamie P., and Joy Phillips. *Racial, Education and Income Segregation in the District of Columbia*. Washington, DC: Office of Planning, 2020. https://planning.dc.gov/sites/default/files/dc/sites/op/page_content/attachments/Segregation%20Report%2011–18–20%20FINAL.pdf.

Cole-Smith, Bethel, and Daniel Muhammad. *The Impact of an Increasing Housing Supply on Housing Prices: The Case of District of Columbia, 2000–2018*. Washington, DC: Office of Revenue Analysis, 2020. https://cfo.dc.gov/sites/default/files/dc/sites/ocfo/publication/attachments/Housing%20Supply%20Bethel%20Cole%20Smith%20April%202020.pdf.

Daniels, Rhonda L. *Fair Housing Compliance Guide*. Washington, DC: Home Builder Press, 1995.

Derthick, Martha. *City Politics in Washington, DC*. Cambridge: Joint Center for Urban Studies of Massachusetts Institute of Technology and Harvard University, 1962.

Diner, Steven J., Jerome S. Paige, Margaret M. Reuss, and Irving Richter. *Housing Washington's People: Public Policy in Retrospect*. Washington, DC: University of the District of Columbia, 1983.

District of Columbia Advisory Committee. *Neighborhood Renewal: Reinvestment and Displacement in DC*. Washington, DC: United States Commission on Civil Rights, 1981.

District of Columbia Redevelopment Land Agency. *Annual Report*. Washington, DC: District of Columbia Redevelopment Land Agency, 1960.

Ellison, Ralph. *Invisible Man*. New York: Vintage, 1952.

Gress, Taryn, Seungjong Cho, and Mark Joseph. *HOPE VI Data Compilation and Analysis*. National Initiative on Mixed-Income Communities and Jack, Joseph and Morton Mandel School of Applied Social Sciences, Case Western Reserve University, September 2016, https://www.huduser.gov/portal/sites/default/files/pdf/HOPE-VI-Data-Compilation-and-Analysis.pdf.

Johnson, Charles S. *Negro Housing: Report of the Committee on Negro Housing*. Washington, DC: President's Conference on Home Building and Home Ownership, 1932.

Joint Center for Housing Studies of Harvard University. *The State of the Nation's Housing, 1999*. Cambridge, MA: Joint Center for Housing Studies of Harvard University, 1999. https://www.jchs.harvard.edu/sites/default/files/media/imp/son99.pdf.

Jones, William Henry. *The Housing of Negroes in Washington, DC: A Study in Human Ecology*. Washington, DC: Howard University Press, 1929.

King, Martin Luther, Jr. *Letter from Birmingham Jail*. New York: Penguin Classics, 2018.

Kober, George Martin. *The History and Development of the Housing Movement in the City of Washington*. Washington, DC: Washington Sanitary Improvement Company, 1927.

Lapp, Joe. *Kenilworth: A DC Neighborhood by the Anacostia River*. Washington, DC: Humanities Council of Washington, DC, 2006. https://planning.dc.gov/sites /default/files/dc/sites/op/publication/attachments/Kenilworth_Brochure.pdf.

Lewis, John. *Walking in the Wind: A Memoir of the Movement*. New York: Simon & Schuster, 1998.

MacDonald, Elizabeth, and Forrester MacDonald. *Homemaking: A Profession for Men and Women*. Boston, MA: Marshall Jones, 1927.

McMichael, Stanley L. *McMichael's Appraising Manual: A Real Estate Appraising Handbook for Fieldwork and Advanced Study Courses*. New York: Prentice-Hall, 1946.

Moynihan, Daniel. *The Negro Family: The Case for National Action*. Washington, DC: Office of Policy Planning and Research, US Department of Labor, 1965.

National Association of Housing and Redevelopment Officials. *The Present State of Housing Code Enforcement*. Washington, DC: Department of Housing and Urban Development, 1968.

National Capital Housing Authority. *Report of the National Capital Housing Authority for the Ten-Year Period 1934–1944*. Washington, DC: Government Printing Office, 1944.

———. *Report on Large Family-Rent Subsidy Demonstration Project*. Washington, DC: National Capital Housing Authority, 1966.

National Capital Park and Planning Commission. *Housing and Redevelopment: A Portion of the Comprehensive Plan for the National Capital and Its Environs*. Washington, DC: Government Printing Office, 1950.

National Commission on Severely Distressed Public Housing. *The Final Report of the National Commission on Severely Distressed Public Housing: A Report to the Congress and Secretary of Housing and Urban Development*. Washington, DC: Government Printing Office, 1992. https://www.huduser.gov/portal//portal /sites/default/files/pdf/The-Final-Report-of-the-National-Commission-on -Severely-Distressed-Public-Housing-.pdf.

Osbourne, C. N. *Public versus Private Housing: A Review of the Washington Slum Clearance Controversy*. New York: National Industrial Conference Board, 1945.

Popkin, Susan J., Bruce Katz, Mary K. Cunningham, Karen D. Brown, Jeremy Gustafson, and Margery A. Turner. *A Decade of HOPE VI: Research Findings and Policy Challenges*. Washington, DC: Urban Institute, 2004. https://webarchive .urban.org/publications/411002.html.

Public Administration Service. *A Housing Program for the United States*. No. 48. Public Administration Service: Chicago, 1935.

Public Utilities Commission of the District of Columbia. *Rent and Housing Conditions in the District of Columbia*. Washington, DC: Government Printing Office, 1934.

Rackley, Lurma. *Laugh If You Like, Ain't a Damn Thing Funny: The Life Story of Ralph "Petey" Greene as Told to Lurma Rackley*. Bloomington, IN: Xlibris, 2003.

Reed, David. *Education for Building a People's Movement*. Boston, MA: South End Press, 1981.

Riis, Jacob A. *How the Other Half Lives: Studies among the Tenements of New York*. 1890. Reprint, New York: Dover, 1971.Stanley, Patrick A., and Roger Y. Dewa. *Public Housing in Hawaii: The Evolution of Housing Policy*. Honolulu: Legislative Reference Bureau, 1967.

State Charities Aid Association. *"Multi-Problem Families": A New Name or a New Problem?* New York: State Charities Aid Association, May 1960.

United States Commission on Civil Rights. *Civil Rights USA: Housing in Washington, DC*. Washington, DC: Government Printing Office, 1962.

United States Department of Commerce. *1990 Census of Population and Housing: Population and Housing Unit Counts, United States*. Washington, DC: Government Printing Office, 1990. https://web.archive.org/web/20080602215230/http://www.census.gov/prod/cen1990/cph2/cph-2-1-1.pdf.

Washington Highlands: A Neighborhood Analysis. Washington, DC: Office of Housing Programs, 1971.

Weller, Frederick C. *Neglected Neighbors: Stories of Life in the Alleys, Tenements, and Shanties of the National Capital*. Philadelphia: J. C. Winston, 1909.

Wood, Elizabeth. *The Small Hard Core: The Housing of Problem Families in New York City. A Study and Recommendations*. New York: Citizens' Housing and Planning Council of New York, 1957.

X, Malcom, and Alex Haley. *The Autobiography of Malcolm X*. New York: One World, 1965.

Congressional Hearings

Alternative Service Delivery: Hearings before the Subcommittee on Intergovernmental Relations of the Committee on Governmental Affairs of the Committee on Governmental Affairs, United States Senate, Ninety-Seventh Congress, First Session. Part 1: July 28, 29, and 30, 1981. Washington, DC: Government Printing Office, 1981.

Antiprofiteering Rent Bill: Hearings before the Subcommittee of the Committee on the District of Columbia, United States Senate, on the Bill H.R. 9248, a Bill to Prevent Extortion, to Impose Taxes on Certain Incomes in the District of Columbia and for Other Purposes, Sixty-Fifth Congress, First Session, March 26, 27, and 28, and April 5, 1918. Washington, DC: Government Printing Office, 1918.

Assessment and Taxation of Real Estate in the District of Columbia: Hearing before Subcommittee of the Committee on the District of Columbia, House of Representatives, under H. Res. 145 and H. Res. 200. Washington, DC: Government Printing Office, 1912.

Barriers to Self-Sufficiency for Single Female Heads of Families. Hearing before the Subcommittee of the Committee on Government Operations, House of Representatives, Ninety-Ninth Congress, First Session, July 9 and 19, 1985. Washington, DC: Government Printing Office, 1985.

DC Housing and Community Development Issues: Hearings before the Subcommittee on Housing and Community Opportunity of the Committee on Banking and

Financial Services, House of Representatives, One Hundred Fourth Congress, First Session, July 14, 1995. Washington, DC: Government Printing Office, 1985.

District of Columbia Appropriations for 1991: Hearings before the Subcommittee of Committee on Appropriations, House of Representatives, One Hundred First Congress, Second Session, Part 1. Washington, DC: Government Printing Office, 1991.

District of Columbia Appropriations for 1997: Hearings before the Subcommittee of the Committee on Appropriations, House of Representatives, One Hundred Fourth Congress, Second Session, Part 1. Washington, DC: Government Printing Office, 1997.

District of Columbia Appropriations for 1999: Hearings before the Subcommittee of the Committee on Appropriations, House of Representatives, One Hundred Fifth Congress, Second Session, Part 1. Washington, DC: Government Printing Office, 1999.

District of Columbia Appropriations for 2002: Hearings before the Subcommittee of the Committee on Appropriations, One Hundred Seventh Congress, First Session, Part 1. Washington, DC: Government Printing Office, 2002.

District of Columbia Urban Renewal Program: Hearing on an Urban Renewal Program for the District of Columbia before the House Committee on the District of Columbia, Eighty-Seventh Congress, First Session, on an Urban Renewal Program for the District of Columbia, April 11, 1961. Washington, DC: Government Printing Office, 1961.

Drug Problem and Public Housing: Hearings before the Committee on Narcotics Abuse and Control, House of Representatives, One Hundred First Congress, First Session, June 15, 1989. Washington, DC: Government Printing Office, 1989.

Drugs and Public Housing: Hearings before the Permanent Subcommittee on Investigations of the Committee on Governmental Affairs, United States Senate, One Hundred First Congress, First Session, May 10, 1989. Washington, DC: Government Printing Office, 1989.

The Extended Family: Society's Forgotten Resources. Hearing before the Subcommittee on Aging, Family and Human Services of the Committee on Labor and Human Resources, Ninety-Seventh Congress, Second Session, May 11, 1982. Washington, DC: Government Printing Office, 1982.

Hearings before the Committee on the District of Columbia. United States Senate, Ninety-Fourth Congress, First Session, on the District of Columbia Revenue Act of 1975, September 8–11, 1975. Washington, DC: Government Printing Office, 1975.

Homeownership Demonstration Program: Hearing before the Subcommittee of the Committee on Government Operations, House of Representatives, Ninety-Ninth Congress, First Session, July 9, 1985. Washington, DC: Government Printing Office, 1989.

Housing Act of 1985: Hearings before the Subcommittee on Housing and Community Development of the Committee on Banking, Finance, and Urban Affairs, House of Representatives, Ninety-Ninth Congress, First Session on H.R. 1, A Bill to Amend and Extend Certain Laws Relating to Housing, and for Other Purposes,

Ninety-Ninth Congress, First Session, Part 2, March 5 and 6, 1985. Washington, DC: Government Printing Office, 1985.

Housing in the District of Columbia: Hearings before the Subcommittee on Business and Commerce of the Committee on the District of Columbia, United States Senate, Eighty-Ninth Congress, Second Session on S.2331, to Provide for Repair by the District of Columbia, at the Expense of the Owner, of Buildings Violating the District of Columbia Housing Regulations, and to Make Tenants Evicted from Unsafe and Insanitary Buildings in the District of Columbia Eligible for Relocation Payments, S.3549 to Amend Certain Provisions of the Act Entitled "An Act to Establish a Code of Law for the District of Columbia," Approved March 3, 1901, Relating to Landlords and Tenants, S.3558 to Require the Publication of the Names of the Owners of Rental Property in the District of Columbia Which Is Used for Residential Purposes, June 28, 29; July 19, 21; August 3 and 4, 1966. Washington, DC: Government Printing Office, 1966.

Inhabited Alleys in the District of Columbia and Housing Unskilled Workingmen: Hearings before a Subcommittee of the Committee on the District of Columbia, United States Senate, Sixty-Third Congress, Second Session, on Senate Bills 1624, 2376, 2397, 2580, 4529, and 4672. Washington, DC: Government Printing Office, 1914.

Investigation of the Program of the National Capital Housing Authority: Hearings before a Subcommittee of the Committee on the District of Columbia, United States Senate, Seventy-Eighth Congress, Second Session, on S. Res. 184: A Resolution Authorizing an Investigation of the Program of the National Capital Housing Authority, and S. 1699: A Bill to Amend the District of Columbia Alley Dwelling Act as Amended. Part 5: June 10, 1944. Washington, DC: Government Printing Office, 1944.

The President's Proposal and Alternative Approaches for the District of Columbia. Hearing before the Subcommittee on Oversight of Government Management, Restructuring, and the District of Columbia of the Committee on Governmental Affairs, One Hundred Fifth Congress, First Session, May 13, 1997. Washington, DC: Government Printing Office, 1997.

Privatization of the Federal Government: Hearing before the Subcommittee on Monetary and Fiscal Policy of the Joint Economic Committee, Congress of the United States, Ninety-Eighth Congress, Second Session, Part 2, September 27 and 28, 1984. Washington, DC: Government Printing Office, 1984.

Rent Commission in the District of Columbia. Hearings Before the Joint Subcommittee of Committees on the District of Columbia, Sixty-Eight Congress, Second Session, January 12, 1925. Washington, DC: Government Printing Office, 1925.

Rent Control Act of 1973: Hearing before the Subcommittee on Public Health, Education, Welfare, and Safety on the Committee on the District of Columbia, United States Senate, Ninety-Third Congress, First Session, on H.R. 4771, to Authorize the District of Columbia Council to Regulate and Stabilize Rents in the District of Columbia, July 24, 1973. Washington, DC: United States Government Printing Office, 1973.

Rental Accommodations Act of 1975 (Council Act No. 1-46): Hearing and Disposition before Subcommittee on Commerce, Housing, and Transportation of the Committee of the District of Columbia, Ninety-Fourth Congress, First Session, on H. Con. Res. 399 to Disapprove the District of Columbia Rental Accommodation Act of 1975, October 1, 1975. Washington, DC: Government Printing Office, 1975.

Tenant Management of Public Housing: Hearing before the Subcommittee on Housing and Community Development of the Committee on Banking, Finance, and Urban Affairs, House of Representatives, Ninety-Ninth Congress, Second Session, March 25, 1986. Washington, DC: Government Printing Office, 1986.

Voluntarism and the Role of Action: Hearings before a Subcommittee of the Committee on Government Operations, House of Representatives, Ninety-seventh Congress, Second Session, February 2 and 3, 1982. Washington, DC: Government Printing Office, 1982.

Miscellaneous Primary Sources

Combahee River Collective. "The Combahee River Collective Statement (1977)." BlackPast. https://www.blackpast.org/african-american-history/combahee -river-collective-statement-1977/.

Danziger, Sheldon, and Robert Haveman. "The Reagan Administration's Budget Cuts: Their Impact on the Poor." *IRP Focus* 5, no. 2 (Winter 1981–82): 13–16. https://www.irp.wisc.edu/publications/focus/pdfs/foc52b.pdf.

Delany, Kevin. *A Walk through Georgetown: A Guided Stroll that Details the History and Charm of Old Georgetown.* Washington, DC: Kevin Delany Publications, 2001.

"District of Columbia: Enact Capital Gains Exclusion, First-Time Homebuyer Credit." *State Tax Review* 58, no. 35 (September 1997).

"Fair Housing for People with Criminal Records." Fair Housing Center for Rights and Research. 2022. https://www.thehousingcenter.org/wp-content/uploads /2022/09/Criminal-Background-Brochure-Update-Final.pdf.

Folbre, Nancy, Shawn Fremstad, and Pilar Gonalons-Pons with Victoria Coan. "Measuring Care Provision in the United States: Resources, Shortfalls, and Possible Improvements." Working paper. Center for Economic and Policy Research and Political Economy Research Institute, University of Massachusetts Amherst, June 7, 2023. https://cepr.net/wp-content/uploads/2023/06 /FINAL-Measuring-Care%E2%80%94Working-Paper-6.7.23.pdf.

Friedman, Lawrence M. "Public Housing and the Poor: An Overview." *California Law Review* 54, no. 2 (May 1966): 642–69.

"Housing of Negroes in Washington, DC." *Monthly Labor Review* 30, no. 5 (May 1930): 13–18.

Jones, Claudia. "An End to the Neglect of the Problems of the Negro Woman!" *Political Affairs* (June 1949): 3–19. https://palmm.digital.flvc.org/islandora /object/ucf%3A4865.

Kelly, Janis. "Yulanda Ward Investigation Continues." *off our backs* 11, no. 1 (January 1981).

Moira, Fran. "Grand Injury." *off our backs* 11, no. 4 (April 1981).

National Housing Association. "House Betterment." *Journal of Housing Advance* 7, no. 1 (February 1918): 25–26.

O'Cleireacain, Carol, and Alice M. Rivlin. "Envisioning a Future Washington." Research brief, Brookings Institution Greater Washington Research Program, Brookings Institution, Washington, DC, June 2001.

United States Census Bureau. "Resident Population in the District of Columbia." Federal Reserve Bank of St. Louis. Accessed April 11, 2025. https://fred .stlouisfed.org/series/DCDIST5POP.

Yulanda Ward Memorial Fund. "Spatial Deconcentration in DC." *Midnight Notes* 2, no. 2 (1981). https://libcom.org/article/spatial-deconcentration-dc-yulanda-ward.

Secondary Sources

Books

Aalbers, Manuel B., ed. *Subprime Cities: The Political Economy of Mortgage Markets.* New York: Wiley-Blackwell Press, 2012.

Agarwala, Rina, and Jennifer Jihye Chun. *Gendering Struggles against Informal and Precarious Work.* Bingley, UK: Emerald Publishing, 2018.

Allen, Robert L., *Black Awakening in Capitalist America: An Analytic History.* New York: Doubleday, 1969.

Arena, John. *Driven from New Orleans: How Nonprofits Betray Public Housing and Promote Privatization.* Minneapolis: University of Minnesota Press, 2015.

Asch, Chris Myers, and George Derek Musgrove. *Chocolate City: A History of Race and Democracy in the Nation's Capital.* Chapel Hill: University of North Carolina Press, 2017.

Austen, Ben. *High-Risers: Cabrini-Green and the Fate of American Public Housing.* New York: Harper, 2019.

Bailey, Moya. *Misogynoir Transformed: Black Women's Digital Resistance.* New York: New York University Press, 2021.

Ballou, Brendan. *Plunder: Private Equity's Plan to Pillage America.* New York: PublicAffairs, 2023.

Baradaran, Mehrsa. *The Color of Money: Black Banks and the Racial Wealth Gap.* New York: Belknap Press, 2017.

Bhattacharya, Tithi, ed. *Social Reproduction Theory: Remapping Class, Recentering Oppression.* London: Pluto Press, 2017.

Bloom, Joshua, and Waldo E. Martin. *Black against Empire: The History and Politics of the Black Panther Party.* Oakland: University of California Press, 2013.

Bloom, Nicholas Dagen, Fritz Umbach, and Lawrence J. Vale, eds. *Public Housing Myths: Perception, Reality, and Social Policy.* Ithaca, NY: Cornell University Press, 2015.

Borchert, James. *Alley Life in Washington: Family, Community, Religion, and Folklife in the City, 1850–1970.* Urbana: University of Illinois Press, 1980.

Branch, Taylor. *Parting the Waters: America in the King Years, 1954–63*. New York: Simon & Schuster, 1989.

———. *Pillar of Fire: America in the King Years, 1963–65*. New York: Simon & Schuster, 2007.

Briggs, Laura. *How All Politics Became Reproductive Politics: From Welfare Reform to Foreclosure to Trump*. Berkeley: University of California Press, 2017.

Brooks, Daphne A. *Liner Notes for the Revolution: The Intellectual Life of Black Feminist Sound*. Cambridge, MA: Harvard University Press, 2021.

Brown, Dorothy A. *The Whiteness of Wealth: How the Tax System Impoverishes Black Americans—and How We Can Fix It*. New York: Penguin Random House, 2022.

Carson, Clayborne. *In Struggle: SNCC and the Black Awakening of the 1960s*. Cambridge, MA: Harvard University Press, 1981.

Chappell, Marisa. *The War on Welfare: Family, Poverty, and Politics in Modern America*. Philadelphia: University of Pennsylvania Press, 2010.

Christian, Mark. *Booker T. Washington: A Life in American History*. Santa Barbara, CA: ABC-CLIO, 2021.

Cohen, Cathy. *The Boundaries of Blackness: AIDS and the Breakdown of Black Politics*. Chicago: University of Chicago Press, 1999.

Collins, Jane L., and Victoria Mayor. *Both Hands Tied: Welfare Reform and the Race to the Bottom in the Low-Wage Labor Market*. Chicago: University of Chicago Press, 2010.

Collins, Patricia Hill. *Black Feminist Thought: Knowledge, Consciousness, and the Politics of Empowerment*. New York: Routledge, 2000.

Connolly, N. D. B. *A World More Concrete: Real Estate and the Remaking of Jim Crow South Florida*. Chicago: University of Chicago Press, 2014.

Contrearas, Edurado. *Latinos and the Liberal City: Politics and Protest in San Francisco*. Philadelphia: University of Pennsylvania Press, 2022.

Cooper, Melinda. *Family Values: Between Neoliberalism and the New Social Conservatism*. Brooklyn, NY: Zone Books, 2017.

Cottom, Tressie McMillan. *Thick: And Other Essays*. New York: New Press, 2019.

Davis, Angela Y. *Women, Race, and Class*. New York: Random House, 1981.

Dawson, Michael C. *Black Visions: The Roots of Contemporary African-American Political Ideologies*. Chicago: University of Chicago Press, 2001.

Desmond, Matthew. *Evicted: Poverty and Profit in the American City*. New York: Crown Publishers, 2016.

Downs, Anthony. *Opening Up the Suburbs: An Urban Strategy for America*. New Haven, CT: Yale University Press, 1975.

Dunning, Claire. *Nonprofit Neighborhoods: An Urban History of Inequality and the American State*. Chicago: University of Chicago Press, 2022.

Ervin, Keona. *Gateway to Equality: Black Women and the Struggle for Economic Justice in St. Louis*. Lexington: University of Kentucky Press, 2017.

Euchner, Charles. *Nobody Turn Me Around: A People's History of the 1963 March on Washington*. New York: Beacon Press, 2011.

Farber, David. *Crack: Rock Cocaine, Street Capitalism, and the Decade of Greed.* Cambridge, UK: Cambridge University Press, 2022.

Ferguson, Karen. *Black Politics in New Deal Atlanta.* Chapel Hill: University of North Carolina Press, 2003.

Ferguson, Roderick A. *Aberrations in Black: Toward a Queer of Color Critique.* Minneapolis: University of Minnesota Press, 2004.

Floyd-Alexander, Nikol G. *Gender, Race, and Nationalism in Contemporary Black Politics.* New York: Palgrave Macmillan, 2007.

Forman, James, Jr. *Locking Up Our Own: Crime and Punishment in Black America.* New York: Farrar, Straus and Ciroux, 2017.

Fox, Cybelle. *Three Worlds of Relief: Race, Immigration, and the American Welfare State from the Progressive Era to the New Deal.* Princeton, NJ: Princeton University Press, 2012.

Frazier, E. Franklin. *Black Bourgeoisie: The Book That Brought the Shock of Self-Revelation to Middle-Class Blacks in America.* New York: The Free Press, 1997.

Ganz, John. *When the Clock Broke: Con Men, Conspiracists, and How America Cracked Up in the Early 1990s.* New York: Farrar, Straus and Giroux, 2024.

Gatewood, Willard. *Aristocrats of Color: The Black Elite, 1880–1920.* Fayetteville: University of Arkansas Press, 1990.

Geary, Daniel. *Beyond Civil Rights: The Moynihan Report and Its Legacy.* Philadelphia: University of Pennsylvania Press, 2015.

Geismer, Lily. *Don't Blame Us: Suburban Liberals and the Transformation of the Democratic Party.* Princeton, NJ: Princeton University Press, 2015.

——. *Left Behind: The Democrats' Failed Attempt to Solve Inequality.* New York: PublicAffairs, 2022.

Giddens, Anthony. *The Third Way: The Renewal of Social Democracy.* Malden, MA: Polity Press, 1998.

Gillette, Howard, Jr. *Between Justice and Beauty: Race, Planning, and the Failure of Urban Policy in Washington, DC.* Philadelphia: University of Pennsylvania Press, 2006.

Gilmore, Ruth Wilson. *Golden Gulag: Prisons, Surplus, Crisis, and Opposition in Globalizing California.* Berkeley: University of California Press, 2007.

Glotzer, Paige. *How the Suburbs Were Segregated: Developers and the Business of Exclusionary Housing, 1890–1960.* New York: Columbia University Press, 2020.

Goetz, Edward G. *New Deal Ruins: Race, Economic Justice, and Public Housing Policy.* Ithaca, NY: Cornell University Press, 2013.

Golash-Boza, Tanya Maria. *Before Gentrification: The Creation of DC's Racial Wealth Gap.* Berkeley: University of California Press, 2023.

Gorlin, Alexander, and Victoria Newhouse, eds. *Housing the Nation: Social Equity, Architecture, and the Future of Affordable Housing.* New York: Rizzoli Press, 2024.

Guy-Sheftall, Beverley, ed. *Words of Fire: An Anthology of African-American Feminist Thought.* New York: The New Press, 1995.

Haley, Sarah. *No Mercy Here: Gender, Punishment, and the Making of Jim Crow Modernity*. Chapel Hill: University of North Carolina Press, 2016.

Hancock, Ange-Marie. *The Politics of Disgust: The Public Identity of the Welfare Queen*. New York: New York University Press, 2004.

Hartman, Saidiya V. *Scenes of Subjection: Terror, Slavery, and Self-Making in Nineteenth-Century America*. New York: Oxford University Press, 1997.

———. *Wayward Lives, Beautiful Experiments: Intimate Histories of Riotous Black Girls, Troublesome Women, and Queer Radicals*. New York: W. W. Norton, 2019.

Harvey, David. *The Urbanization of Capital: Studies in the History and Theory of Capitalist Urbanization*. Baltimore, MD: John Hopkins University Press, 1985.

Hays, R. Allen. *The Federal Government and Urban Housing*. 3rd ed. Albany: State University of New York Press, 2012.

Hennessy, Rosemary, and Chrys Ingraham, eds. *Materialist Feminism: A Reader in Class, Difference, and Women's Lives*. New York: Routledge, 1997.

Higginbotham, Evelyn Brooks. *Righteous Discontent: The Women's Movement in the Black Baptist Church, 1880–1920*. Cambridge, MA: Harvard University Press, 1994.

Hicks, Cheryl. *Talk with You Like a Woman: African American Women, Justice, and Reform in New York, 1890–1935*. Chapel Hill: University of North Carolina Press, 2010.

Hinton, Elizabeth. *America on Fire: The Untold History of Police Violence and Black Rebellion since the 1960s*. New York: W. W. Norton, 2021.

———. *From the War on Poverty to the War on Crime: The Making of Mass Incarceration in America*. Cambridge, MA: Harvard University Press, 2016.

Hirsch, Arnold. *Making the Second Ghetto: Race and Housing in Chicago, 1940–1960*. Chicago: University of Chicago Press, 2021.

Holsaert, Faith S., Martha Prescod Norman Noonan, Judy Richardson, Betty Garman Robinson, Jean Smith Young, and Dorothy M. Zellner, eds. *Hands on the Freedom Plow: Personal Accounts by Women in SNCC*. Urbana: University of Illinois Press, 2010.

hooks, bell. *Ain't I a Woman: Black Women and Feminism*. New York: Routledge, 1981.

———. *Outlaw Culture: Resisting Representations*. New York: Routledge, 1994.

Hunt, D. Bradford. *Blueprint for Disaster: The Unraveling of Chicago Public Housing*. Chicago: University of Chicago Press, 2010.

Hunter, Marcus Anthony, and Zandria F. Robinson. *Chocolate Cites: The Black Map of American Life*. Oakland: University of California Press, 2018.

Huron, Amanda. *Carving Out the Commons: Tenant Organizing and Housing Cooperatives in Washington, DC*. Minneapolis: University of Minnesota Press, 2019.

Hyra, Derek S. *Race, Class, and Politics in the Cappuccino City*. Chicago: University of Chicago Press, 2017.

Jackson, John L., Jr. *Harlemworld: Doing Race and Class in Contemporary Black America*. Chicago: University of Chicago Press, 2001.

Jackson, Kenneth. *Crabgrass Frontier: The Suburbanization of the United States.* New York: Oxford University Press, 1985.

Jaffe, Harry, and Tom Sherwood. *Dream City: Race, Power, and the Decline of Washington DC.* New York: Simon & Schuster, 1994.

James, Joy. *Shadowboxing: Representations of Black Feminist Politics.* New York: Palgrave, 2002.

Jones, Daniel Stedman. *Masters of the Universe: Hayek, Friedman, and the Birth of Neoliberal Politics.* Princeton, NJ: Princeton University Press, 2013.

Jordan, June. *Civil Wars: Observations from the Front Lines of America.* New York: Simon & Schuster, 1981.

Jordan-Zachery, Julia, and Nikol Alexander-Floyd, eds. *Black Women in Politics: Demanding Citizenship, Challenging Power, and Seeking Justice.* New York: State University of New York, 2018.

Katznelson, Ira. *Fear Itself: The New Deal and the Origins of Our Time.* New York: Liveright, 2013.

Kelley, Robin D. G. *Hammer and Hoe: Alabama Communists During the Great Depression.* Chapel Hill: University of North Carolina Press, 1990.

Kohler-Hausmann, Julilly. *Getting Tough: Welfare and Imprisonment in 1970s America.* Princeton, NJ: Princeton University Press, 2017.

Lamis, Alexander P., ed. *Southern Politics in the 1990s.* Baton Rouge: Louisiana State University Press, 1999.

Lawson, Ronald, ed. *The Tenant Movement in New York City, 1904–1984.* New Brunswick, NJ: Rutgers University Press, 1986.

Lesko, Kathleen M., Valeria Babb, and Carroll R. Gibbs. *Black Georgetown Remembered: A History of Its Black Community from the Founding of "The Town of George" in 1751 to the Present Day.* Washington, DC: Georgetown University Press, 1991.

Levin, Josh. *The Queen: The Forgotten Life behind an American Myth.* New York: Little, Brown and Company, 2019.

Levine, Lawrence W. *Black Culture and Black Consciousness: Afro-American Folk Thought from Slavery to Freedom.* New York: Oxford University Press, 1977.

Lorde, Audre. *Sister Outsider: Essays and Speeches.* Berkeley, CA: Crossing Press, 1984.

Lusane, Clarence. *Pipe Dream Blues: Racism and the War on Drugs.* Boston, MA: South End Press, 1991.

Marable, Manning. *How Capitalism Underdeveloped Black America: Problems in Race, Political Economy, and Society.* New York: Haymarket Books, 2015.

Masur, Kate. *An Example for All the Land: Emancipation and the Struggle over Equality in Washington, D.C.* Chapel Hill: University of North Carolina Press, 2010.

———. *Until Justice Be Done: America's First Civil Rights Movement, from Revolution to Reconstruction.* New York: W. W. Norton & Company, 2021.

Mayer, Jane. *Dark Money: The Hidden History of the Billionaires Behind the Rise of the Radical Right.* New York: Vintage Books, 2016.

McKenzie, Evan. *Privatopia: Homeowner Associations and the Rise of Residential Private Government.* New Haven, CT: Yale University Press, 1996.

Mies, Maria. *Patriarchy and Accumulation on a World Scale: Women in the International Division of Labour.* London: Zed Books, 1986.

Mirowski, Philip. *Never Let a Serious Crisis Go to Waste: How Neoliberalism Survived the Financial Meltdown.* New York: Verso, 2013.

Mohanty, Chandra Talpade. *Feminism without Borders: Decolonizing Theory, Practicing Solidarity.* Durham, NC: Duke University Press, 2003.

Moskowitz, Peter. *How to Kill a City: Gentrification, Inequality, and the Fight for the Neighborhood.* New York: Bold Type Books, 2017.

Murakawa, Naomi. *The First Civil Right: How Liberals Built Prison America.* New York: Oxford University Press, 2014.

Murch, Donna. *Assata Taught Me: State Violence, Racial Capitalism, and the Movement for Black Lives.* Chicago: Haymarket Press, 2022.

Murch, Donna, ed. *Racist Logic: Markets, Drugs, Sex.* Boston, MA: Boston Review, 2019.

Nadasen, Premilla. *Care: The Highest Stage of Capitalism.* Chicago: Haymarket Press, 2023.

O'Conner, Alice. *Poverty Knowledge: Social Science, Social Policy, and the Poor in Twentieth-Century US History.* Princeton, NJ: Princeton University Press, 2001.

Oakley, Ann. *Woman's Work: The Housewife, Past and Present.* New York: Random House, 1976.

Omi, Michael, and Howard Winant. *Racial Formation in the United States.* New York: Routledge, 2015.

Orleck, Annelise. *Storming Caesars Palace: How Black Mothers Fought Their Own War on Poverty.* New York: Beacon Press, 2006.

Patterson, James T. *Freedom Is Not Enough: The Moynihan Report and America's Struggle over Black Family Life—from LBJ to Obama.* New York: Basic Books, 2010.

——. *Grand Expectations: The United States, 1945–1974.* New York: Oxford University Press, 1996.

Pattillo, Mary. *Black Picket Fences: Privilege and Peril among the Black Middle Class.* Chicago: University of Chicago Press, 2013.

Pearlman, Lauren. *Democracy's Capital: Black Political Power in Washington, DC, 1960s–1970s.* Chapel Hill: University of North Carolina Press, 2019.

Phillips-Fein, Kim. *Fear City: New York's Fiscal Crisis and the Rise of Austerity Politics.* New York: Metropolitan Books, 2017.

——. *Invisible Hands: The Making of the Conservative Movement from the New Deal to Reagan.* New York: W. W. Norton & Company, 2009.

Piven, Frances Fox, and Richard A. Cloward. *Poor People's Movements: Why They Succeed, How They Fail.* New York: Vintage Books, 1977.

——. *Regulating the Poor: The Functions of Public Welfare.* New York: Vintage Books, 1971.

Quadango, Jill. *The Color of Welfare: How Racism Undermined the War on Poverty.* New York: Oxford University Press, 1996.

Ransby, Barbara. *Ella Baker and the Black Freedom Movement: A Radical Democratic Vision*. Chapel Hill: University of North Carolina Press, 2003.

——. *Making All Black Lives Matter: Reimagining Freedom in the 21st Century*. Oakland: University of California Press, 2018.

Red Nation. *The Red Deal: Indigenous Action to Save Our Earth*. New York: Common Notions, 2021.

Reed, Adolph, Jr. *Class Notes: Posing as Politics and Other Thoughts on the American Scene*. New York: The New Press, 2001.

——. *The Jesse Jackson Phenomenon: The Crisis of Purpose in Afro-American Politics*. New Haven, CT: Yale University Press, 1986.

Richie, Beth E. *Arrested Justice: Black Women, Violence, and America's Prison Nation*. New York: New York University Press, 2012.

Riguer, Leah Wright. *The Loneliness of the Black Republican: Pragmatic Politics and the Pursuit of Power*. Princeton, NJ: Princeton University Press, 2016.

Roberts, Dorothy. *Torn Apart: How the Child Welfare System Destroys Black Families—and How Abolition Can Build a Safer World*. New York: Basic Books, 2022.

Robinson, Cedric. *Black Marxism: The Making of the Black Radical Tradition*. Chapel Hill: University of North Carolina Press, 1983.

Robinson, Dean E. *Black Nationalism in American Politics and Thought*. Cambridge, UK: Cambridge University Press, 2001.

Rodriguez, Akira Drake. *Diverging Space for Deviants: The Politics of Atlanta's Public Housing*. Athens: University of Georgia Press, 2021.

Ross, Loretta J., and Rickie Solinger. *Reproductive Justice: An Introduction*. Oakland: University of California Press, 2017.

Rothstein, Richard. *The Color of Law: A Forgotten History of How Our Government Segregated America*. New York: Liveright, 2017.

Rubin, Corey. *The Reactionary Mind: Conservatism from Edmund Burke to Sarah Palin*. New York: Oxford University Press, 2011.

Ruble, Blair A. *Washington's U Street: A Biography*. Baltimore, MD: Johns Hopkins University Press, 2012.

Satter, Beryl. *Family Properties: Race, Real Estate, and the Exploitation of Black Urban America*. New York: Metropolitan Books, 2009.

Skocpol, Theda. *Protecting Soldiers and Mothers: The Political Origins of Social Policy in the United States*. Cambridge, MA: Harvard University Press, 1992.

Slater, Gene. *Freedom to Discriminate: How Realtors Conspired to Segregate Housing and Divide America*. Berkeley, CA: Heyday, 2021.

Smith, Neil. *Uneven Development: Nature, Capital, and the Production of Space*. New York: Verso, 2010.

Sorkin, Andrew, and Ross Sorkin, *Too Big to Fail: The Inside Story of How Wall Street and Washington Fought to Save the Financial System—and Themselves*. New York: Viking Press, 2009.

Squires, Gregory D., ed. *The Fight for Fair Housing: Causes, Consequences, and Future Implications of the 1968 Federal Housing Act*. New York: Routledge, 2018.

Stack, Carol B. *All Our Kin: Strategies for Survival in a Black Community*. New York: Basic Books, 1974.

Standing, Guy. *The Precariat: The New Dangerous Class*. London: Bloomsbury, 2011.

Stanford, Jim. *Economics for Everyone: A Short Guide to the Economics of Capitalism*. London: Pluto Press, 2008.

Stein, Samuel. *Capital City: Gentrification and the Real Estate State*. New York: Verso, 2019.

Sugrue, Thomas. *The Origins of the Urban Crisis: Race and Inequality in Postwar Detroit*. Princeton, NJ: Princeton University Press, 1996.

Summers, Brandi Thompson. *Black in Place: The Spatial Aesthetics of Race in a Post-Chocolate City*. Chapel Hill: University of North Carolina Press, 2019.

Táíwò, Olúfémi O. *Elite Capture: How the Powerful Took Over Identity Politics (and Everything Else)*. New York: Haymarket Press, 2022.

Taylor, Keeanga-Yamahtta. *From #BlackLivesMatter to Black Liberation*. Chicago: Haymarket Books, 2021.

———. *How We Get Free: Black Feminism and the Combahee River Collective*. Chicago: Haymarket Books, 2017.

———. *Race to Profit: How Banks and the Real Estate Industry Undermined Black Homeownership*. Chapel Hill: University of North Carolina Press, 2019.

Taylor, Ula Yvette. *The Promise of Patriarchy: Women and the Nation of Islam*. Chapel Hill: University of North Carolina Press, 2017.

Vale, Lawrence J. *From the Puritans to the Projects: Public Housing and Public Neighbors*. Cambridge, MA: Harvard University Press, 2000.

———. *Purging the Poorest: Public Housing and the Design Politics of Twice-Cleared Communities*. Chicago: University of Chicago Press, 2013.

Valk, Anne. *Radical Sisters: Second Wave Feminism and Black Liberation in Washington, DC*. Urbana: University of Illinois Press, 2008.

Walker, Alice. *In Search of Our Mothers' Gardens: Womanist Prose*. San Diego, CA: Harcourt Brace Jovanovich, 1983.

Wilchins, Riki Anne. *Queer Theory, Gender Theory*. New York: Alyson Publications, 2004.

Williams, Rhonda Y. *The Politics of Public Housing: Black Women's Struggles against Urban Inequality*. New York: Oxford University Press, 2004.

Yergin, Daniel, and Joseph Stanislaw. *The Commanding Heights: The Battle for the World Economy*. New York: Simon & Schuster, 1998.

Journal Articles, Book Chapters, and Dissertations

Asch, Chris Myers, and George Derek Musgrove. "'We Are Headed for Some Bad Trouble': Gentrification and Displacement in Washington, DC, 1920–2014." In *Capital Dilemma: Growth and Inequality in Washington, DC*, edited by Derek Hyra and Sabiyha Price, 107–36. New York: Routledge Press, 2015.

Bailey, Moya. "On Misogynoir: Citation, Erasure, and Plagiarism." *Feminist Media Studies* 18, no. 4 (2018): 762–68.

Baker, Catherine, Debbie Ging, and Maja Brandt Andreasen. "Recommending Toxicity: The Role of Algorithmic Recommender Functions on YouTube Shorts and TikTok in Promoting Male Supremacist Influencers." *DCU Centre* (April 2024). https://antibullyingcentre.ie/wp-content/uploads/2024/04/DCU-Toxicity-Full-Report.pdf.

Bockman, Johanna. "Removing the Public from Public Housing: Public-Private Redevelopment of the Ellen Wilson Dwellings in Washington, DC." *Journal of Urban Affairs* 43, no. 2 (2021): 308–28. https://doi.org/10.1080/07352166.2018.1457406.

Brewer, Rose M. "21st-Century Capitalism, Austerity, and Black Economic Dispossession." *Souls* 14, no. 3–4 (July 2012): 227–39. http://dx.doi.org/10.1080/10999949.2013.766119.

Chennault, Carrie, and Lynn Sutton. "At Home: Black Women's Collective Claims to Environmentally Just Rental Housing." *Annals of American Association of Geographers* 113, no. 7 (August 2023): 1682–98. https://doi.org/10.1080/24694452.2022.2157238.

Choflet, Robert. "'Unfit for Family Life': How Regimes of Accumulation, Sexuality, and Antiblackness Built (and Rebuilt) West Baltimore." PhD diss., University of Maryland-College Park, 2018.

Cohen, Cathy. "Deviance as Resistance: A New Research Agenda for the Study of Black Politics." *Du Bois Review* 1, no. 1 (March 2004): 27–45. https://doi.org/10.1017/S1742058X04040044.

———. "Punks, Bulldaggers, and Welfare Queens: The Radical Potential of Queer Politics?" *GLQ* 3, no. 4 (May 1997): 437–65.

Collins, Patricia Hill. "Gender, Black Feminism, and Black Political Economy." *Annals of the American Academy of Political and Social Science* 563 (March 2000): 41–53.

Cooper, Brittany, Tanisha C. Ford, Treva B. Lindsey, Joan Morgan, and Kaila A. Story, eds. "On the Future of Black Feminism, Part 1." Special issue, *The Black Scholar* 45, no. 4 (2015).

———. "On the Future of Black Feminism, Part 2." Special issue, *The Black Scholar* 46, no. 3 (2016).

Crenshaw, Kimberle. "Demarginalizing the Intersection of Race and Sex: A Black Feminist Critique of Antidiscrimination Doctrine." *University of Chicago Legal Forum* 1 (1989): 139–67.

Dill, Bonnie Thornton. "Our Mothers' Grief: Racial Ethnic Women and Maintenance of Families," *Journal of Family History* 13 no. 4 (October 1988): 415–31. https://doi.org/10.1177/036319908801300 4.

Fraser, Nancy. "Contradictions of Capital and Care." *New Left Review* 100 (July/August 2016). https://newleftreview.org/issues/ii100/articles/nancy-fraser-contradictions-of-capital-and-care.

Friedman, Lawrence M. "Public Housing and the Poor: An Overview." *California Law Review* 54, no. 2 (May 1966): 642–69.

Guild, Joshua, George Derek Musgrove, Benjamin Talton, Keeanga-Yamahtta Taylor, and Leah Wright Rigueur, eds. "The Black 1980s." Special issue, *Journal of African American History* 108, no. 3 (Summer 2023).

Harrison, Rashida L., Mary Frances Phillips, and Nicole M. Jackson, eds. "Black Love." Special issue, *Women's Studies Quarterly,* 50 no.1/2 (Spring/Summer 2022).

Hirsch, Arnold R. "Containment on the Home Front: Race and Federal Housing Policy from the New Deal to the Cold War." *Journal of Urban History* 26, no. 2 (January 2000): 158–80. https://doi.org/10.1177 /009614420002600202.

Hoagland, Alison K. "Nineteenth-Century Building Regulations in Washington, DC." *Records of Columbia Historical Society* 52 (1989): 57–77.

hooks, bell. "Homeplace: A Site of Resistance." In bell hooks, *Yearning: Race, Gender, and Cultural Politics,* 41–50. Boston, MA: South End Press, 1990.

Huron, Amanda. "Defending Tenants in the Midst of Plague." *Washington History* 32, no. 1/2 (Fall 2020): 41–43.

Karp, Michael. "The St. Louis Rent Strike of 1969: Transforming Black Activism and American Low-Income Housing." *Journal of Urban History* 40, no. 4 (July 2014): 648–70. https://doi.org/10.1177/0096144213516082.

Kelley, Robin D. G. "On Violence and Carcerality." Signs 42 no. 3 (2017): 590–600. https://doi.org/10.1086/689623.

Kumfer, Timothy D. "Counter-Capital: Black Power, the New Left, and the Struggle to Remake Washington, DC from Below, 1964–1994." PhD diss., University of Maryland-College Park, 2023.

La Rue, Linda. "The Black Movement and Women's Liberation." In *Words of Fire: An Anthology of African-American Feminist Thought,* edited by Beverly Guy-Sheftall, 164–74. New York: The New Press, 1995.

Nardone, Thomas, Diane Herz, Earl Mellor, and Steven Hipple. "1992: Job Market in the Doldrums." *Monthly Labor Review* 116, no. 2 (February 1993): 3–14.

Nayak, Suryia. "For Women of Colour in Social Work: Black Feminist Self-Care Practice Based on Audre Lorde's Radical Pioneering Principles." *Critical and Radical Social Work* 8, no. 3 (2020): 405–21. https://doi.org/10.1332 /204986020X15945755847234.

Ndubuizu, Rosemary. "Faux Heads of Households and the Gendered and Racialized Politics of Housing Reform." *Feminist Formations* 33, no. 1 (Spring 2021): 142–64. https://doi.org/10.1353/ff.2021.0007.

———. "In the State's Shadow of Fair Housing: DC (White) Businesses and Their Revanchist Desires." *Urban Affairs Review* 57, no. 6 (July 2020): 1–32. https:// doi.org/10.1177/1078087420935515.

———. "Reagan's Austerity Bureaucrats: Examining the Racial and Gender Bias of Ronald Reagan's Housing Vouchers." *Du Bois Review* 16, no. 2 (January 2019): 535–54. https://doi.org/10.1017/S1742058X19000274.

———. "Where Shall the Monsters Live? Black Women and the Politics of Urban Disposability." PhD diss., Rutgers University, 2017.

Padgett, Deborah K. "Homelessness, Housing Instability and Mental Health." *BJPsych Bulletin* 44, no. 5 (October 2020): 197–201. https://doi.org/10.1192/bjb.2020.49.

Reese, Ashanté M., and Dara Cooper. "Making Spaces Something Like Freedom: Black Feminist Praxis in the Re/Imagining of a Just Food System." In *Beyond the Kitchen Table: Black Women and Global Food Systems*, edited by Priscilla McCutcheon, Latricia E. Best, and Theresa Rajack-Talley, 92–105. Chapel Hill: University of North Carolina Press, 2023.

Robinson, Kenneth J. "Savings and Loan Crisis: 1980–1989." Federal Reserve History, November 22, 2013. https://www.federalreservehistory.org/essays/savings-and-loan-crisis.

Schaller, Susanna. "Situating Entrepreneurial Place Making in DC: Business Improvement Districts and Urban (Re)Development in Washington, DC." In *Capital Dilemma: Growth and Inequality in Washington, DC*, edited by Derek Hyra and Sabiyha Price, 139–58. New York: Routledge Press, 2015.

Spillers, Hortense. "Mama's Baby, Papa's Maybe: An American Grammar Book." *Diacritics* 17, no. 2 (Summer 1987): 64–81.

Summers, Brandi. "La douleur exquise: Neoliberalism, Race, and the Un/Making of Blackness in the 21st Century." PhD diss., University of California-Santa Cruz, 2014.

Van Wormer, Katherine. "Restorative Justice as Social Justice for Victims of Gendered Violence: A Standpoint Feminist Perspective." *Social Work* 54, no. 2 (April 2009): 107–16. https://doi.org/10.1093/sw/54.2.107.

Wagner, Robert F., Jr., and Julia Vitullo-Martin. "New Hope for Old Projects, Vince Lane and the Revival of Public Housing." *City Journal* (Spring 1994). https://www.city-journal.org/article/new-hope-for-old-projects-vince-lane-and-the-revival-of-public-housing.

Walsh, Carl E. "What Caused the 1990–1991 Recession?" *Economic Review, Federal Reserve Bank of San Francisco*, no. 2 (1993): 33–48. https://www.frbsf.org/wp-content/uploads/93-2_34-48.pdf.

Wells, Katie Jeanne. "A Decent Place to Stay: Housing Crises, Failed Laws, and Property Conflicts in Washington, DC." PhD diss., Syracuse University, 2013.

———. "A Housing Crisis, a Failed Law, and a Property Conflict: The US Urban Speculation Tax." *Antipode* 47, no. 4 (September 2015): 1043–61. https://doi.org/10.1111/anti.12146.

Winston, Celeste. "Maroon Geographies." *Annals of the American Association of Geographers* 111, no. 7 (May 2021): 2185–99. https://doi.org/10.1080/24694452.2021.1894087.

Yeager, Matthew G. "The Political Economy of Illicit Drugs." *Contemporary Drug Problems* 4, no. 2 (Summer 1975): 141–78.

Index

Baugh, James, 175
behavioral approaches to governance, 87, 99, 194–95; "problem families," 55–56; contrasted with rent control, 118; housing voucher programs, 142. *See also* disciplinary housing governance
Bell, Eugenia, 73
Bellevue neighborhood, 119
Better Homes Movement, 36
Birmingham, AL, 63
Black entrepreneurship, 155, 160, 257n49
Black feminism, 159, 232n15
Black feminist materialism, 6–11, 62, 183–84, 228
Black middle class: and working class, 132; expansion of, 128; and inner city, 135; and lower-income tenants, 137–38
Black mothers, 158–159; as base of resistance, 63–64; desirable/undesirable binary, 187–188; and illicit drug economy, 174–75; individual vs. structural critiques, 44–45, 64; moral character impugned, 73, 173, 202–3; and welfare assistance in DC, 126–27. *See also* Black women; "desirable" vs. "undesirable" tenant binary
Black populations: Black conservatism, 117; Black cultural nationalism, 167; Black wealth, growth in, 252n97; character development, 27; cultural deficiencies, alleged, 81–82; desirable/undesirable binary, 15, 24, 88, 102–3, 114–15, 137, 184, 197–98, 201–6; racial uplift ideology, 96, 116, 145; restricted residential mobility, 29
Black Power, 90, 173
Black tenant irresponsibility trope: background and overview of, 12–15, 20–21, 23–24, 28; and gentrification, 220–21; impact of, 145; in Kemp and Butler public housing proposal, 163–64; and landlord acceptance of rent control, 143; landlords' use of,

44–45, 68; media depictions, 202–4; and opposition to rent control, 136–37; political exploitation of, 60–62, 98, 195; and public housing management, 114–15, 116–17; pushback against, 86–87; advocacy groups' use of, 217–18; "welfare queens," 127, 187
Black women: leadership skills, 7, 119; political development of, 120, 124; and rent control enforcement, 117–24; testimonies of victimization, 217–18. *See also* Black mothers
Blagden's Alley, 36
Bockman, Johanna, 201–2
Boston, MA, 183; Boston Housing Authority, 183; Combahee River Collective, 7
Bowser, Muriel, 225, 226–27
Brentwood neighborhood, 131
Brewer, Rose, 9
Briscoe, Betty, 112, 118
Broadus, Rosa, 67
Bromley-Heath management group, 183
Brooke, Edward, 92, 93
Brooke Amendment (HUD Act), 92–93, 150
Brookings Institution, 210
Brown, Pat, 90
Buchanan, Pat, 190
Building Owners and Managers Association, 111
Burroughs, Nannie Helen, 35
Bush, George H. W., 178, 189; austerity policies, 179
Butler, Stuart, 161, 162–63, 258n68
Byrd, Marion, 83
Byrd, Rosetta, 118

Calcara, Frank, 68
capital flight, 150–51
capitalism: capitalist structures, 120; social reproduction, 9
Capitol East Housing Coalition, 110
Capitol Hill neighborhood, 49, 109

Downs, Anthony, 138

drug distribution and use, illegal, 172–73, 174–75; anti-drug initiatives, 179; Kenilworth-Parkside, 179–80; Operation Safehome, 197

Duke, David, 190

Du Pont, Samuel Francis, 67

Dupont Circle neighborhood, *43*, 67

Durenberger, David, 157–58

East Capitol Dwellings, 173

East Shaw neighborhood, 81

economics: exchange rates, 107; interest rates, 107; knowledge-based service economy in United States, 10; savings and loan deregulation, 189; social and political aspects, 8

Edmond, Rayful, 174

Eisen, Jacob, 128

elderly residents and homeowners, 49–50, 137

Ellen Wilson Dwellings, 198–202, 205

Ellen Wilson Neighborhood Redevelopment Corporation, 199

Ellington, Duke, 19, 42

Emancipation Proclamation, 100th anniversary, 69

Emergency Committee to Save Rental Housing, 133, 139, 141

EMPOWER DC, 215, 221

entitlement: concept of, 127–28; men's, 10

environmental issues, 229

environmental racism, 150–51

evictions: during 1971 rent strike, 98–99; DC Court of Appeals ruling on thirty-day notices, 109; HUD's disciplinary efforts (1986), 175–77; "nuisance behavior," 134; police support for, 73–74; during rent strikes (1971), 101–2; Schuler family's experience, 70–74, *71*; of Jacqueline Williams, 186–87

Executive Order 8801, 41

extermination and rat-proofing, 79, 81–82, 83, 124

fair housing, 250n55

Fair Housing Act (1968), 116–17

Falwell, Jerry, 130

family structures: Black vs. white, 24–25; Black maternal care, 45–46; Black men, criminalization of, 8; cohabitation, 59; employment and marriage, 167; family size, 19–20, 50–51, 81–82, 85, 114–15, 185–86; and gender, 10; heteronormative models, 10–11, 97; heteropatriarchal norms, 166–68; male role models for sons, 96; matriarchal structures, 95; single mothers, 50–52, 57–59, 95, 129; social reproduction, 9; structural factors, 96–97

Farrell, Robert, 136

"father substitutes," 96

Fauntroy, Walter, 41, 110, 160, 167, 262n136; proposed legislation, 168–71

Federal City College (University of the District of Columbia), 110

Federal City Council (lobby group), 207

federal enterprise zones, 206

Federal Housing Administration (FHA), 50–51, 107, 168

Federal National Mortgage Association (Fannie Mae), 108

Federal Reserve, 107

feminism, 90; Black feminist materialism, 6–11, 62, 183–84, 228

Fenty, Adrian, 2

Fertig, Ralph, 75

Fiscal Affairs Committee, 100

Fisher, Leroy, 131

Fisk University, 126

Fitzgerald, Ella, 42

Florida Avenue, 29

Floyd, Maggie, 46

Foggy Bottom neighborhood, 26, 45

Ford Foundation, 153

Ford's Theatre, 67

Forman, James, Jr., 176

Fort Greble Apartments, 119

Foster, Rosa, 133